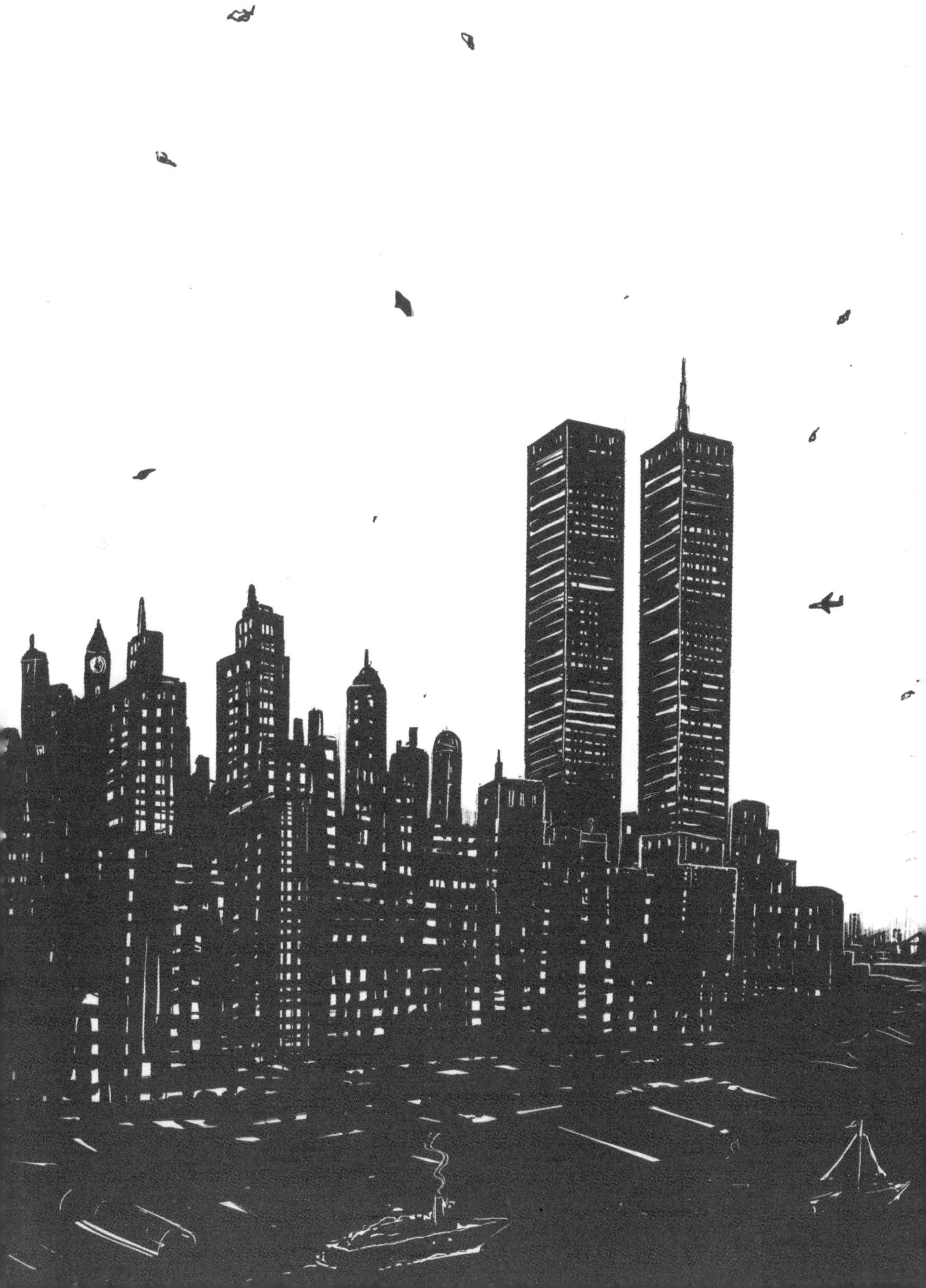

STOP FORGETTING TO REMEMBER

The Autobiography of Walter Kurtz

PETER KUPER

CROWN PUBLISHERS

NEW YORK

This is a work of fiction.
Names, characters, places, and incidents either are
the product of the author's fevered imagination
or are used fictitiously.
Any resemblance to actual persons, living or dead,
events, or locales is entirely coincidental.
No animals were harmed in the making of this book.

Copyright © 2007 by Peter Kuper
All rights reserved.
Photo on page 132 © 1995 Dominique Wirz
Author photo © 2007 Ilona Leiberman

Published in the United States by Crown Publishers,
an imprint of the Crown Publishing Group,
a division of Random House, Inc., New York.
www.crownpublishing.com

Library of Congress Cataloging-in-Publication
Data is available upon request.

ISBN 978-0-307-33950-8

Printed in Singapore

Design by Walter Kurtz

10 9 8 7 6 5 4 3 2 1

First Edition

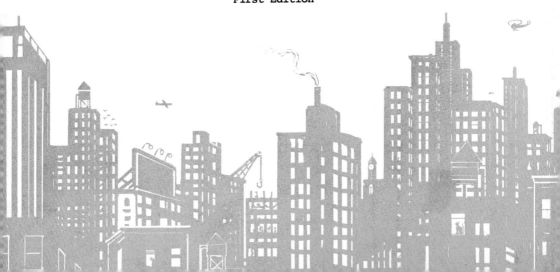

**Dedicated to
the girls who let me get past first base,
and my wife, who got me home.**

ACKNOWLEDGEMENTS

For endless scanning, halftoning, technical and psychological assistance: **Tiffany Pilgrim and Ryan Inzana.**
For editorial suggestions, inspiration, encouragement and unlimited patience: **Emily Russell, Tony Stonier, Scott Cunningham, Jim Rasenberger, Steve Ross, Emily Kuper, Betty Russell, and Seth Tobocman.**
For legal expertise: **John Thomas.**
For a lifetime of fortification: **Alan, Virginia, Holly, and Kate Kuper.**
For past and present publishing: **Gary Groth** and **Kim Thompson.**
Road scholars: **Mark Owen and Dominique Wirz.**
For aiding and abetting: **Kyle Baker, Jason Pinter, Gregory Benton, Genoveva Llosa, Linnea Knollmueller, Erin Schell, Rocky Maffit, and David Tran.**
Guiding lightbulbs: **Winsor McCay, Will Eisner, Harvey Kurtzman, Jack Kirby, Jules Feiffer, Antonio Prohias, and R.Crumb,**
to name but a few.

I have been working on this book for over 13 years, so if you're one of the hundreds of people who've helped me, and I've forgotten to remember you here; i'm sorry, *snif.*

Ceci n'est pas une pipe.

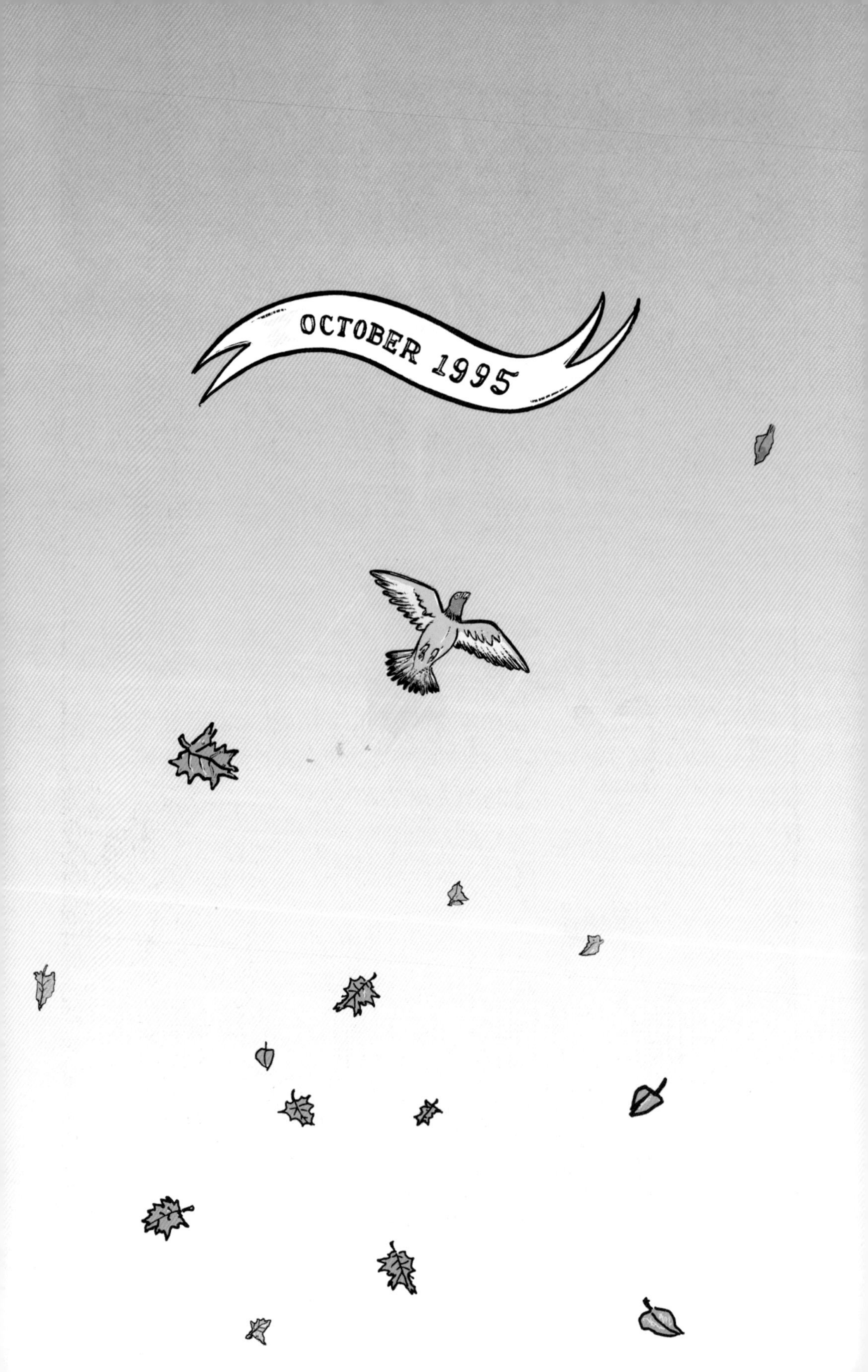
OCTOBER 1995

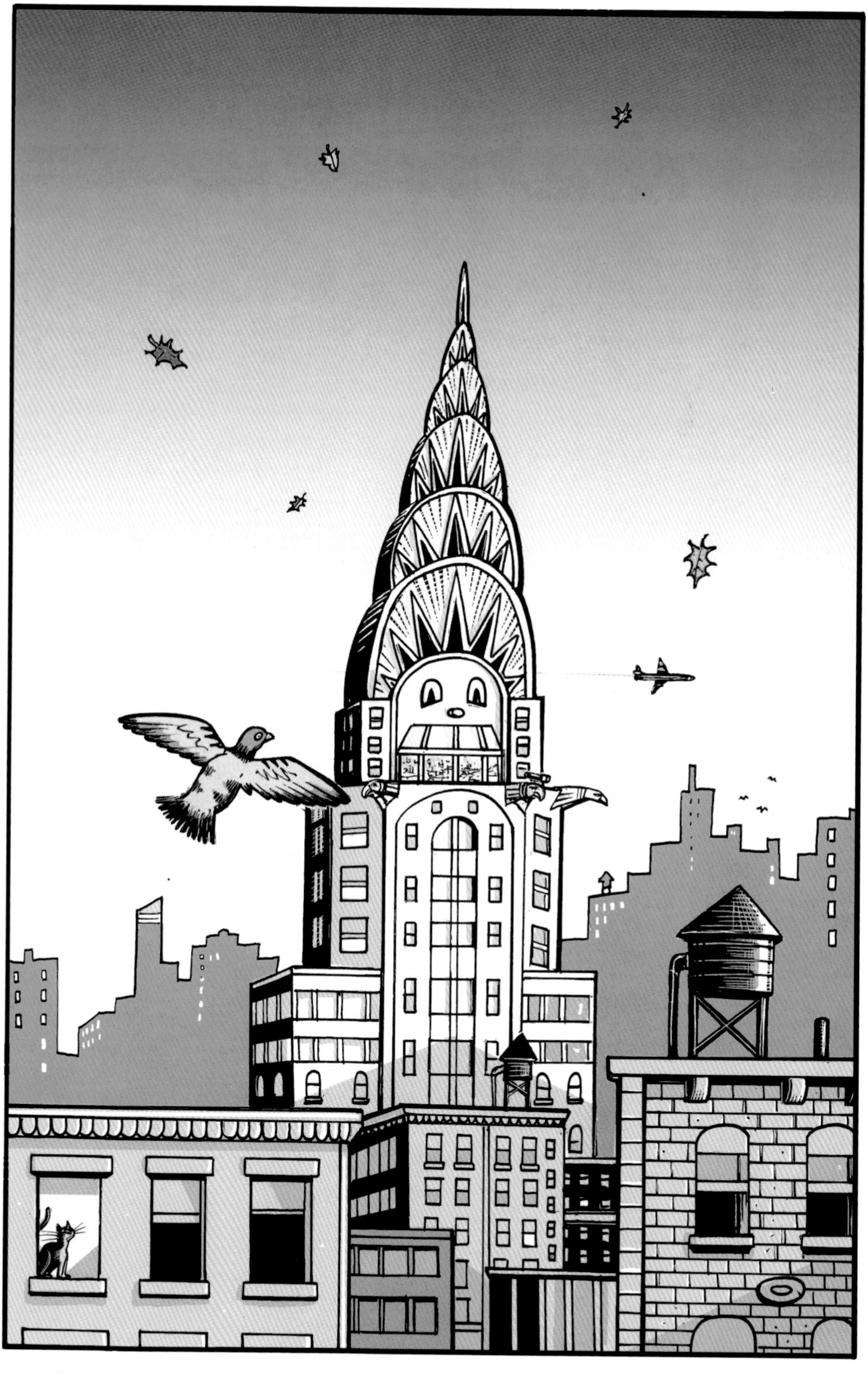

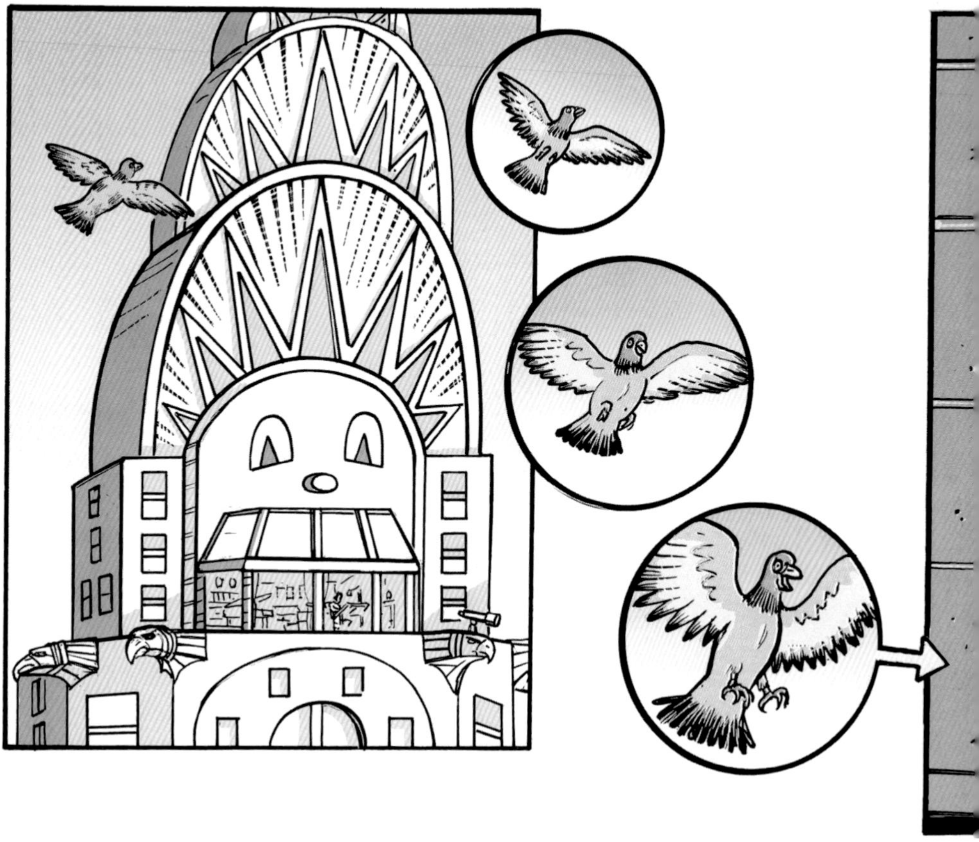

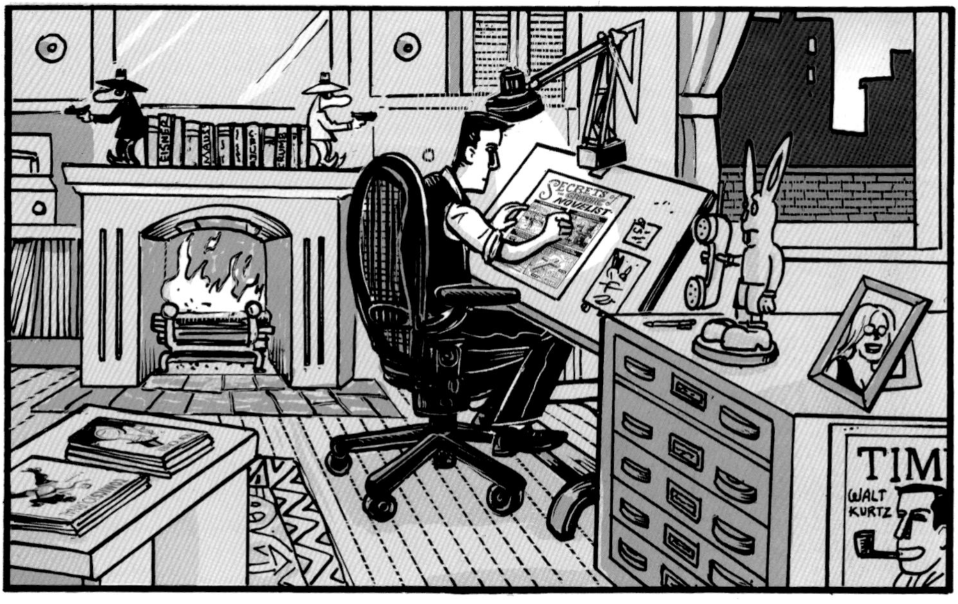

EISNER
CRUMB
SECRETS of the GRAPHIC NOVELIST
TIM
WALT KURTZ

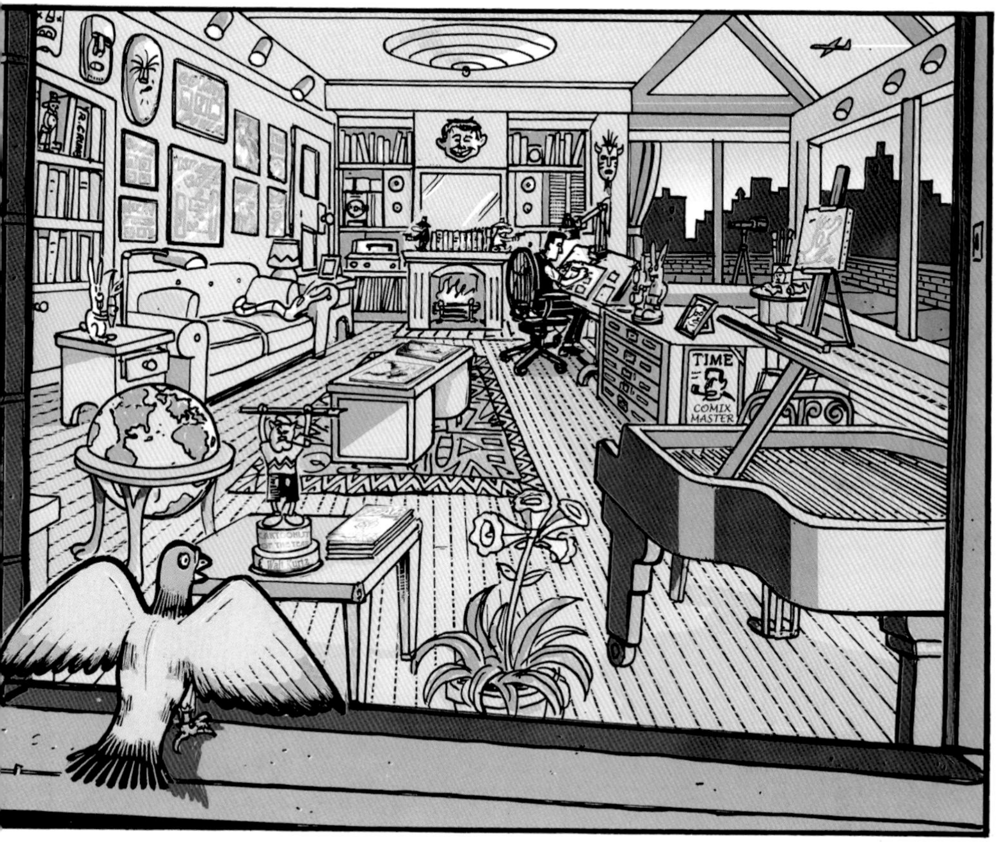
TIME
COMIX MASTER

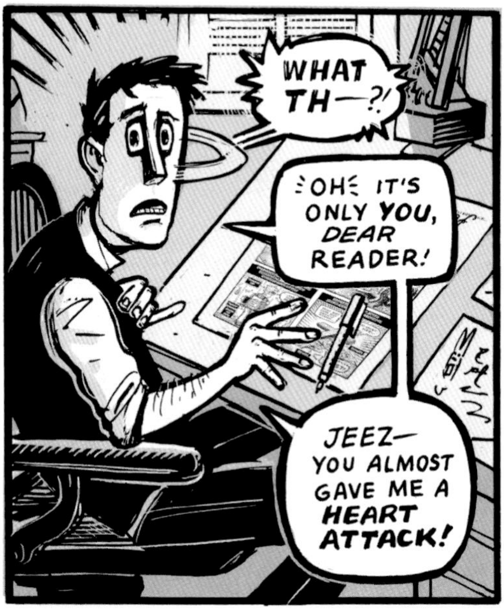
WHAT TH—?!
OH! IT'S ONLY YOU, DEAR READER!
JEEZ— YOU ALMOST GAVE ME A HEART ATTACK!

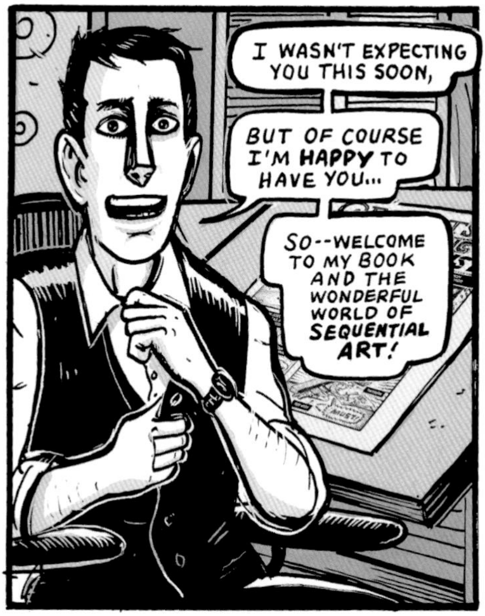
I WASN'T EXPECTING YOU THIS SOON,
BUT OF COURSE I'M HAPPY TO HAVE YOU...
SO--WELCOME TO MY BOOK AND THE WONDERFUL WORLD OF SEQUENTIAL ART!

AS YOU'VE PROBABLY SURMISED, I'M WALTER KURTZ--

CALL ME WALT.

I'LL BE YOUR GUIDE FOR A BEHIND THE SCENES LOOK INTO THE LIFE OF A WORKING CARTOONIST...

AS A LONG-TIME PRACTITIONER, I HAVE MANY INSIGHTS TO SHARE...

FROM THE HISTORY TO THE MECHANICS OF THIS GREAT AMERICAN ART FORM.

LIKE JAZZ, COMIC BOOKS ARE ONE OF THE FEW ARTS INVENTED IN THIS COUNTRY...

Keep on Truckin'

AND SADLY, LIKE JAZZ, COMICS GET MORE RESPECT IN EUROPE AND JAPAN THAN THEY EVER HAVE HERE.

WHEN MOST AMERICANS HEAR THE TERM "COMICS" THEY THINK ONLY OF BATMAN* OR GARFIELD...

UNAWARE OF THE MEDIUM'S VAST POTENTIAL BEYOND SUPER-HEROES AND ONE-LINERS...

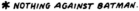

* NOTHING AGAINST BATMAN.

IT'S ALSO IRONIC THAT COMICS HAVE ALWAYS BEEN VIEWED AS "LOW ART"...

DREAM OF THE RAREBIT FIEND

WHEN SO MUCH "HIGH ART" CAN'T HOLD A CANDLE TO THE PIONEERS OF THIS MEDIUM!

WHEN IT COMES DOWN TO IT, COMICS ARE PROBABLY **THE** MOST DEMANDING ART FORM.

THE GRAPHIC NOVELIST MUST HAVE THE ABILITY TO WRITE, DRAW, LETTER, AND DESIGN WITH EQUAL SKILL...

Lettering needs work

IT'S NO WONDER IT TAKES DECADES TO MASTER ONE'S CRAFT!

HAPPILY, AS MORE AND MORE PEOPLE DISCOVER THE POSSIBILITIES OF COMICS...

ART SCHOOLS HAVE BEGUN OFFERING COURSES ON THE SUBJECT AND A WHOLE NEW GENERATION OF CARTOONISTS ARE EMERGING.

AS A LECTURER AND TEACHER, I'VE TRIED TO DISSECT THIS MEDIUM TO UNLOCK *ITS* SECRETS FOR MY STUDENTS...

PANEL SHAPE

TRAGEDY + TIME = COMIX

KIRBY + DITKO

NO   NO   NO   NO

McCAY: 'GERTIE'

WHILE THERE ARE NO SHORTCUTS TO OBTAINING THE KNOWLEDGE...

I HAVE DISCOVERED NUMEROUS SIMILAR-ITIES BETWEEN THE ARTISTS WHO HAVE BEEN SUCCESSFUL IN THIS FIELD...

QUEBECOR
TO: PRINTING
"SECRETS" 100 COPIES
TO: WALTER KURT

QUEBECOR   QUEBECOR   "SECRETS"

I'VE NARROWED IT DOWN TO *TEN* POINTS THAT THE ENDURING *PRACTITIONERS* SEEM TO HAVE IN COMMON...

SECRETS OF THE GRAPHIC NOVELIST
WALTER KURT

LET ME READ THEM TO YOU...

SECRETS of THE GRAPHIC NOVELIST*

* BOY'S CLUB VERSION

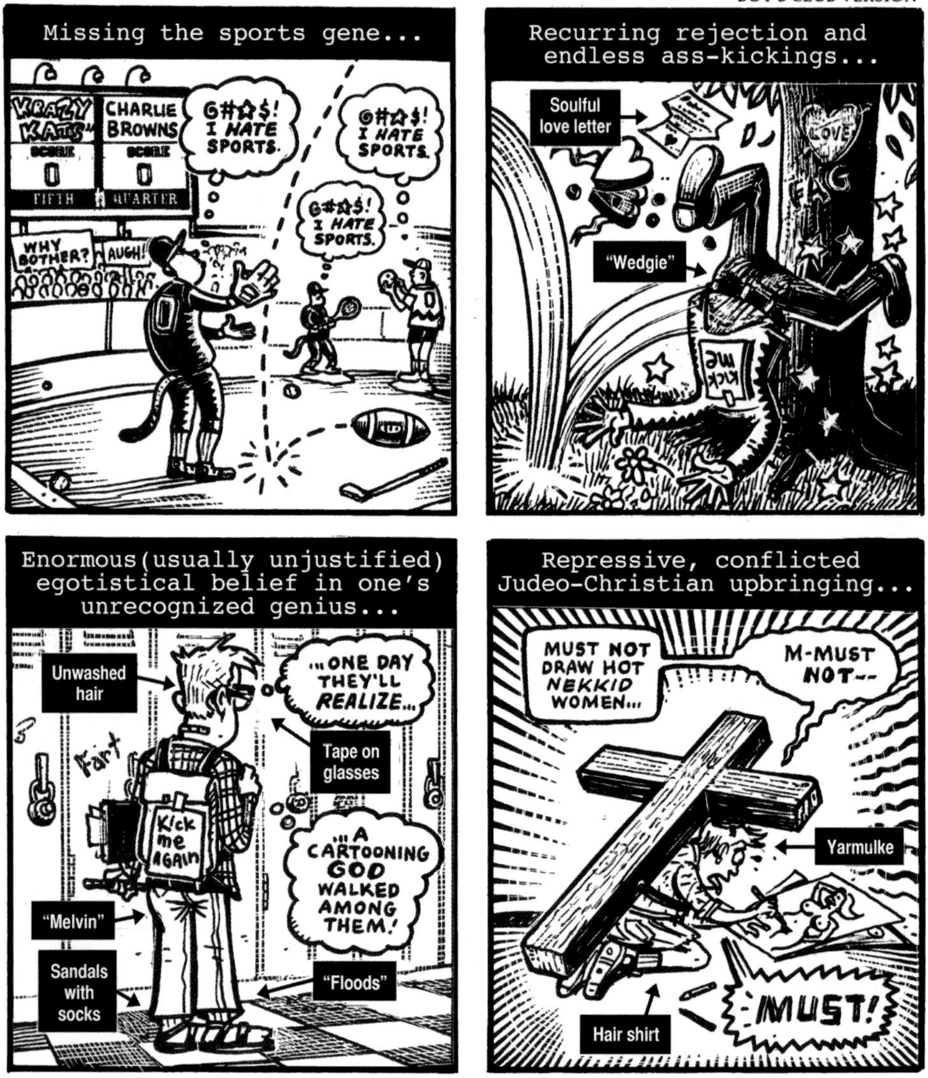

Missing the sports gene...
KRAZY KATS
SCORE
0
CHARLIE BROWNS
SCORE
0
FIFTH QUARTER
WHY BOTHER?
AUGH!
G#✩$! I HATE SPORTS.
G#✩$! I HATE SPORTS.
G#✩$! I HATE SPORTS.
Recurring rejection and endless ass-kickings...
Soulful love letter
LOVE
FAG
"Wedgie"
KICK ME
Enormous(usually unjustified) egotistical belief in one's unrecognized genius...
Unwashed hair
...ONE DAY THEY'LL REALIZE...
Tape on glasses
Fart
Kick me AGAIN
...A CARTOONING GOD WALKED AMONG THEM!
"Melvin"
Sandals with socks
"Floods"
Repressive, conflicted Judeo-Christian upbringing...
MUST NOT DRAW HOT NEKKID WOMEN...
M-MUST NOT--
Yarmulke
Hair shirt
MUST!

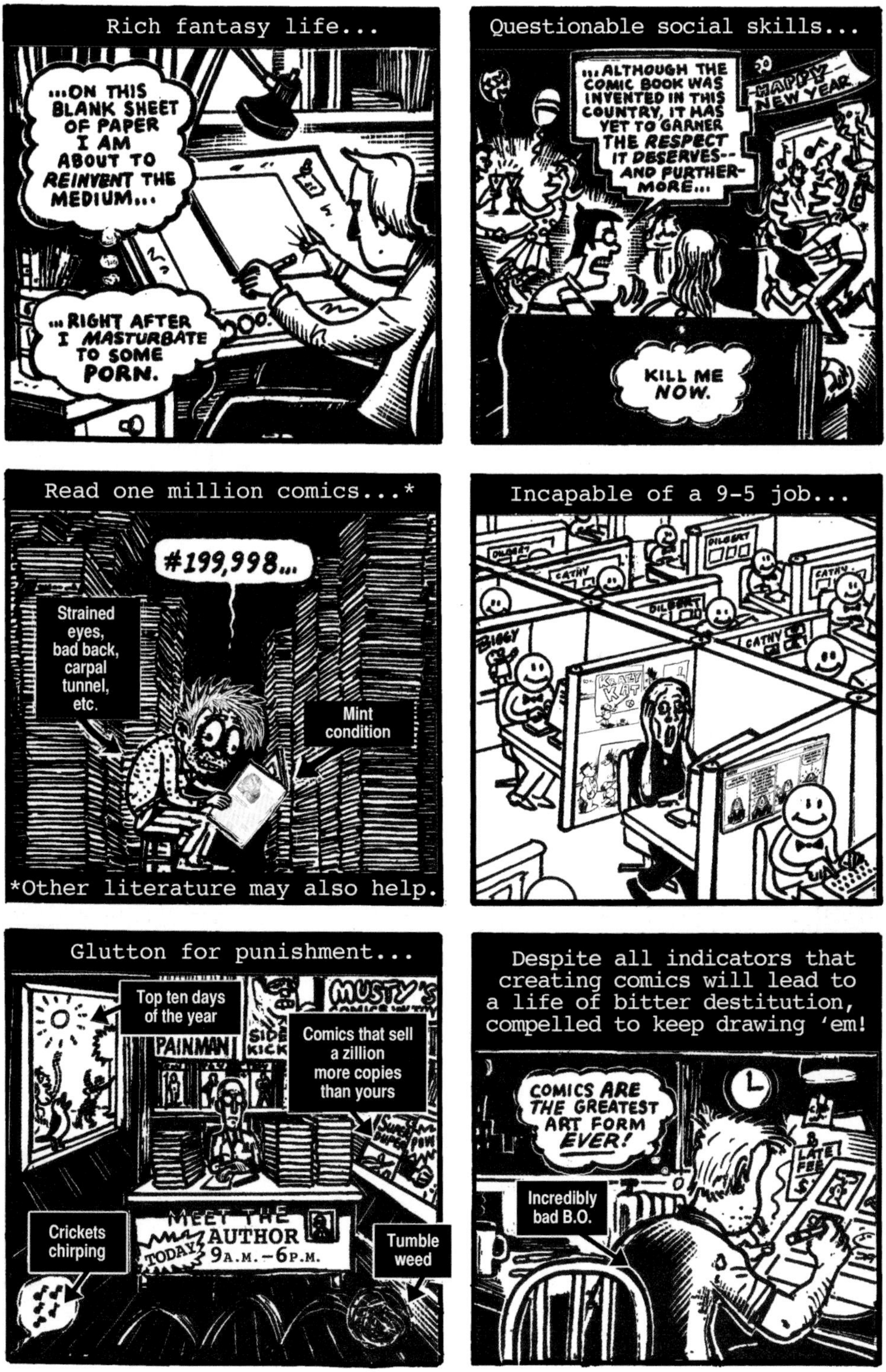
Rich fantasy life...
...ON THIS BLANK SHEET OF PAPER I AM ABOUT TO REINVENT THE MEDIUM...
...RIGHT AFTER I MASTURBATE TO SOME PORN.
Questionable social skills...
...ALTHOUGH THE COMIC BOOK WAS INVENTED IN THIS COUNTRY, IT HAS YET TO GARNER THE RESPECT IT DESERVES-- AND FURTHERMORE...
HAPPY NEW YEAR
KILL ME NOW.
Read one million comics...*
#199,998...
Strained eyes, bad back, carpal tunnel, etc.
Mint condition
*Other literature may also help.
Incapable of a 9-5 job...
Glutton for punishment...
Top ten days of the year
MUSTY'S
PAINMAN
SIDE KICK
Comics that sell a zillion more copies than yours
MEET THE AUTHOR
TODAY 9A.M.-6P.M.
Crickets chirping
Tumble weed
Despite all indicators that creating comics will lead to a life of bitter destitution, compelled to keep drawing 'em!
COMICS ARE THE GREATEST ART FORM EVER!
LATE FEE $
Incredibly bad B.O.

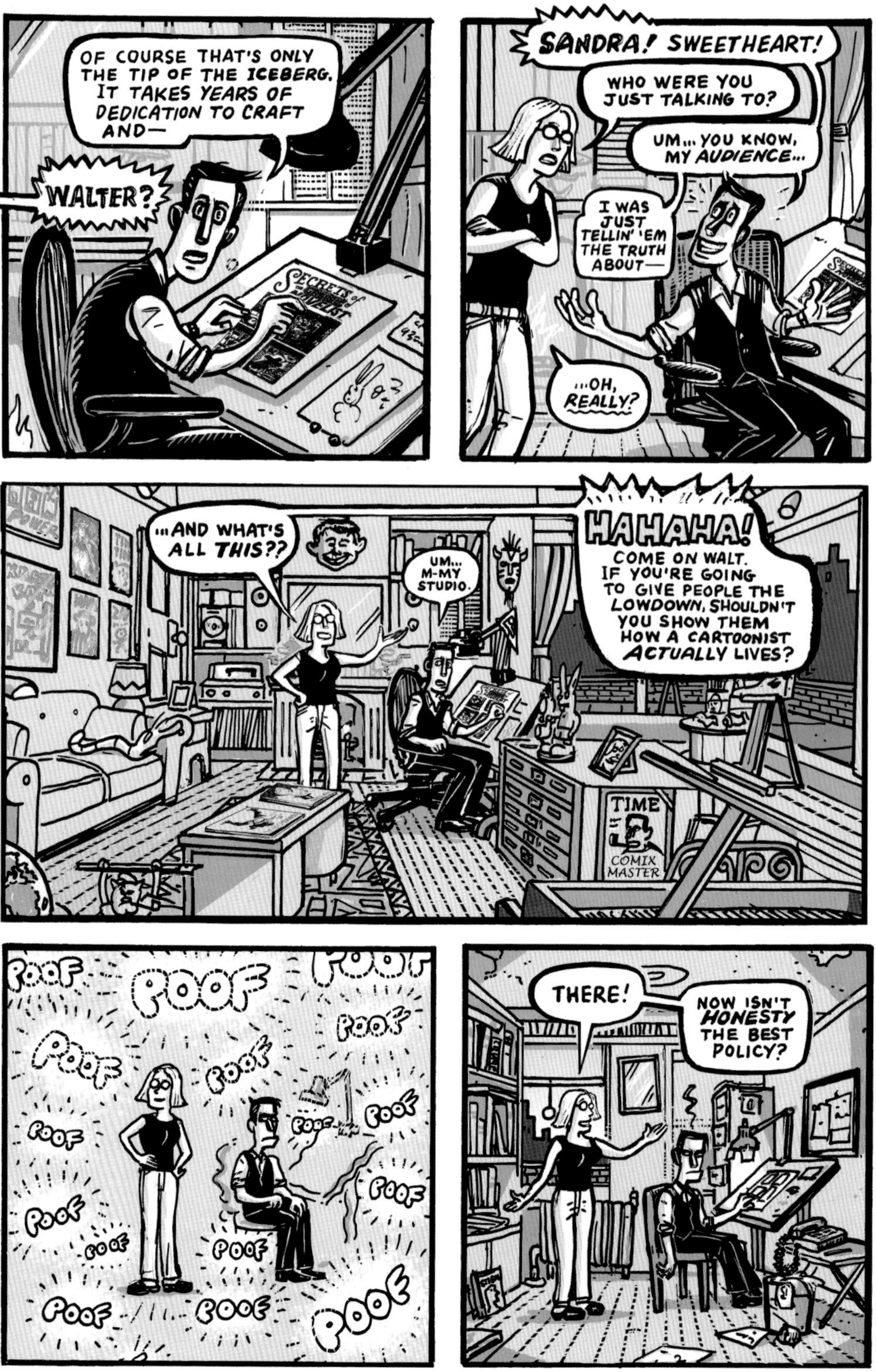
OF COURSE THAT'S ONLY THE TIP OF THE ICEBERG. IT TAKES YEARS OF DEDICATION TO CRAFT AND—
WALTER?
SANDRA! SWEETHEART!
WHO WERE YOU JUST TALKING TO?
UM... YOU KNOW, MY AUDIENCE...
I WAS JUST TELLIN' 'EM THE TRUTH ABOUT—
...OH, REALLY?
...AND WHAT'S ALL THIS??
UM... M-MY STUDIO.
HAHAHA! COME ON WALT. IF YOU'RE GOING TO GIVE PEOPLE THE LOWDOWN, SHOULDN'T YOU SHOW THEM HOW A CARTOONIST ACTUALLY LIVES?
TIME
COMIX MASTER
POOF POOF POOF POOF POOF POOF POOF POOF POOF POOF POOF POOF POOF POOF POOF POOF
THERE!
NOW ISN'T HONESTY THE BEST POLICY?

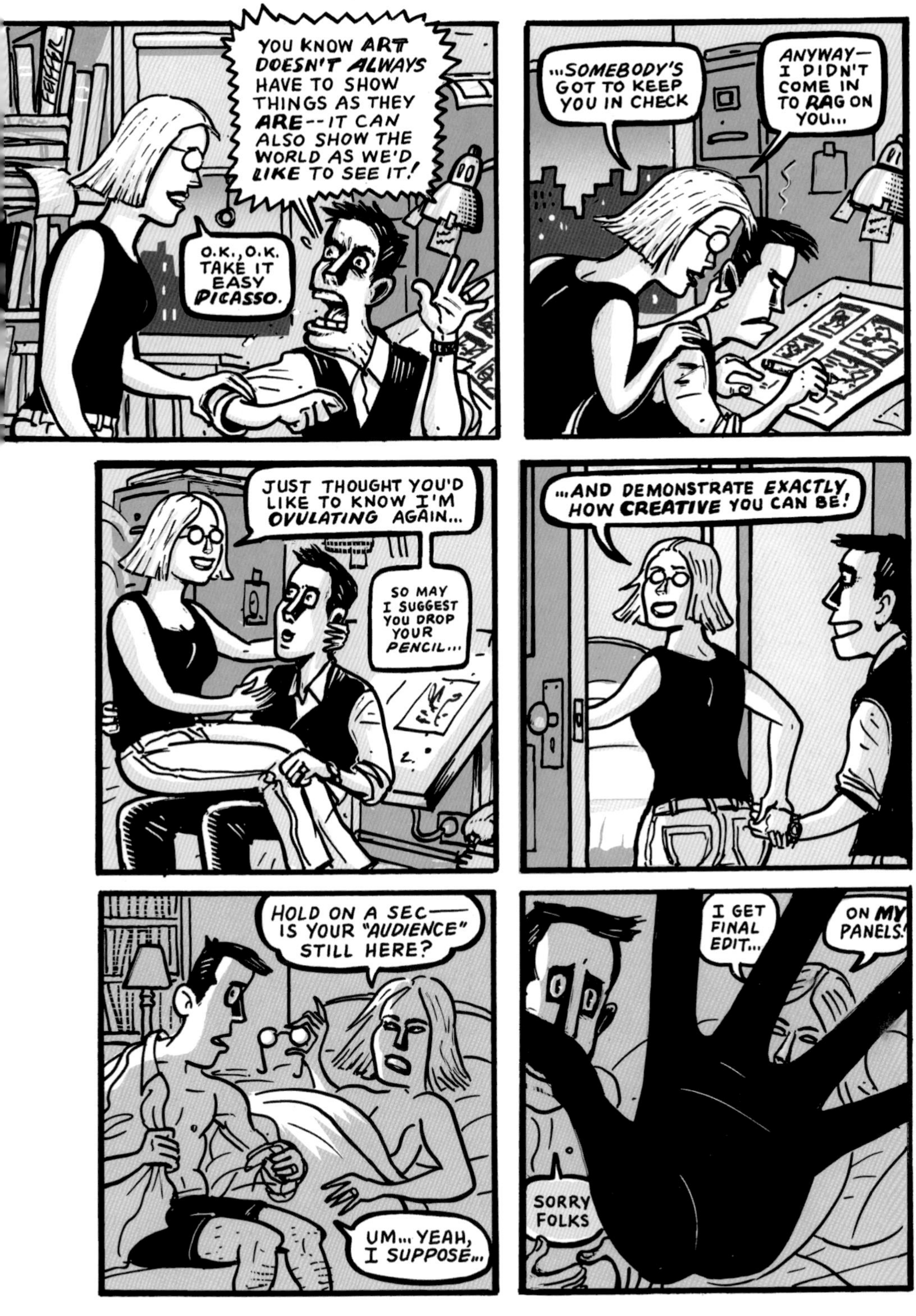
YOU KNOW ART DOESN'T ALWAYS HAVE TO SHOW THINGS AS THEY ARE--IT CAN ALSO SHOW THE WORLD AS WE'D LIKE TO SEE IT!
O.K., O.K. TAKE IT EASY PICASSO.
...SOMEBODY'S GOT TO KEEP YOU IN CHECK
ANYWAY— I DIDN'T COME IN TO RAG ON YOU...
JUST THOUGHT YOU'D LIKE TO KNOW I'M OVULATING AGAIN...
SO MAY I SUGGEST YOU DROP YOUR PENCIL...
...AND DEMONSTRATE EXACTLY HOW CREATIVE YOU CAN BE!
HOLD ON A SEC— IS YOUR "AUDIENCE" STILL HERE?
UM... YEAH, I SUPPOSE...
I GET FINAL EDIT...
ON MY PANELS!
SORRY FOLKS

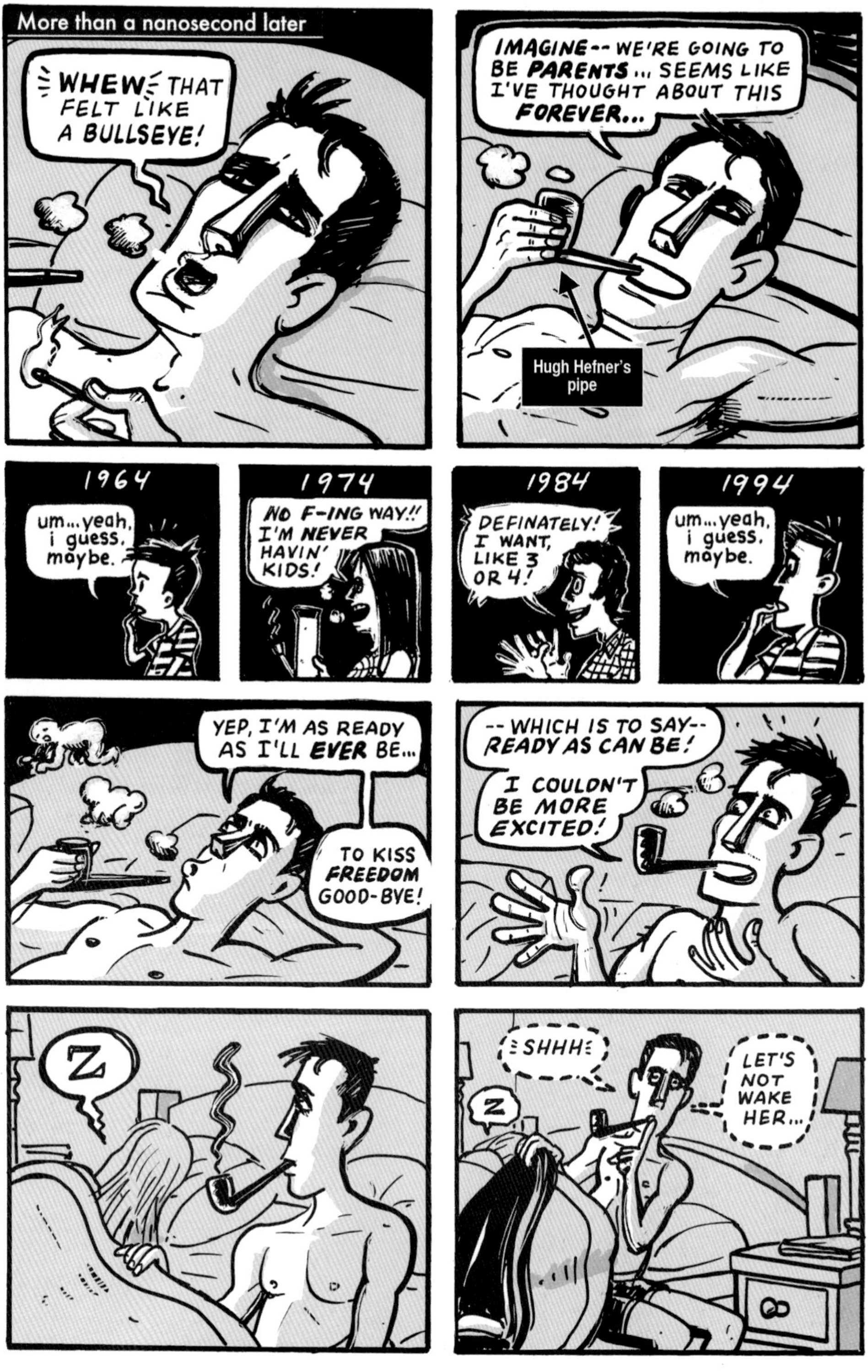
More than a nanosecond later
WHEW THAT FELT LIKE A BULLSEYE!
IMAGINE -- WE'RE GOING TO BE PARENTS... SEEMS LIKE I'VE THOUGHT ABOUT THIS FOREVER...
Hugh Hefner's pipe
1964
um...yeah, i guess, maybe.
1974
NO F-ING WAY!! I'M NEVER HAVIN' KIDS!
1984
DEFINATELY! I WANT, LIKE 3 OR 4!
1994
um...yeah, i guess, maybe.
YEP, I'M AS READY AS I'LL EVER BE...
TO KISS FREEDOM GOOD-BYE!
-- WHICH IS TO SAY-- READY AS CAN BE!
I COULDN'T BE MORE EXCITED!
Z
SHHH
Z
LET'S NOT WAKE HER...

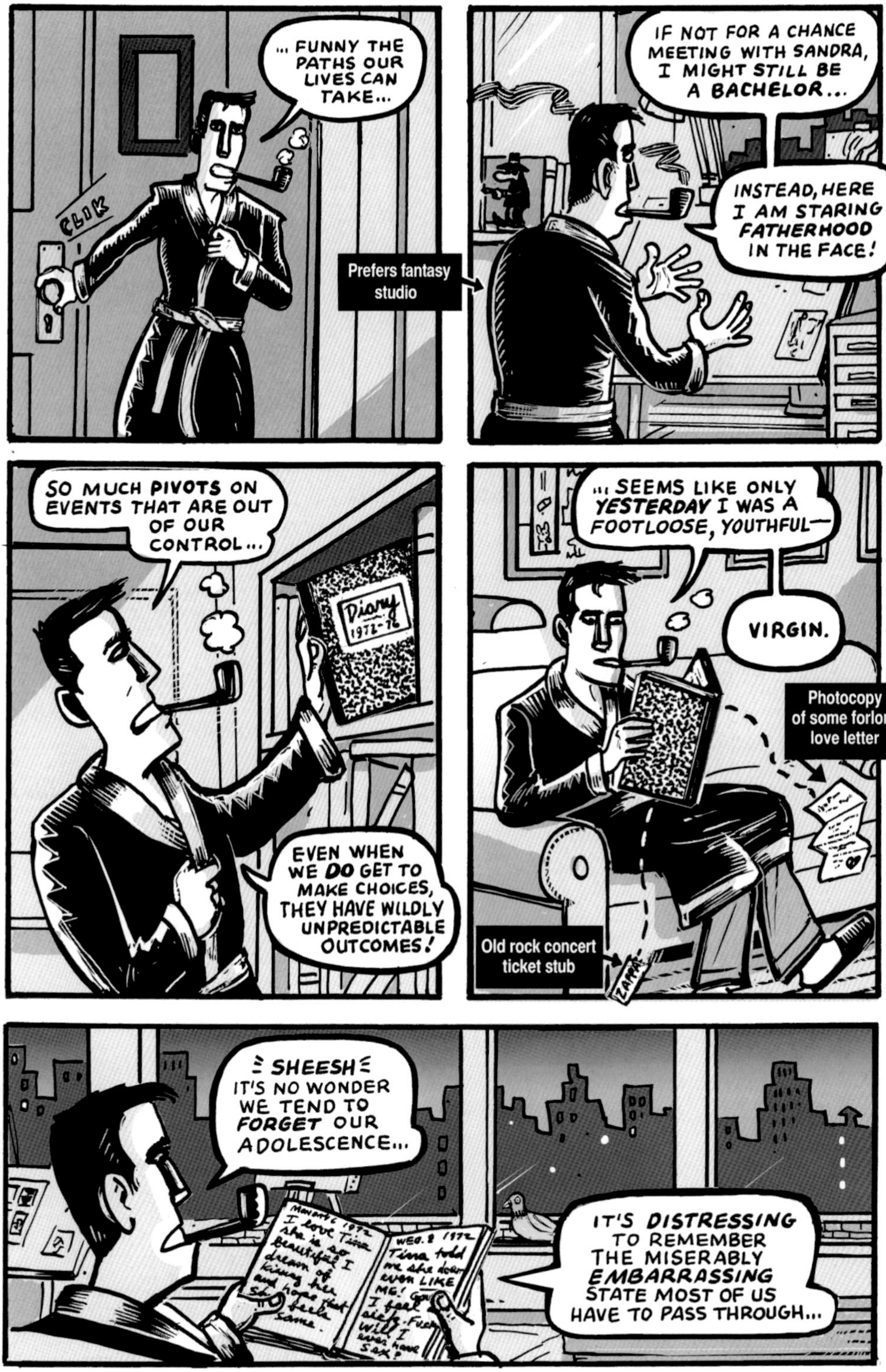
...FUNNY THE PATHS OUR LIVES CAN TAKE...
CLIK
IF NOT FOR A CHANCE MEETING WITH SANDRA, I MIGHT STILL BE A BACHELOR...
INSTEAD, HERE I AM STARING FATHERHOOD IN THE FACE!
Prefers fantasy studio
SO MUCH PIVOTS ON EVENTS THAT ARE OUT OF OUR CONTROL...
Diary 1972-76
EVEN WHEN WE DO GET TO MAKE CHOICES, THEY HAVE WILDLY UNPREDICTABLE OUTCOMES!
...SEEMS LIKE ONLY YESTERDAY I WAS A FOOTLOOSE, YOUTHFUL—
VIRGIN.
Photocopy of some forlorn love letter
Old rock concert ticket stub
ZAPPA
SHEESH IT'S NO WONDER WE TEND TO FORGET OUR ADOLESCENCE...
IT'S DISTRESSING TO REMEMBER THE MISERABLY EMBARRASSING STATE MOST OF US HAVE TO PASS THROUGH...

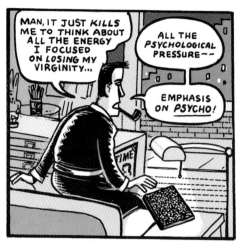

MAN, IT JUST *KILLS* ME TO THINK ABOUT ALL THE ENERGY I FOCUSED ON *LOSING MY VIRGINITY*...

ALL THE PSYCHOLOGICAL PRESSURE--

EMPHASIS ON *PSYCHO!*

NOT TO MENTION *DESIRE*-- GOD, I WAS *CONSUMED* BY MY DESIRE FOR SEX...

YET I JUST ABOUT HAD TO BE *HOG-TIED* INTO HAVING IT...

Still true

SOMETIMES IT *AMAZES* ME THAT I *EVER* GOT OVER THAT *HUMP!*

AFTER ALL THIS TIME IT'S *STILL* PAINFUL TO RECALL.

BUT WE CAN'T IGNORE OUR *HISTORY*...

THEN AGAIN, THOSE THAT *REMEMBER* THEIR PAST ARE *DOOMED* TO RELIVE...

Eat Joe

IT!

≈WHEW≈

SO... LET'S TAKE A TRIP DOWN *MEMORY LANE*...

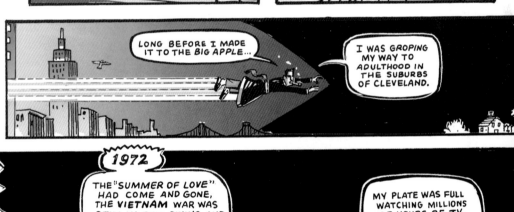

LONG BEFORE I MADE IT TO THE *BIG APPLE*...

I WAS GROPING MY WAY TO ADULTHOOD IN THE SUBURBS OF CLEVELAND.

1972

THE "*SUMMER OF LOVE*" HAD COME AND GONE, THE *VIETNAM* WAR WAS STILL IN *FULL SWING* AND "*TRICKY DICK*" NIXON WAS IN THE WHITE HOUSE...

MY PLATE WAS FULL WATCHING MILLIONS OF HOURS OF TV, READING EVERY COMIC I COULD LAY MY HANDS ON...

AND *FLUBBING* EVERY OPPORTUNITY TO GAIN SEXUAL EXPERIENCE...

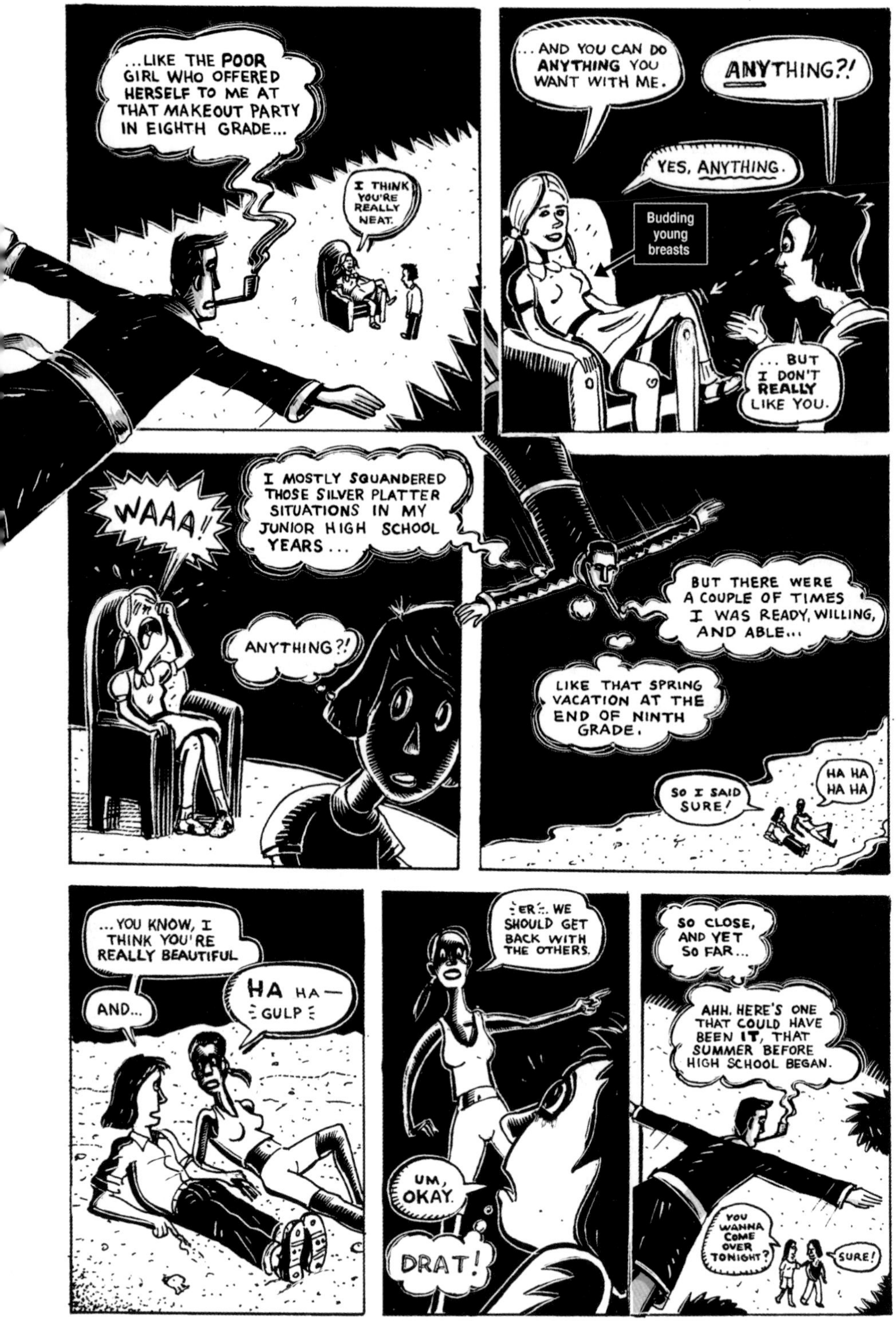
...LIKE THE POOR GIRL WHO OFFERED HERSELF TO ME AT THAT MAKEOUT PARTY IN EIGHTH GRADE...
I THINK YOU'RE REALLY NEAT.
...AND YOU CAN DO ANYTHING YOU WANT WITH ME.
ANYTHING?!
YES, ANYTHING.
Budding young breasts
...BUT I DON'T REALLY LIKE YOU.
WAAA!
I MOSTLY SQUANDERED THOSE SILVER PLATTER SITUATIONS IN MY JUNIOR HIGH SCHOOL YEARS...
ANYTHING?!
BUT THERE WERE A COUPLE OF TIMES I WAS READY, WILLING, AND ABLE...
LIKE THAT SPRING VACATION AT THE END OF NINTH GRADE.
SO I SAID SURE!
HA HA HA HA
...YOU KNOW, I THINK YOU'RE REALLY BEAUTIFUL
AND...
HA HA—GULP
ER... WE SHOULD GET BACK WITH THE OTHERS.
UM, OKAY.
DRAT!
SO CLOSE, AND YET SO FAR...
AHH, HERE'S ONE THAT COULD HAVE BEEN IT, THAT SUMMER BEFORE HIGH SCHOOL BEGAN.
YOU WANNA COME OVER TONIGHT?
SURE!

MARY HAD LONG SINCE LOST HER VIRGINITY, AND WASN'T SEXUALLY INHIBITED...

THIS POT IS GREAT!

YEAH... MY MOM GETS THE BEST STUFF...

... WOW, THIS IS WEIRD... I CAN'T FEEL MY HEART BEATING —

R-REALLY?

HERE, FEEL...

Super skinny arms →

SEE?

⫷GULP⫸ I-I GUESS SO!

OF COURSE SCARED LIL' BUNNY-BOY® MANAGED TO HIGHTAIL IT OUT OF THERE BEFORE THINGS GOT OUT OF HAND...

I-I REALLY MUST BE GOING!

HIP

HOP

ALTHOUGH I WAS DYING TO HAVE SEX, MY DESIRE WAS NECK-IN-NECK WITH MY UNADULTERATED FEAR...

GO! GO! GO!

WE LOVE LUST

LUST

FEAR

VIRG SLIMS

THE NEXT NIGHT I GOT MY COURAGE UP AND PAID MARY ANOTHER VISIT...

UM... HI MARY! WHATCHA DOIN' TONIGHT?

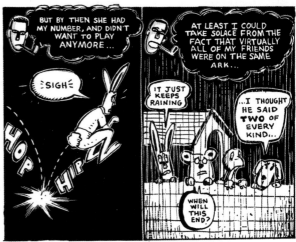

BUT BY THEN SHE HAD MY NUMBER, AND DIDN'T WANT TO PLAY ANYMORE...

⫷SIGH⫸

HOP

HIP

AT LEAST I COULD TAKE SOLACE FROM THE FACT THAT VIRTUALLY ALL OF MY FRIENDS WERE ON THE SAME ARK...

IT JUST KEEPS RAINING

...I THOUGHT HE SAID TWO OF EVERY KIND...

WHEN WILL THIS END?

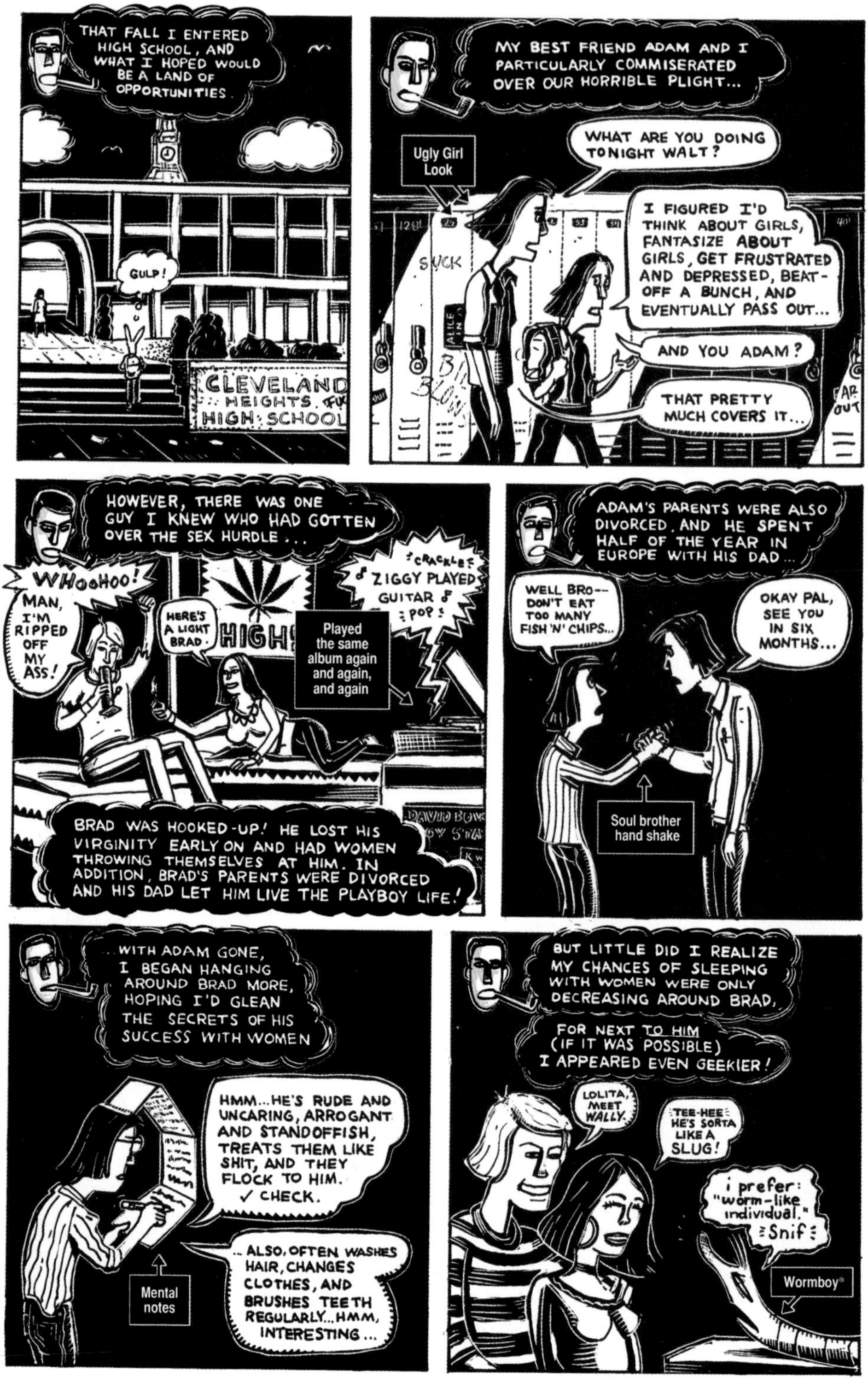
THAT FALL I ENTERED HIGH SCHOOL, AND WHAT I HOPED WOULD BE A LAND OF OPPORTUNITIES.
GULP!
CLEVELAND HEIGHTS HIGH SCHOOL
MY BEST FRIEND ADAM AND I PARTICULARLY COMMISERATED OVER OUR HORRIBLE PLIGHT...
Ugly Girl Look
WHAT ARE YOU DOING TONIGHT WALT?
I FIGURED I'D THINK ABOUT GIRLS, FANTASIZE ABOUT GIRLS, GET FRUSTRATED AND DEPRESSED, BEAT-OFF A BUNCH, AND EVENTUALLY PASS OUT...
AND YOU ADAM?
THAT PRETTY MUCH COVERS IT...
HOWEVER, THERE WAS ONE GUY I KNEW WHO HAD GOTTEN OVER THE SEX HURDLE...
WHOOHOO! MAN, I'M RIPPED OFF MY ASS!
HERE'S A LIGHT BRAD.
HIGH!
CRACKLE ZIGGY PLAYED GUITAR POP
Played the same album again and again, and again
BRAD WAS HOOKED-UP! HE LOST HIS VIRGINITY EARLY ON AND HAD WOMEN THROWING THEMSELVES AT HIM. IN ADDITION, BRAD'S PARENTS WERE DIVORCED AND HIS DAD LET HIM LIVE THE PLAYBOY LIFE!
ADAM'S PARENTS WERE ALSO DIVORCED, AND HE SPENT HALF OF THE YEAR IN EUROPE WITH HIS DAD...
WELL BRO-- DON'T EAT TOO MANY FISH 'N' CHIPS...
OKAY PAL, SEE YOU IN SIX MONTHS...
Soul brother hand shake
...WITH ADAM GONE, I BEGAN HANGING AROUND BRAD MORE, HOPING I'D GLEAN THE SECRETS OF HIS SUCCESS WITH WOMEN
HMM...HE'S RUDE AND UNCARING, ARROGANT AND STANDOFFISH, TREATS THEM LIKE SHIT, AND THEY FLOCK TO HIM. ✓ CHECK.
...ALSO, OFTEN WASHES HAIR, CHANGES CLOTHES, AND BRUSHES TEETH REGULARLY...HMM, INTERESTING...
Mental notes
BUT LITTLE DID I REALIZE MY CHANCES OF SLEEPING WITH WOMEN WERE ONLY DECREASING AROUND BRAD,
FOR NEXT TO HIM (IF IT WAS POSSIBLE) I APPEARED EVEN GEEKIER!
LOLITA, MEET WALLY.
TEE-HEE HE'S SORTA LIKE A SLUG!
i prefer: "worm-like individual." Snif
Wormboy®

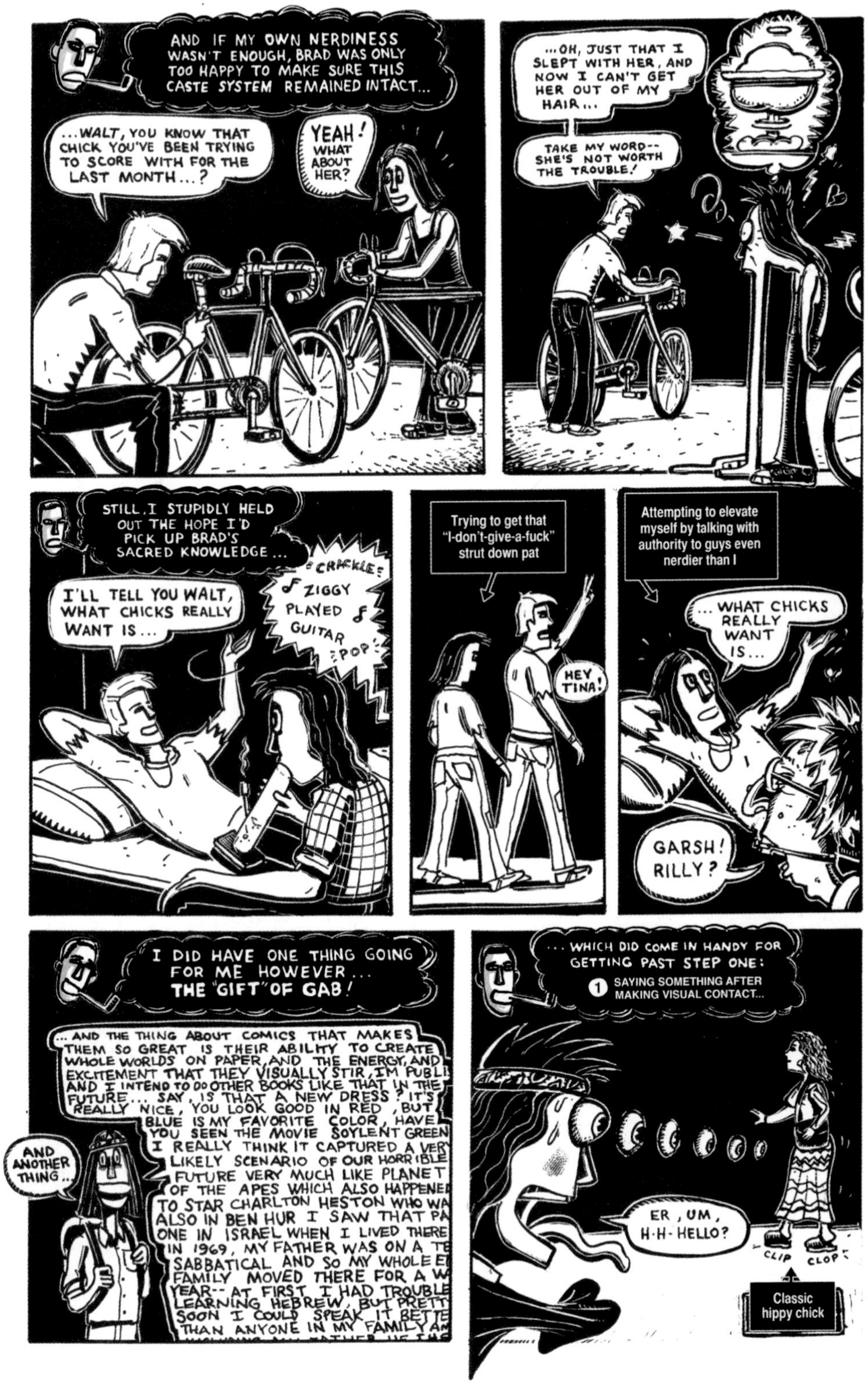
AND IF MY OWN NERDINESS WASN'T ENOUGH, BRAD WAS ONLY TOO HAPPY TO MAKE SURE THIS CASTE SYSTEM REMAINED INTACT...
...WALT, YOU KNOW THAT CHICK YOU'VE BEEN TRYING TO SCORE WITH FOR THE LAST MONTH...?
YEAH! WHAT ABOUT HER?
...OH, JUST THAT I SLEPT WITH HER, AND NOW I CAN'T GET HER OUT OF MY HAIR...
TAKE MY WORD-- SHE'S NOT WORTH THE TROUBLE!
STILL, I STUPIDLY HELD OUT THE HOPE I'D PICK UP BRAD'S SACRED KNOWLEDGE...
I'LL TELL YOU WALT, WHAT CHICKS REALLY WANT IS...
CRACKLE! ZIGGY PLAYED GUITAR POP!
Trying to get that "I-don't-give-a-fuck" strut down pat
HEY TINA!
Attempting to elevate myself by talking with authority to guys even nerdier than I
...WHAT CHICKS REALLY WANT IS...
GARSH! RILLY?
I DID HAVE ONE THING GOING FOR ME HOWEVER... THE "GIFT" OF GAB!
...AND THE THING ABOUT COMICS THAT MAKES THEM SO GREAT IS THEIR ABILITY TO CREATE WHOLE WORLDS ON PAPER, AND THE ENERGY, AND EXCITEMENT THAT THEY VISUALLY STIR, I'M PUBLI AND I INTEND TO DO OTHER BOOKS LIKE THAT IN THE FUTURE... SAY, IS THAT A NEW DRESS? IT'S REALLY NICE, YOU LOOK GOOD IN RED, BUT BLUE IS MY FAVORITE COLOR, HAVE YOU SEEN THE MOVIE SOYLENT GREEN I REALLY THINK IT CAPTURED A VERY LIKELY SCENARIO OF OUR HORRIBLE FUTURE VERY MUCH LIKE PLANET OF THE APES WHICH ALSO HAPPENED TO STAR CHARLTON HESTON WHO WA ALSO IN BEN HUR I SAW THAT PA ONE IN ISRAEL WHEN I LIVED THERE IN 1969, MY FATHER WAS ON A TE SABBATICAL AND SO MY WHOLE E FAMILY MOVED THERE FOR A W YEAR-- AT FIRST I HAD TROUBLE LEARNING HEBREW, BUT PRETTY SOON I COULD SPEAK IT BETTE THAN ANYONE IN MY FAMILY A
AND ANOTHER THING...
...WHICH DID COME IN HANDY FOR GETTING PAST STEP ONE:
1 SAYING SOMETHING AFTER MAKING VISUAL CONTACT...
ER, UM, H-H-HELLO?
CLIP CLOP
Classic hippy chick

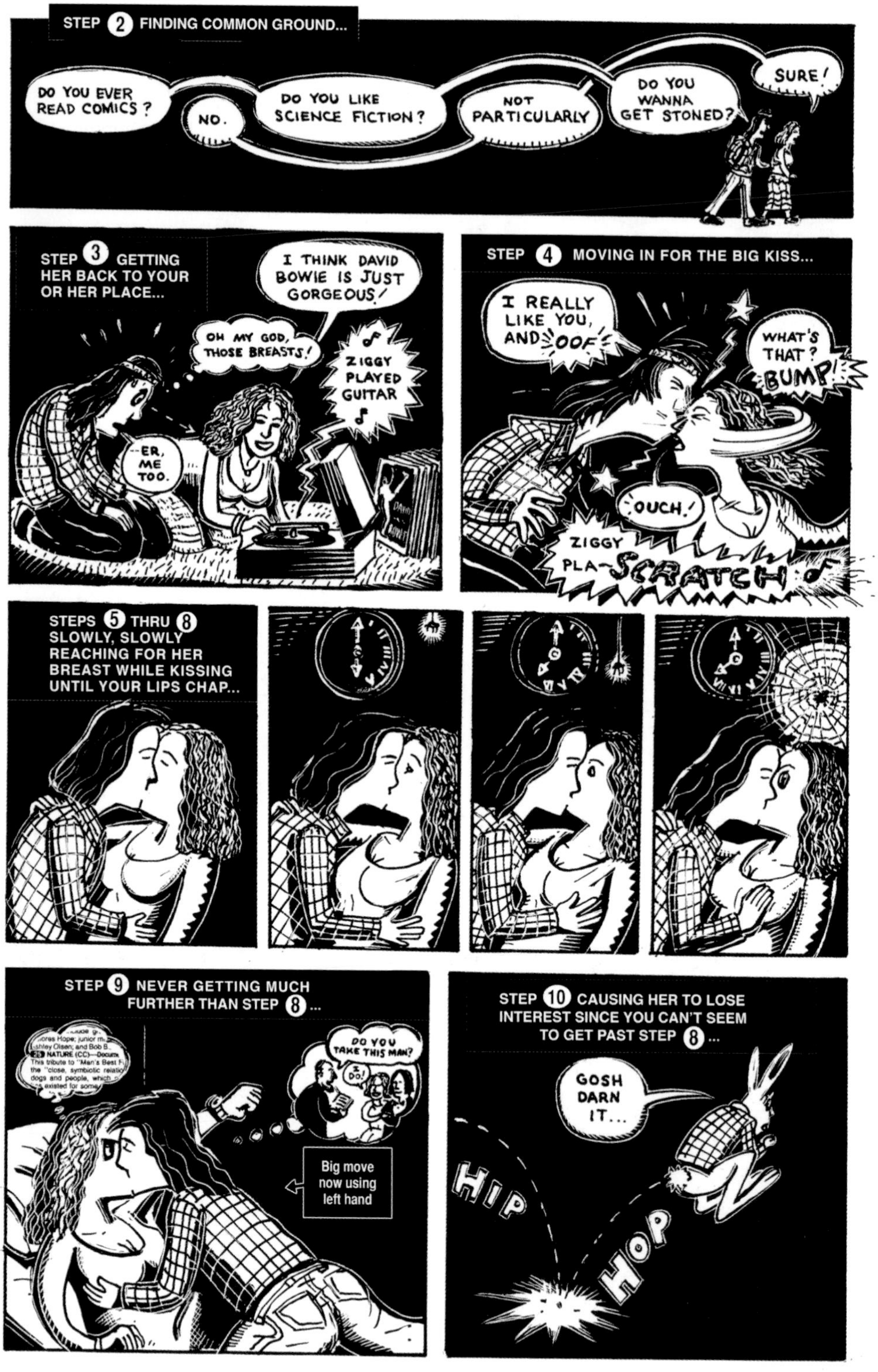

STEP 2 FINDING COMMON GROUND...
DO YOU EVER READ COMICS?
NO.
DO YOU LIKE SCIENCE FICTION?
NOT PARTICULARLY
DO YOU WANNA GET STONED?
SURE!
STEP 3 GETTING HER BACK TO YOUR OR HER PLACE...
I THINK DAVID BOWIE IS JUST GORGEOUS!
OH MY GOD, THOSE BREASTS!
ZIGGY PLAYED GUITAR
--ER, ME TOO.
DAVID BOWIE
STEP 4 MOVING IN FOR THE BIG KISS...
I REALLY LIKE YOU, AND OOF
WHAT'S THAT? BUMP!
OUCH!
ZIGGY PLA-SCRATCH
STEPS 5 THRU 8 SLOWLY, SLOWLY REACHING FOR HER BREAST WHILE KISSING UNTIL YOUR LIPS CHAP...
STEP 9 NEVER GETTING MUCH FURTHER THAN STEP 8...
DO YOU TAKE THIS MAN?
I DO!
Big move now using left hand
STEP 10 CAUSING HER TO LOSE INTEREST SINCE YOU CAN'T SEEM TO GET PAST STEP 8...
GOSH DARN IT...
HIP
HOP

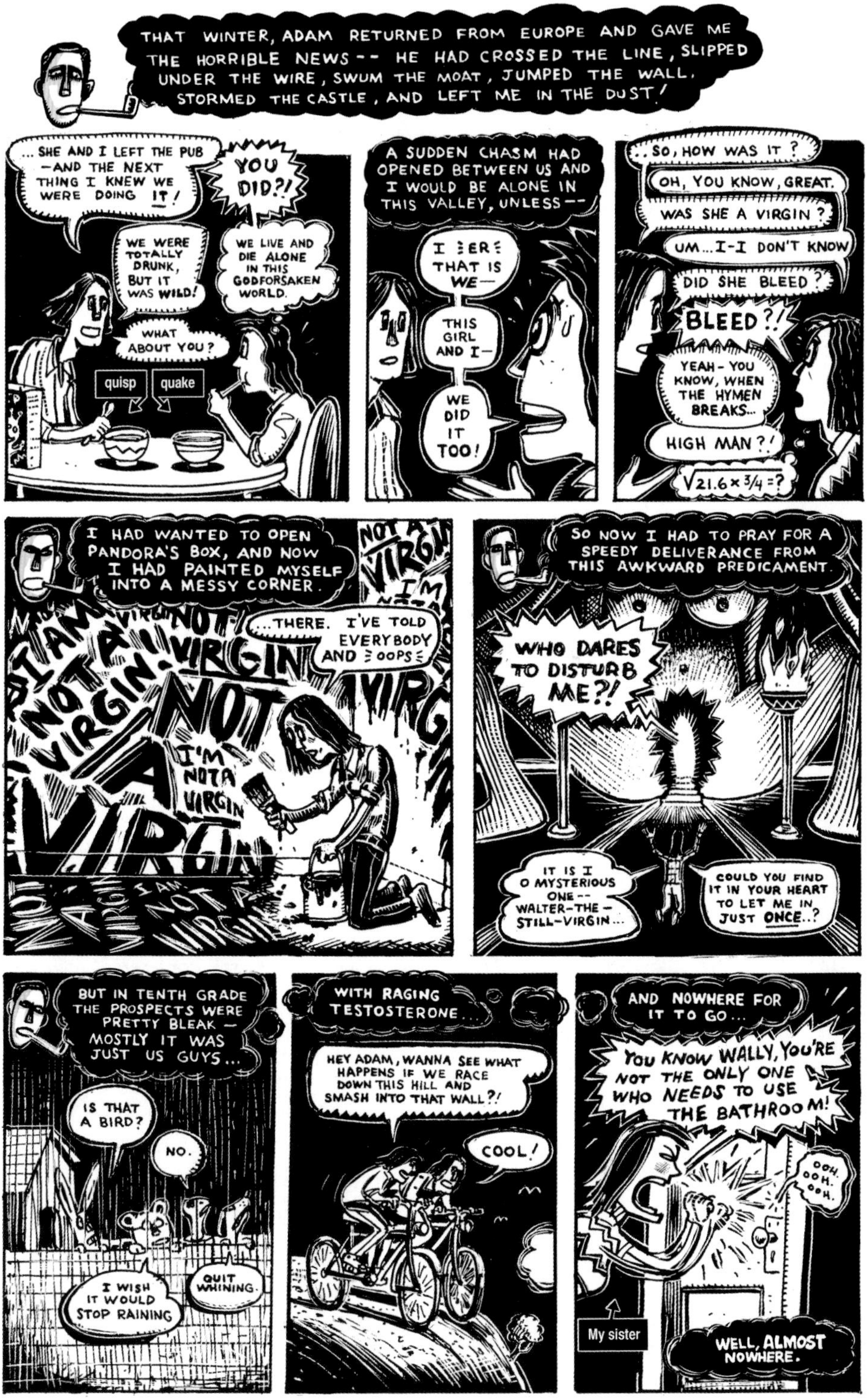
THAT WINTER, ADAM RETURNED FROM EUROPE AND GAVE ME THE HORRIBLE NEWS -- HE HAD CROSSED THE LINE, SLIPPED UNDER THE WIRE, SWUM THE MOAT, JUMPED THE WALL, STORMED THE CASTLE, AND LEFT ME IN THE DUST!
... SHE AND I LEFT THE PUB —AND THE NEXT THING I KNEW WE WERE DOING IT!
YOU DID?!
WE WERE TOTALLY DRUNK, BUT IT WAS WILD!
WE LIVE AND DIE ALONE IN THIS GODFORSAKEN WORLD.
WHAT ABOUT YOU?
quisp
quake
A SUDDEN CHASM HAD OPENED BETWEEN US AND I WOULD BE ALONE IN THIS VALLEY, UNLESS --
I ER THAT IS WE—
THIS GIRL AND I—
WE DID IT TOO!
SO, HOW WAS IT?
OH, YOU KNOW, GREAT.
WAS SHE A VIRGIN?
UM... I-I DON'T KNOW
DID SHE BLEED?
BLEED?!
YEAH - YOU KNOW, WHEN THE HYMEN BREAKS...
HIGH MAN?!
√21.6 × 3/4 = ?
I HAD WANTED TO OPEN PANDORA'S BOX, AND NOW I HAD PAINTED MYSELF INTO A MESSY CORNER.
...THERE. I'VE TOLD EVERYBODY AND OOPS
I AM NOT A VIRGIN!
NOT A VIRGIN
I'M NOT A VIRGIN
SO NOW I HAD TO PRAY FOR A SPEEDY DELIVERANCE FROM THIS AWKWARD PREDICAMENT.
WHO DARES TO DISTURB ME?!
IT IS I O MYSTERIOUS ONE -- WALTER-THE-STILL-VIRGIN...
COULD YOU FIND IT IN YOUR HEART TO LET ME IN JUST ONCE..?
BUT IN TENTH GRADE THE PROSPECTS WERE PRETTY BLEAK — MOSTLY IT WAS JUST US GUYS...
IS THAT A BIRD?
NO.
I WISH IT WOULD STOP RAINING
QUIT WHINING.
WITH RAGING TESTOSTERONE...
HEY ADAM, WANNA SEE WHAT HAPPENS IF WE RACE DOWN THIS HILL AND SMASH INTO THAT WALL?!
COOL!
AND NOWHERE FOR IT TO GO...
YOU KNOW WALLY, YOU'RE NOT THE ONLY ONE WHO NEEDS TO USE THE BATHROOM!
OOH. OOH. OOH.
My sister
WELL, ALMOST NOWHERE.

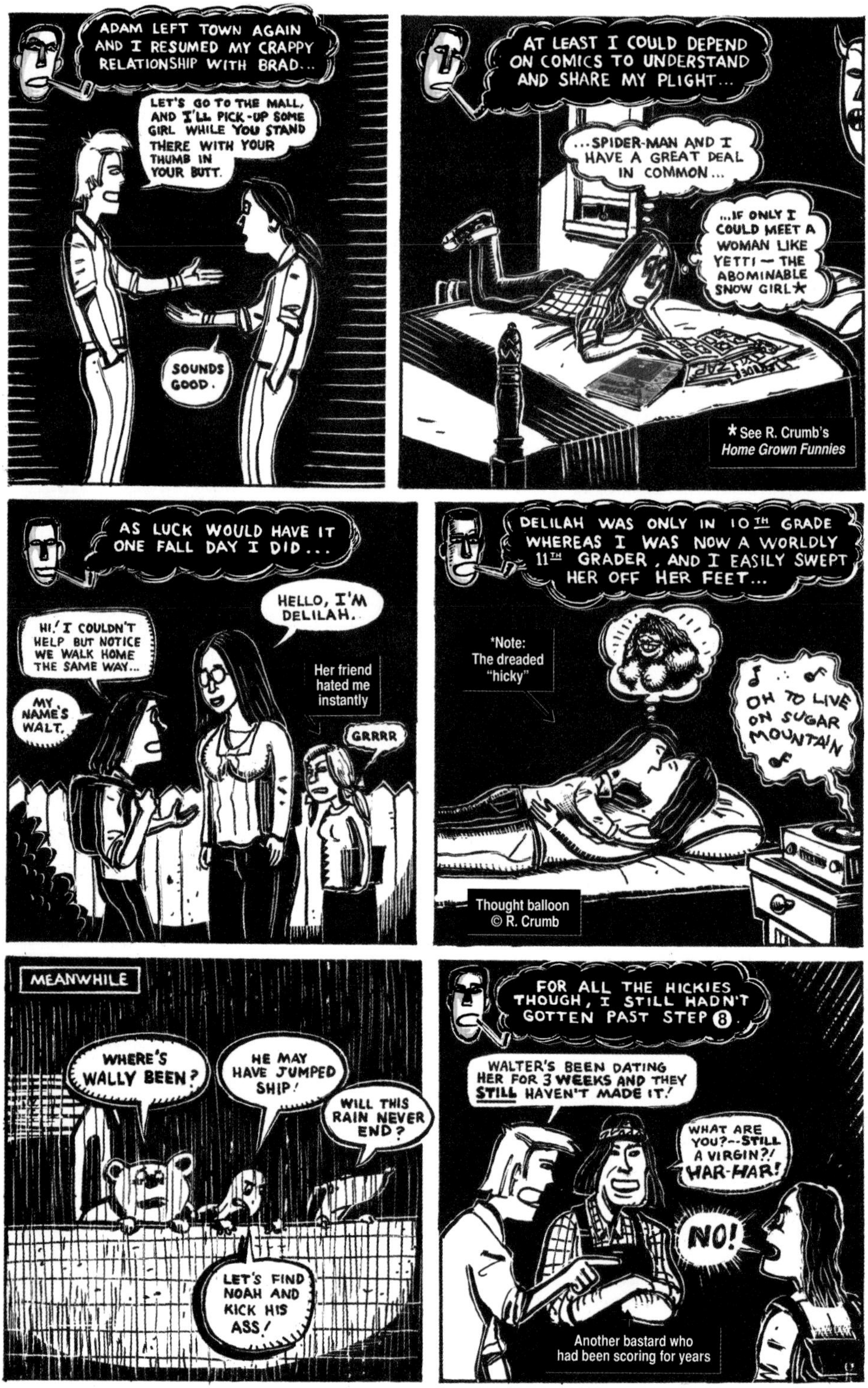
ADAM LEFT TOWN AGAIN AND I RESUMED MY CRAPPY RELATIONSHIP WITH BRAD...
LET'S GO TO THE MALL, AND I'LL PICK-UP SOME GIRL WHILE YOU STAND THERE WITH YOUR THUMB IN YOUR BUTT.
SOUNDS GOOD.
AT LEAST I COULD DEPEND ON COMICS TO UNDERSTAND AND SHARE MY PLIGHT...
...SPIDER-MAN AND I HAVE A GREAT DEAL IN COMMON...
...IF ONLY I COULD MEET A WOMAN LIKE YETTI — THE ABOMINABLE SNOW GIRL*
* See R. Crumb's *Home Grown Funnies*
AS LUCK WOULD HAVE IT ONE FALL DAY I DID...
HI! I COULDN'T HELP BUT NOTICE WE WALK HOME THE SAME WAY...
MY NAME'S WALT.
HELLO, I'M DELILAH.
Her friend hated me instantly
GRRRR
DELILAH WAS ONLY IN 10TH GRADE WHEREAS I WAS NOW A WORLDLY 11TH GRADER, AND I EASILY SWEPT HER OFF HER FEET...
*Note: The dreaded "hicky"
OH TO LIVE ON SUGAR MOUNTAIN
Thought balloon © R. Crumb
MEANWHILE
WHERE'S WALLY BEEN?
HE MAY HAVE JUMPED SHIP!
WILL THIS RAIN NEVER END?
LET'S FIND NOAH AND KICK HIS ASS!
FOR ALL THE HICKIES THOUGH, I STILL HADN'T GOTTEN PAST STEP 8.
WALTER'S BEEN DATING HER FOR 3 WEEKS AND THEY STILL HAVEN'T MADE IT!
WHAT ARE YOU?--STILL A VIRGIN?! HAR-HAR!
NO!
Another bastard who had been scoring for years

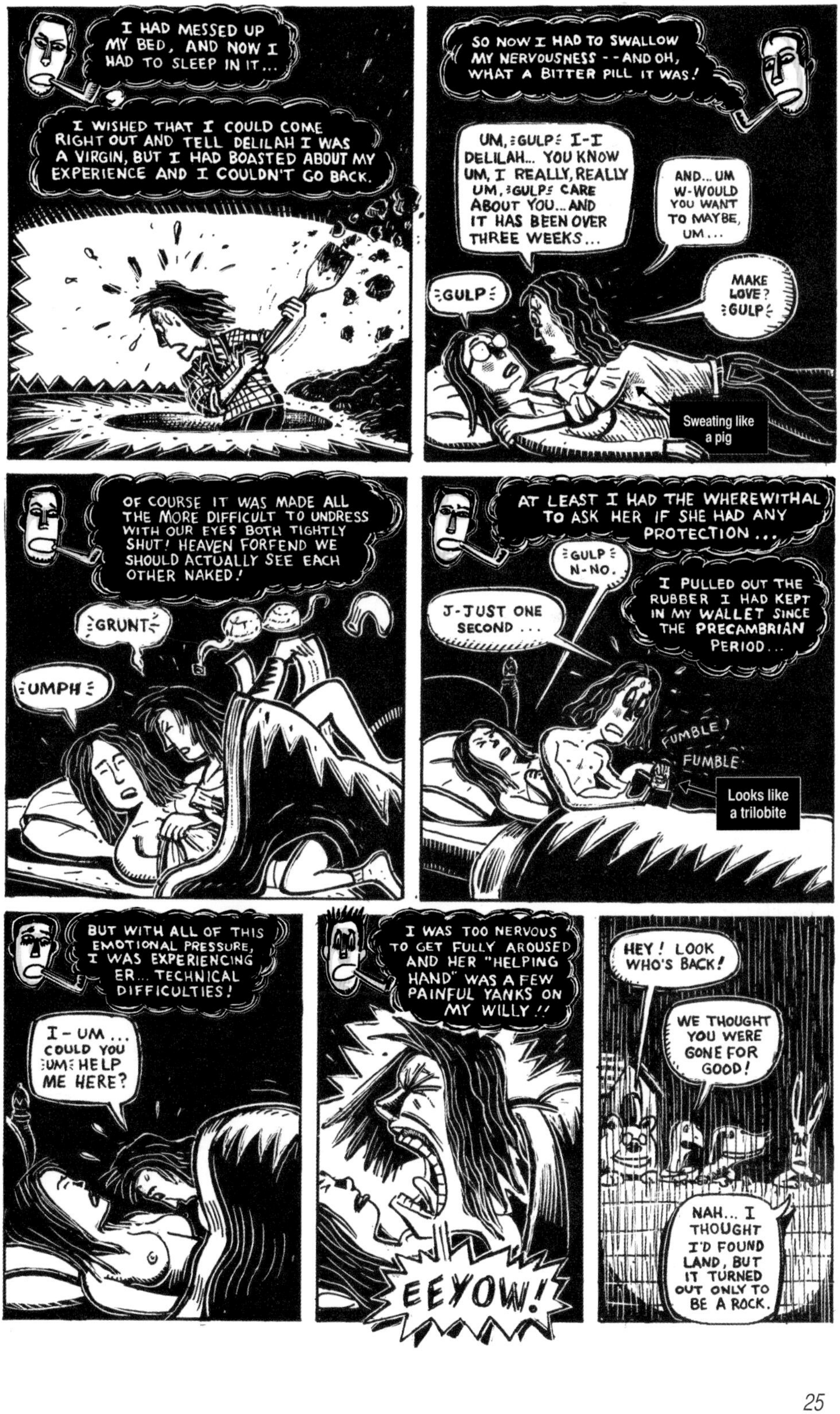
I HAD MESSED UP MY BED, AND NOW I HAD TO SLEEP IN IT...
I WISHED THAT I COULD COME RIGHT OUT AND TELL DELILAH I WAS A VIRGIN, BUT I HAD BOASTED ABOUT MY EXPERIENCE AND I COULDN'T GO BACK.
SO NOW I HAD TO SWALLOW MY NERVOUSNESS -- AND OH, WHAT A BITTER PILL IT WAS!
UM, GULP I-I DELILAH... YOU KNOW UM, I REALLY, REALLY UM, GULP CARE ABOUT YOU... AND IT HAS BEEN OVER THREE WEEKS...
AND... UM W-WOULD YOU WANT TO MAYBE, UM...
GULP
MAKE LOVE? GULP
Sweating like a pig
OF COURSE IT WAS MADE ALL THE MORE DIFFICULT TO UNDRESS WITH OUR EYES BOTH TIGHTLY SHUT! HEAVEN FORFEND WE SHOULD ACTUALLY SEE EACH OTHER NAKED!
GRUNT
UMPH
AT LEAST I HAD THE WHEREWITHAL TO ASK HER IF SHE HAD ANY PROTECTION...
GULP N-NO.
I PULLED OUT THE RUBBER I HAD KEPT IN MY WALLET SINCE THE PRECAMBRIAN PERIOD...
J-JUST ONE SECOND...
FUMBLE
FUMBLE
Looks like a trilobite
BUT WITH ALL OF THIS EMOTIONAL PRESSURE, I WAS EXPERIENCING ER... TECHNICAL DIFFICULTIES!
I-UM... COULD YOU UM HELP ME HERE?
I WAS TOO NERVOUS TO GET FULLY AROUSED AND HER "HELPING HAND" WAS A FEW PAINFUL YANKS ON MY WILLY!!
EEYOW!
HEY! LOOK WHO'S BACK!
WE THOUGHT YOU WERE GONE FOR GOOD!
NAH... I THOUGHT I'D FOUND LAND, BUT IT TURNED OUT ONLY TO BE A ROCK.

SO THERE I WAS BACK AT SQUARE ONE, STILL HANGING OUT WITH BRAD, STILL A VIRGIN. I HAD TO GIVE BRAD CREDIT THOUGH, HE WAS INVENTIVE WHEN IT CAME TO MEETING THE OPPOSITE SEX, AND ONE OF HIS BETTER IDEAS WAS TO GO DIRECTLY TO AN UNCHALLENGED SOURCE...

THAT CAR'S STOPPING!

WHOOHOO! GIRLS, HERE WE COME!

SCREEEEEE

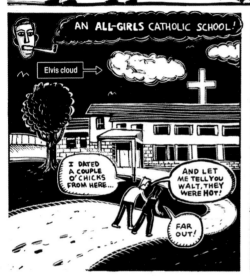

AN **ALL-GIRLS** CATHOLIC SCHOOL!

Elvis cloud →

I DATED A COUPLE O' CHICKS FROM HERE...

AND LET ME TELL YOU WALT, THEY WERE HOT!

FAR OUT!

IT WAS FUNNY HOW A PLACE THAT PREACHED SUCH A STRICT MORAL CODE REGULARLY PRODUCED GIRLS WHO SMOKED, DRANK, DID MORE DRUGS, AND HAD MORE SEX THAN THEIR PUBLIC SCHOOL COUNTERPARTS!

VERONICA, CAN YOU MEET US IN THE WOODS WITH BETTY?

NEXT PERIOD.

I DON'T WANT TO SEE YOU WITH THOSE DIME STORE EYES AGAIN YOUNG LADY!

BITCH

BOY, THAT IS SOME REALLY GOOD REEFER BETTY!

THANKS.

DO YOU GUYS WANT TO COME OVER TONIGHT?

MY PARENTS ARE OUT OF TOWN!

BEAUTIFUL!

THAT NIGHT WHILE BRAD COMFORTABLY MADE THE MOVES ON BETTY, I UNCOMFORTABLY PLAYED PING-PONG WITH VERONICA...

JEEZ! VERONICA HAS ENORMOUS BREASTS, AND SHE'S NOT WEARING A BRA!

TOUCHÉ!

OH, BRAD!

I NEVER NOTICED HOW BLUE YOUR EYES ARE...

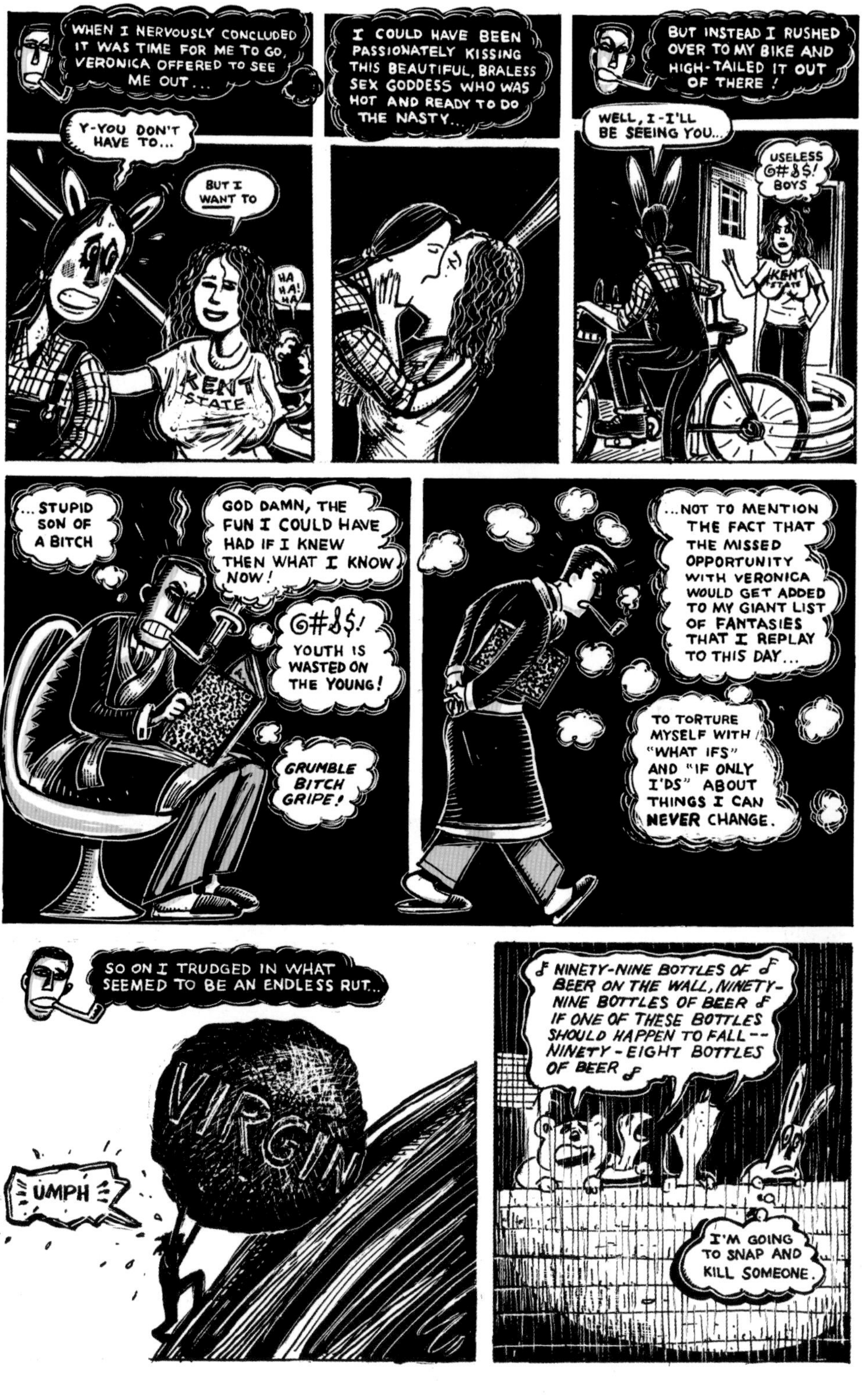

WHEN I NERVOUSLY CONCLUDED IT WAS TIME FOR ME TO GO, VERONICA OFFERED TO SEE ME OUT...
Y-YOU DON'T HAVE TO...
BUT I WANT TO
HA HA! HA
I COULD HAVE BEEN PASSIONATELY KISSING THIS BEAUTIFUL, BRALESS SEX GODDESS WHO WAS HOT AND READY TO DO THE NASTY...
BUT INSTEAD I RUSHED OVER TO MY BIKE AND HIGH-TAILED IT OUT OF THERE!
WELL, I-I'LL BE SEEING YOU...
USELESS G#$$! BOYS
KENT STATE
...STUPID SON OF A BITCH
GOD DAMN, THE FUN I COULD HAVE HAD IF I KNEW THEN WHAT I KNOW NOW!
G#$$! YOUTH IS WASTED ON THE YOUNG!
GRUMBLE BITCH GRIPE!
...NOT TO MENTION THE FACT THAT THE MISSED OPPORTUNITY WITH VERONICA WOULD GET ADDED TO MY GIANT LIST OF FANTASIES THAT I REPLAY TO THIS DAY...
TO TORTURE MYSELF WITH "WHAT IFS" AND "IF ONLY I'DS" ABOUT THINGS I CAN NEVER CHANGE.
SO ON I TRUDGED IN WHAT SEEMED TO BE AN ENDLESS RUT...
VIRGIN
UMPH
NINETY-NINE BOTTLES OF BEER ON THE WALL, NINETY-NINE BOTTLES OF BEER IF ONE OF THESE BOTTLES SHOULD HAPPEN TO FALL-- NINETY-EIGHT BOTTLES OF BEER
I'M GOING TO SNAP AND KILL SOMEONE.

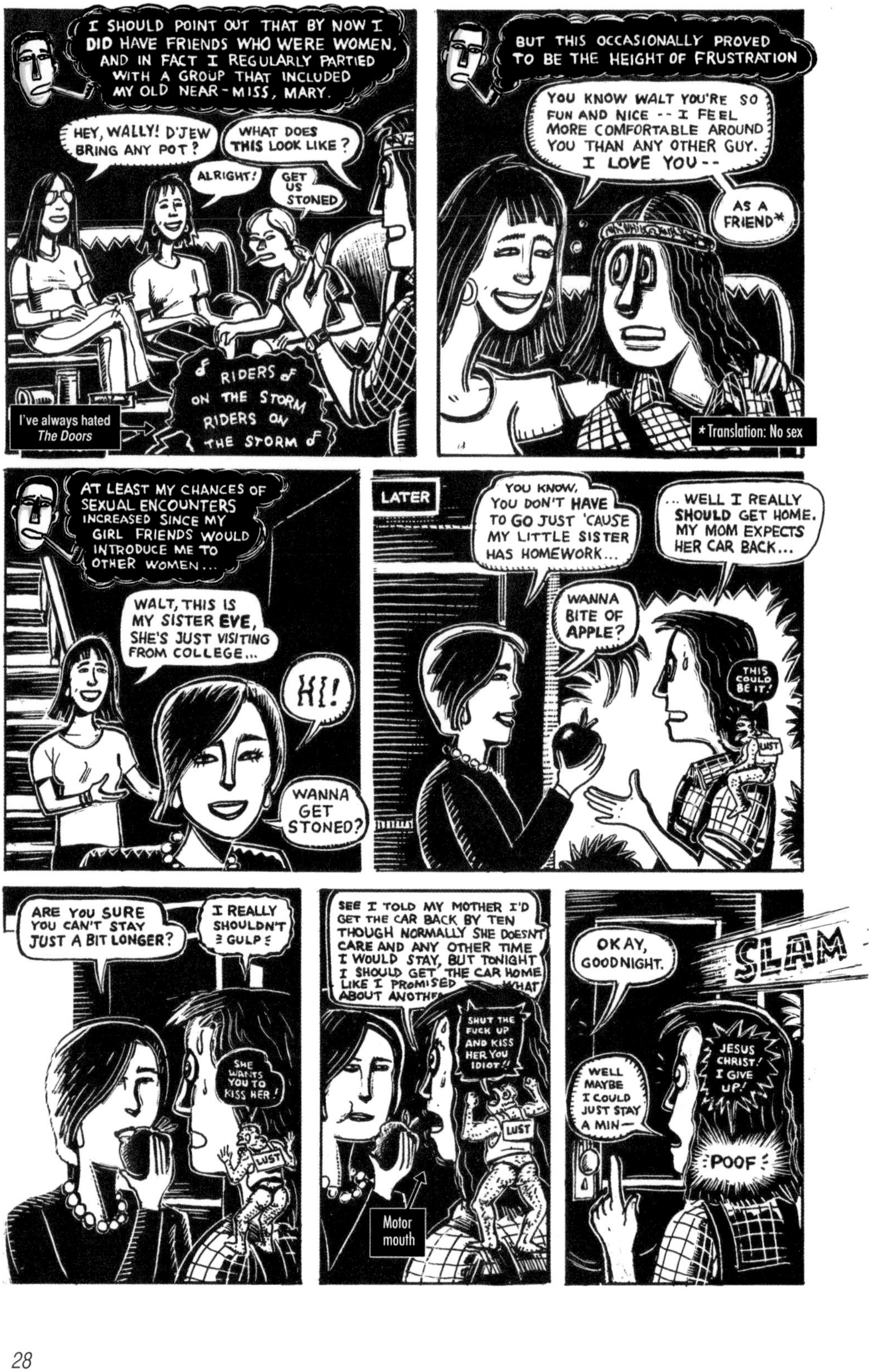
I SHOULD POINT OUT THAT BY NOW I DID HAVE FRIENDS WHO WERE WOMEN, AND IN FACT I REGULARLY PARTIED WITH A GROUP THAT INCLUDED MY OLD NEAR-MISS, MARY.
HEY, WALLY! D'JEW BRING ANY POT?
WHAT DOES THIS LOOK LIKE?
ALRIGHT!
GET US STONED
RIDERS ON THE STORM RIDERS ON THE STORM
I've always hated The Doors
BUT THIS OCCASIONALLY PROVED TO BE THE HEIGHT OF FRUSTRATION
YOU KNOW WALT YOU'RE SO FUN AND NICE -- I FEEL MORE COMFORTABLE AROUND YOU THAN ANY OTHER GUY. I LOVE YOU --
AS A FRIEND*
*Translation: No sex
AT LEAST MY CHANCES OF SEXUAL ENCOUNTERS INCREASED SINCE MY GIRL FRIENDS WOULD INTRODUCE ME TO OTHER WOMEN...
WALT, THIS IS MY SISTER EVE, SHE'S JUST VISITING FROM COLLEGE...
HI!
WANNA GET STONED?
LATER
YOU KNOW, YOU DON'T HAVE TO GO JUST 'CAUSE MY LITTLE SISTER HAS HOMEWORK...
...WELL I REALLY SHOULD GET HOME. MY MOM EXPECTS HER CAR BACK...
WANNA BITE OF APPLE?
THIS COULD BE IT!
LUST
ARE YOU SURE YOU CAN'T STAY JUST A BIT LONGER?
I REALLY SHOULDN'T GULP
SHE WANTS YOU TO KISS HER!
LUST
SEE I TOLD MY MOTHER I'D GET THE CAR BACK BY TEN THOUGH NORMALLY SHE DOESN'T CARE AND ANY OTHER TIME I WOULD STAY, BUT TONIGHT I SHOULD GET THE CAR HOME LIKE I PROMISED WHAT ABOUT ANOTHE
SHUT THE FUCK UP AND KISS HER YOU IDIOT!!
LUST
Motor mouth
OKAY, GOODNIGHT.
SLAM
WELL MAYBE I COULD JUST STAY A MIN—
JESUS CHRIST! I GIVE UP!
POOF

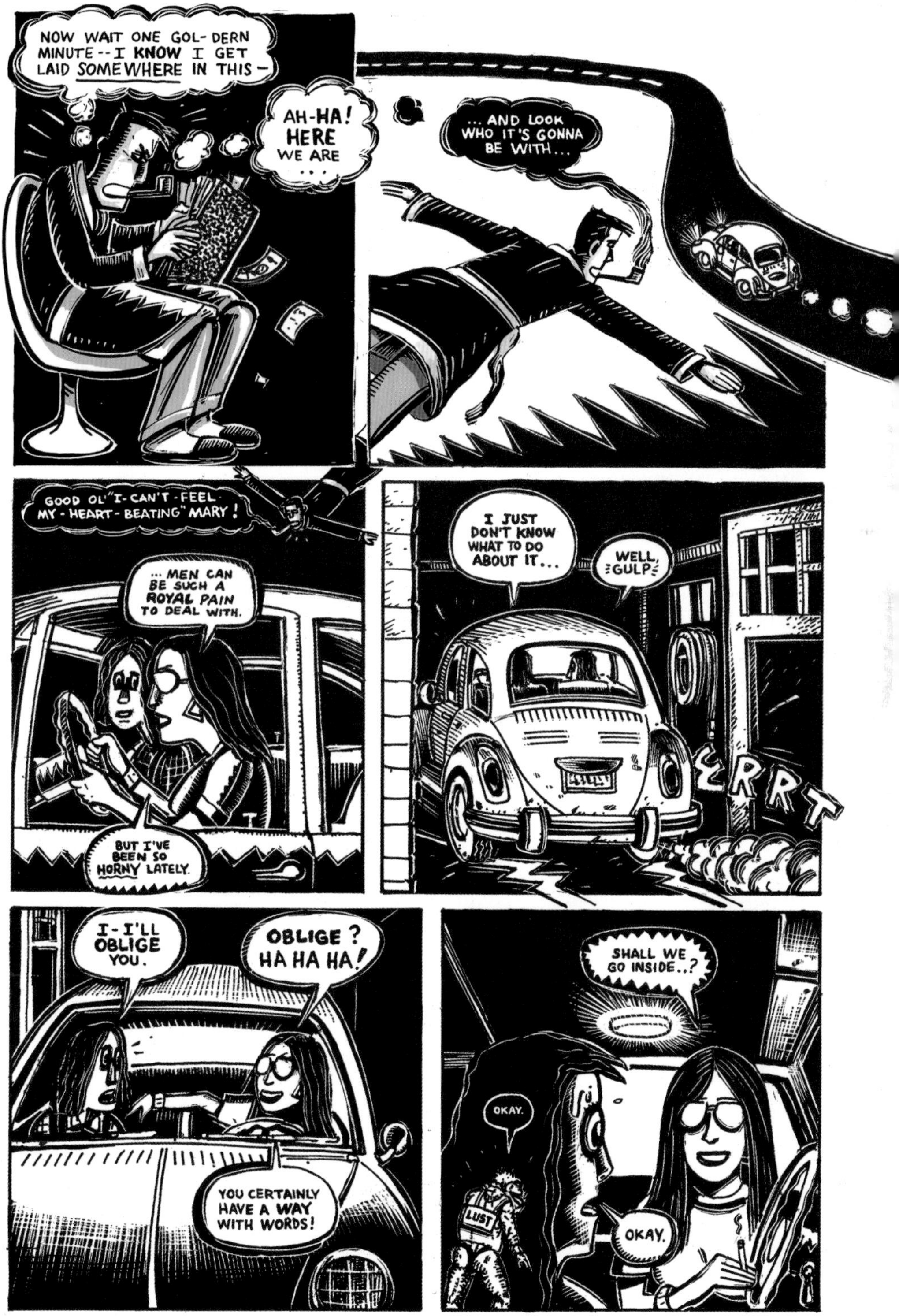
NOW WAIT ONE GOL-DERN MINUTE--I KNOW I GET LAID SOMEWHERE IN THIS—
AH-HA! HERE WE ARE . . .
...AND LOOK WHO IT'S GONNA BE WITH...
GOOD OL' "I-CAN'T-FEEL-MY-HEART-BEATING" MARY!
...MEN CAN BE SUCH A ROYAL PAIN TO DEAL WITH.
BUT I'VE BEEN SO HORNY LATELY.
I JUST DON'T KNOW WHAT TO DO ABOUT IT...
WELL, GULP
ERRT
I-I'LL OBLIGE YOU.
OBLIGE? HA HA HA!
YOU CERTAINLY HAVE A WAY WITH WORDS!
SHALL WE GO INSIDE..?
OKAY.
LUST
OKAY.

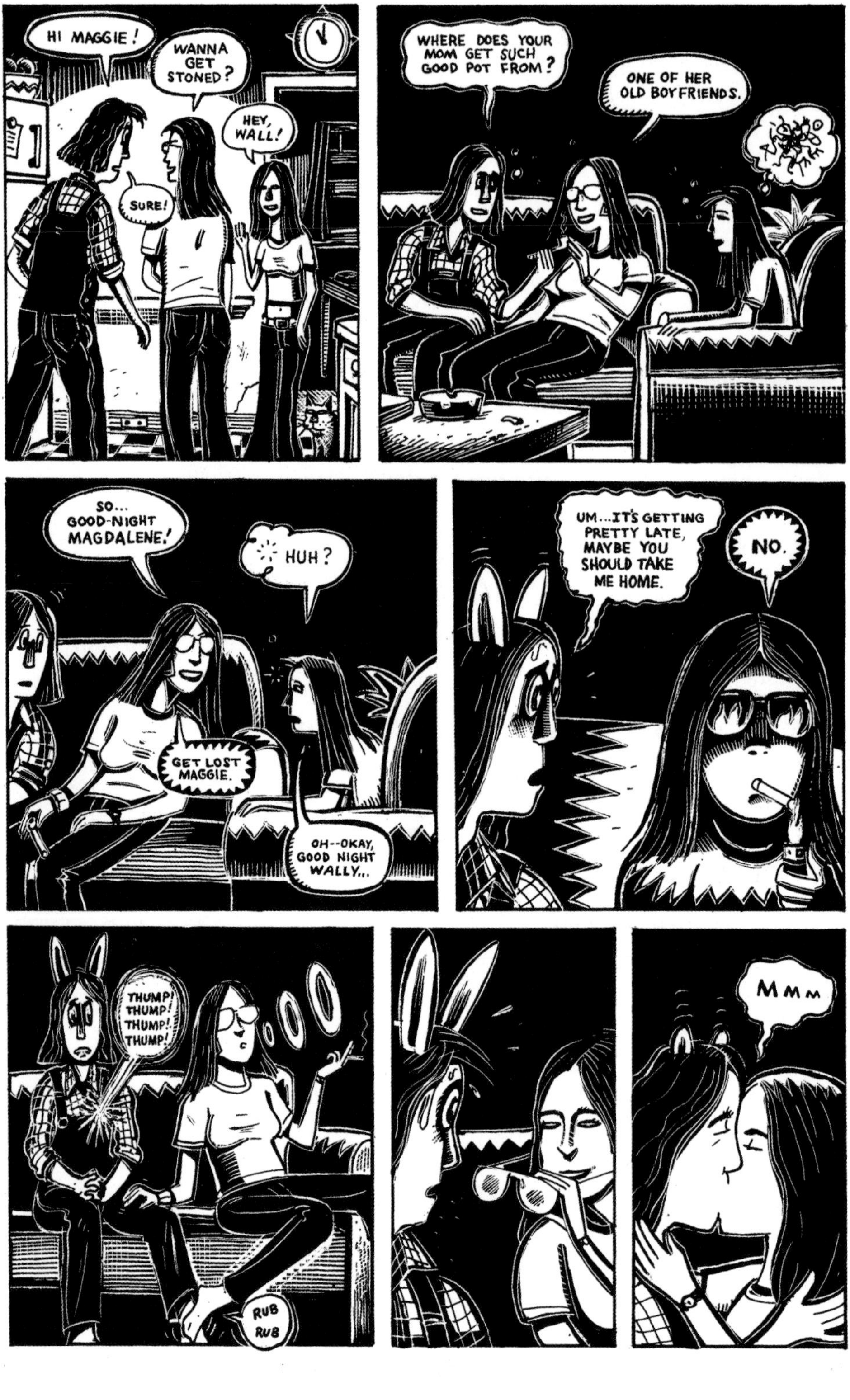
HI MAGGIE!
WANNA GET STONED?
SURE!
HEY, WALL!
WHERE DOES YOUR MOM GET SUCH GOOD POT FROM?
ONE OF HER OLD BOYFRIENDS.
SO... GOOD-NIGHT MAGDALENE!
HUH?
GET LOST MAGGIE.
OH--OKAY, GOOD NIGHT WALLY...
UM...IT'S GETTING PRETTY LATE, MAYBE YOU SHOULD TAKE ME HOME.
NO.
THUMP! THUMP! THUMP! THUMP!
RUB RUB
Mmm

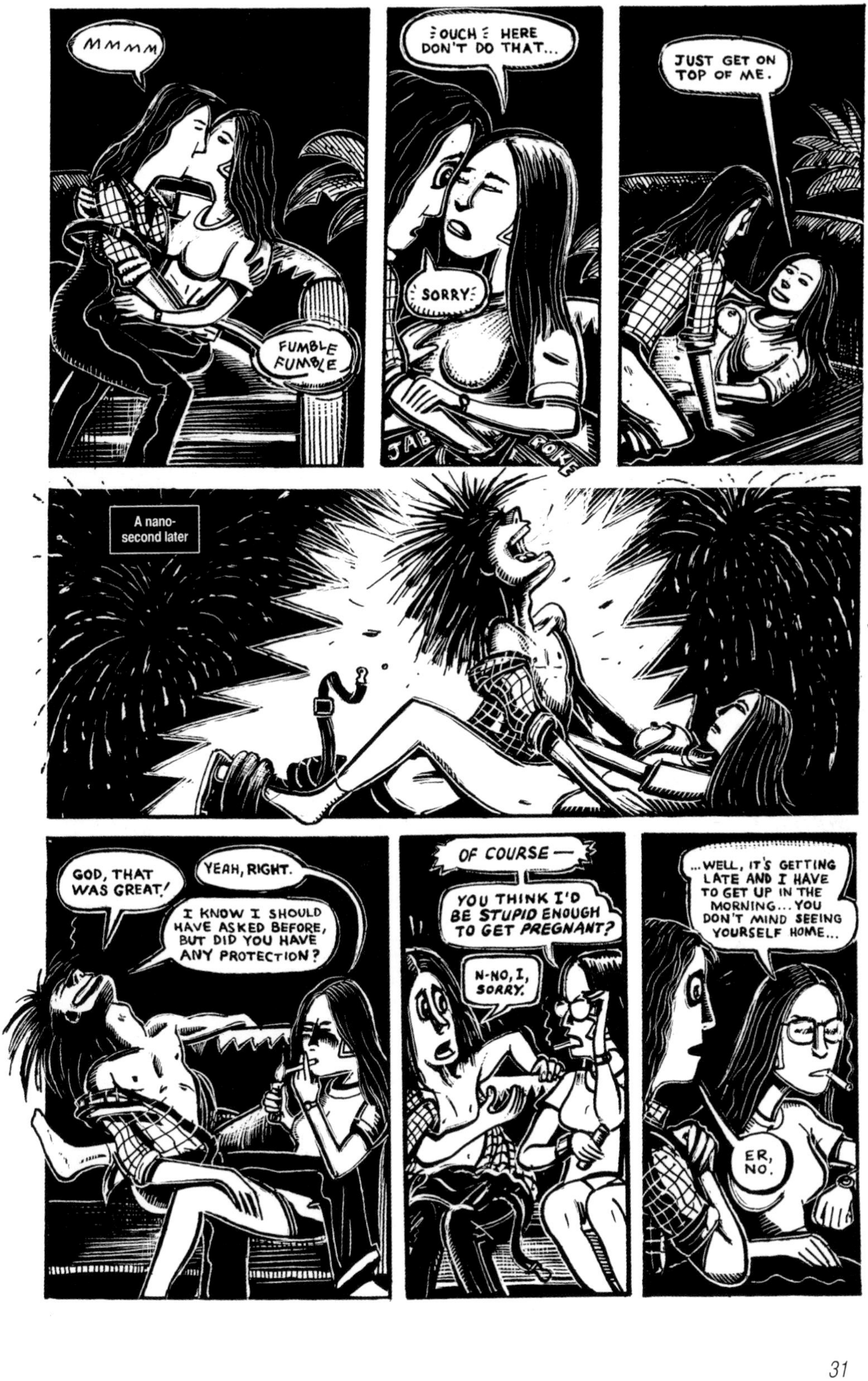
MMMM
FUMBLE FUMBLE
OUCH HERE DON'T DO THAT...
SORRY
JAB
POKE
JUST GET ON TOP OF ME.
A nano-second later
GOD, THAT WAS GREAT!
YEAH, RIGHT.
I KNOW I SHOULD HAVE ASKED BEFORE, BUT DID YOU HAVE ANY PROTECTION?
OF COURSE —
YOU THINK I'D BE STUPID ENOUGH TO GET PREGNANT?
N-NO, I, SORRY.
...WELL, IT'S GETTING LATE AND I HAVE TO GET UP IN THE MORNING... YOU DON'T MIND SEEING YOURSELF HOME...
ER, NO.

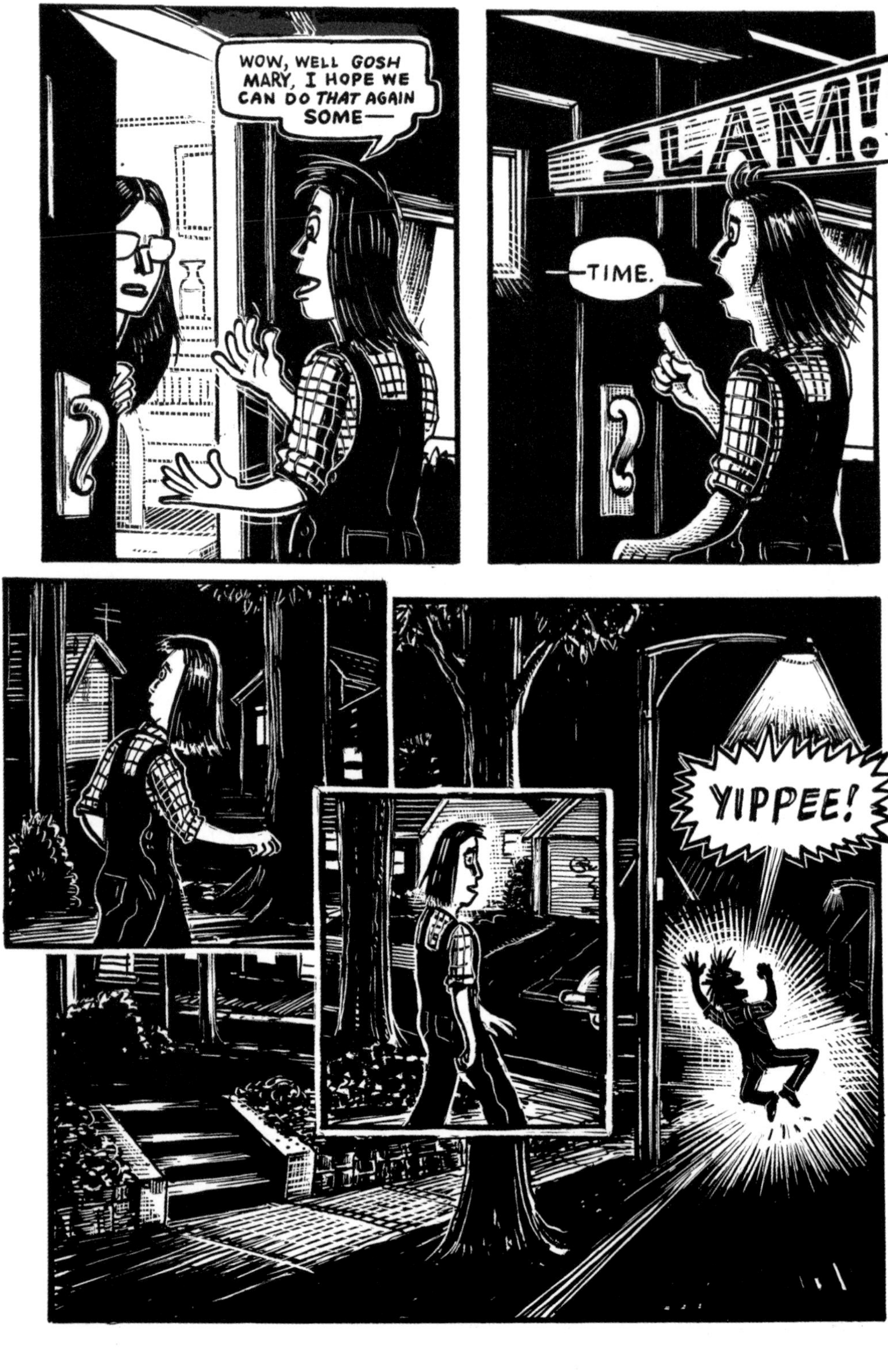
WOW, WELL GOSH MARY, I HOPE WE CAN DO THAT AGAIN SOME—
SLAM!
—TIME.
YIPPEE!

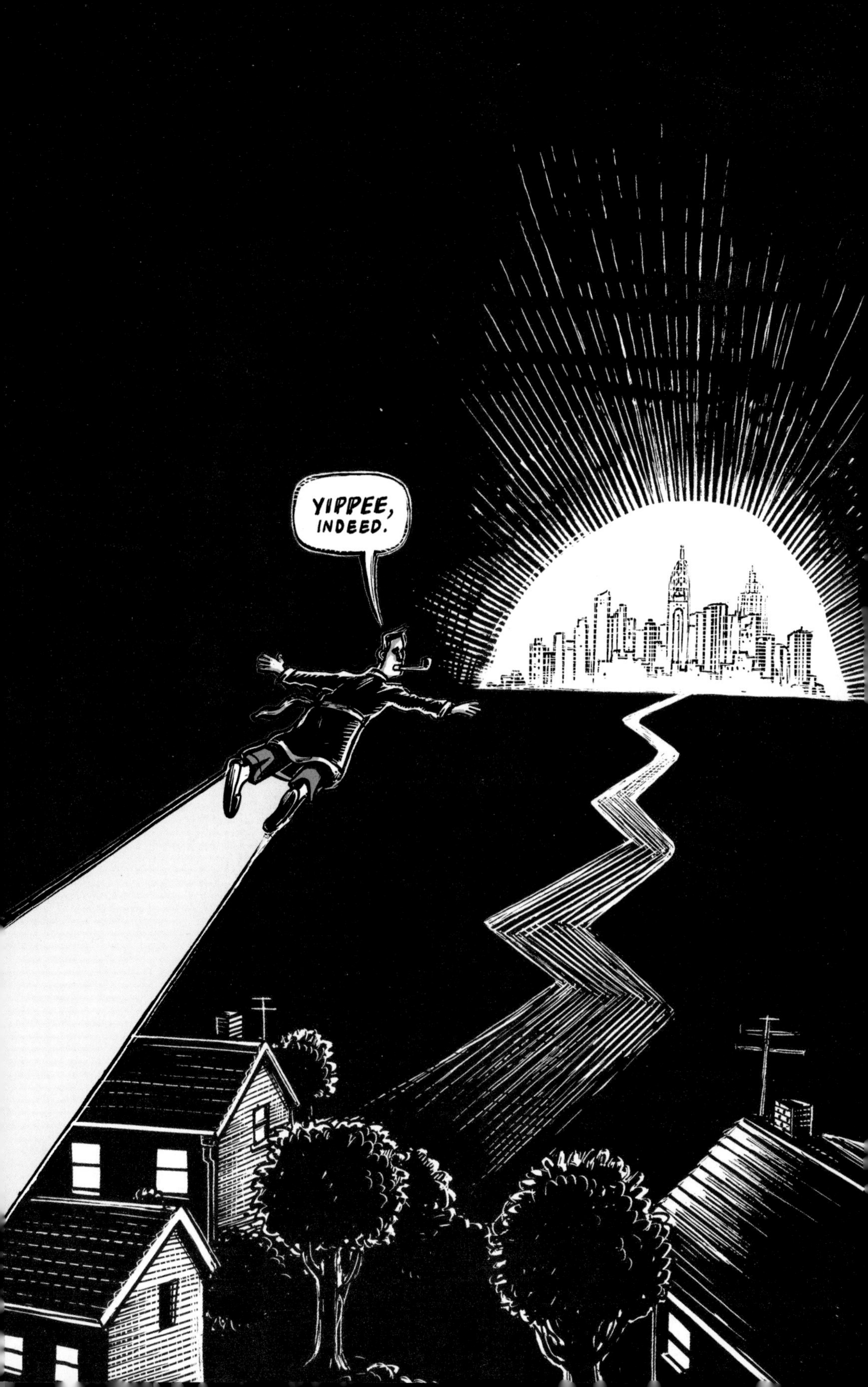
YIPPEE, INDEED.

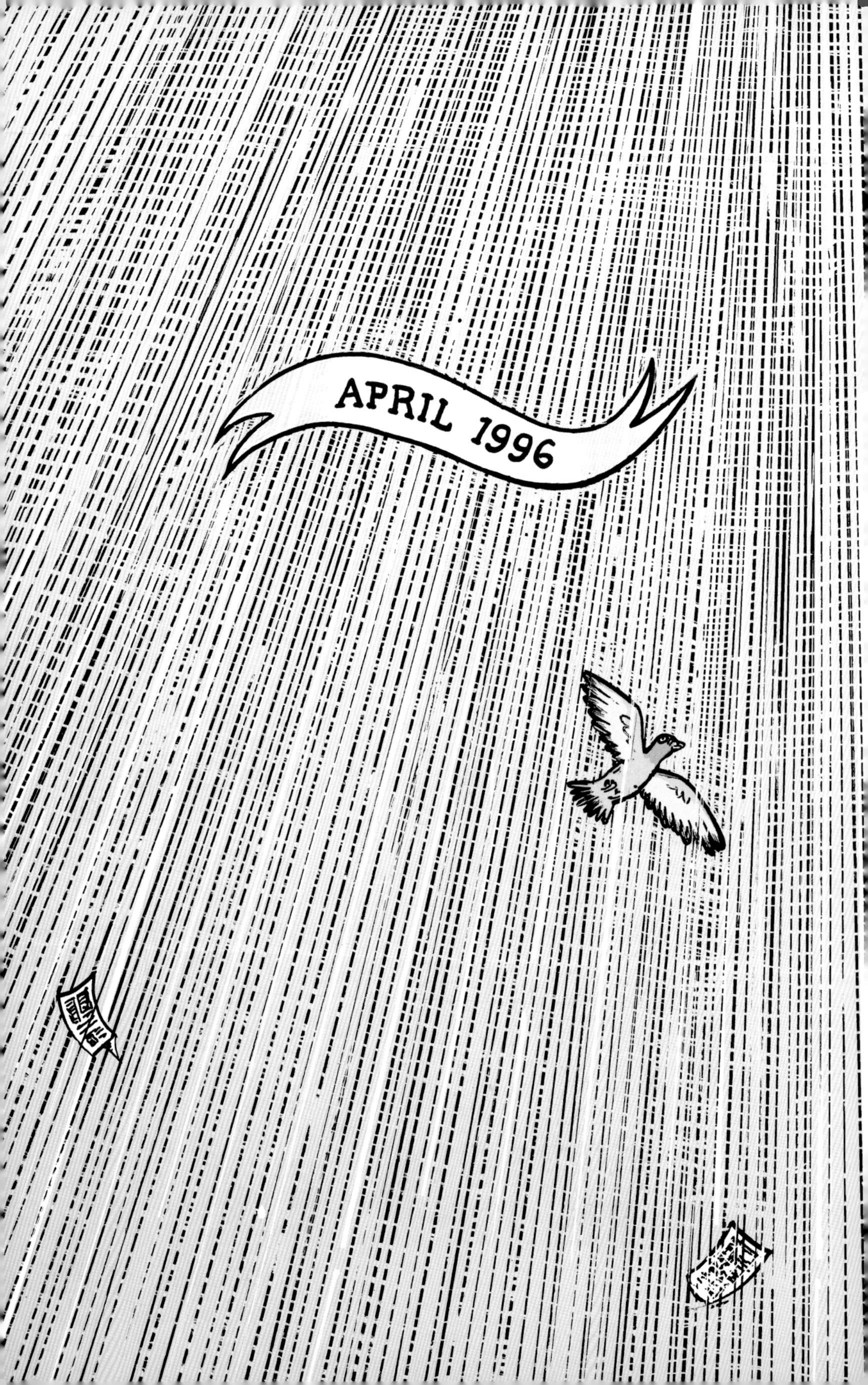
APRIL 1996

... AND THAT'S WHAT SEPARATES THE MERELY GOOD CARTOONIST, FROM THE GREAT ONES...

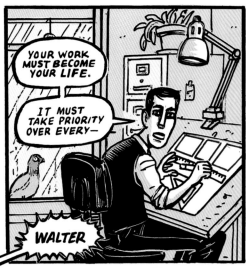

YOUR WORK MUST BECOME YOUR LIFE.

IT MUST TAKE PRIORITY OVER EVERY—

WALTER

SORRY TO INTERRUPT, BUT I'M LATE FOR WORK AND— OH!

WHAT?

YOUR PROGENY IS VERY KICKY THIS MORNING.

LEMMIE FEEL...

KNOCK, KNOCK. CAN BABY COME OUT AND PLAY?

O.K. MR. FUNNYMAN...

CAN YOU PICK UP THE DRY CLEANING AND SOME MILK AND PLEASE—DO THE DISHES BEFORE I GET HOME?

SIR, YES SIR!

CALL ME LATER!

SHUT

... SO, WHERE WERE WE?

UM...

LET'S TALK ABOUT INSPIRATION...

STORIES CAN COME FROM ANYWHERE-- PERSONAL EXPERIENCES, DREAMS, FANTASIES, YOU NAME IT...

I FIND THE NEWSPAPER IS GREAT FOR SOURCE MATERIAL.

LET'S SEE... AIDS, GLOBAL WARMING, OVERPOPULATION, MASS EXTINCTIONS, FAMINE, WARS...

JESUS CHRIST, WE'RE DOOMED!

Symbol for an idea

HOLD ON...

SOMETHING'S COMING TO ME...

I'VE GOT IT!

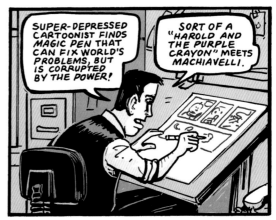

SUPER-DEPRESSED CARTOONIST FINDS MAGIC PEN THAT CAN FIX WORLD'S PROBLEMS, BUT IS CORRUPTED BY THE POWER!

SORT OF A "HAROLD AND THE PURPLE CRAYON" MEETS MACHIAVELLI.

HMM... ON SECOND THOUGHT...

I WANNA KEEP MY STORIES MORE PERSONAL, MORE...

RING!

OOPS

'SCUSE ME A SECOND.

ADAM--HEY!

OH, YOU KNOW, DRAWING...

A BLANK.

UM... O.K., MEET YOU AT THE USUAL BENCH...

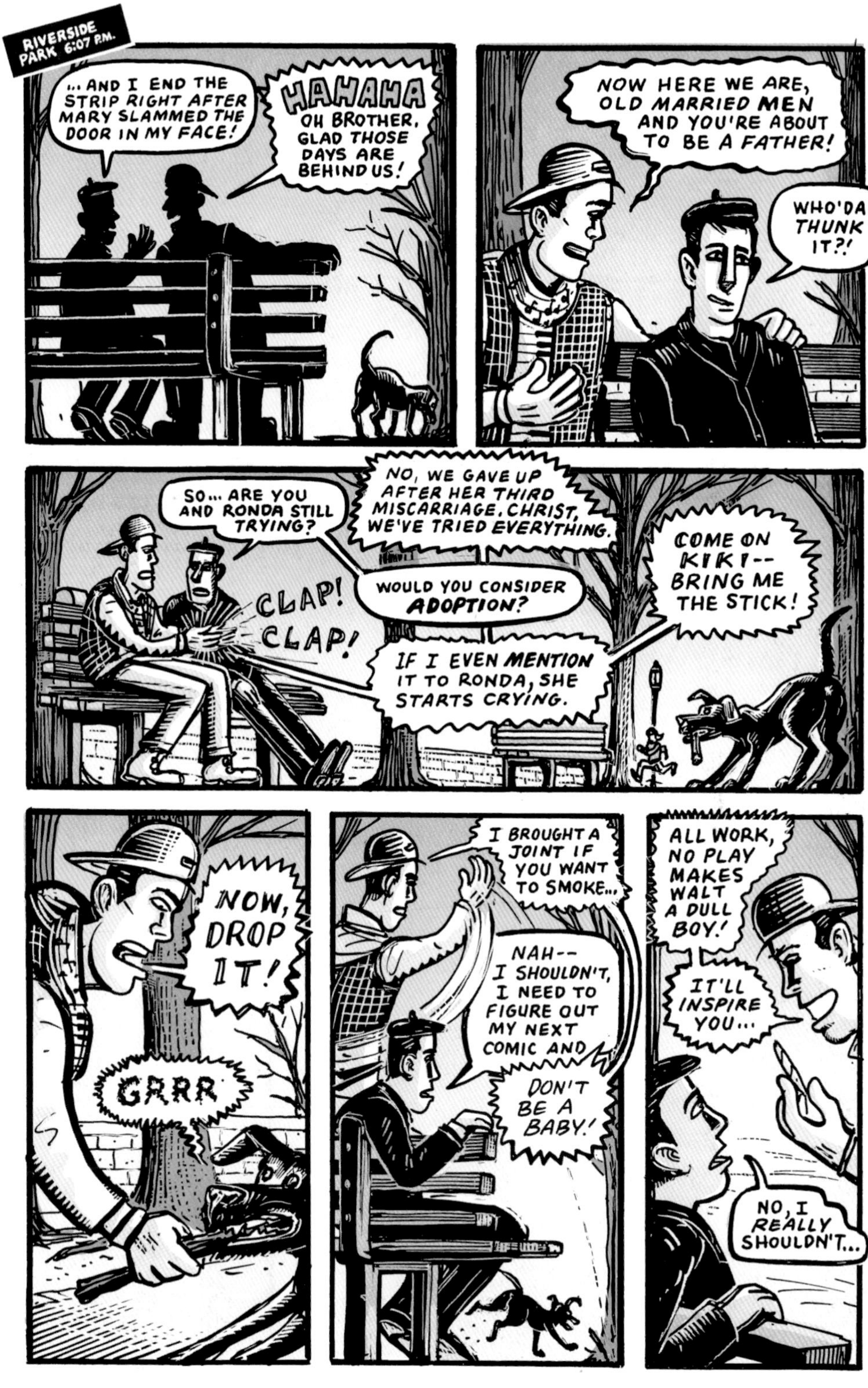
RIVERSIDE PARK 6:07 P.M.
...AND I END THE STRIP RIGHT AFTER MARY SLAMMED THE DOOR IN MY FACE!
HAHAHA OH BROTHER, GLAD THOSE DAYS ARE BEHIND US!
NOW HERE WE ARE, OLD MARRIED MEN AND YOU'RE ABOUT TO BE A FATHER!
WHO'DA THUNK IT?!
SO... ARE YOU AND RONDA STILL TRYING?
NO, WE GAVE UP AFTER HER THIRD MISCARRIAGE. CHRIST, WE'VE TRIED EVERYTHING.
CLAP! CLAP!
WOULD YOU CONSIDER ADOPTION?
IF I EVEN MENTION IT TO RONDA, SHE STARTS CRYING.
COME ON KIKI-- BRING ME THE STICK!
NOW, DROP IT!
GRRR
I BROUGHT A JOINT IF YOU WANT TO SMOKE...
NAH-- I SHOULDN'T, I NEED TO FIGURE OUT MY NEXT COMIC AND
DON'T BE A BABY!
ALL WORK, NO PLAY MAKES WALT A DULL BOY!
IT'LL INSPIRE YOU...
NO, I REALLY SHOULDN'T...

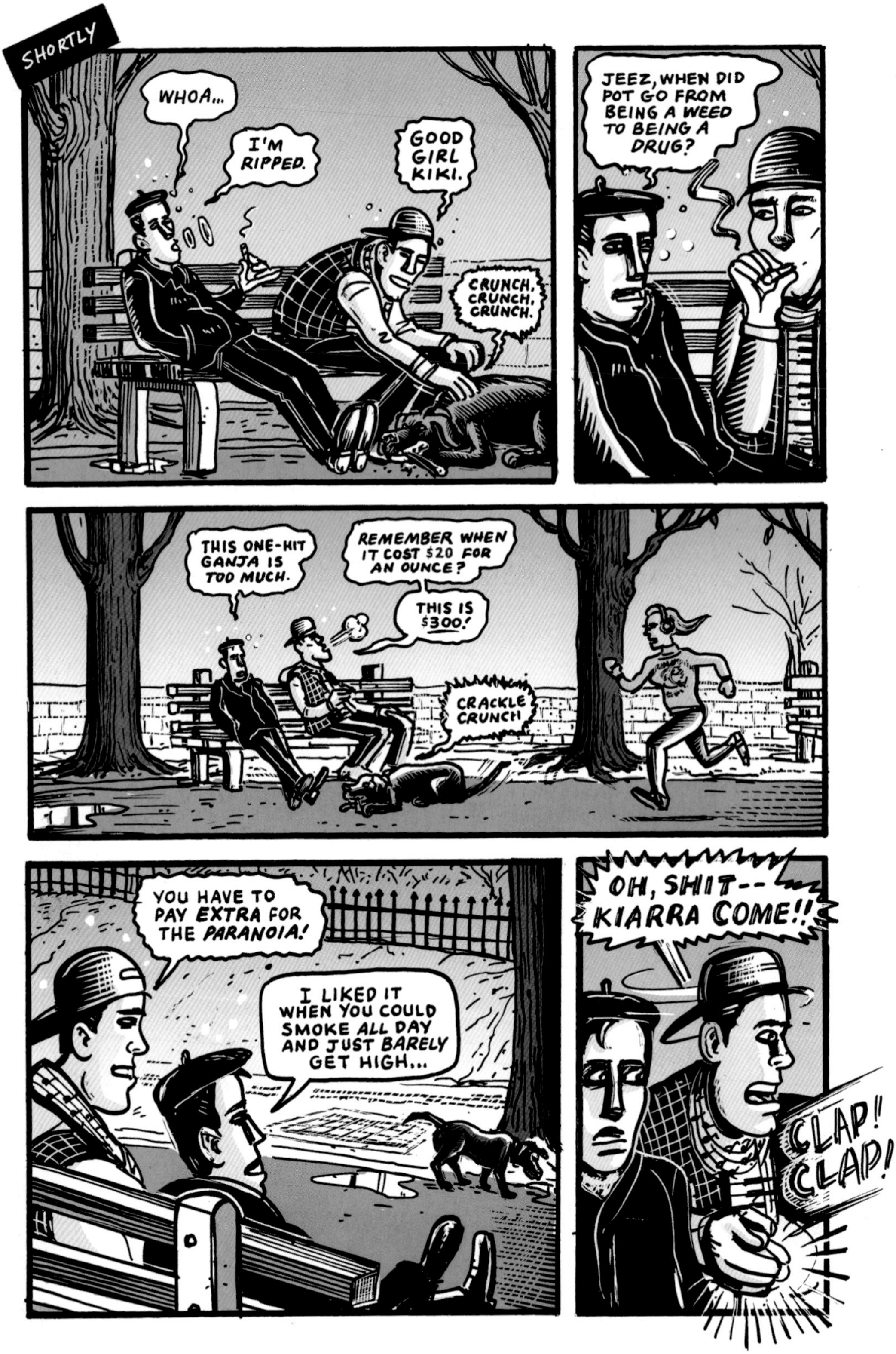
SHORTLY
WHOA...
I'M RIPPED.
GOOD GIRL KIKI.
CRUNCH, CRUNCH, CRUNCH.
JEEZ, WHEN DID POT GO FROM BEING A WEED TO BEING A DRUG?
THIS ONE-HIT GANJA IS TOO MUCH.
REMEMBER WHEN IT COST $20 FOR AN OUNCE?
THIS IS $300!
CRACKLE CRUNCH
YOU HAVE TO PAY EXTRA FOR THE PARANOIA!
I LIKED IT WHEN YOU COULD SMOKE ALL DAY AND JUST BARELY GET HIGH...
OH, SHIT-- KIARRA COME!!
CLAP! CLAP!

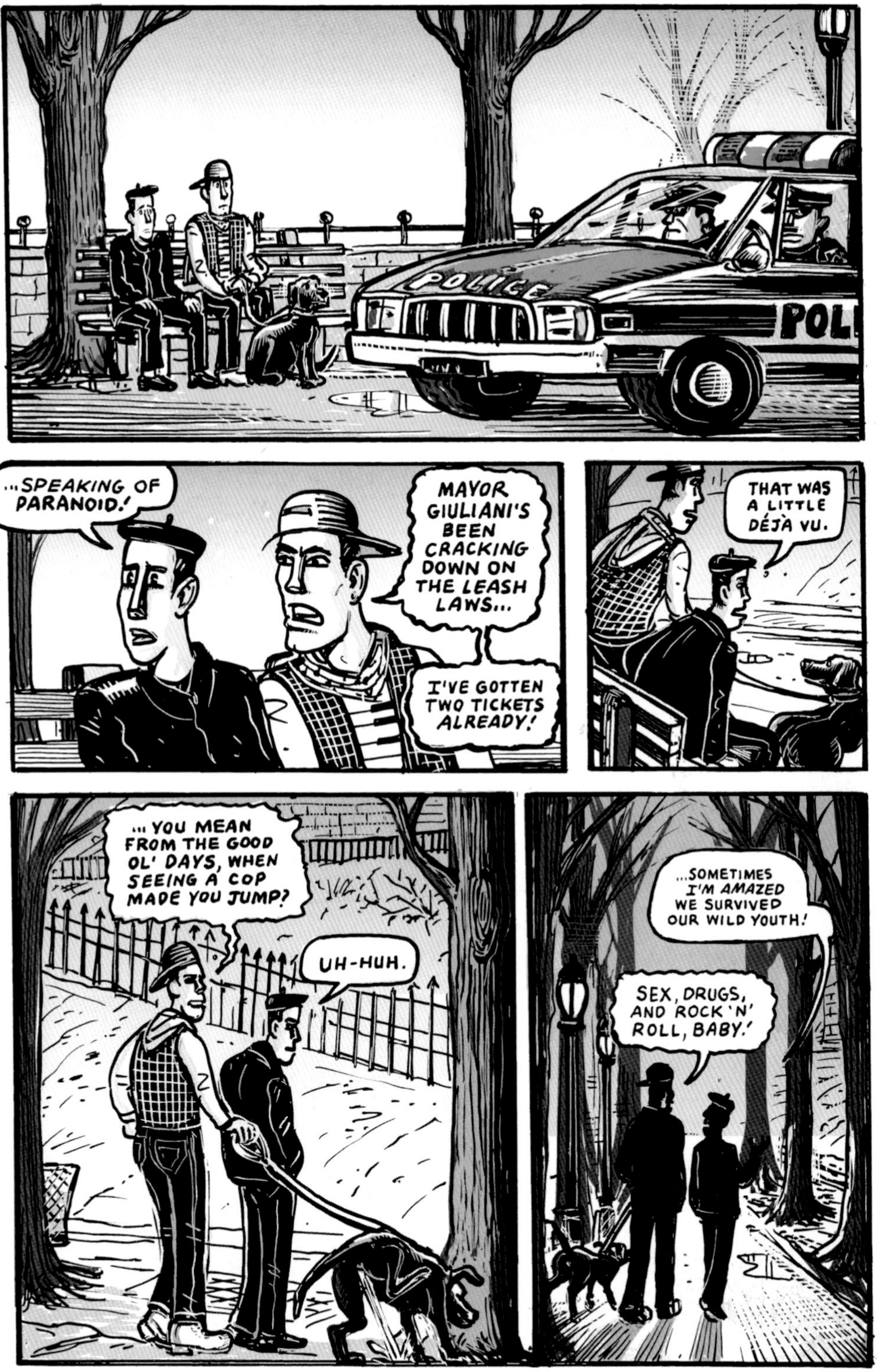
POLICE
POL
...SPEAKING OF PARANOID!
MAYOR GIULIANI'S BEEN CRACKING DOWN ON THE LEASH LAWS...
I'VE GOTTEN TWO TICKETS ALREADY!
THAT WAS A LITTLE DÉJÀ VU.
...YOU MEAN FROM THE GOOD OL' DAYS, WHEN SEEING A COP MADE YOU JUMP?
UH-HUH.
...SOMETIMES I'M AMAZED WE SURVIVED OUR WILD YOUTH!
SEX, DRUGS, AND ROCK 'N' ROLL, BABY!

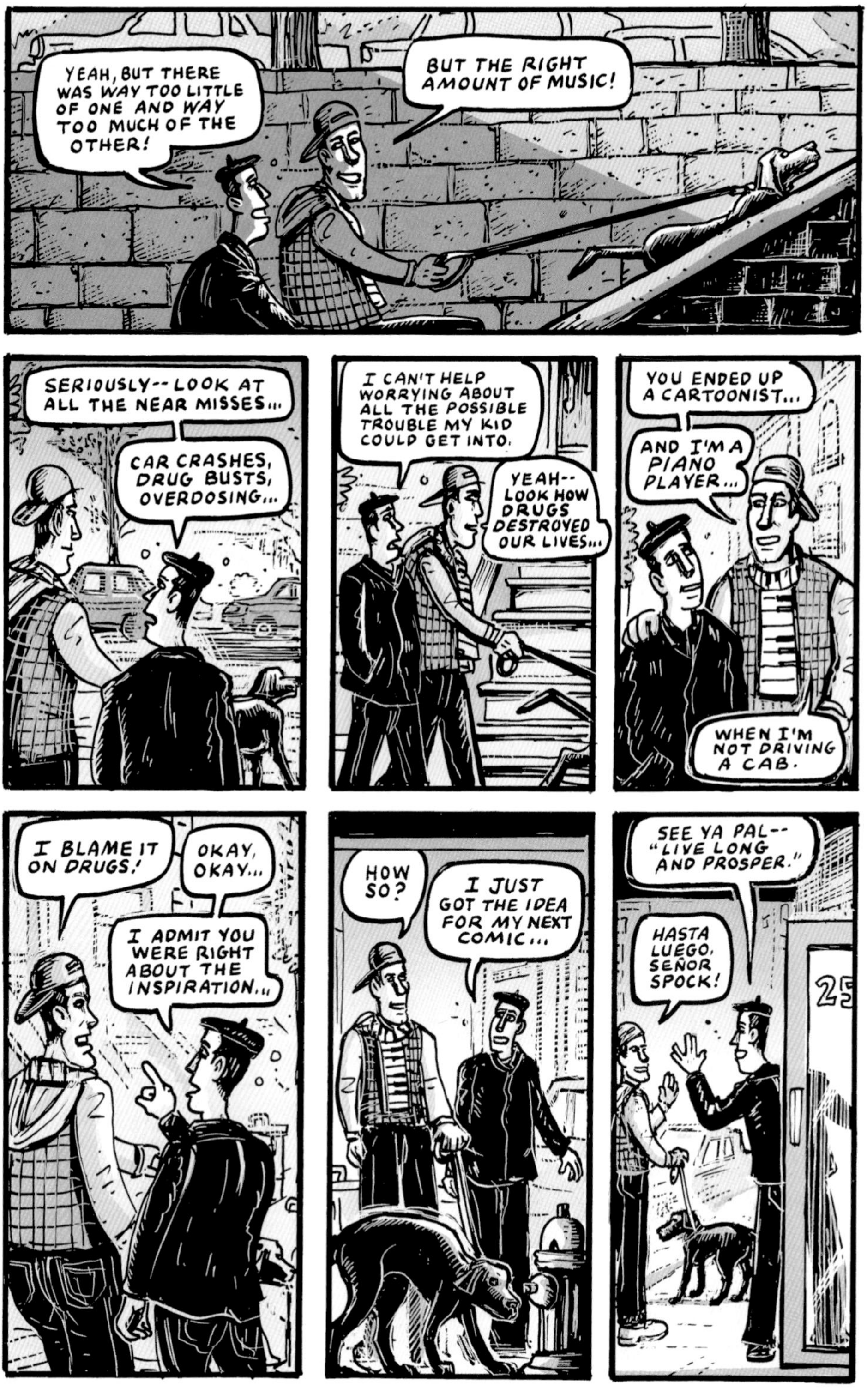
YEAH, BUT THERE WAS WAY TOO LITTLE OF ONE AND WAY TOO MUCH OF THE OTHER!
BUT THE RIGHT AMOUNT OF MUSIC!
SERIOUSLY-- LOOK AT ALL THE NEAR MISSES...
CAR CRASHES, DRUG BUSTS, OVERDOSING...
I CAN'T HELP WORRYING ABOUT ALL THE POSSIBLE TROUBLE MY KID COULD GET INTO.
YEAH-- LOOK HOW DRUGS DESTROYED OUR LIVES...
YOU ENDED UP A CARTOONIST...
AND I'M A PIANO PLAYER...
WHEN I'M NOT DRIVING A CAB.
I BLAME IT ON DRUGS!
OKAY, OKAY...
I ADMIT YOU WERE RIGHT ABOUT THE INSPIRATION...
HOW SO?
I JUST GOT THE IDEA FOR MY NEXT COMIC...
SEE YA PAL-- "LIVE LONG AND PROSPER."
HASTA LUEGO, SEÑOR SPOCK!
25

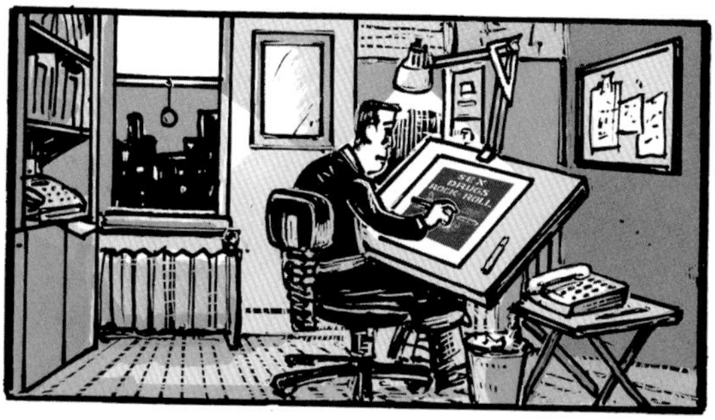

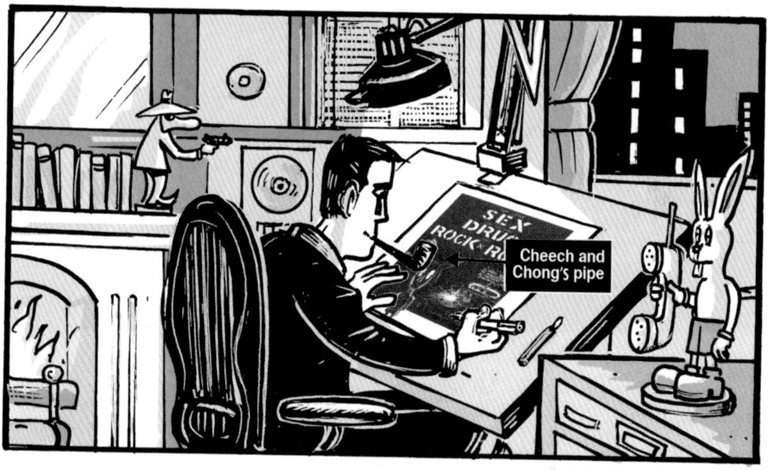
Cheech and Chong's pipe

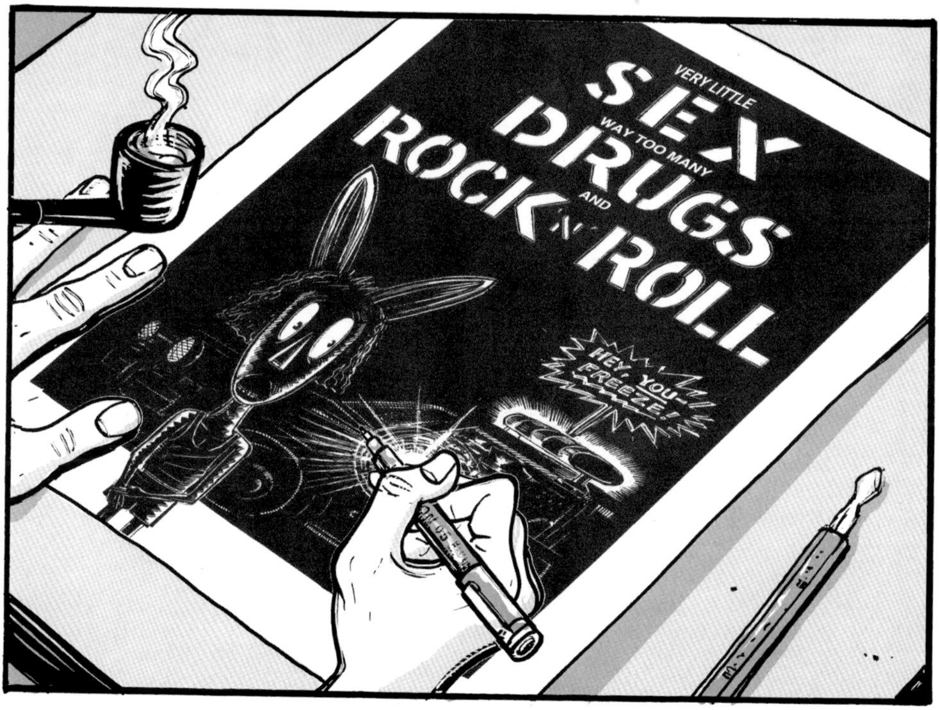
VERY LITTLE
SEX
WAY TOO MANY
DRUGS
AND
ROCK N' ROLL
HEY, YOU— FREEZE!

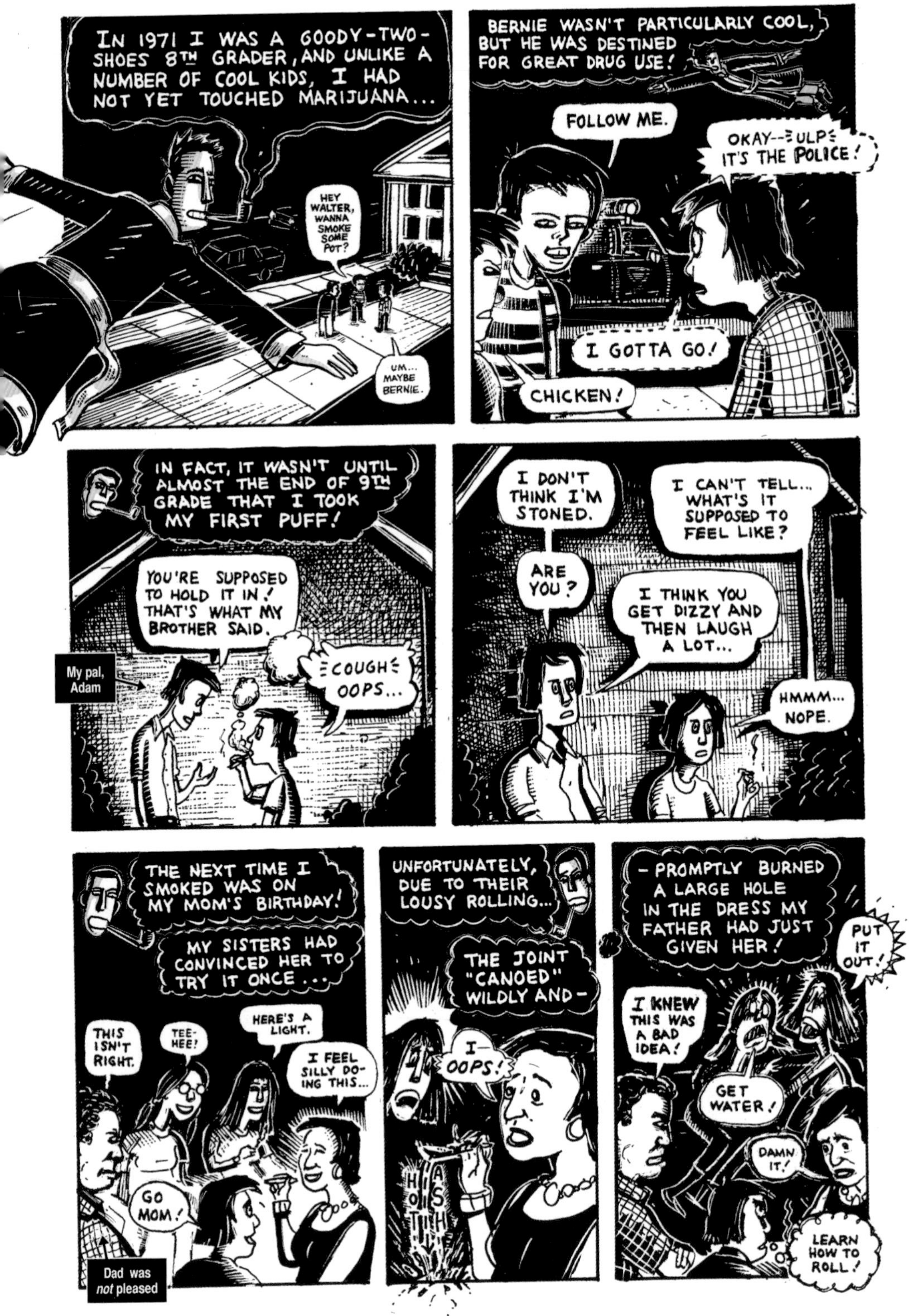
IN 1971 I WAS A GOODY-TWO-SHOES 8TH GRADER, AND UNLIKE A NUMBER OF COOL KIDS, I HAD NOT YET TOUCHED MARIJUANA...
HEY WALTER, WANNA SMOKE SOME POT?
UM... MAYBE BERNIE.
BERNIE WASN'T PARTICULARLY COOL, BUT HE WAS DESTINED FOR GREAT DRUG USE!
FOLLOW ME.
OKAY-- ULP IT'S THE POLICE!
I GOTTA GO!
CHICKEN!
IN FACT, IT WASN'T UNTIL ALMOST THE END OF 9TH GRADE THAT I TOOK MY FIRST PUFF!
YOU'RE SUPPOSED TO HOLD IT IN! THAT'S WHAT MY BROTHER SAID.
My pal, Adam
COUGH OOPS...
I DON'T THINK I'M STONED.
I CAN'T TELL... WHAT'S IT SUPPOSED TO FEEL LIKE?
ARE YOU?
I THINK YOU GET DIZZY AND THEN LAUGH A LOT...
HMMM... NOPE.
THE NEXT TIME I SMOKED WAS ON MY MOM'S BIRTHDAY!
MY SISTERS HAD CONVINCED HER TO TRY IT ONCE...
THIS ISN'T RIGHT.
TEE-HEE!
HERE'S A LIGHT.
I FEEL SILLY DOING THIS...
GO MOM!
Dad was *not* pleased
UNFORTUNATELY, DUE TO THEIR LOUSY ROLLING...
THE JOINT "CANOED" WILDLY AND—
I— OOPS!
HOT ASH
—PROMPTLY BURNED A LARGE HOLE IN THE DRESS MY FATHER HAD JUST GIVEN HER!
PUT IT OUT!
I KNEW THIS WAS A BAD IDEA!
GET WATER!
DAMN IT!
LEARN HOW TO ROLL!

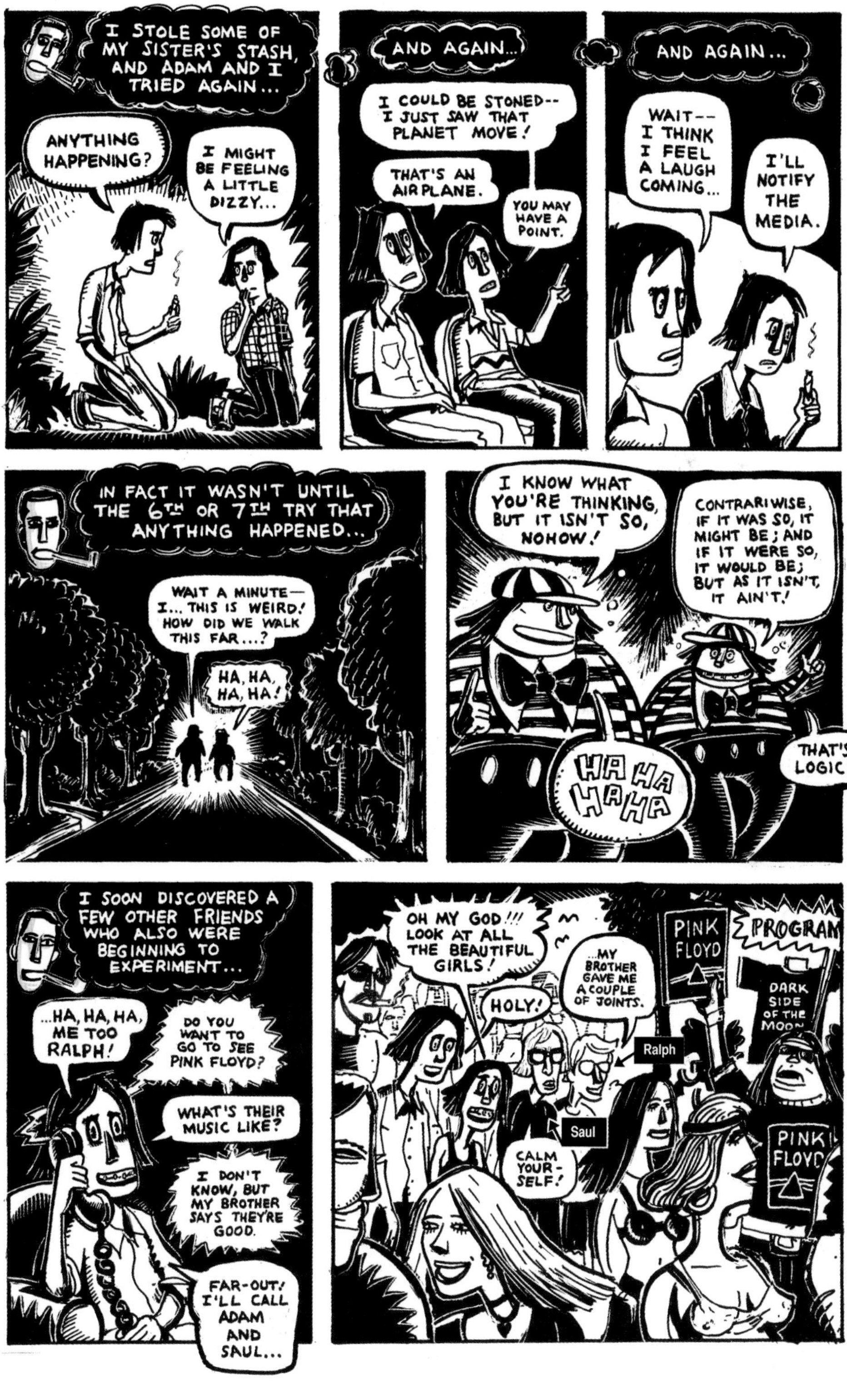
I STOLE SOME OF MY SISTER'S STASH, AND ADAM AND I TRIED AGAIN...
ANYTHING HAPPENING?
I MIGHT BE FEELING A LITTLE DIZZY...
AND AGAIN...
I COULD BE STONED-- I JUST SAW THAT PLANET MOVE!
THAT'S AN AIRPLANE.
YOU MAY HAVE A POINT.
AND AGAIN...
WAIT-- I THINK I FEEL A LAUGH COMING...
I'LL NOTIFY THE MEDIA.
IN FACT IT WASN'T UNTIL THE 6TH OR 7TH TRY THAT ANYTHING HAPPENED...
WAIT A MINUTE— I... THIS IS WEIRD! HOW DID WE WALK THIS FAR...?
HA, HA, HA, HA!
I KNOW WHAT YOU'RE THINKING, BUT IT ISN'T SO, NOHOW!
CONTRARIWISE, IF IT WAS SO, IT MIGHT BE; AND IF IT WERE SO, IT WOULD BE; BUT AS IT ISN'T, IT AIN'T!
HA HA HA HA
THAT'S LOGIC!
I SOON DISCOVERED A FEW OTHER FRIENDS WHO ALSO WERE BEGINNING TO EXPERIMENT...
...HA, HA, HA, ME TOO RALPH!
DO YOU WANT TO GO TO SEE PINK FLOYD?
WHAT'S THEIR MUSIC LIKE?
I DON'T KNOW, BUT MY BROTHER SAYS THEY'RE GOOD.
FAR-OUT! I'LL CALL ADAM AND SAUL...
OH MY GOD!!! LOOK AT ALL THE BEAUTIFUL GIRLS!
HOLY!
...MY BROTHER GAVE ME A COUPLE OF JOINTS.
CALM YOURSELF!
PINK FLOYD
PROGRAM
DARK SIDE OF THE MOON
Ralph
Saul
PINK FLOYD

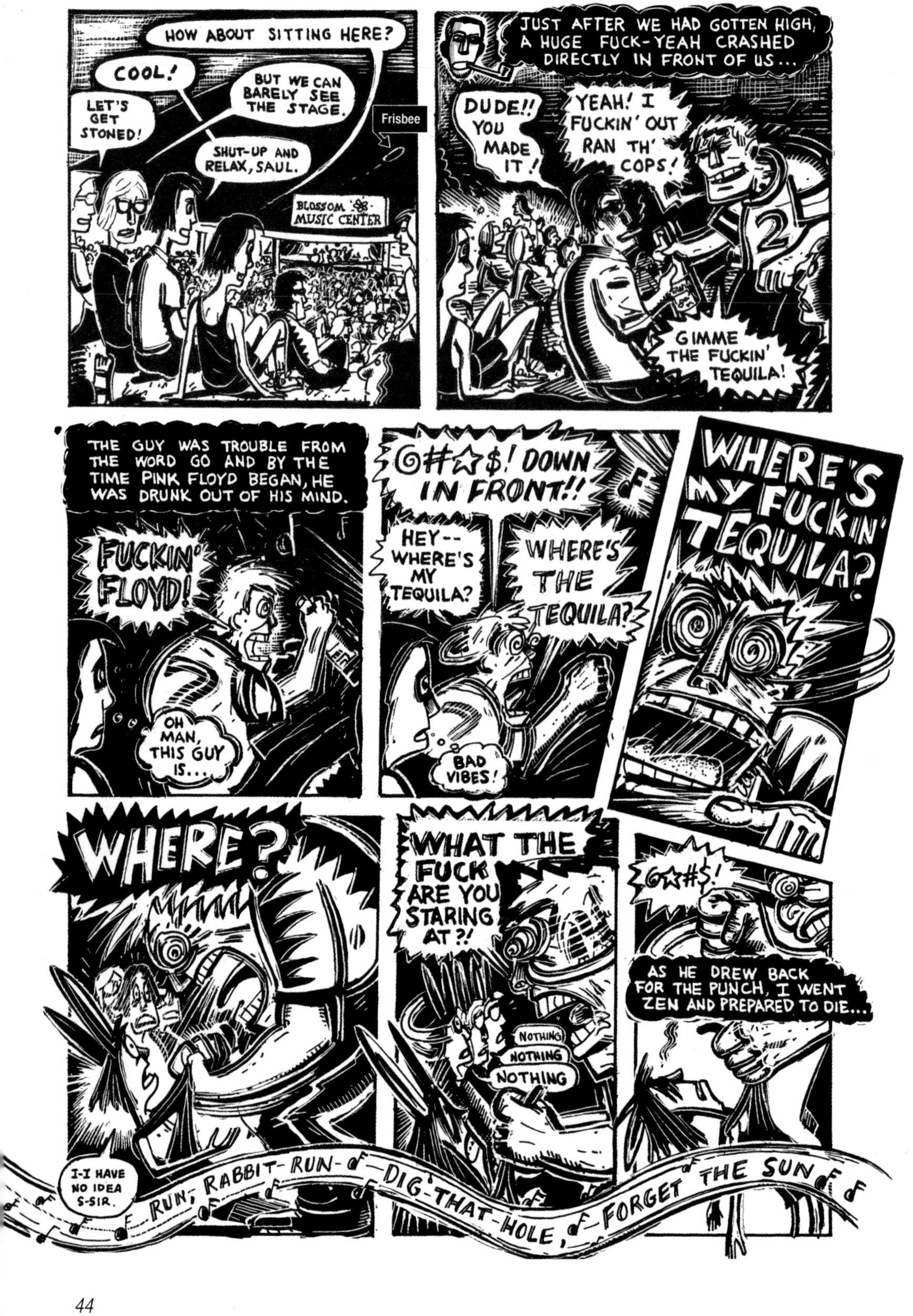
HOW ABOUT SITTING HERE?
COOL!
LET'S GET STONED!
BUT WE CAN BARELY SEE THE STAGE.
SHUT-UP AND RELAX, SAUL.
Frisbee
BLOSSOM MUSIC CENTER
JUST AFTER WE HAD GOTTEN HIGH, A HUGE FUCK-YEAH CRASHED DIRECTLY IN FRONT OF US...
DUDE!! YOU MADE IT!
YEAH! I FUCKIN' OUT RAN TH' COPS!
GIMME THE FUCKIN' TEQUILA!
THE GUY WAS TROUBLE FROM THE WORD GO AND BY THE TIME PINK FLOYD BEGAN, HE WAS DRUNK OUT OF HIS MIND.
FUCKIN' FLOYD!
OH MAN, THIS GUY IS...
@#☆$! DOWN IN FRONT!!
HEY-- WHERE'S MY TEQUILA?
WHERE'S THE TEQUILA?
BAD VIBES!
WHERE'S MY FUCKIN' TEQUILA?
WHERE?
I-I HAVE NO IDEA S-SIR.
WHAT THE FUCK ARE YOU STARING AT?!
NOTHING
NOTHING
NOTHING
@☆#$!
AS HE DREW BACK FOR THE PUNCH, I WENT ZEN AND PREPARED TO DIE...
RUN, RABBIT-RUN-DIG-THAT-HOLE, FORGET THE SUN

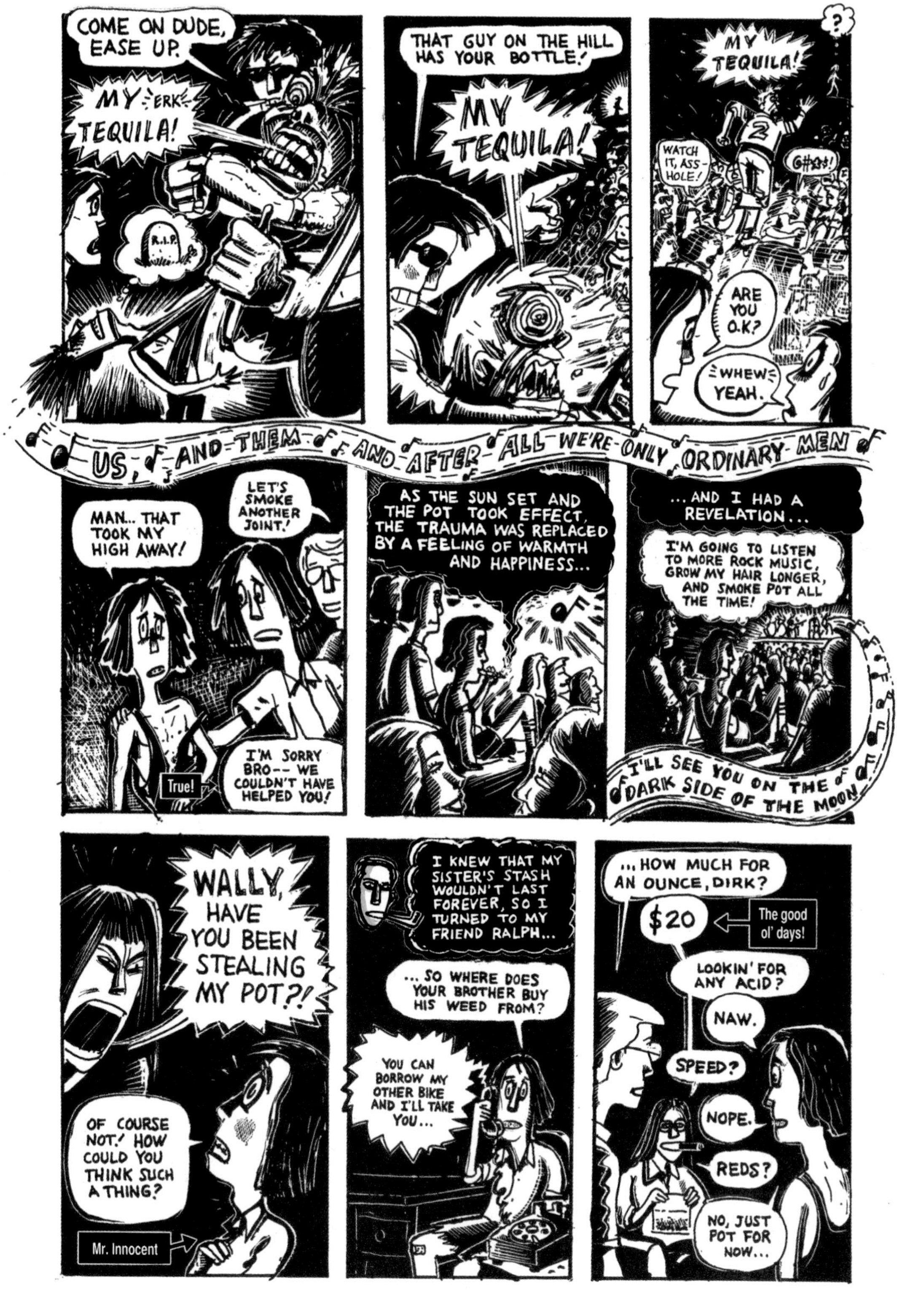
COME ON DUDE, EASE UP.
MY ERK TEQUILA!
R.I.P.
THAT GUY ON THE HILL HAS YOUR BOTTLE!
MY TEQUILA!
MY TEQUILA!
?
WATCH IT, ASS HOLE!
G#@*!
ARE YOU O.K.?
WHEW YEAH.
US, AND THEM AND AFTER ALL WE'RE ONLY ORDINARY MEN
MAN... THAT TOOK MY HIGH AWAY!
LET'S SMOKE ANOTHER JOINT!
I'M SORRY BRO-- WE COULDN'T HAVE HELPED YOU!
True!
AS THE SUN SET AND THE POT TOOK EFFECT, THE TRAUMA WAS REPLACED BY A FEELING OF WARMTH AND HAPPINESS...
... AND I HAD A REVELATION...
I'M GOING TO LISTEN TO MORE ROCK MUSIC, GROW MY HAIR LONGER, AND SMOKE POT ALL THE TIME!
I'LL SEE YOU ON THE DARK SIDE OF THE MOON
WALLY, HAVE YOU BEEN STEALING MY POT?!
OF COURSE NOT! HOW COULD YOU THINK SUCH A THING?
Mr. Innocent
I KNEW THAT MY SISTER'S STASH WOULDN'T LAST FOREVER, SO I TURNED TO MY FRIEND RALPH...
... SO WHERE DOES YOUR BROTHER BUY HIS WEED FROM?
YOU CAN BORROW MY OTHER BIKE AND I'LL TAKE YOU...
... HOW MUCH FOR AN OUNCE, DIRK?
$20
The good ol' days!
LOOKIN' FOR ANY ACID?
NAW.
SPEED?
NOPE.
REDS?
NO, JUST POT FOR NOW...

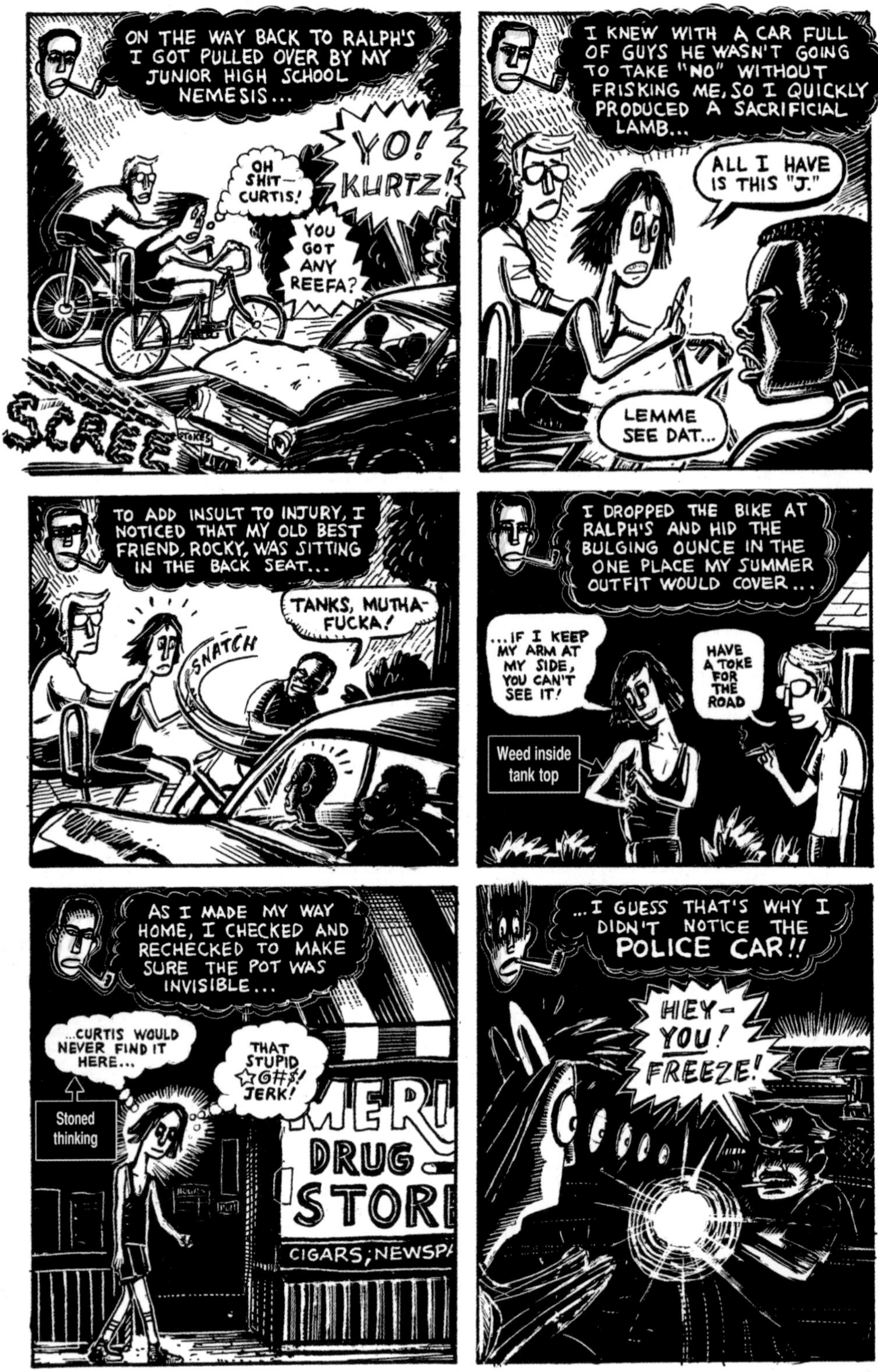

ON THE WAY BACK TO RALPH'S I GOT PULLED OVER BY MY JUNIOR HIGH SCHOOL NEMESIS...
OH SHIT—CURTIS!
YO! KURTZ!
YOU GOT ANY REEFA?
SCREE
I KNEW WITH A CAR FULL OF GUYS HE WASN'T GOING TO TAKE "NO" WITHOUT FRISKING ME, SO I QUICKLY PRODUCED A SACRIFICIAL LAMB...
ALL I HAVE IS THIS "J."
LEMME SEE DAT...
TO ADD INSULT TO INJURY, I NOTICED THAT MY OLD BEST FRIEND, ROCKY, WAS SITTING IN THE BACK SEAT...
TANKS, MUTHA-FUCKA!
SNATCH
I DROPPED THE BIKE AT RALPH'S AND HID THE BULGING OUNCE IN THE ONE PLACE MY SUMMER OUTFIT WOULD COVER...
...IF I KEEP MY ARM AT MY SIDE, YOU CAN'T SEE IT!
HAVE A TOKE FOR THE ROAD
Weed inside tank top
AS I MADE MY WAY HOME, I CHECKED AND RECHECKED TO MAKE SURE THE POT WAS INVISIBLE...
...CURTIS WOULD NEVER FIND IT HERE...
THAT STUPID ☆@#$! JERK!
Stoned thinking
DRUG STOR
CIGARS; NEWSP
...I GUESS THAT'S WHY I DIDN'T NOTICE THE POLICE CAR!!
HEY-YOU! FREEZE!

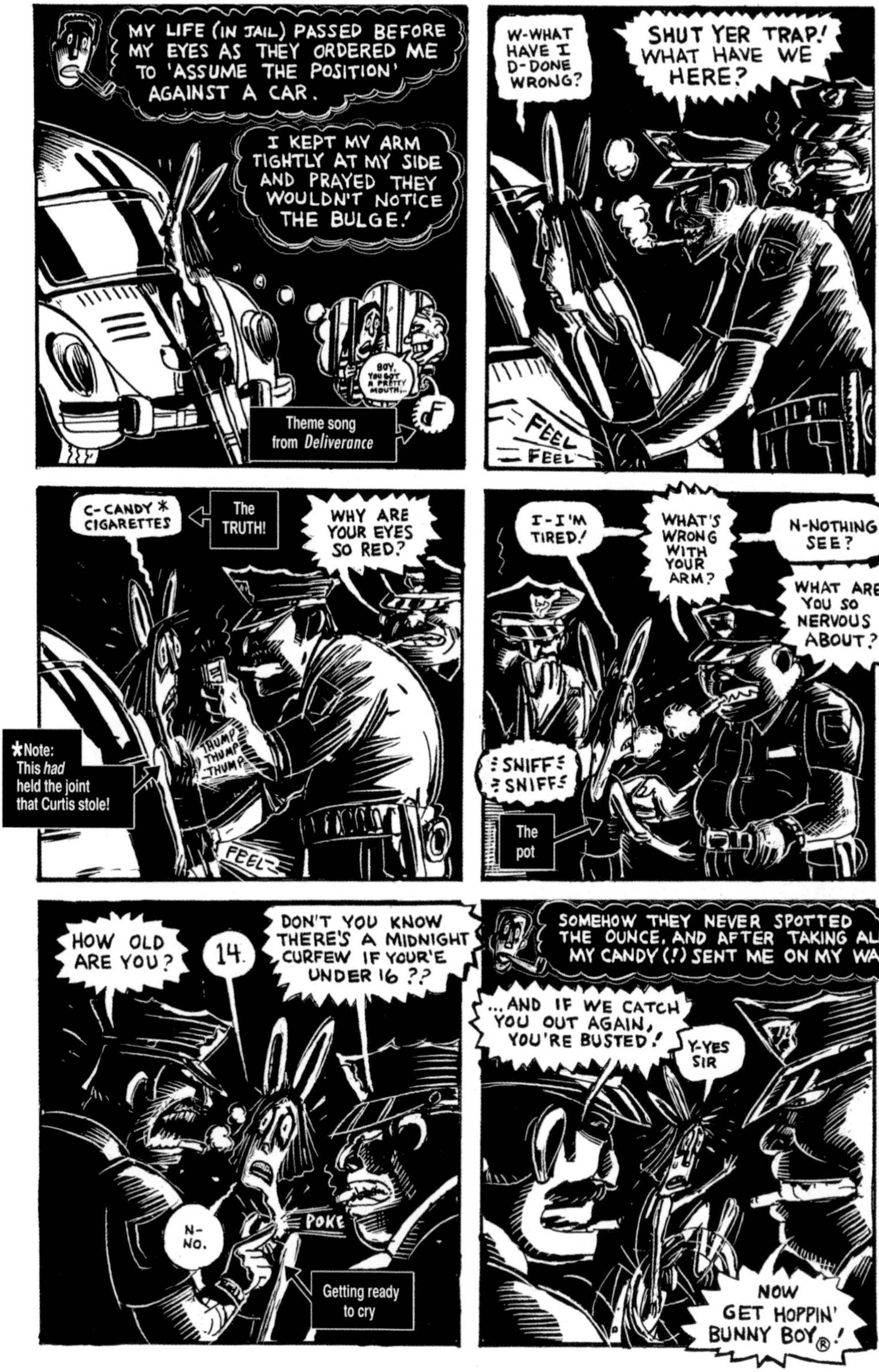
MY LIFE (IN JAIL) PASSED BEFORE MY EYES AS THEY ORDERED ME TO 'ASSUME THE POSITION' AGAINST A CAR.
I KEPT MY ARM TIGHTLY AT MY SIDE AND PRAYED THEY WOULDN'T NOTICE THE BULGE!
BOY, YOU GOT A PRETTY MOUTH...
Theme song from *Deliverance*
W-WHAT HAVE I D-DONE WRONG?
SHUT YER TRAP! WHAT HAVE WE HERE?
FEEL
FEEL
C-CANDY * CIGARETTES
The TRUTH!
WHY ARE YOUR EYES SO RED?
THUMP THUMP THUMP
FEEL
*Note: This *had* held the joint that Curtis stole!
I-I'M TIRED!
WHAT'S WRONG WITH YOUR ARM?
N-NOTHING SEE?
WHAT ARE YOU SO NERVOUS ABOUT?
SNIFF SNIFF
The pot
HOW OLD ARE YOU?
14.
DON'T YOU KNOW THERE'S A MIDNIGHT CURFEW IF YOUR'E UNDER 16 ??
N-NO.
POKE
Getting ready to cry
SOMEHOW THEY NEVER SPOTTED THE OUNCE, AND AFTER TAKING ALL MY CANDY (!) SENT ME ON MY WAY!
...AND IF WE CATCH YOU OUT AGAIN, YOU'RE BUSTED!
Y-YES SIR
NOW GET HOPPIN' BUNNY BOY®!

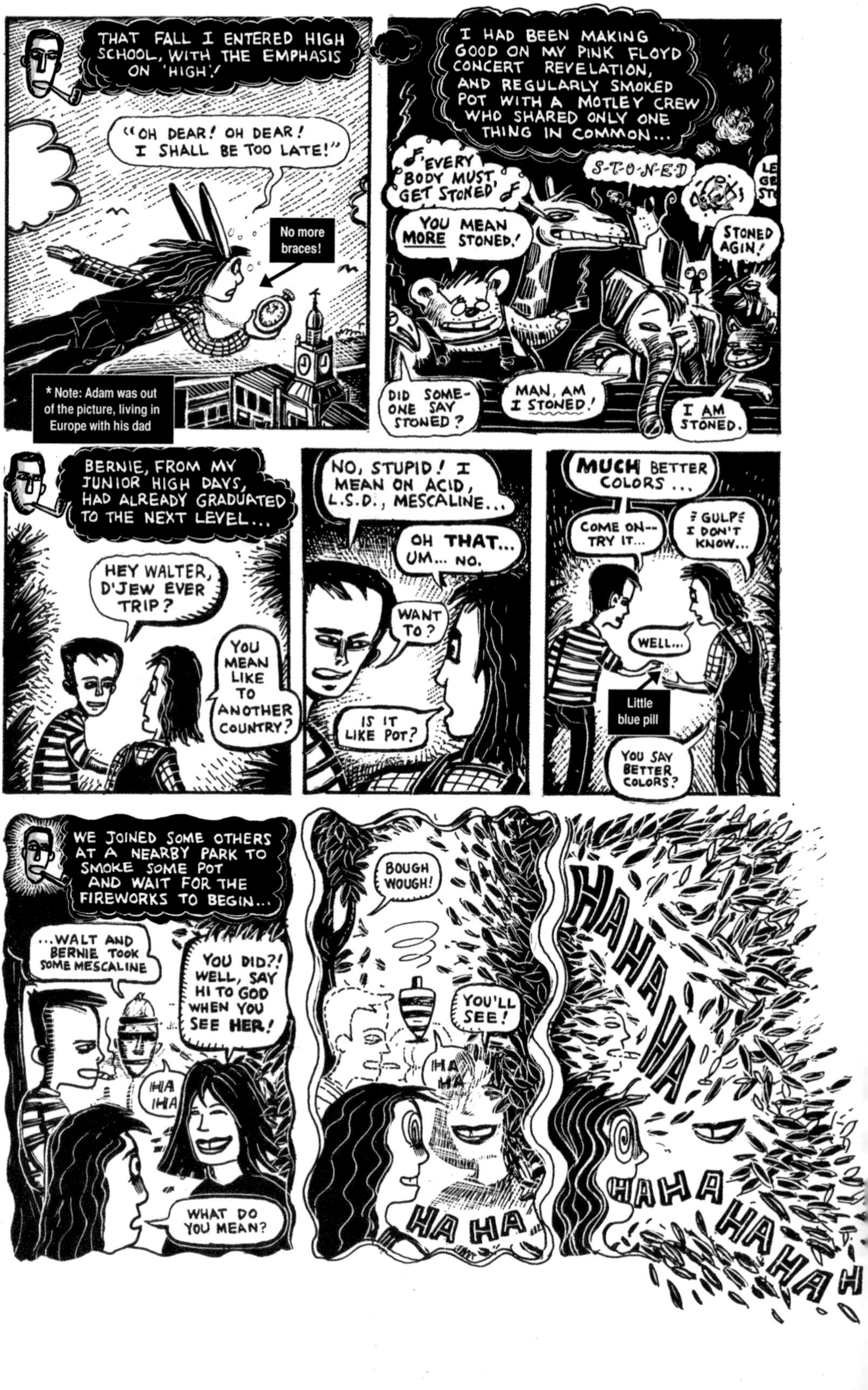

THAT FALL I ENTERED HIGH SCHOOL, WITH THE EMPHASIS ON 'HIGH'!
"OH DEAR! OH DEAR! I SHALL BE TOO LATE!"
No more braces!
* Note: Adam was out of the picture, living in Europe with his dad
I HAD BEEN MAKING GOOD ON MY PINK FLOYD CONCERT REVELATION, AND REGULARLY SMOKED POT WITH A MOTLEY CREW WHO SHARED ONLY ONE THING IN COMMON...
'EVERY BODY MUST GET STONED'
S-T-O-N-E-D
YOU MEAN MORE STONED!
STONED AGIN!
DID SOME-ONE SAY STONED?
MAN, AM I STONED!
I AM STONED.
BERNIE, FROM MY JUNIOR HIGH DAYS, HAD ALREADY GRADUATED TO THE NEXT LEVEL...
HEY WALTER, D'JEW EVER TRIP?
YOU MEAN LIKE TO ANOTHER COUNTRY?
NO, STUPID! I MEAN ON ACID, L.S.D., MESCALINE...
OH THAT... UM... NO.
WANT TO?
IS IT LIKE POT?
MUCH BETTER COLORS...
COME ON-- TRY IT...
GULP I DON'T KNOW...
WELL...
Little blue pill
YOU SAY BETTER COLORS?
WE JOINED SOME OTHERS AT A NEARBY PARK TO SMOKE SOME POT AND WAIT FOR THE FIREWORKS TO BEGIN...
...WALT AND BERNIE TOOK SOME MESCALINE
YOU DID?! WELL, SAY HI TO GOD WHEN YOU SEE HER!
HA HA
WHAT DO YOU MEAN?
BOUGH WOUGH!
YOU'LL SEE!
HA HA
HA HA
HA HA HA HA HA
HAHA HA
HA HA HA H

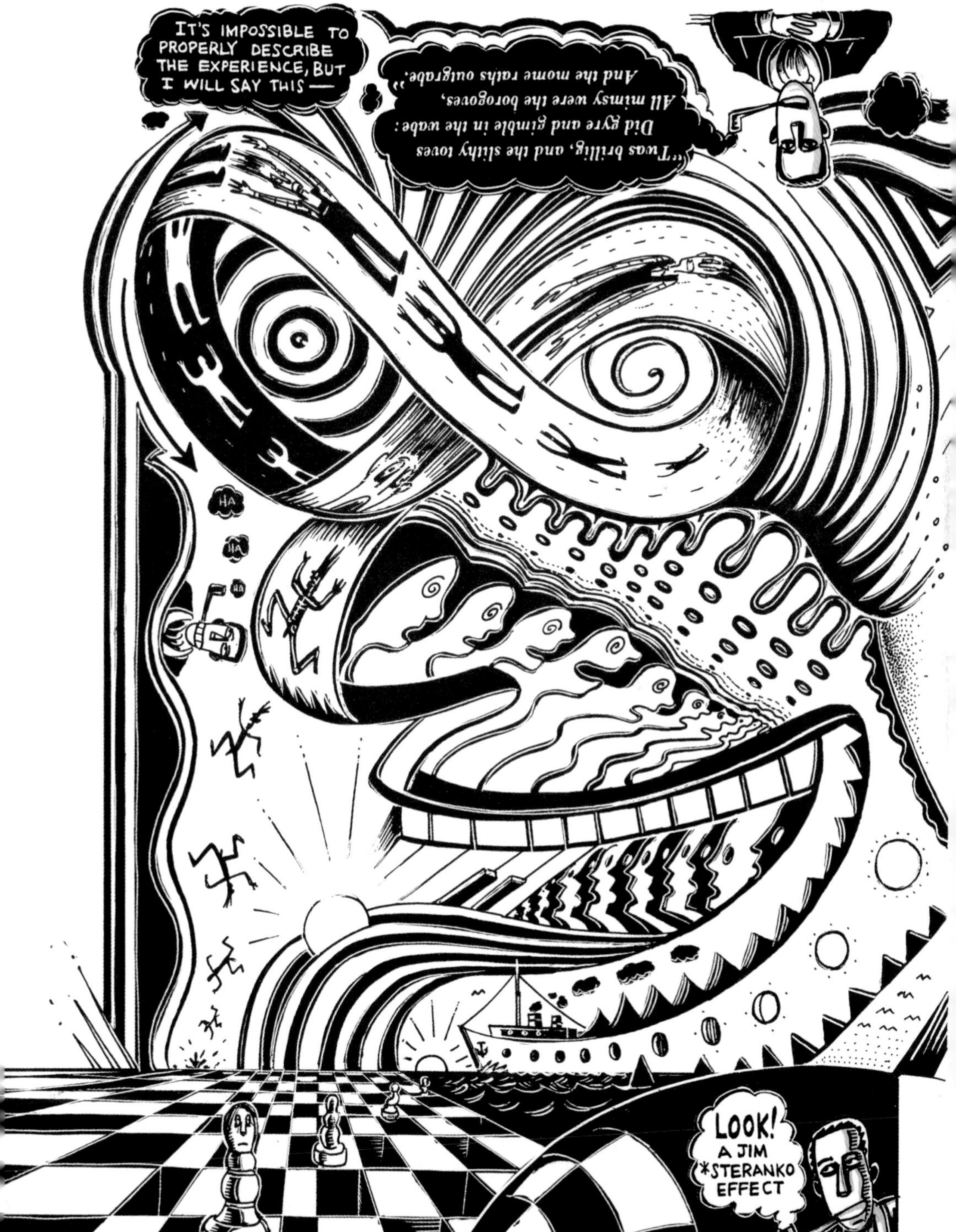
IT'S IMPOSSIBLE TO PROPERLY DESCRIBE THE EXPERIENCE, BUT I WILL SAY THIS —
"'Twas brillig, and the slithy toves
Did gyre and gimble in the wabe:
All mimsy were the borogoves,
And the mome raths outgrabe."
HA
HA
HA
LOOK! A JIM *STERANKO EFFECT

* NOTED EXPERIMENTAL SUPERHERO COMIC BOOK ARTIST

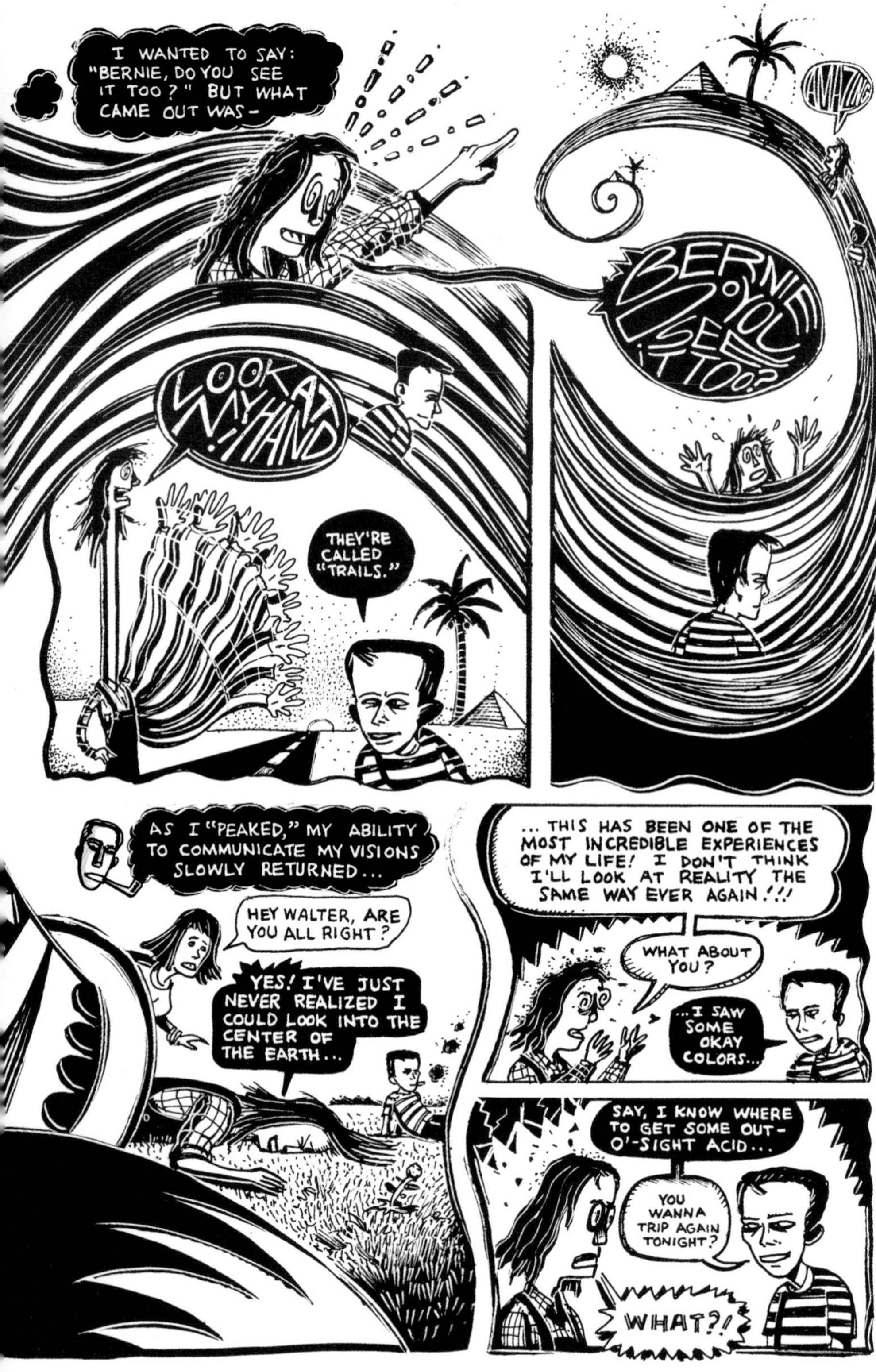
I WANTED TO SAY: "BERNIE, DO YOU SEE IT TOO?" BUT WHAT CAME OUT WAS-
AMAZING
BERNIE DO YOU SEE IT TOO?
LOOK AT MY HAND!
THEY'RE CALLED "TRAILS."
AS I "PEAKED," MY ABILITY TO COMMUNICATE MY VISIONS SLOWLY RETURNED...
HEY WALTER, ARE YOU ALL RIGHT?
YES! I'VE JUST NEVER REALIZED I COULD LOOK INTO THE CENTER OF THE EARTH...
... THIS HAS BEEN ONE OF THE MOST INCREDIBLE EXPERIENCES OF MY LIFE! I DON'T THINK I'LL LOOK AT REALITY THE SAME WAY EVER AGAIN!!!
WHAT ABOUT YOU?
...I SAW SOME OKAY COLORS...
SAY, I KNOW WHERE TO GET SOME OUT-O'-SIGHT ACID...
YOU WANNA TRIP AGAIN TONIGHT?
WHAT?!

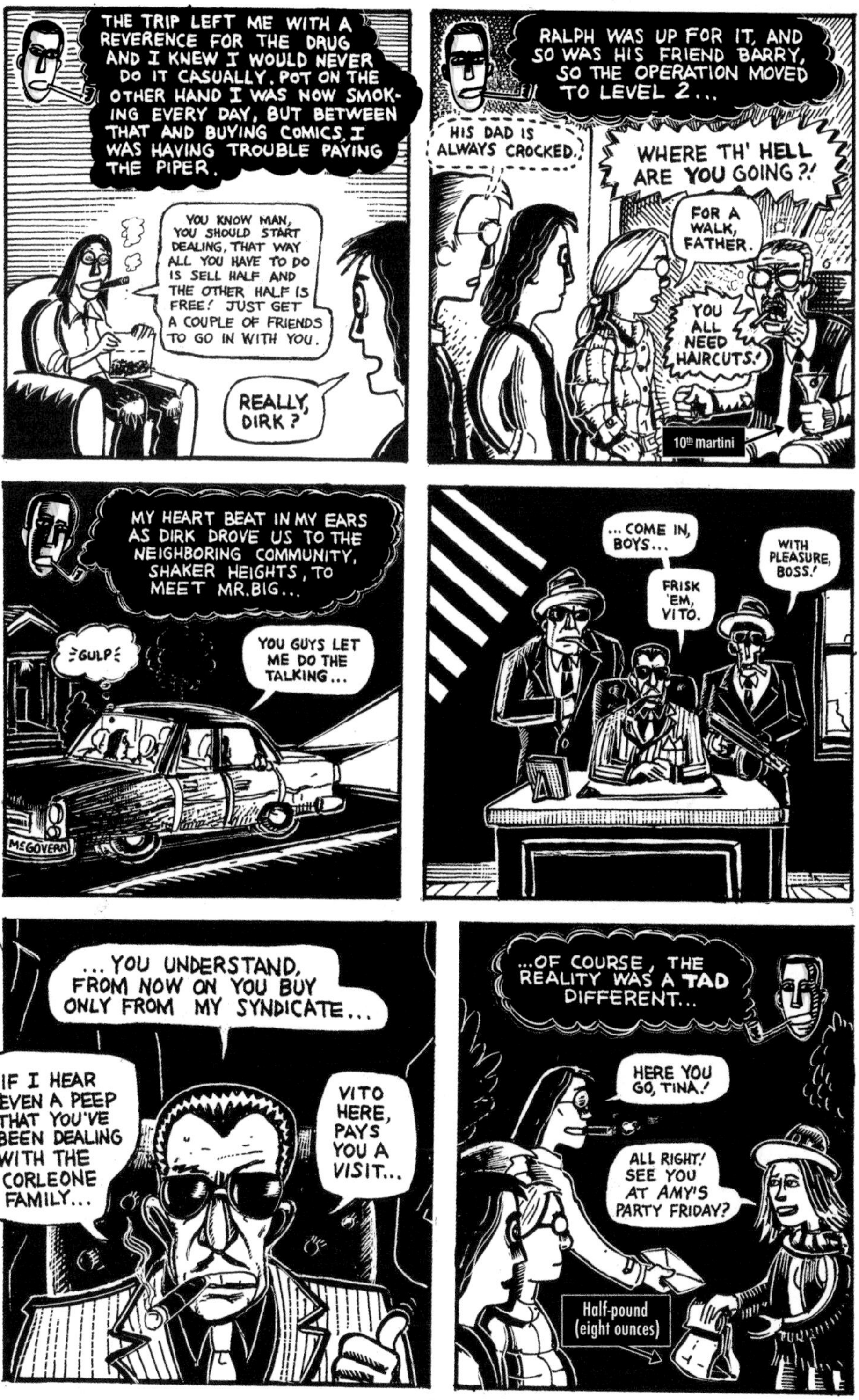
THE TRIP LEFT ME WITH A REVERENCE FOR THE DRUG AND I KNEW I WOULD NEVER DO IT CASUALLY. POT ON THE OTHER HAND I WAS NOW SMOKING EVERY DAY, BUT BETWEEN THAT AND BUYING COMICS, I WAS HAVING TROUBLE PAYING THE PIPER.
YOU KNOW MAN, YOU SHOULD START DEALING, THAT WAY ALL YOU HAVE TO DO IS SELL HALF AND THE OTHER HALF IS FREE! JUST GET A COUPLE OF FRIENDS TO GO IN WITH YOU.
REALLY, DIRK?
RALPH WAS UP FOR IT, AND SO WAS HIS FRIEND BARRY, SO THE OPERATION MOVED TO LEVEL 2...
HIS DAD IS ALWAYS CROCKED.
WHERE TH' HELL ARE YOU GOING?!
FOR A WALK, FATHER.
YOU ALL NEED HAIRCUTS!
10th martini
MY HEART BEAT IN MY EARS AS DIRK DROVE US TO THE NEIGHBORING COMMUNITY, SHAKER HEIGHTS, TO MEET MR. BIG...
GULP
YOU GUYS LET ME DO THE TALKING...
McGOVERN
...COME IN, BOYS...
FRISK 'EM, VITO.
WITH PLEASURE, BOSS!
...YOU UNDERSTAND, FROM NOW ON YOU BUY ONLY FROM MY SYNDICATE...
IF I HEAR EVEN A PEEP THAT YOU'VE BEEN DEALING WITH THE CORLEONE FAMILY...
VITO HERE, PAYS YOU A VISIT...
...OF COURSE, THE REALITY WAS A TAD DIFFERENT...
HERE YOU GO, TINA!
ALL RIGHT! SEE YOU AT AMY'S PARTY FRIDAY?
Half-pound (eight ounces)

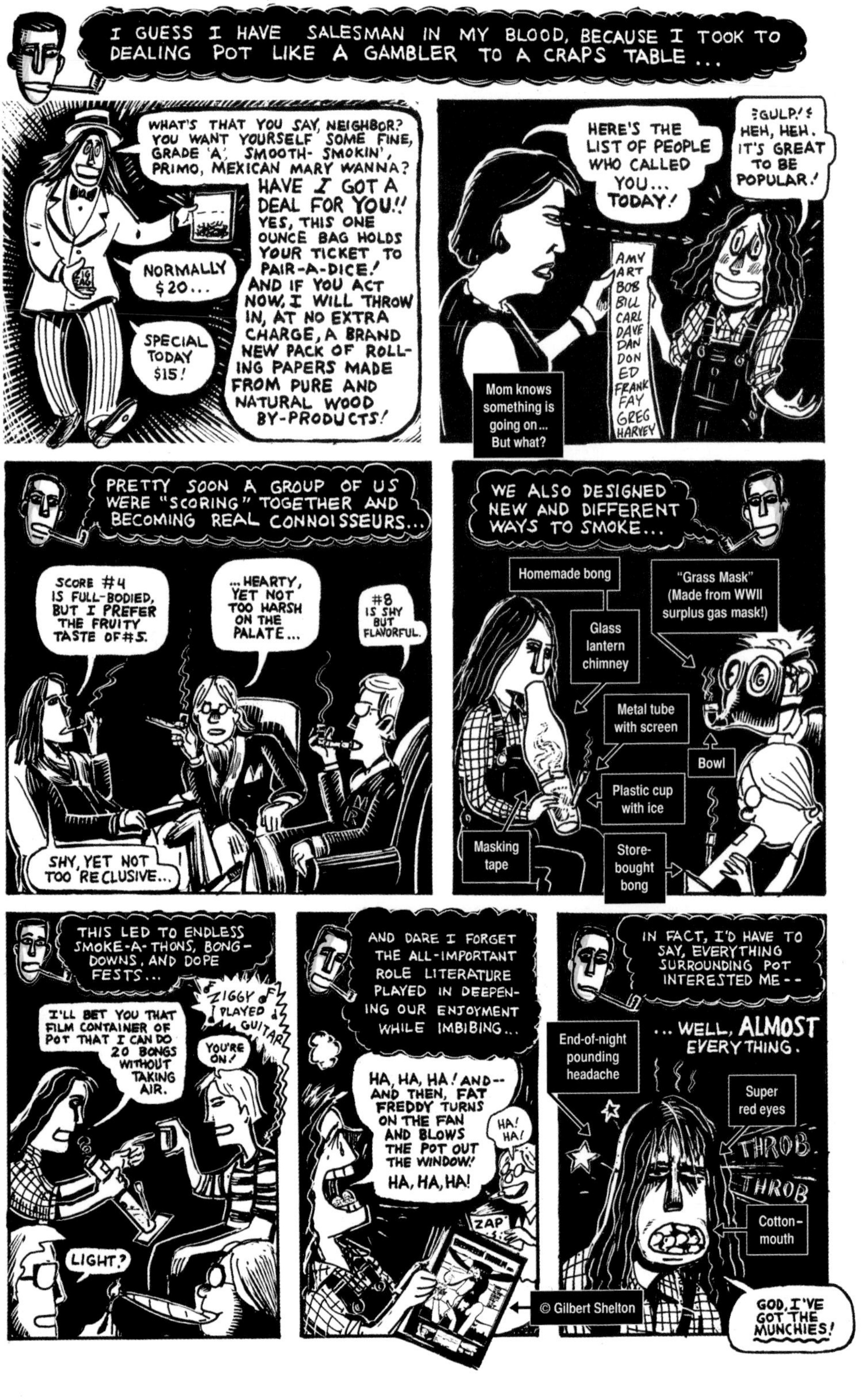

I GUESS I HAVE SALESMAN IN MY BLOOD, BECAUSE I TOOK TO DEALING POT LIKE A GAMBLER TO A CRAPS TABLE...
WHAT'S THAT YOU SAY, NEIGHBOR? YOU WANT YOURSELF SOME FINE, GRADE 'A', SMOOTH-SMOKIN', PRIMO, MEXICAN MARY WANNA?
HAVE I GOT A DEAL FOR YOU!! YES, THIS ONE OUNCE BAG HOLDS YOUR TICKET TO PAIR-A-DICE! AND IF YOU ACT NOW, I WILL THROW IN, AT NO EXTRA CHARGE, A BRAND NEW PACK OF ROLLING PAPERS MADE FROM PURE AND NATURAL WOOD BY-PRODUCTS!
NORMALLY $20...
SPECIAL TODAY $15!
HERE'S THE LIST OF PEOPLE WHO CALLED YOU... TODAY!
AMY
ART
BOB
BILL
CARL
DAVE
DAN
DON
ED
FRANK
FAY
GREG
HARVEY
≷GULP!≶ HEH, HEH. IT'S GREAT TO BE POPULAR!
Mom knows something is going on... But what?
PRETTY SOON A GROUP OF US WERE "SCORING" TOGETHER AND BECOMING REAL CONNOISSEURS...
SCORE #4 IS FULL-BODIED, BUT I PREFER THE FRUITY TASTE OF #5.
...HEARTY, YET NOT TOO HARSH ON THE PALATE...
#8 IS SHY BUT FLAVORFUL.
SHY, YET NOT TOO RECLUSIVE...
WE ALSO DESIGNED NEW AND DIFFERENT WAYS TO SMOKE...
Homemade bong
Glass lantern chimney
"Grass Mask" (Made from WWII surplus gas mask!)
Metal tube with screen
Bowl
Plastic cup with ice
Masking tape
Store-bought bong
THIS LED TO ENDLESS SMOKE-A-THONS, BONG-DOWNS, AND DOPE FESTS...
I'LL BET YOU THAT FILM CONTAINER OF POT THAT I CAN DO 20 BONGS WITHOUT TAKING AIR.
ZIGGY PLAYED GUITAR
YOU'RE ON!
LIGHT?
AND DARE I FORGET THE ALL-IMPORTANT ROLE LITERATURE PLAYED IN DEEPENING OUR ENJOYMENT WHILE IMBIBING...
HA, HA, HA! AND-- AND THEN, FAT FREDDY TURNS ON THE FAN AND BLOWS THE POT OUT THE WINDOW! HA, HA, HA!
HA! HA!
ZAP
© Gilbert Shelton
IN FACT, I'D HAVE TO SAY, EVERYTHING SURROUNDING POT INTERESTED ME--
...WELL, ALMOST EVERYTHING.
End-of-night pounding headache
Super red eyes
THROB
THROB
Cotton-mouth
GOD, I'VE GOT THE MUNCHIES!

UNFORTUNATELY, ALL OF THIS PARTYING WAS TAKING ITS TOLL...

=COUGH=

(I suppose hitching a ride in the freezing rain also didn't help)

HONEY-- ARE YOU ALL RIGHT? YOU LOOK AWFUL!!

I'M =COUGH= JUST A BIT TIRED =COUGH=

I'D BETTER TAKE YOUR TEMPERATURE.

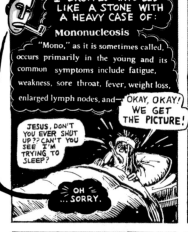

I DROPPED INTO BED LIKE A STONE WITH A HEAVY CASE OF:

Mononucleosis

"Mono," as it is sometimes called, occurs primarily in the young and its common symptoms include fatigue, weakness, sore throat, fever, weight loss, enlarged lymph nodes, and—

OKAY, OKAY! WE GET THE PICTURE!

JESUS, DON'T YOU EVER SHUT UP?? CAN'T YOU SEE I'M TRYING TO SLEEP?

OH ...SORRY.

AT THE TIME I HAPPENED TO HAVE BEEN READING THE POPULAR CARLOS CASTANEDA BOOKS THAT DEALT WITH A MYSTICAL DRUG-TAKING CHARACTER...

HOLA AMIGO, ME LLAMO ES DON JUAN...

EAT THIS PEYOTE.

Z

Vaporizer

SO IT WAS PERFECTLY FITTING THAT MY DOCTOR HAD PRESCRIBED THE OPIUM DERIVATIVE, CODEINE, TO RELIEVE MY SYMPTOMS, WITH A SIDE EFFECT OF WILD, VIVID DREAMS...

IT WILL HELP YOU SEE THE WORLD INSIDE!

=UGH= THIS TASTES TERRIBLE!

YOU MUST FIND YOUR SPACE, A PLACE WHERE YOU ARE COMFORTABLE.

BUT HOW?

WHERE?

CONTROLLED ABANDON...

WAIT, DON JUAN!

DON'T GO!

I'M LOST!

SON, SON, WAKE UP...

I--DAD! I WAS HAVING A HORRIBLE DREAM...

I KNOW. IT'S OKAY NOW...

53

I DREAMT THAT I MET DON JUAN AND...

GO ON.

WHAT ARE YOU DOING?

Margarine

EEYAAA

HOLY SHIT!

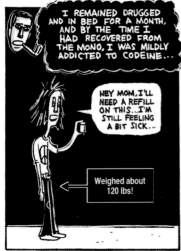

I REMAINED DRUGGED AND IN BED FOR A MONTH, AND BY THE TIME I HAD RECOVERED FROM THE MONO, I WAS MILDLY ADDICTED TO CODEINE...

HEY MOM, I'LL NEED A REFILL ON THIS...I'M STILL FEELING A BIT SICK...

Weighed about 120 lbs!

BUT I HAD A FULL-BODY HALLUCINATION THAT DISENCHANTED ME WITH THE DRUG...

HUH? WHO'S THERE?

HEE, HEE, HEE

OH MY GOD!

MY FEET WERE GRABBED, AND MY BODY WAS CORKSCREWED AS I WAS YANKED INTO (WHAT I SURMISED TO BE) THE DEPTHS OF HELL!

MOMMY

HA HA HA !!

Held on to the panel border for dear life!

UM.. MOM, YOU WON'T HAVE TO BE REFILLING THAT PRESCRIPTION.

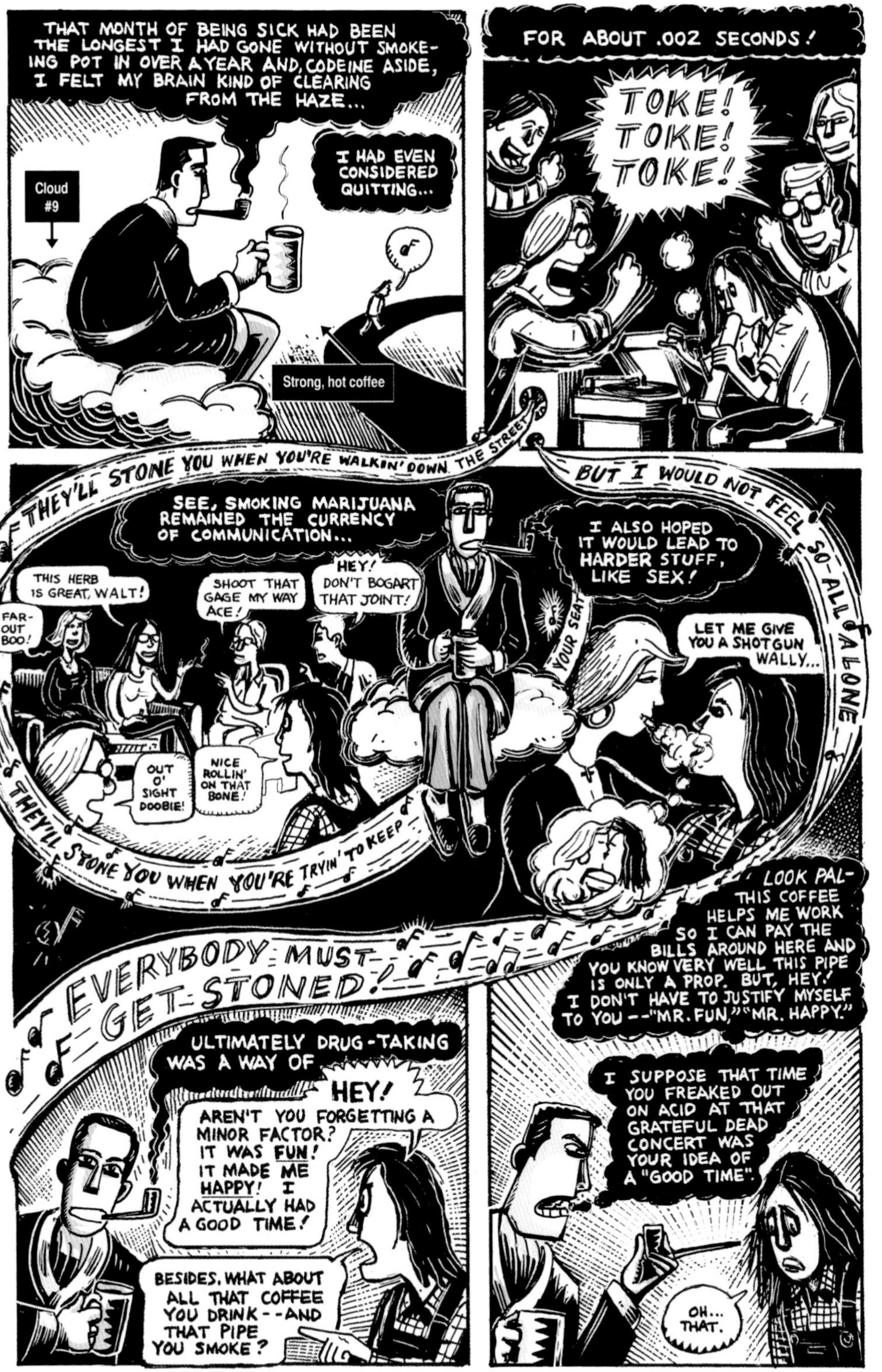
THAT MONTH OF BEING SICK HAD BEEN THE LONGEST I HAD GONE WITHOUT SMOKE-ING POT IN OVER A YEAR AND, CODEINE ASIDE, I FELT MY BRAIN KIND OF CLEARING FROM THE HAZE...
I HAD EVEN CONSIDERED QUITTING...
Cloud #9
Strong, hot coffee
FOR ABOUT .002 SECONDS!
TOKE! TOKE! TOKE!
THEY'LL STONE YOU WHEN YOU'RE WALKIN' DOWN THE STREET
BUT I WOULD NOT FEEL SO-ALL ALONE
SEE, SMOKING MARIJUANA REMAINED THE CURRENCY OF COMMUNICATION...
I ALSO HOPED IT WOULD LEAD TO HARDER STUFF, LIKE SEX!
THIS HERB IS GREAT, WALT!
FAR-OUT BOO!
SHOOT THAT GAGE MY WAY ACE!
HEY! DON'T BOGART THAT JOINT!
YOUR SEAT
LET ME GIVE YOU A SHOTGUN WALLY...
OUT O' SIGHT DOOBIE!
NICE ROLLIN' ON THAT BONE!
THEY'LL STONE YOU WHEN YOU'RE TRYIN' TO KEEP
EVERYBODY MUST GET STONED!
LOOK PAL- THIS COFFEE HELPS ME WORK SO I CAN PAY THE BILLS AROUND HERE AND YOU KNOW VERY WELL THIS PIPE IS ONLY A PROP. BUT, HEY! I DON'T HAVE TO JUSTIFY MYSELF TO YOU --"MR. FUN," "MR. HAPPY."
ULTIMATELY DRUG-TAKING WAS A WAY OF
HEY!
AREN'T YOU FORGETTING A MINOR FACTOR? IT WAS FUN! IT MADE ME HAPPY! I ACTUALLY HAD A GOOD TIME!
BESIDES, WHAT ABOUT ALL THAT COFFEE YOU DRINK--AND THAT PIPE YOU SMOKE?
I SUPPOSE THAT TIME YOU FREAKED OUT ON ACID AT THAT GRATEFUL DEAD CONCERT WAS YOUR IDEA OF A "GOOD TIME".
OH... THAT.

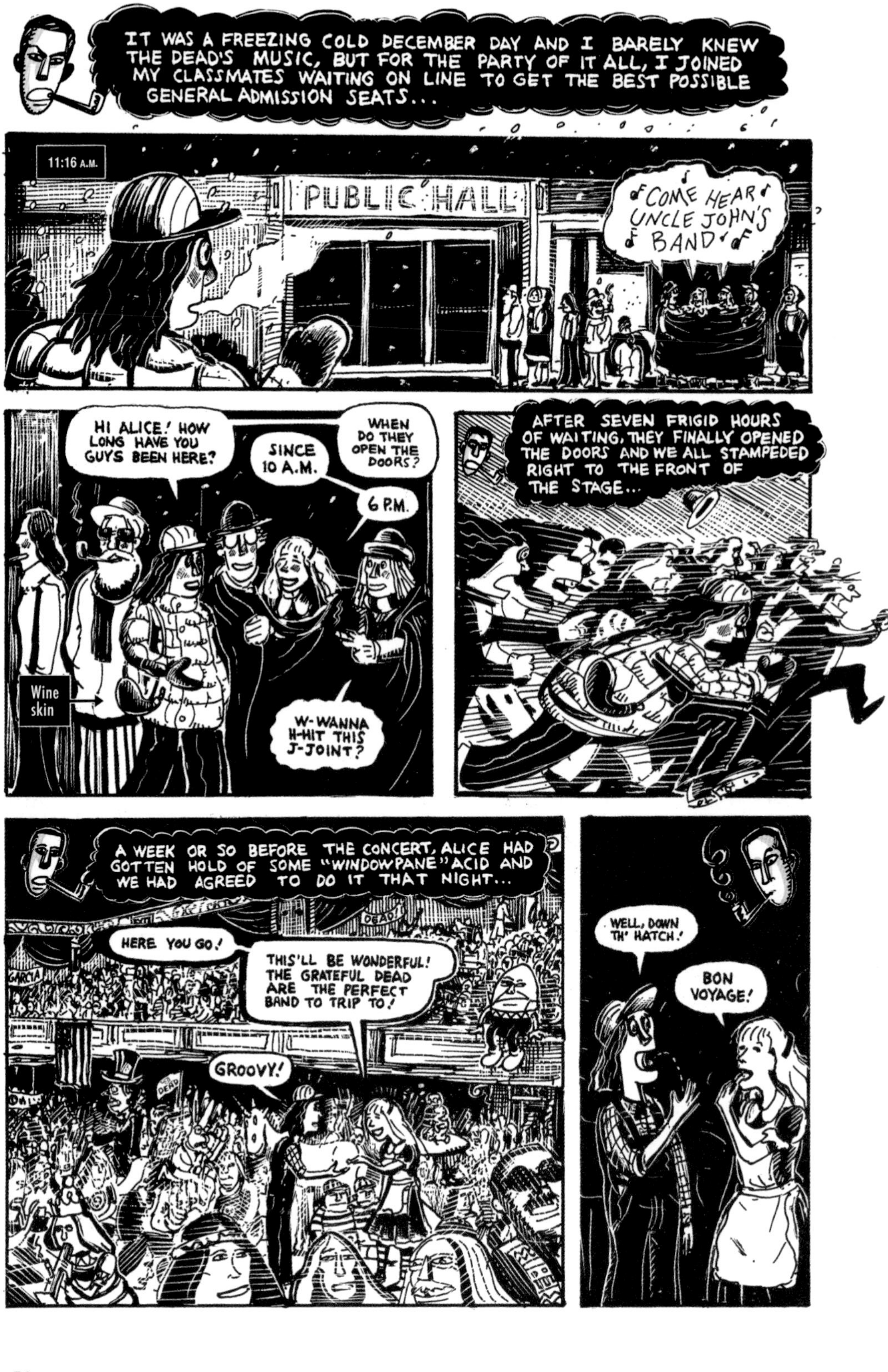
IT WAS A FREEZING COLD DECEMBER DAY AND I BARELY KNEW THE DEAD'S MUSIC, BUT FOR THE PARTY OF IT ALL, I JOINED MY CLASSMATES WAITING ON LINE TO GET THE BEST POSSIBLE GENERAL ADMISSION SEATS...
11:16 A.M.
PUBLIC HALL
COME HEAR UNCLE JOHN'S BAND
HI ALICE! HOW LONG HAVE YOU GUYS BEEN HERE?
SINCE 10 A.M.
WHEN DO THEY OPEN THE DOORS?
6 P.M.
Wine skin
W-WANNA H-HIT THIS J-JOINT?
AFTER SEVEN FRIGID HOURS OF WAITING, THEY FINALLY OPENED THE DOORS AND WE ALL STAMPEDED RIGHT TO THE FRONT OF THE STAGE...
A WEEK OR SO BEFORE THE CONCERT, ALICE HAD GOTTEN HOLD OF SOME "WINDOWPANE" ACID AND WE HAD AGREED TO DO IT THAT NIGHT...
HERE YOU GO!
THIS'LL BE WONDERFUL! THE GRATEFUL DEAD ARE THE PERFECT BAND TO TRIP TO!
GROOVY!
WELL, DOWN TH' HATCH!
BON VOYAGE!

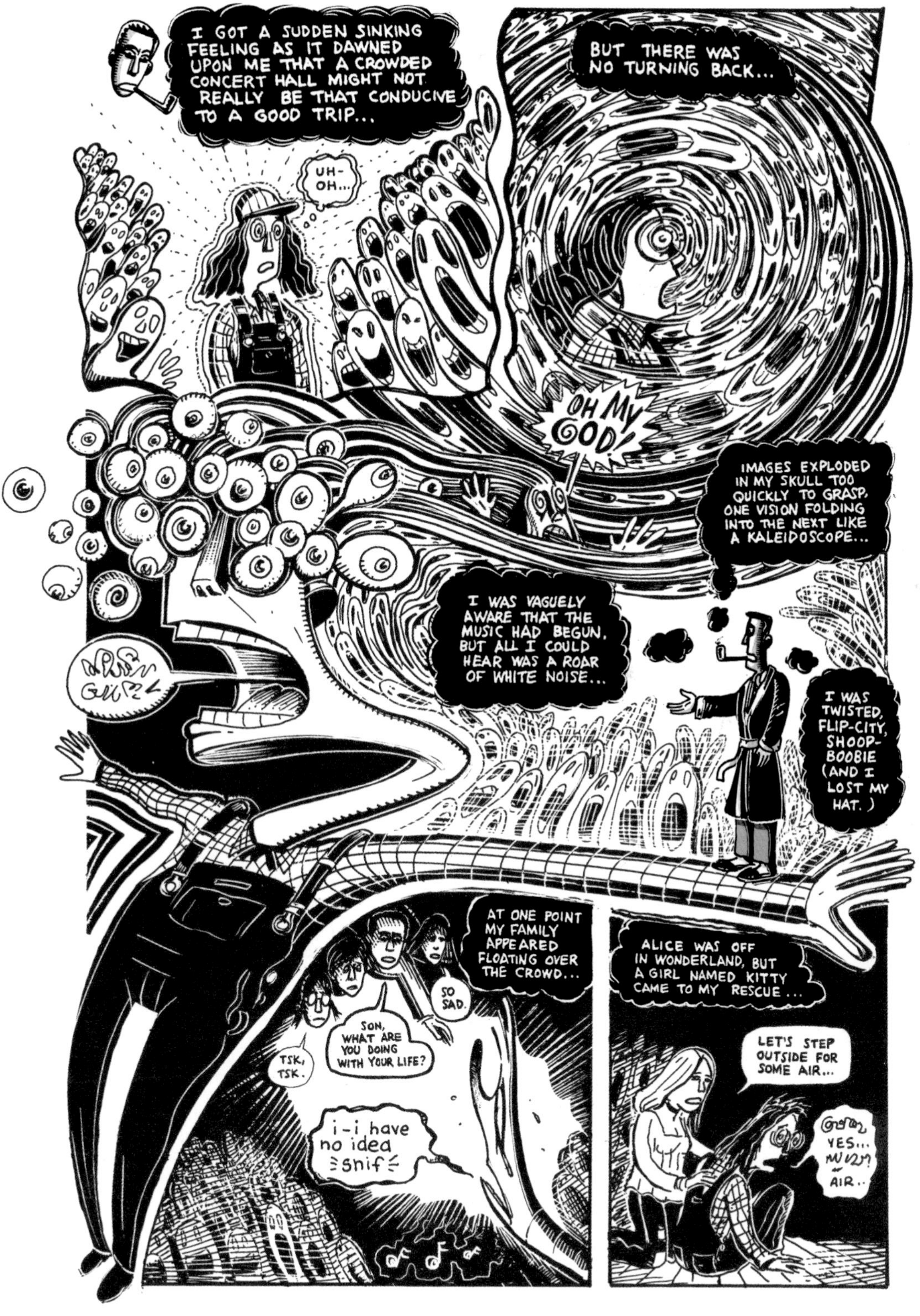
I GOT A SUDDEN SINKING FEELING AS IT DAWNED UPON ME THAT A CROWDED CONCERT HALL MIGHT NOT REALLY BE THAT CONDUCIVE TO A GOOD TRIP...
UH-OH...
BUT THERE WAS NO TURNING BACK...
OH MY GOD!
IMAGES EXPLODED IN MY SKULL TOO QUICKLY TO GRASP, ONE VISION FOLDING INTO THE NEXT LIKE A KALEIDOSCOPE...
I WAS VAGUELY AWARE THAT THE MUSIC HAD BEGUN, BUT ALL I COULD HEAR WAS A ROAR OF WHITE NOISE...
I WAS TWISTED, FLIP-CITY, SHOOP-BOOBIE (AND I LOST MY HAT.)
AT ONE POINT MY FAMILY APPEARED FLOATING OVER THE CROWD...
SO SAD.
SON, WHAT ARE YOU DOING WITH YOUR LIFE?
TSK, TSK.
i-i have no idea
snif
ALICE WAS OFF IN WONDERLAND, BUT A GIRL NAMED KITTY CAME TO MY RESCUE...
LET'S STEP OUTSIDE FOR SOME AIR...
YES...
AIR..

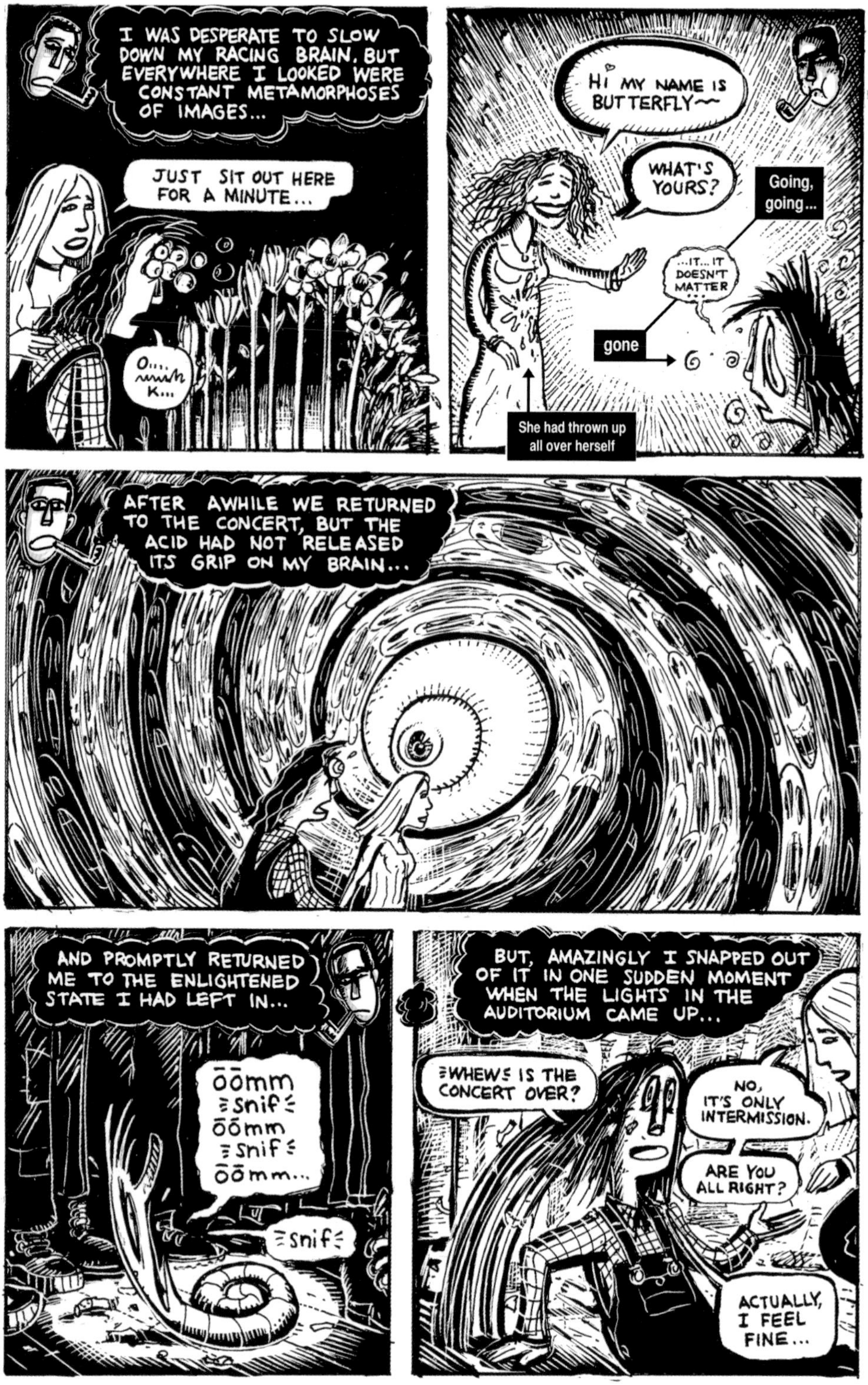
I WAS DESPERATE TO SLOW DOWN MY RACING BRAIN, BUT EVERYWHERE I LOOKED WERE CONSTANT METAMORPHOSES OF IMAGES...
JUST SIT OUT HERE FOR A MINUTE...
O.... K...
HI MY NAME IS BUTTERFLY~~
WHAT'S YOURS?
Going, going...
...IT... IT DOESN'T MATTER...
gone
She had thrown up all over herself
AFTER AWHILE WE RETURNED TO THE CONCERT, BUT THE ACID HAD NOT RELEASED ITS GRIP ON MY BRAIN...
AND PROMPTLY RETURNED ME TO THE ENLIGHTENED STATE I HAD LEFT IN...
ŌŌMM SNIF ŌŌMM SNIF ŌŌMM...
SNIF
BUT, AMAZINGLY I SNAPPED OUT OF IT IN ONE SUDDEN MOMENT WHEN THE LIGHTS IN THE AUDITORIUM CAME UP...
WHEW IS THE CONCERT OVER?
NO, IT'S ONLY INTERMISSION.
ARE YOU ALL RIGHT?
ACTUALLY, I FEEL FINE...

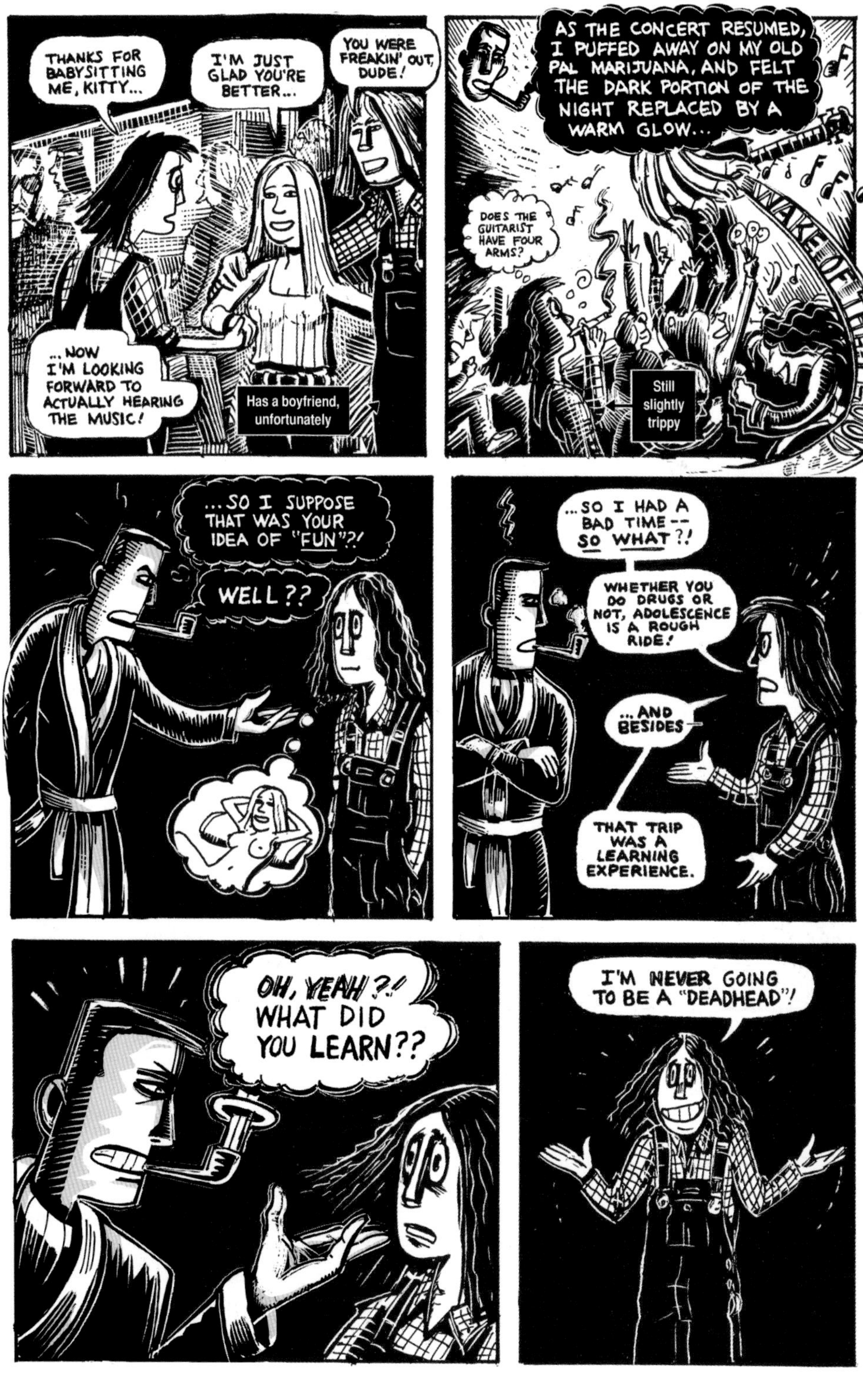
THANKS FOR BABYSITTING ME, KITTY...
I'M JUST GLAD YOU'RE BETTER...
YOU WERE FREAKIN' OUT, DUDE!
...NOW I'M LOOKING FORWARD TO ACTUALLY HEARING THE MUSIC!
Has a boyfriend, unfortunately
AS THE CONCERT RESUMED, I PUFFED AWAY ON MY OLD PAL MARIJUANA, AND FELT THE DARK PORTION OF THE NIGHT REPLACED BY A WARM GLOW...
DOES THE GUITARIST HAVE FOUR ARMS?
WAKE OF THE FLOOD
Still slightly trippy
...SO I SUPPOSE THAT WAS YOUR IDEA OF "FUN"?!
WELL??
...SO I HAD A BAD TIME -- SO WHAT?!
WHETHER YOU DO DRUGS OR NOT, ADOLESCENCE IS A ROUGH RIDE!
...AND BESIDES—
THAT TRIP WAS A LEARNING EXPERIENCE.
OH, YEAH?! WHAT DID YOU LEARN??
I'M NEVER GOING TO BE A "DEADHEAD"!

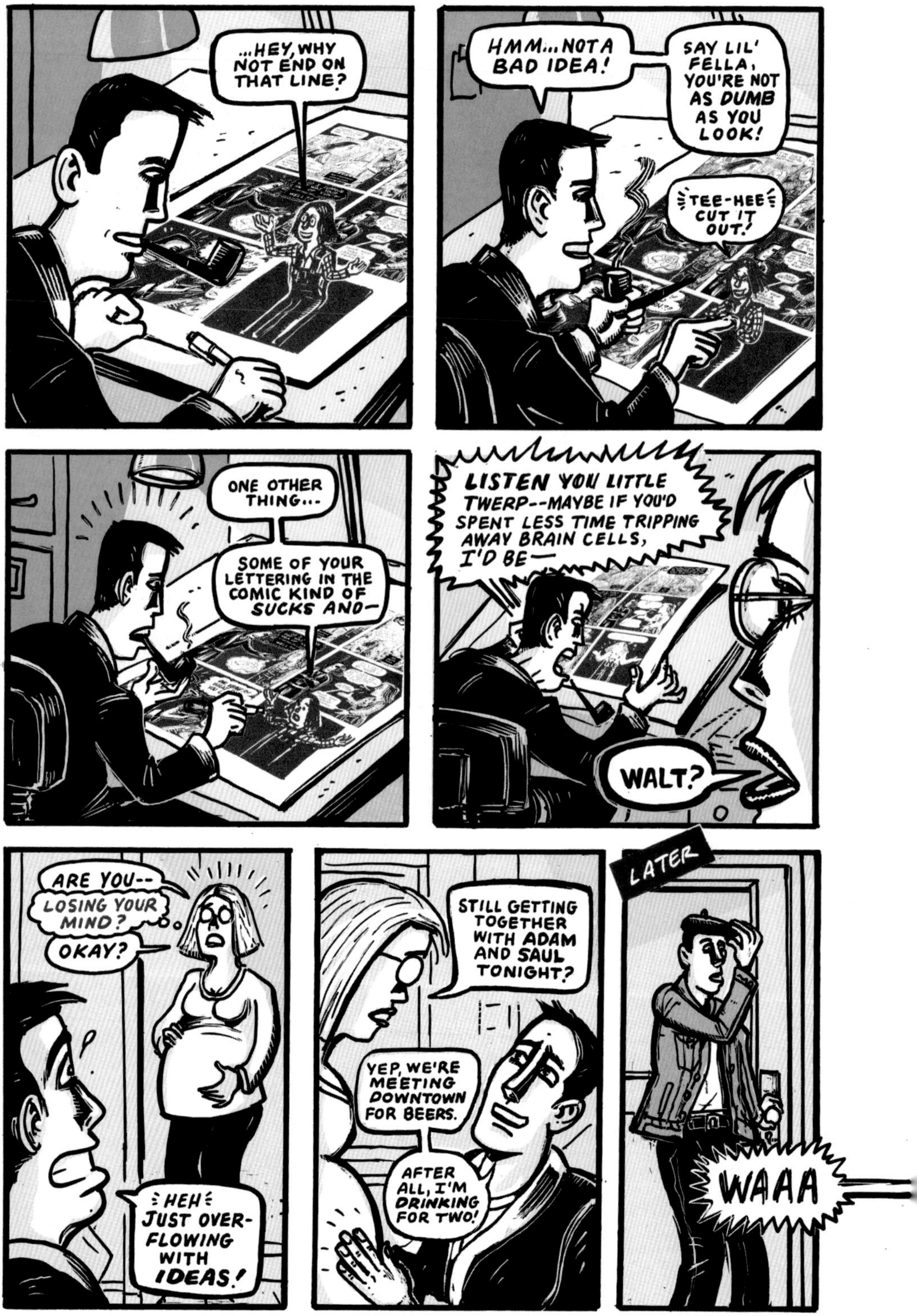
...HEY, WHY NOT END ON THAT LINE?
HMM... NOT A BAD IDEA!
SAY LIL' FELLA, YOU'RE NOT AS DUMB AS YOU LOOK!
TEE-HEE CUT IT OUT!
ONE OTHER THING...
SOME OF YOUR LETTERING IN THE COMIC KIND OF SUCKS AND—
LISTEN YOU LITTLE TWERP--MAYBE IF YOU'D SPENT LESS TIME TRIPPING AWAY BRAIN CELLS, I'D BE—
WALT?
ARE YOU--
LOSING YOUR MIND?
OKAY?
HEH JUST OVER-FLOWING WITH IDEAS!
STILL GETTING TOGETHER WITH ADAM AND SAUL TONIGHT?
YEP, WE'RE MEETING DOWNTOWN FOR BEERS.
AFTER ALL, I'M DRINKING FOR TWO!
LATER
WAAA

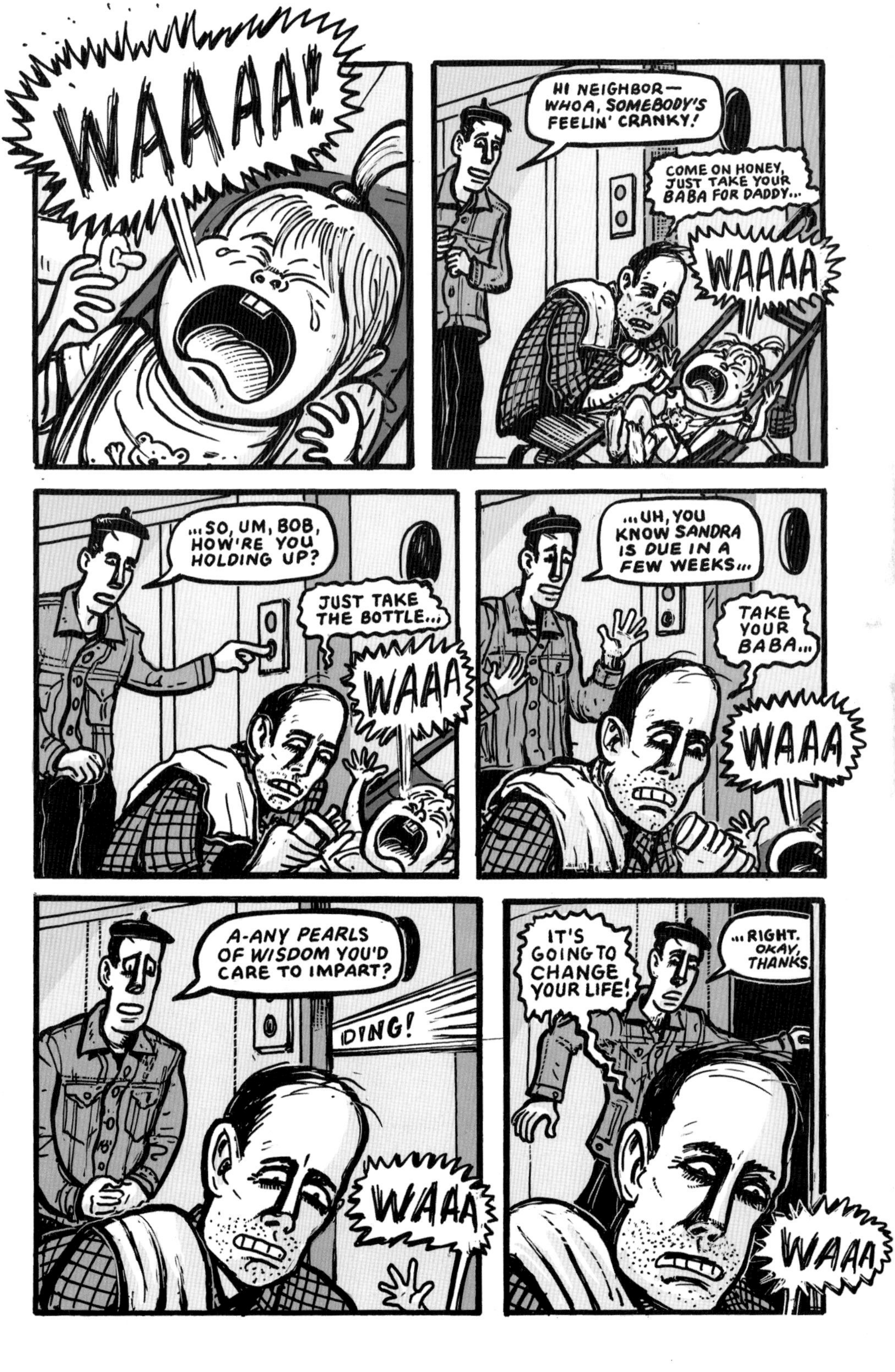
WAAAA!
HI NEIGHBOR—WHOA, SOMEBODY'S FEELIN' CRANKY!
COME ON HONEY, JUST TAKE YOUR BABA FOR DADDY...
WAAAA
...SO, UM, BOB, HOW'RE YOU HOLDING UP?
JUST TAKE THE BOTTLE...
WAAA
...UH, YOU KNOW SANDRA IS DUE IN A FEW WEEKS...
TAKE YOUR BABA...
WAAA
A-ANY PEARLS OF WISDOM YOU'D CARE TO IMPART?
DING!
WAAA
IT'S GOING TO CHANGE YOUR LIFE!
...RIGHT. OKAY, THANKS.
WAAA

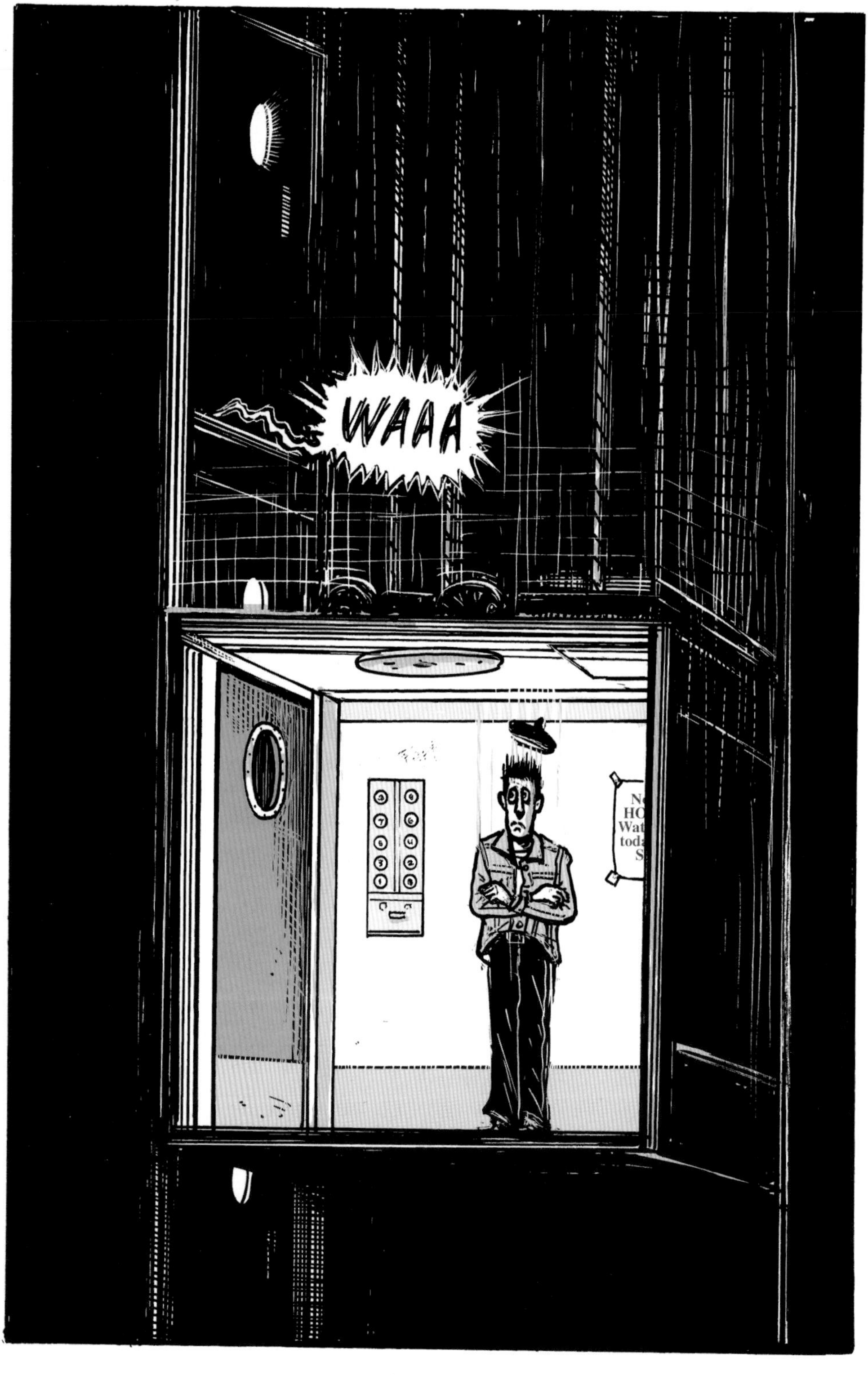
WAAA

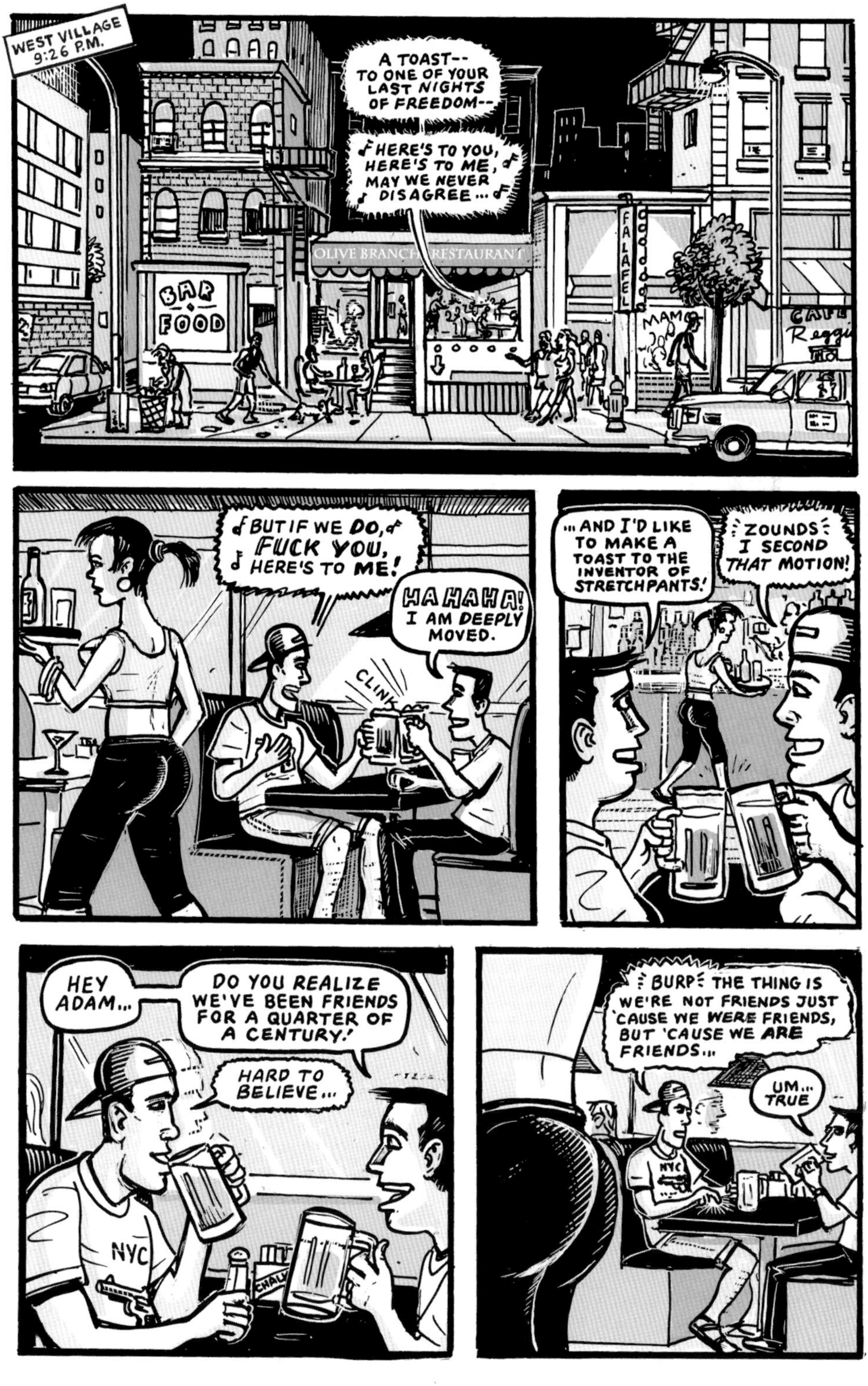
WEST VILLAGE 9:26 P.M.
A TOAST-- TO ONE OF YOUR LAST NIGHTS OF FREEDOM--
HERE'S TO YOU, HERE'S TO ME, MAY WE NEVER DISAGREE...
OLIVE BRANCH RESTAURANT
BAR FOOD
FALAFEL
CAFE Reggio
BUT IF WE DO, FUCK YOU, HERE'S TO ME!
HA HA HA! I AM DEEPLY MOVED.
CLINK
...AND I'D LIKE TO MAKE A TOAST TO THE INVENTOR OF STRETCHPANTS!
ZOUNDS I SECOND THAT MOTION!
HEY ADAM...
DO YOU REALIZE WE'VE BEEN FRIENDS FOR A QUARTER OF A CENTURY!
HARD TO BELIEVE...
NYC
BURP THE THING IS WE'RE NOT FRIENDS JUST 'CAUSE WE WERE FRIENDS, BUT 'CAUSE WE ARE FRIENDS...
UM... TRUE

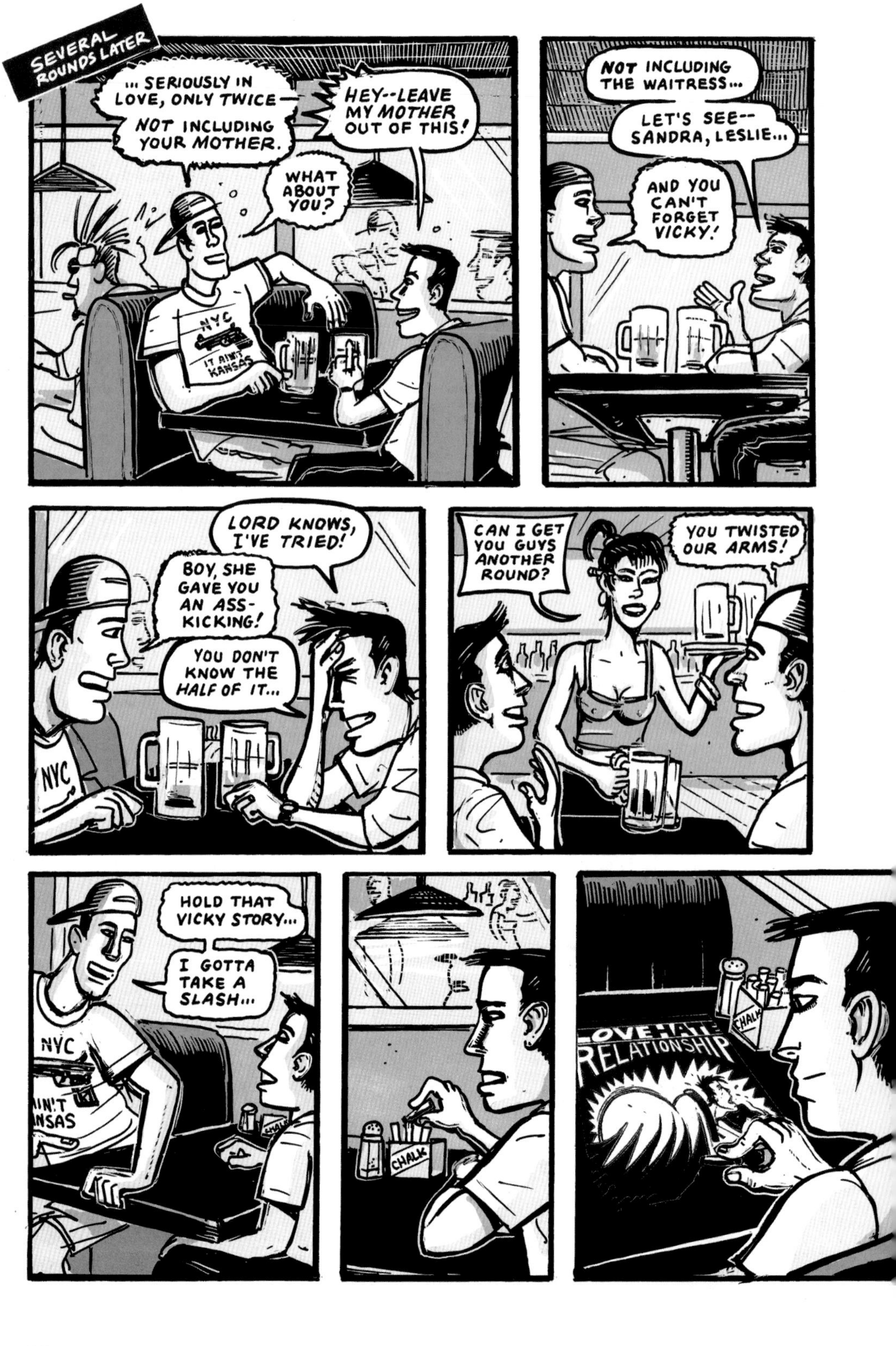
SEVERAL ROUNDS LATER
... SERIOUSLY IN LOVE, ONLY TWICE—
NOT INCLUDING YOUR MOTHER.
HEY--LEAVE MY MOTHER OUT OF THIS!
WHAT ABOUT YOU?
NYC IT AIN'T KANSAS
NOT INCLUDING THE WAITRESS...
LET'S SEE-- SANDRA, LESLIE...
AND YOU CAN'T FORGET VICKY!
LORD KNOWS, I'VE TRIED!
BOY, SHE GAVE YOU AN ASS-KICKING!
YOU DON'T KNOW THE HALF OF IT...
NYC
CAN I GET YOU GUYS ANOTHER ROUND?
YOU TWISTED OUR ARMS!
HOLD THAT VICKY STORY...
I GOTTA TAKE A SLASH...
CHALK
LOVE HATE RELATIONSHIP

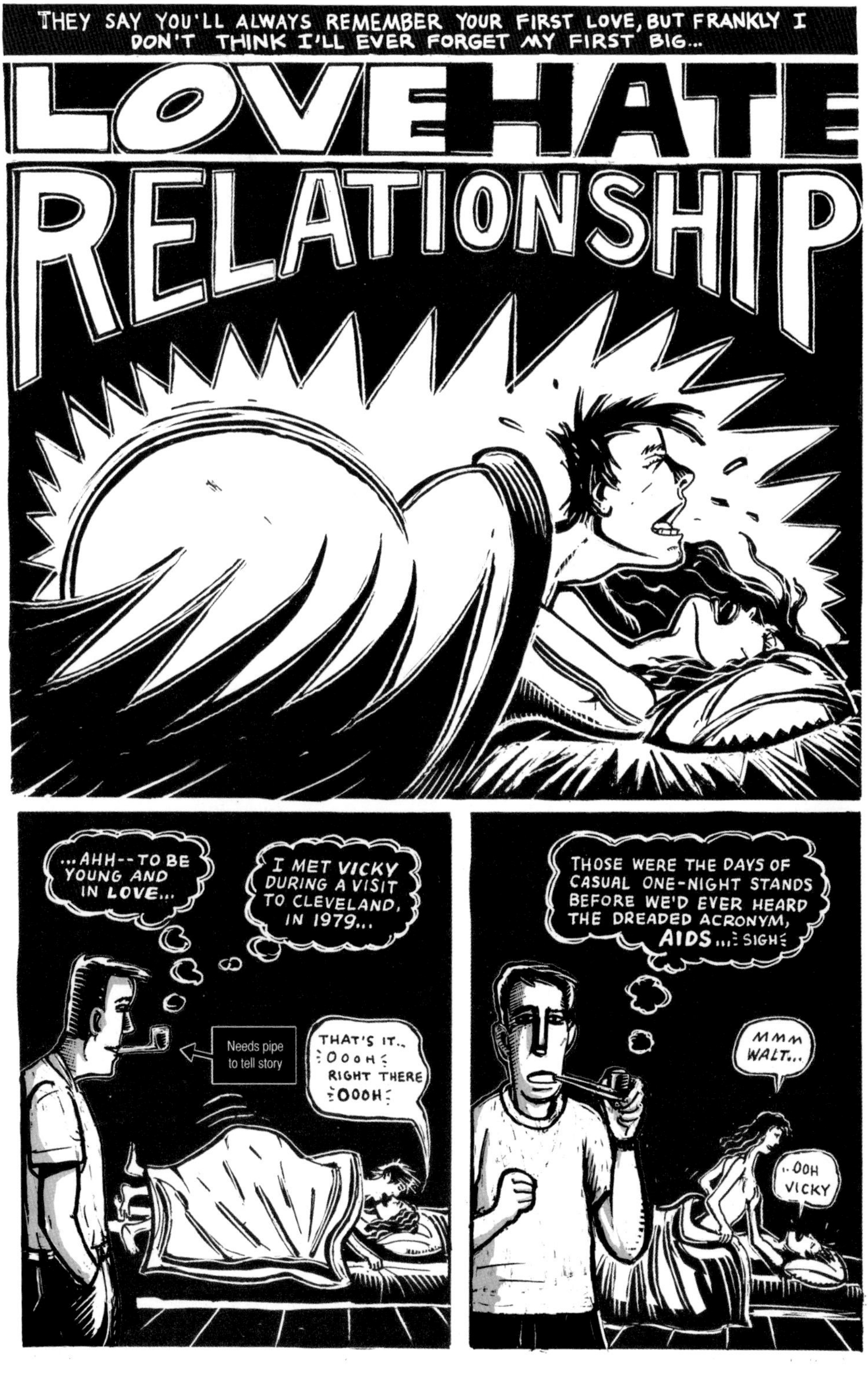
THEY SAY YOU'LL ALWAYS REMEMBER YOUR FIRST LOVE, BUT FRANKLY I DON'T THINK I'LL EVER FORGET MY FIRST BIG...
LOVE HATE RELATIONSHIP
...AHH--TO BE YOUNG AND IN LOVE...
I MET VICKY DURING A VISIT TO CLEVELAND, IN 1979...
Needs pipe to tell story
THAT'S IT.. OOOH RIGHT THERE OOOH
THOSE WERE THE DAYS OF CASUAL ONE-NIGHT STANDS BEFORE WE'D EVER HEARD THE DREADED ACRONYM, AIDS... SIGH
MMM WALT...
..OOH VICKY

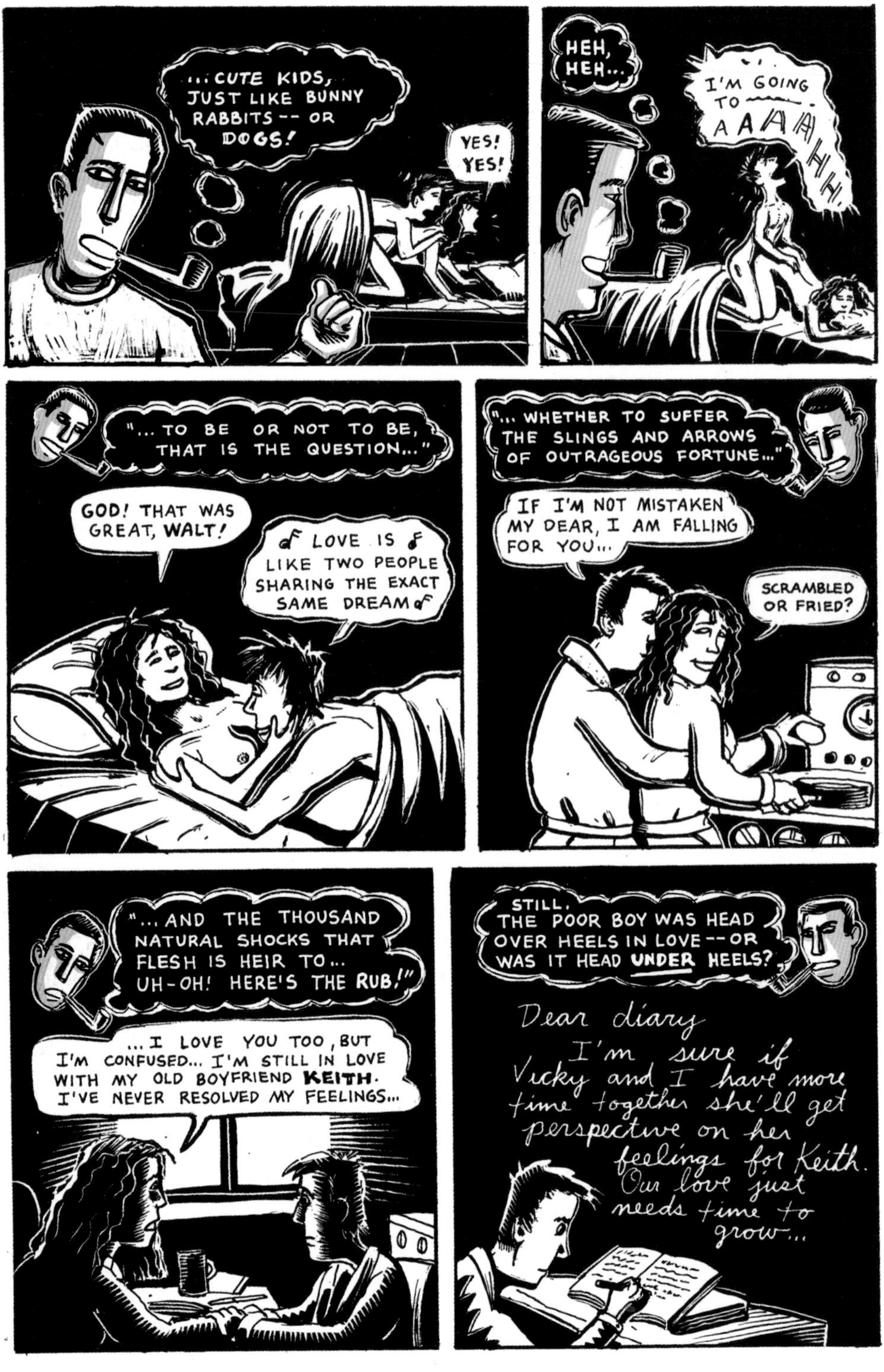
...CUTE KIDS, JUST LIKE BUNNY RABBITS -- OR DOGS!
YES! YES!
HEH, HEH...
I'M GOING TO AAAAHHH.
"...TO BE OR NOT TO BE, THAT IS THE QUESTION..."
GOD! THAT WAS GREAT, WALT!
LOVE IS LIKE TWO PEOPLE SHARING THE EXACT SAME DREAM
"...WHETHER TO SUFFER THE SLINGS AND ARROWS OF OUTRAGEOUS FORTUNE..."
IF I'M NOT MISTAKEN MY DEAR, I AM FALLING FOR YOU...
SCRAMBLED OR FRIED?
"...AND THE THOUSAND NATURAL SHOCKS THAT FLESH IS HEIR TO... UH-OH! HERE'S THE RUB!"
...I LOVE YOU TOO, BUT I'M CONFUSED... I'M STILL IN LOVE WITH MY OLD BOYFRIEND KEITH. I'VE NEVER RESOLVED MY FEELINGS...
STILL, THE POOR BOY WAS HEAD OVER HEELS IN LOVE -- OR WAS IT HEAD UNDER HEELS?
Dear diary
I'm sure if Vicky and I have more time together she'll get perspective on her feelings for Keith. Our love just needs time to grow...

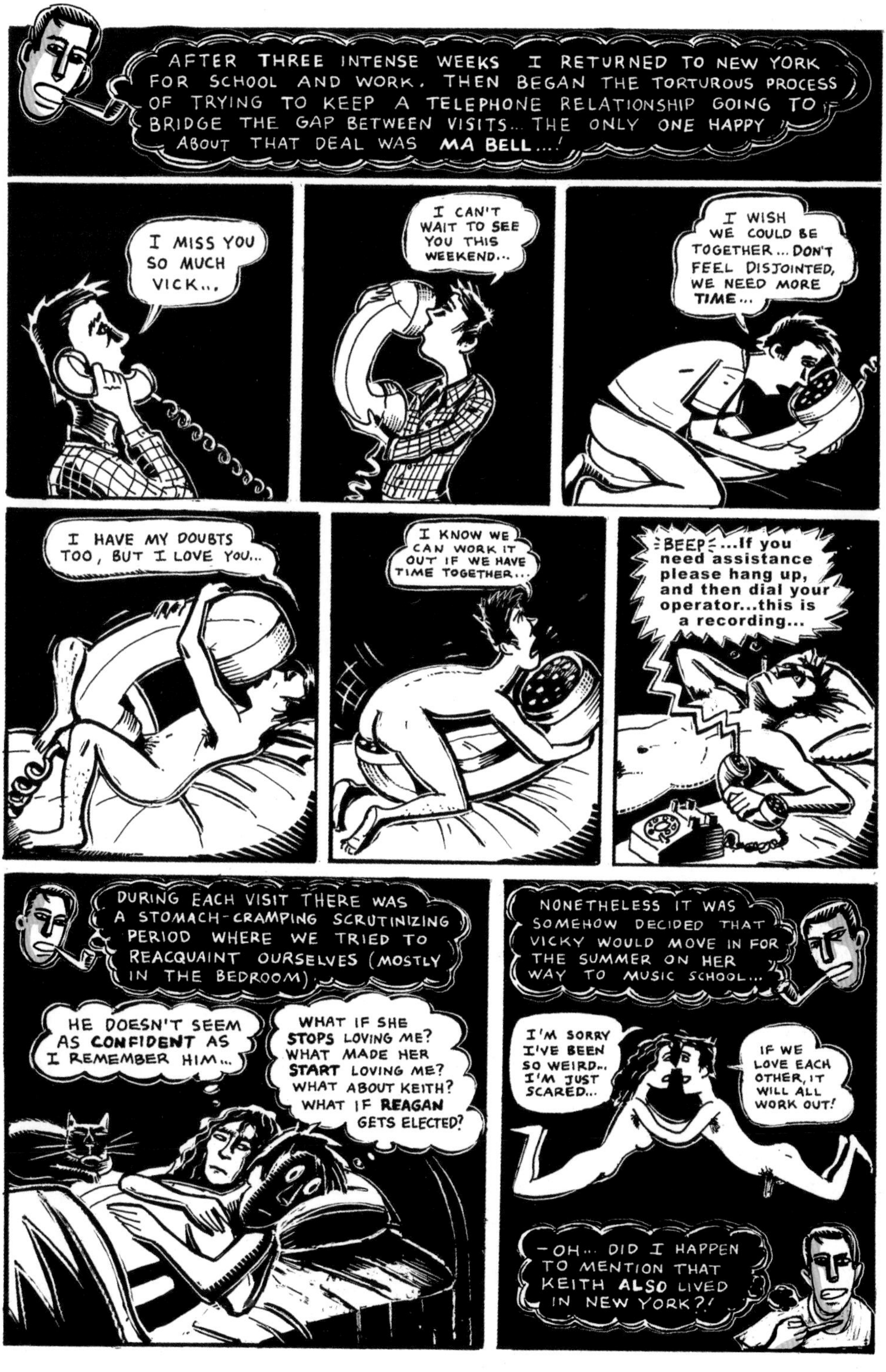
AFTER THREE INTENSE WEEKS I RETURNED TO NEW YORK FOR SCHOOL AND WORK. THEN BEGAN THE TORTUROUS PROCESS OF TRYING TO KEEP A TELEPHONE RELATIONSHIP GOING TO BRIDGE THE GAP BETWEEN VISITS... THE ONLY ONE HAPPY ABOUT THAT DEAL WAS MA BELL...!
I MISS YOU SO MUCH VICK...
I CAN'T WAIT TO SEE YOU THIS WEEKEND...
I WISH WE COULD BE TOGETHER... DON'T FEEL DISJOINTED, WE NEED MORE TIME...
I HAVE MY DOUBTS TOO, BUT I LOVE YOU...
I KNOW WE CAN WORK IT OUT IF WE HAVE TIME TOGETHER...
BEEP ...If you need assistance please hang up, and then dial your operator...this is a recording...
DURING EACH VISIT THERE WAS A STOMACH-CRAMPING SCRUTINIZING PERIOD WHERE WE TRIED TO REACQUAINT OURSELVES (MOSTLY IN THE BEDROOM).
HE DOESN'T SEEM AS CONFIDENT AS I REMEMBER HIM...
WHAT IF SHE STOPS LOVING ME? WHAT MADE HER START LOVING ME? WHAT ABOUT KEITH? WHAT IF REAGAN GETS ELECTED?
NONETHELESS IT WAS SOMEHOW DECIDED THAT VICKY WOULD MOVE IN FOR THE SUMMER ON HER WAY TO MUSIC SCHOOL...
I'M SORRY I'VE BEEN SO WEIRD.. I'M JUST SCARED...
IF WE LOVE EACH OTHER, IT WILL ALL WORK OUT!
—OH... DID I HAPPEN TO MENTION THAT KEITH ALSO LIVED IN NEW YORK?!

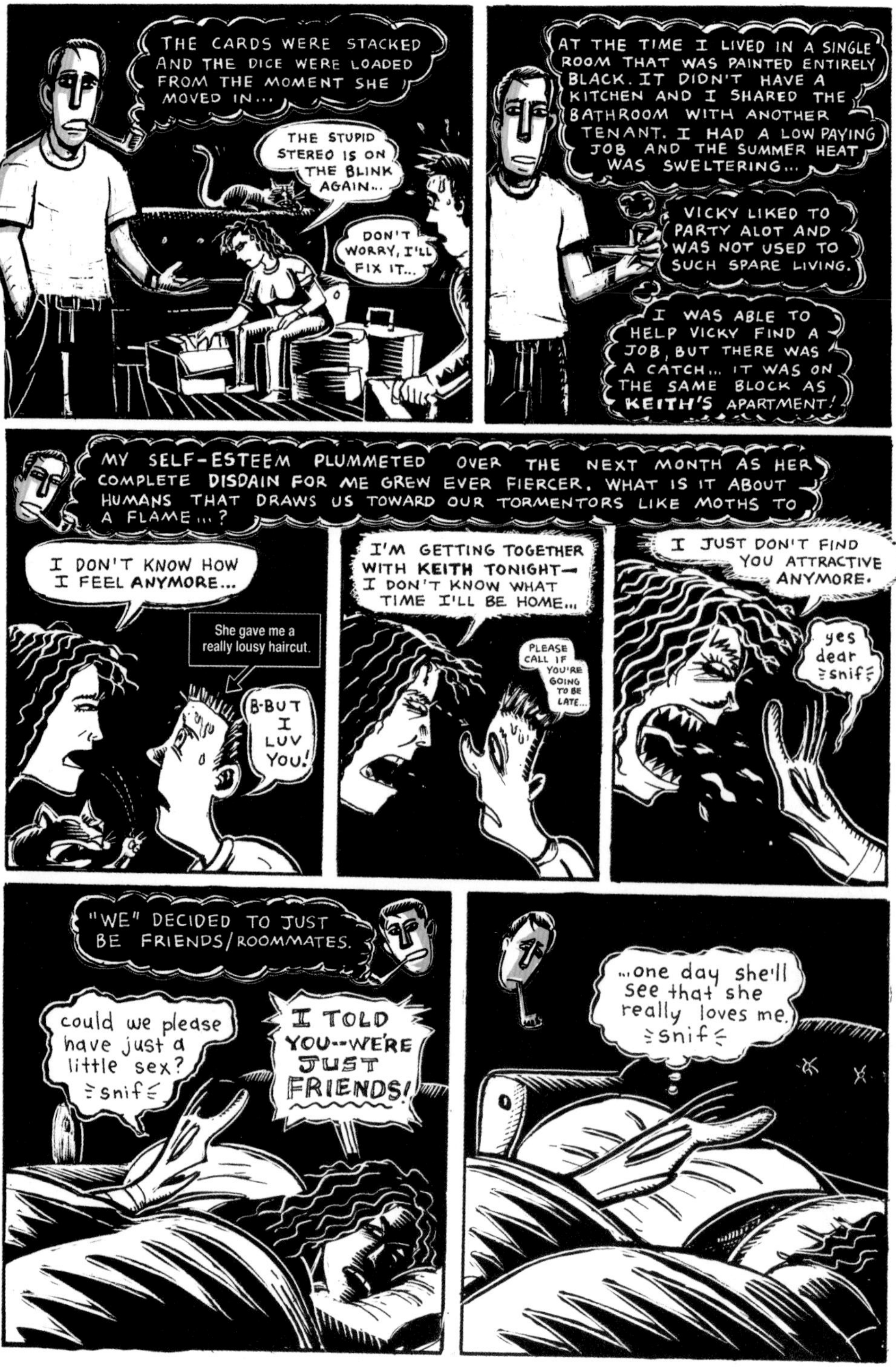
THE CARDS WERE STACKED AND THE DICE WERE LOADED FROM THE MOMENT SHE MOVED IN...
THE STUPID STEREO IS ON THE BLINK AGAIN...
DON'T WORRY, I'LL FIX IT...
AT THE TIME I LIVED IN A SINGLE ROOM THAT WAS PAINTED ENTIRELY BLACK. IT DIDN'T HAVE A KITCHEN AND I SHARED THE BATHROOM WITH ANOTHER TENANT. I HAD A LOW PAYING JOB AND THE SUMMER HEAT WAS SWELTERING...
VICKY LIKED TO PARTY ALOT AND WAS NOT USED TO SUCH SPARE LIVING.
I WAS ABLE TO HELP VICKY FIND A JOB, BUT THERE WAS A CATCH... IT WAS ON THE SAME BLOCK AS KEITH'S APARTMENT!
MY SELF-ESTEEM PLUMMETED OVER THE NEXT MONTH AS HER COMPLETE DISDAIN FOR ME GREW EVER FIERCER. WHAT IS IT ABOUT HUMANS THAT DRAWS US TOWARD OUR TORMENTORS LIKE MOTHS TO A FLAME...?
I DON'T KNOW HOW I FEEL ANYMORE...
She gave me a really lousy haircut.
B-BUT I LUV YOU!
I'M GETTING TOGETHER WITH KEITH TONIGHT— I DON'T KNOW WHAT TIME I'LL BE HOME...
PLEASE CALL IF YOU'RE GOING TO BE LATE...
I JUST DON'T FIND YOU ATTRACTIVE ANYMORE.
yes dear snif
"WE" DECIDED TO JUST BE FRIENDS/ROOMMATES.
could we please have just a little sex? snif
I TOLD YOU--WE'RE JUST FRIENDS!
...one day she'll see that she really loves me. snif

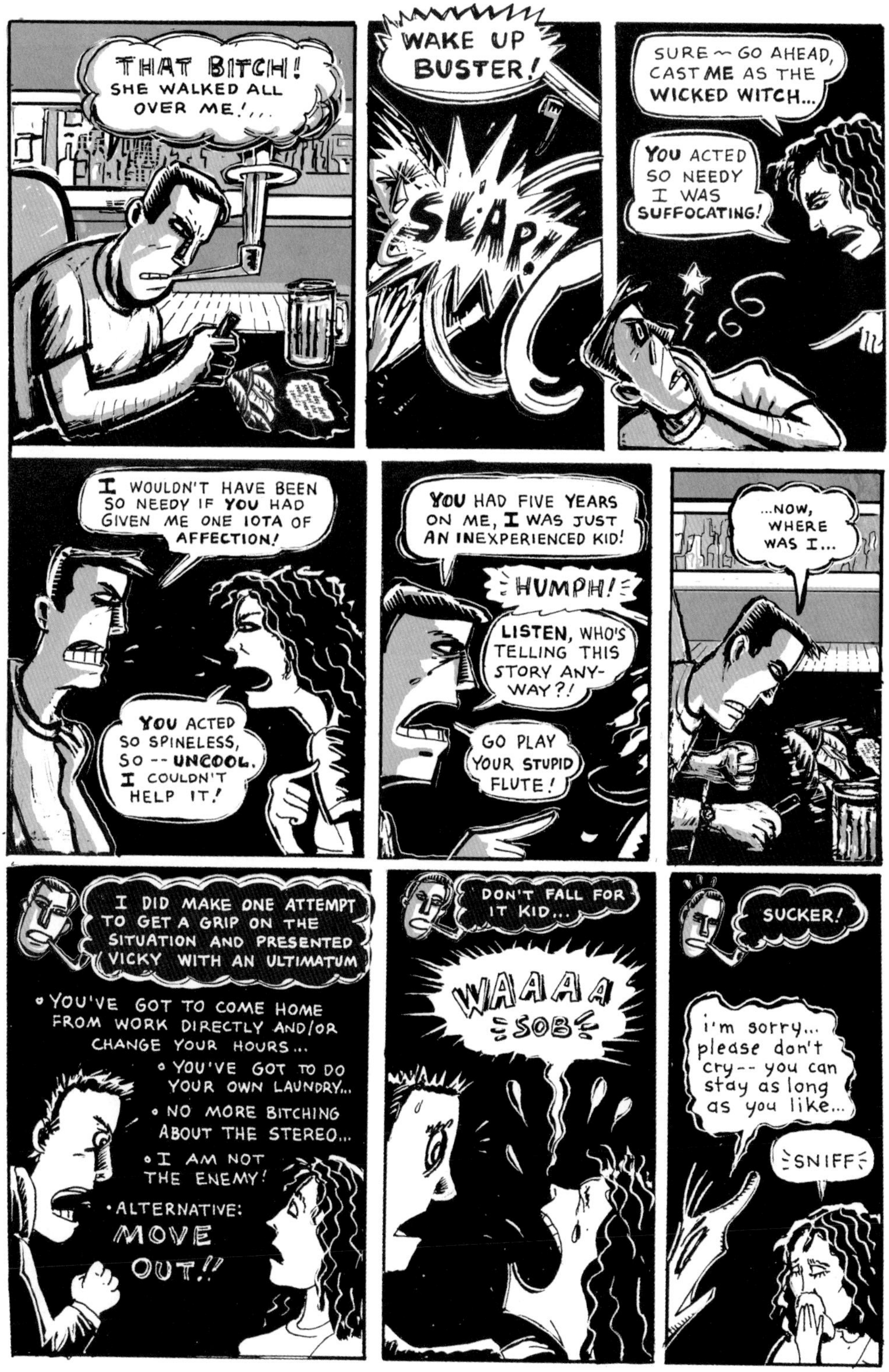
THAT BITCH! SHE WALKED ALL OVER ME!...
WAKE UP BUSTER!
SLAP!
SURE ~ GO AHEAD, CAST ME AS THE WICKED WITCH...
YOU ACTED SO NEEDY I WAS SUFFOCATING!
I WOULDN'T HAVE BEEN SO NEEDY IF YOU HAD GIVEN ME ONE IOTA OF AFFECTION!
YOU ACTED SO SPINELESS, SO -- UNCOOL. I COULDN'T HELP IT!
YOU HAD FIVE YEARS ON ME, I WAS JUST AN INEXPERIENCED KID!
HUMPH!
LISTEN, WHO'S TELLING THIS STORY ANY-WAY?!
GO PLAY YOUR STUPID FLUTE!
...NOW, WHERE WAS I...
I DID MAKE ONE ATTEMPT TO GET A GRIP ON THE SITUATION AND PRESENTED VICKY WITH AN ULTIMATUM
• YOU'VE GOT TO COME HOME FROM WORK DIRECTLY AND/OR CHANGE YOUR HOURS...
• YOU'VE GOT TO DO YOUR OWN LAUNDRY...
• NO MORE BITCHING ABOUT THE STEREO...
• I AM NOT THE ENEMY!
• ALTERNATIVE: MOVE OUT!!
DON'T FALL FOR IT KID...
WAAAA
SOB
SUCKER!
i'm sorry... please don't cry-- you can stay as long as you like...
SNIFF

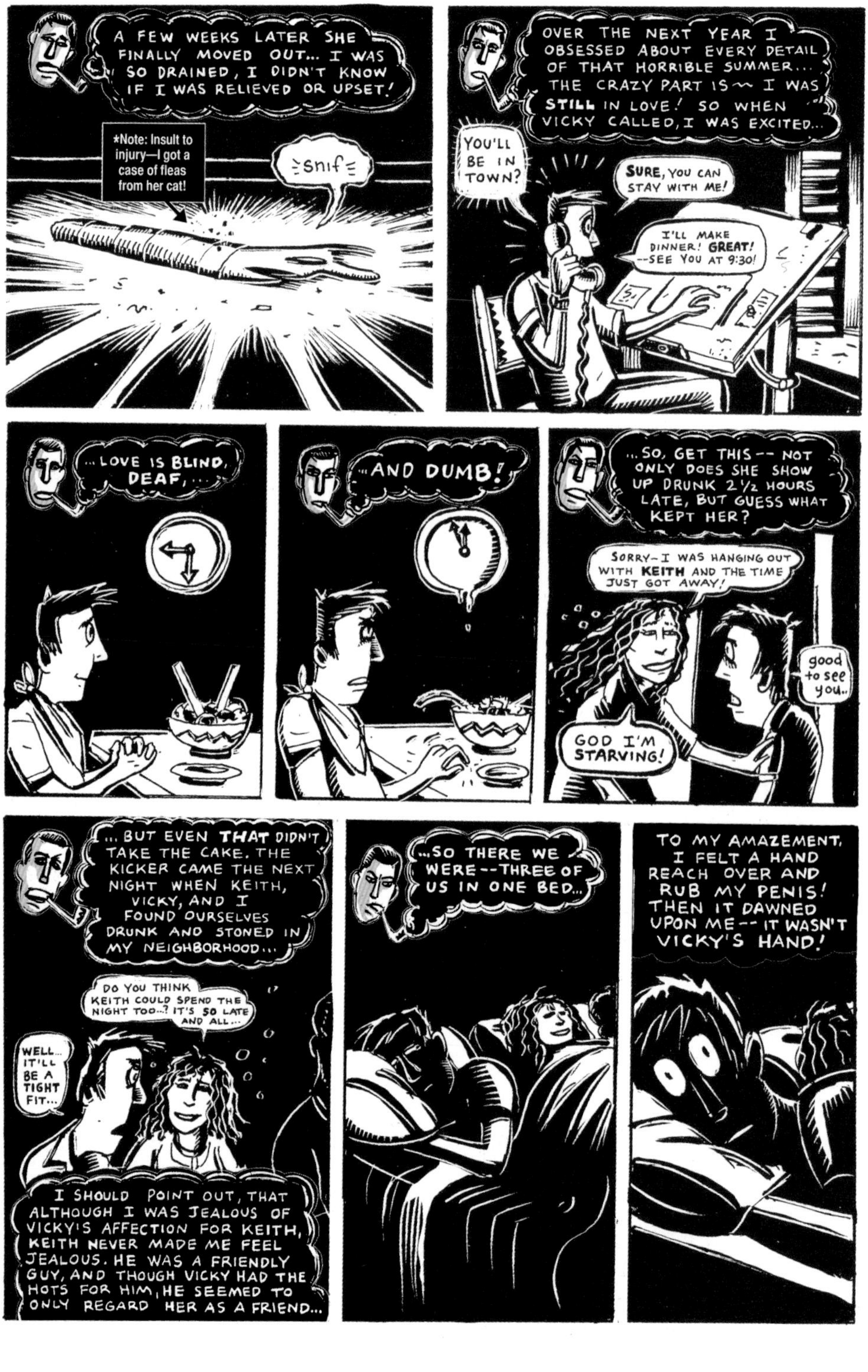
A FEW WEEKS LATER SHE FINALLY MOVED OUT... I WAS SO DRAINED, I DIDN'T KNOW IF I WAS RELIEVED OR UPSET!
*Note: Insult to injury—I got a case of fleas from her cat!
snif
OVER THE NEXT YEAR I OBSESSED ABOUT EVERY DETAIL OF THAT HORRIBLE SUMMER... THE CRAZY PART IS ~ I WAS STILL IN LOVE! SO WHEN VICKY CALLED, I WAS EXCITED...
YOU'LL BE IN TOWN?
SURE, YOU CAN STAY WITH ME!
I'LL MAKE DINNER! GREAT! --SEE YOU AT 9:30!
...LOVE IS BLIND, DEAF,...
...AND DUMB!
...SO, GET THIS-- NOT ONLY DOES SHE SHOW UP DRUNK 2 1/2 HOURS LATE, BUT GUESS WHAT KEPT HER?
SORRY- I WAS HANGING OUT WITH KEITH AND THE TIME JUST GOT AWAY!
good to see you..
GOD I'M STARVING!
...BUT EVEN THAT DIDN'T TAKE THE CAKE. THE KICKER CAME THE NEXT NIGHT WHEN KEITH, VICKY, AND I FOUND OURSELVES DRUNK AND STONED IN MY NEIGHBORHOOD...
DO YOU THINK KEITH COULD SPEND THE NIGHT TOO..? IT'S SO LATE AND ALL...
WELL... IT'LL BE A TIGHT FIT...
I SHOULD POINT OUT, THAT ALTHOUGH I WAS JEALOUS OF VICKY'S AFFECTION FOR KEITH, KEITH NEVER MADE ME FEEL JEALOUS. HE WAS A FRIENDLY GUY, AND THOUGH VICKY HAD THE HOTS FOR HIM, HE SEEMED TO ONLY REGARD HER AS A FRIEND...
...SO THERE WE WERE--THREE OF US IN ONE BED...
TO MY AMAZEMENT, I FELT A HAND REACH OVER AND RUB MY PENIS! THEN IT DAWNED UPON ME-- IT WASN'T VICKY'S HAND!

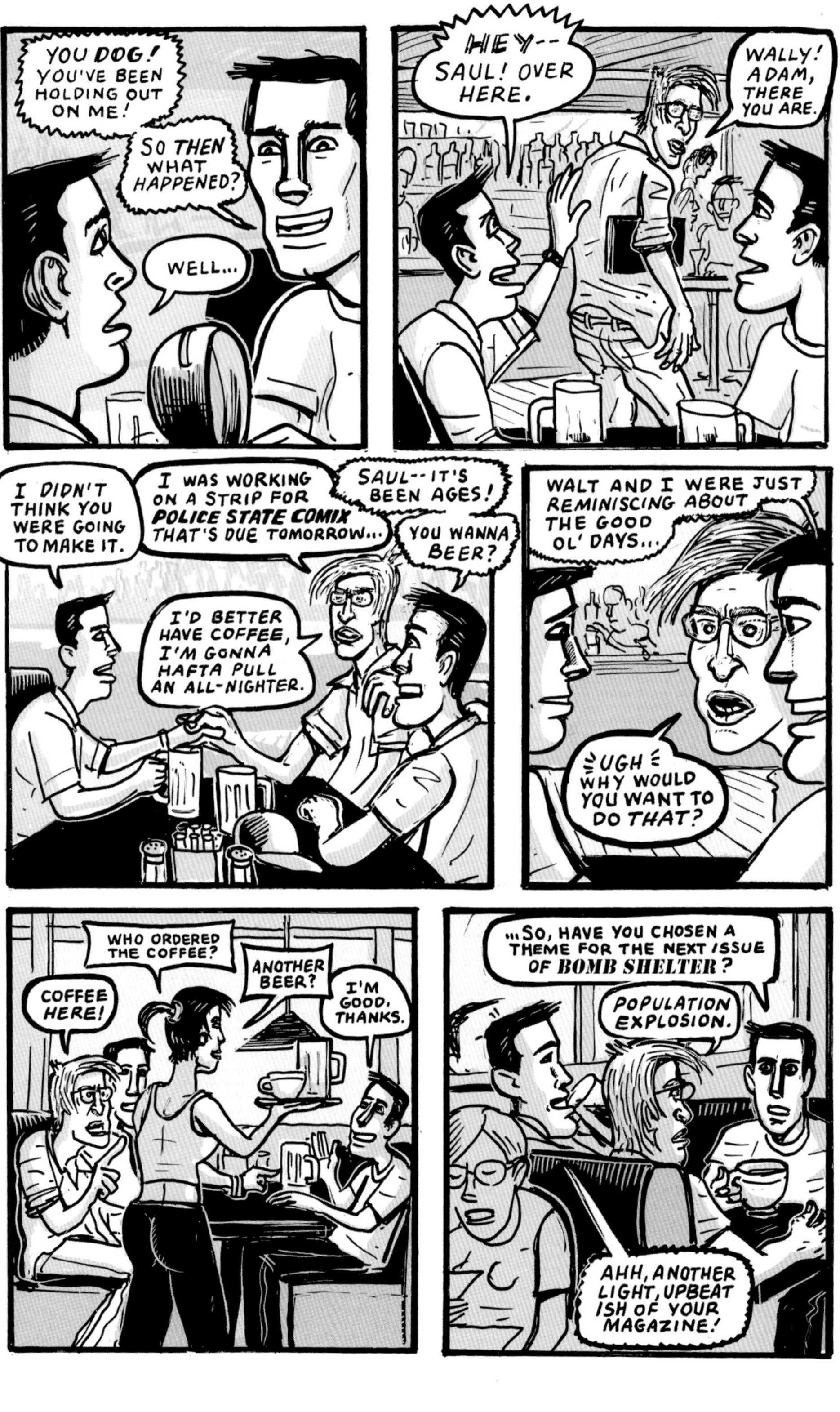
YOU DOG! YOU'VE BEEN HOLDING OUT ON ME!
SO THEN WHAT HAPPENED?
WELL...
HEY-- SAUL! OVER HERE.
WALLY! ADAM, THERE YOU ARE.
I DIDN'T THINK YOU WERE GOING TO MAKE IT.
I WAS WORKING ON A STRIP FOR POLICE STATE COMIX THAT'S DUE TOMORROW...
SAUL--IT'S BEEN AGES!
YOU WANNA BEER?
I'D BETTER HAVE COFFEE, I'M GONNA HAFTA PULL AN ALL-NIGHTER.
WALT AND I WERE JUST REMINISCING ABOUT THE GOOD OL' DAYS...
UGH WHY WOULD YOU WANT TO DO THAT?
WHO ORDERED THE COFFEE?
COFFEE HERE!
ANOTHER BEER?
I'M GOOD, THANKS.
...SO, HAVE YOU CHOSEN A THEME FOR THE NEXT ISSUE OF BOMB SHELTER?
POPULATION EXPLOSION.
AHH, ANOTHER LIGHT, UPBEAT ISH OF YOUR MAGAZINE!

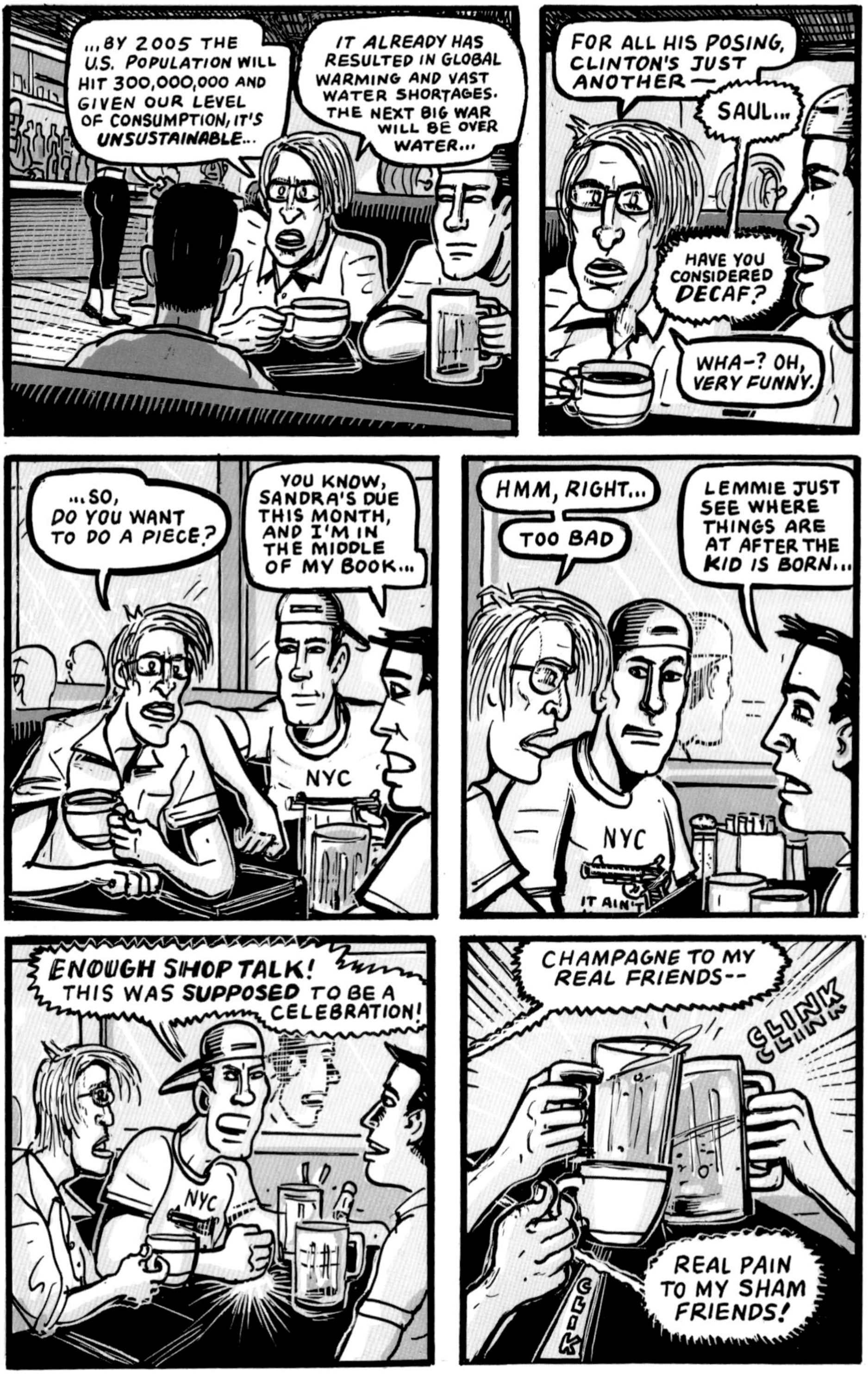
...BY 2005 THE U.S. POPULATION WILL HIT 300,000,000 AND GIVEN OUR LEVEL OF CONSUMPTION, IT'S UNSUSTAINABLE...
IT ALREADY HAS RESULTED IN GLOBAL WARMING AND VAST WATER SHORTAGES. THE NEXT BIG WAR WILL BE OVER WATER...
FOR ALL HIS POSING, CLINTON'S JUST ANOTHER—
SAUL...
HAVE YOU CONSIDERED DECAF?
WHA-? OH, VERY FUNNY.
...SO, DO YOU WANT TO DO A PIECE?
YOU KNOW, SANDRA'S DUE THIS MONTH, AND I'M IN THE MIDDLE OF MY BOOK...
NYC
HMM, RIGHT...
TOO BAD
LEMMIE JUST SEE WHERE THINGS ARE AT AFTER THE KID IS BORN...
NYC
IT AIN'T
ENOUGH SHOP TALK! THIS WAS SUPPOSED TO BE A CELEBRATION!
NYC
CHAMPAGNE TO MY REAL FRIENDS--
CLINK CLINK
REAL PAIN TO MY SHAM FRIENDS!
CLINK

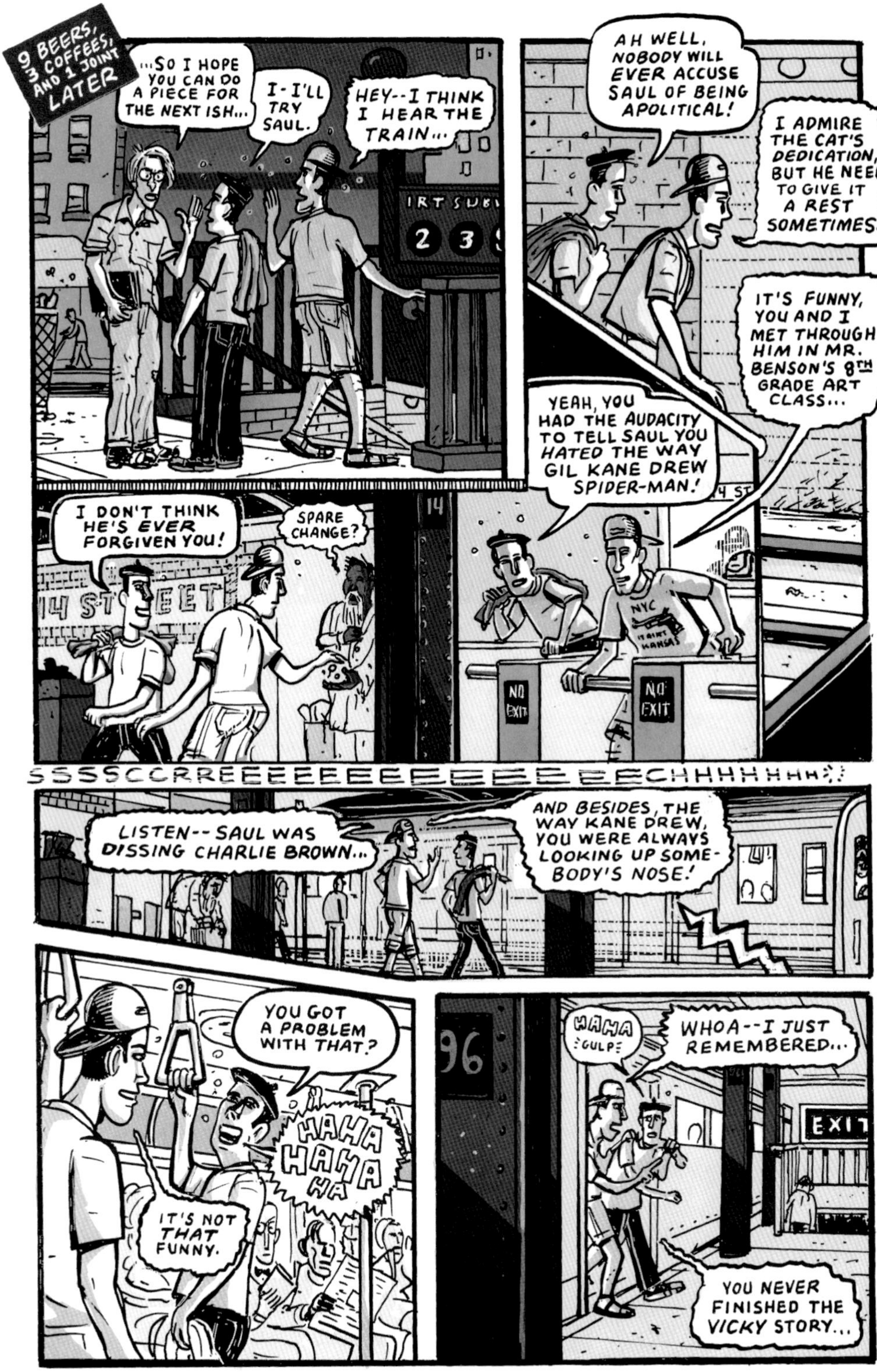

9 BEERS, 3 COFFEES, AND 1 JOINT LATER
...SO I HOPE YOU CAN DO A PIECE FOR THE NEXT ISH...
I-I'LL TRY SAUL.
HEY--I THINK I HEAR THE TRAIN...
IRT SUBW
2 3
AH WELL, NOBODY WILL EVER ACCUSE SAUL OF BEING APOLITICAL!
I ADMIRE THE CAT'S DEDICATION, BUT HE NEEDS TO GIVE IT A REST SOMETIMES...
IT'S FUNNY, YOU AND I MET THROUGH HIM IN MR. BENSON'S 8TH GRADE ART CLASS...
YEAH, YOU HAD THE AUDACITY TO TELL SAUL YOU HATED THE WAY GIL KANE DREW SPIDER-MAN!
I DON'T THINK HE'S EVER FORGIVEN YOU!
SPARE CHANGE?
14 STREET
14
NYC
NO EXIT
NO EXIT
SSSSCCRREEEEEEEEEEEEEEEEECHHHHHHHH
LISTEN--SAUL WAS DISSING CHARLIE BROWN...
AND BESIDES, THE WAY KANE DREW, YOU WERE ALWAYS LOOKING UP SOMEBODY'S NOSE!
YOU GOT A PROBLEM WITH THAT?
HAHA HAHA HA
IT'S NOT THAT FUNNY.
96
HAHA GULP
WHOA--I JUST REMEMBERED...
EXIT
YOU NEVER FINISHED THE VICKY STORY...

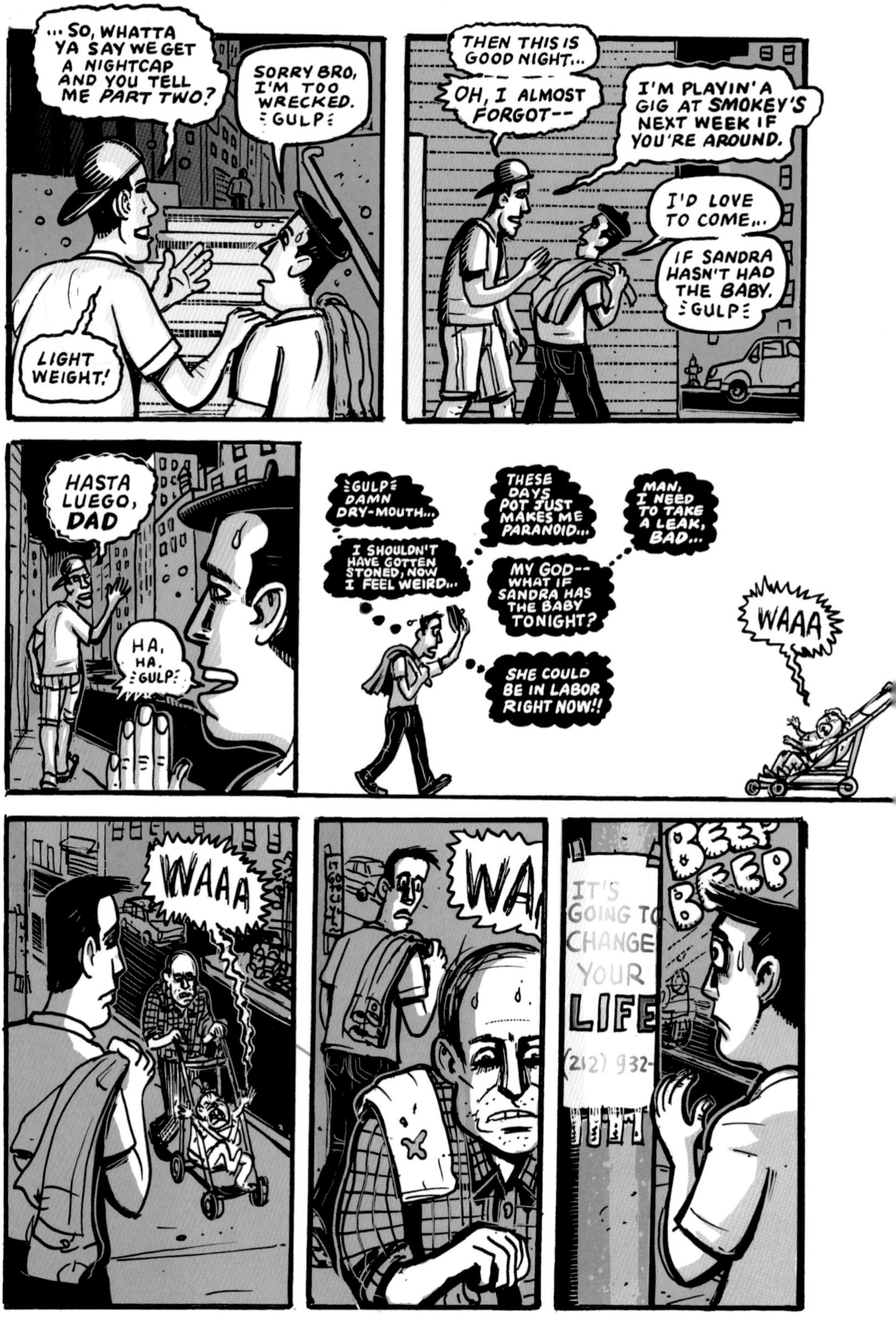
... SO, WHATTA YA SAY WE GET A NIGHTCAP AND YOU TELL ME PART TWO?
SORRY BRO, I'M TOO WRECKED. GULP
LIGHT WEIGHT!
THEN THIS IS GOOD NIGHT...
OH, I ALMOST FORGOT--
I'M PLAYIN' A GIG AT SMOKEY'S NEXT WEEK IF YOU'RE AROUND.
I'D LOVE TO COME...
IF SANDRA HASN'T HAD THE BABY. GULP
HASTA LUEGO, DAD
HA, HA. GULP
GULP DAMN DRY-MOUTH...
I SHOULDN'T HAVE GOTTEN STONED, NOW I FEEL WEIRD...
THESE DAYS POT JUST MAKES ME PARANOID...
MY GOD-- WHAT IF SANDRA HAS THE BABY TONIGHT?
MAN, I NEED TO TAKE A LEAK, BAD...
SHE COULD BE IN LABOR RIGHT NOW!!
WAAA
WAAA
WA
IT'S GOING TO CHANGE YOUR LIFE
(212) 932-
BEEP BEEP

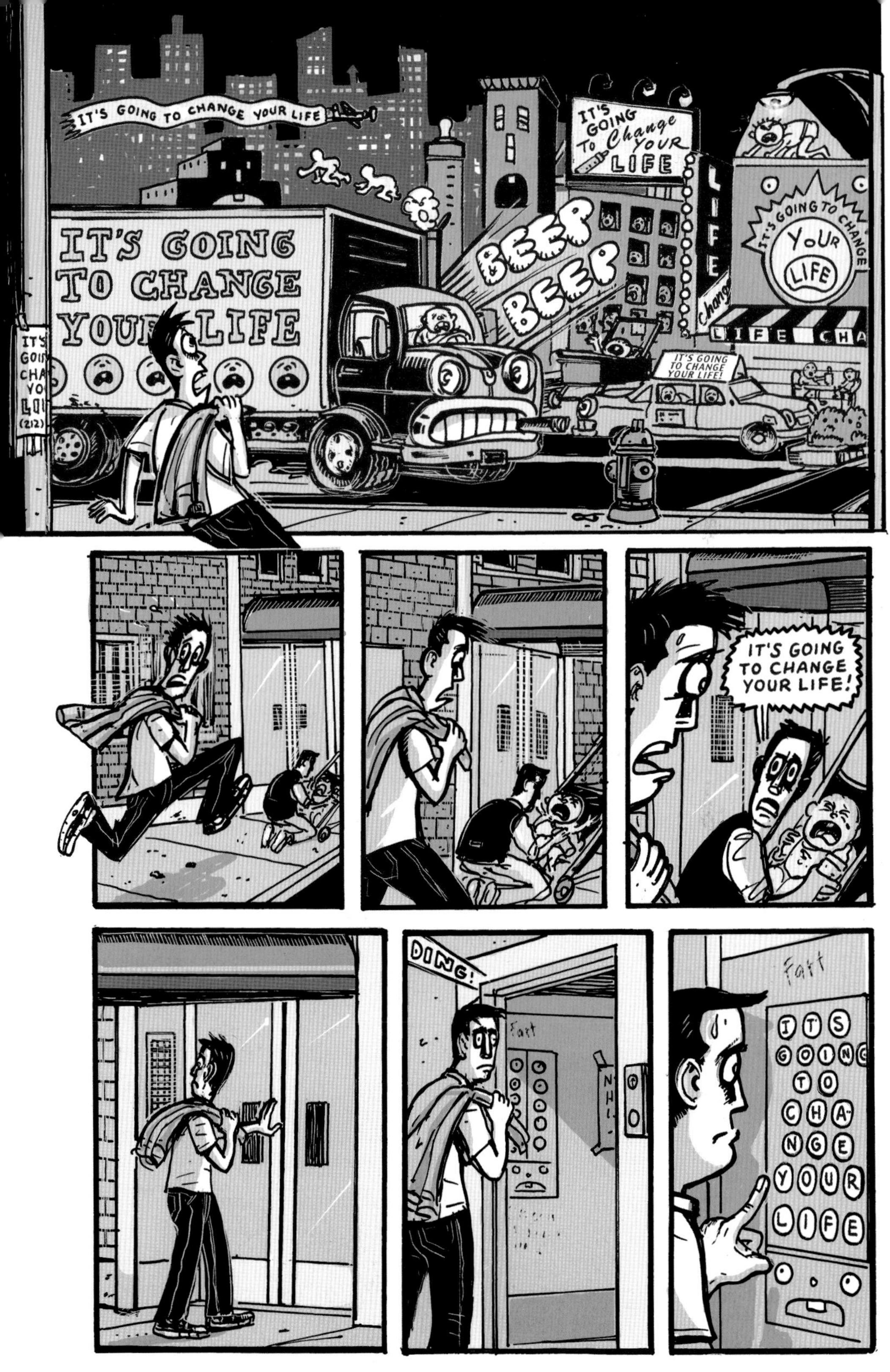
IT'S GOING TO CHANGE YOUR LIFE
IT'S GOING To Change YOUR LIFE
LIFE
IT'S GOING TO CHANGE YOUR LIFE
IT'S GOING TO CHANGE YOUR LIFE
BEEP BEEP
Change
LIFE CHA
IT'S GOING TO CHANGE YOUR LIFE!
(212)
IT'S GOING TO CHANGE YOUR LIFE!
DING!
Fart
Fart
IT'S GOING TO CHANGE YOUR LIFE

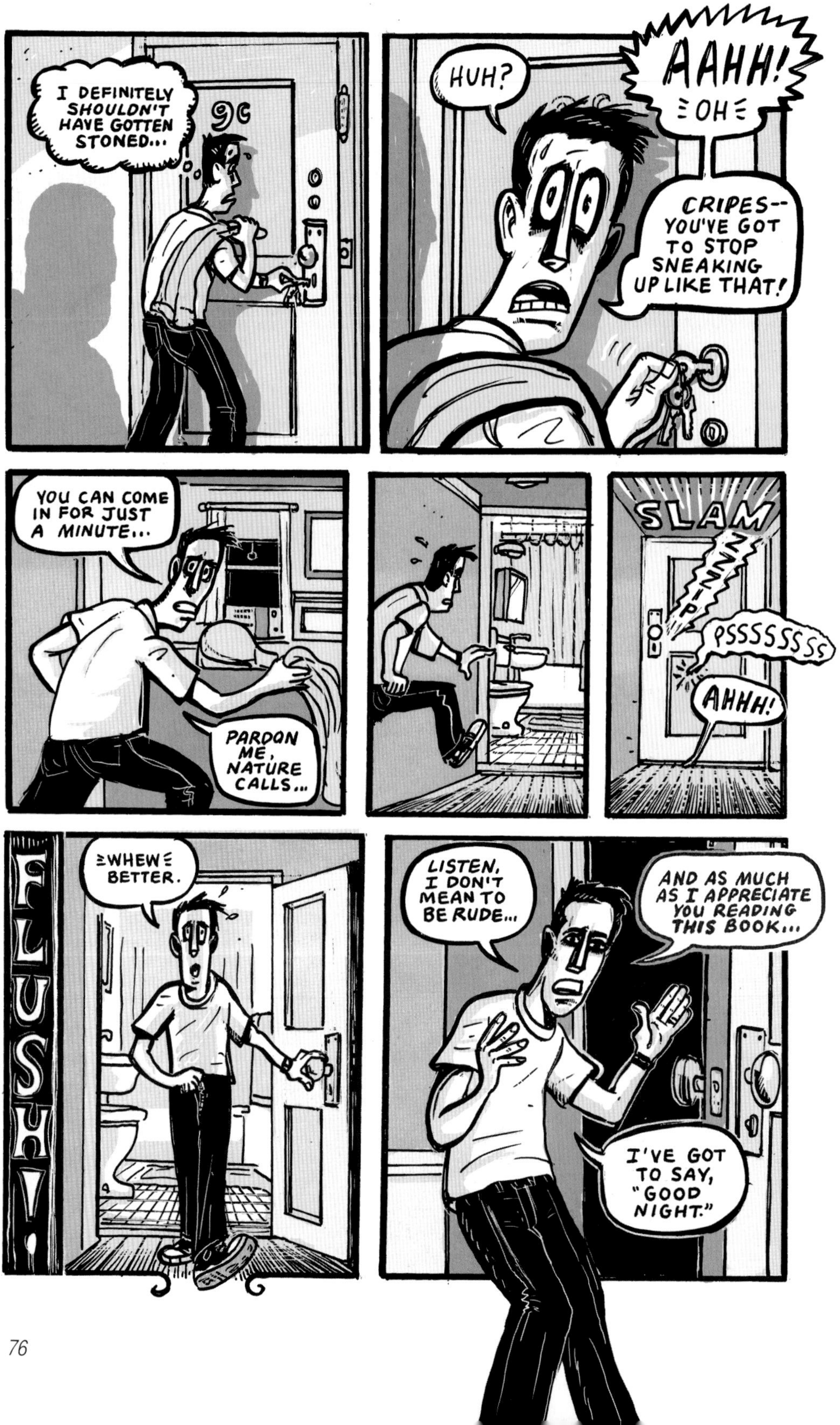

I DEFINITELY SHOULDN'T HAVE GOTTEN STONED...
9C
HUH?
AAHH! OH
CRIPES-- YOU'VE GOT TO STOP SNEAKING UP LIKE THAT!
YOU CAN COME IN FOR JUST A MINUTE...
PARDON ME, NATURE CALLS...
SLAM
ZZZIP
PSSSSSSSS
AHHH!
FLUSH!
WHEW BETTER.
LISTEN, I DON'T MEAN TO BE RUDE...
AND AS MUCH AS I APPRECIATE YOU READING THIS BOOK...
I'VE GOT TO SAY, "GOOD NIGHT."

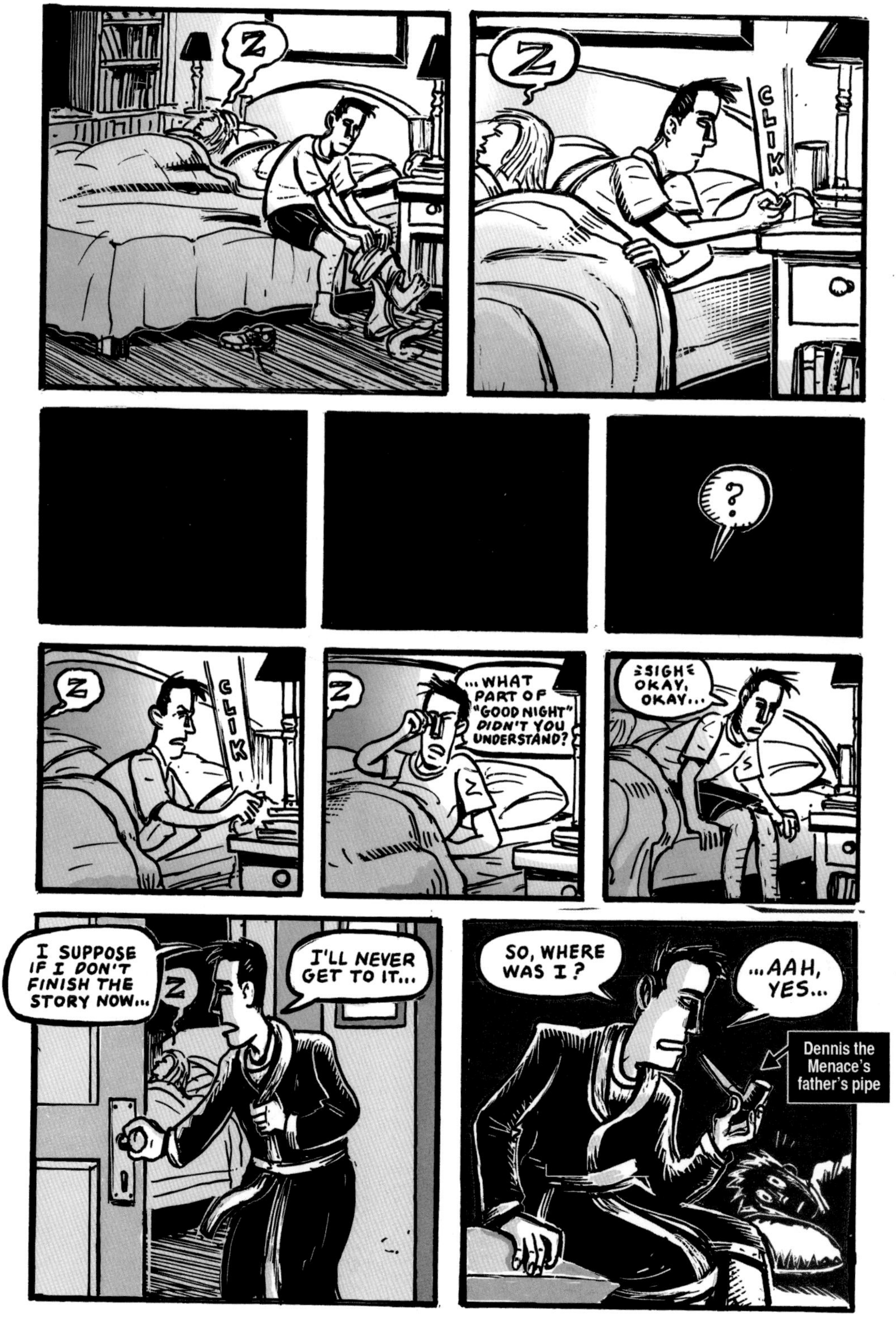
Z
Z
CLIK
?
Z
CLIK
Z
...WHAT PART OF "GOOD NIGHT" DIDN'T YOU UNDERSTAND?
≶SIGH≷ OKAY, OKAY...
I SUPPOSE IF I DON'T FINISH THE STORY NOW...
Z
I'LL NEVER GET TO IT...
SO, WHERE WAS I?
...AAH, YES...
Dennis the Menace's father's pipe

LOVEHATE

love (luv) *n.* [ME. < OE. *lufu*, akin to OHG. *luba*, Goth. *lubo* < IE. base **leubh-*, to be fond of, desire, whence LIBIDO, LIEF, LUST] **1.** a deep and tender feeling of affection for or attachment or devotion to a person or persons

SYN.—**hate** implies a feeling of great dislike or aversion, and, with persons as the object, connotes the bearing of malice; **detest** implies vehement dislike or antipathy; **despise** suggests a looking down with great contempt upon the person or thing one hates; **abhor** implies a feeling of great repugnance or disgust; **loathe** implies utter abhorrence —*ANT.* **love, like**

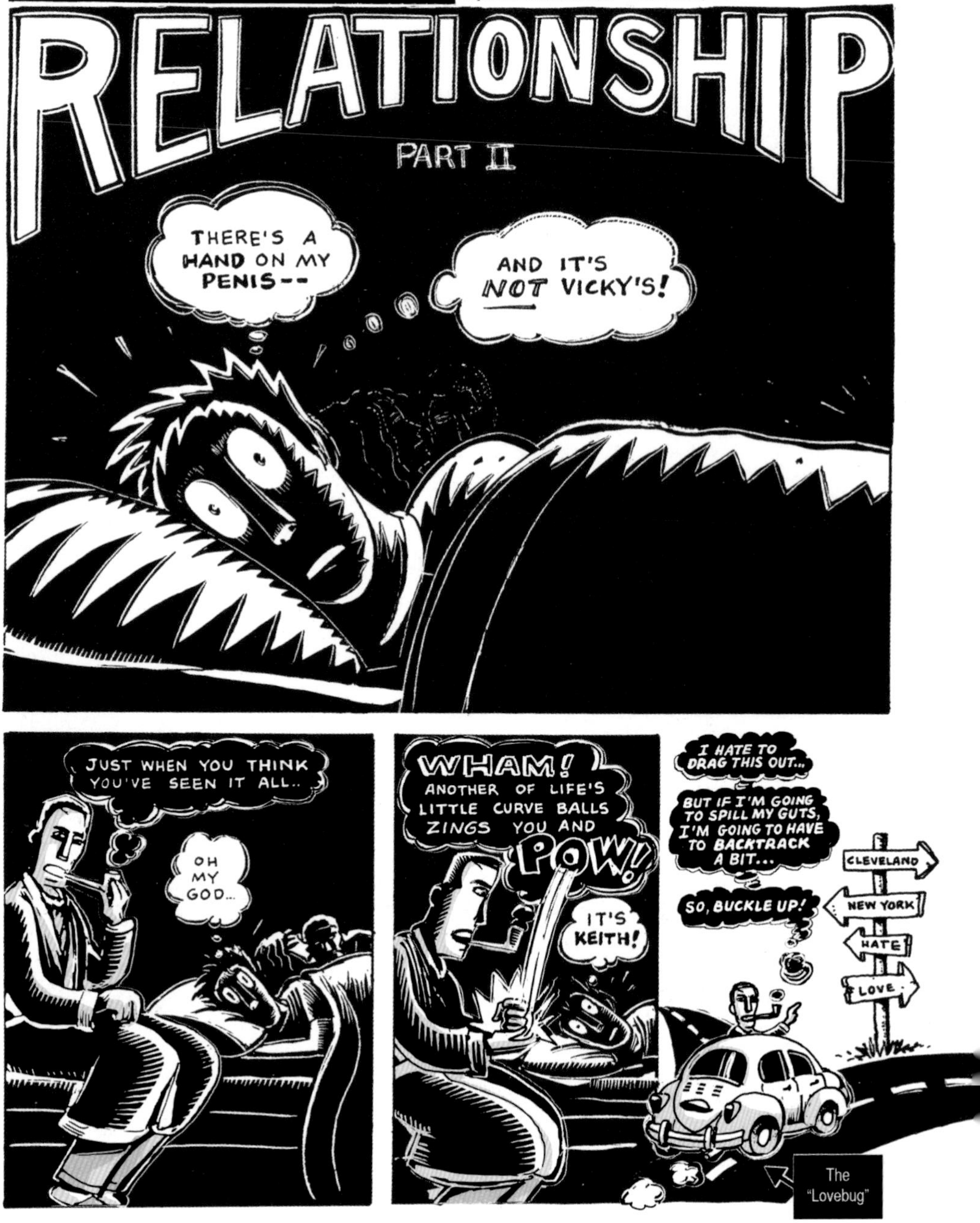

RELATIONSHIP
PART II
THERE'S A HAND ON MY PENIS--
AND IT'S NOT VICKY'S!
JUST WHEN YOU THINK YOU'VE SEEN IT ALL..
OH MY GOD...
WHAM! ANOTHER OF LIFE'S LITTLE CURVE BALLS ZINGS YOU AND
POW!
IT'S KEITH!
I HATE TO DRAG THIS OUT...
BUT IF I'M GOING TO SPILL MY GUTS, I'M GOING TO HAVE TO BACKTRACK A BIT...
SO, BUCKLE UP!
CLEVELAND
NEW YORK
HATE
LOVE

The "Lovebug"

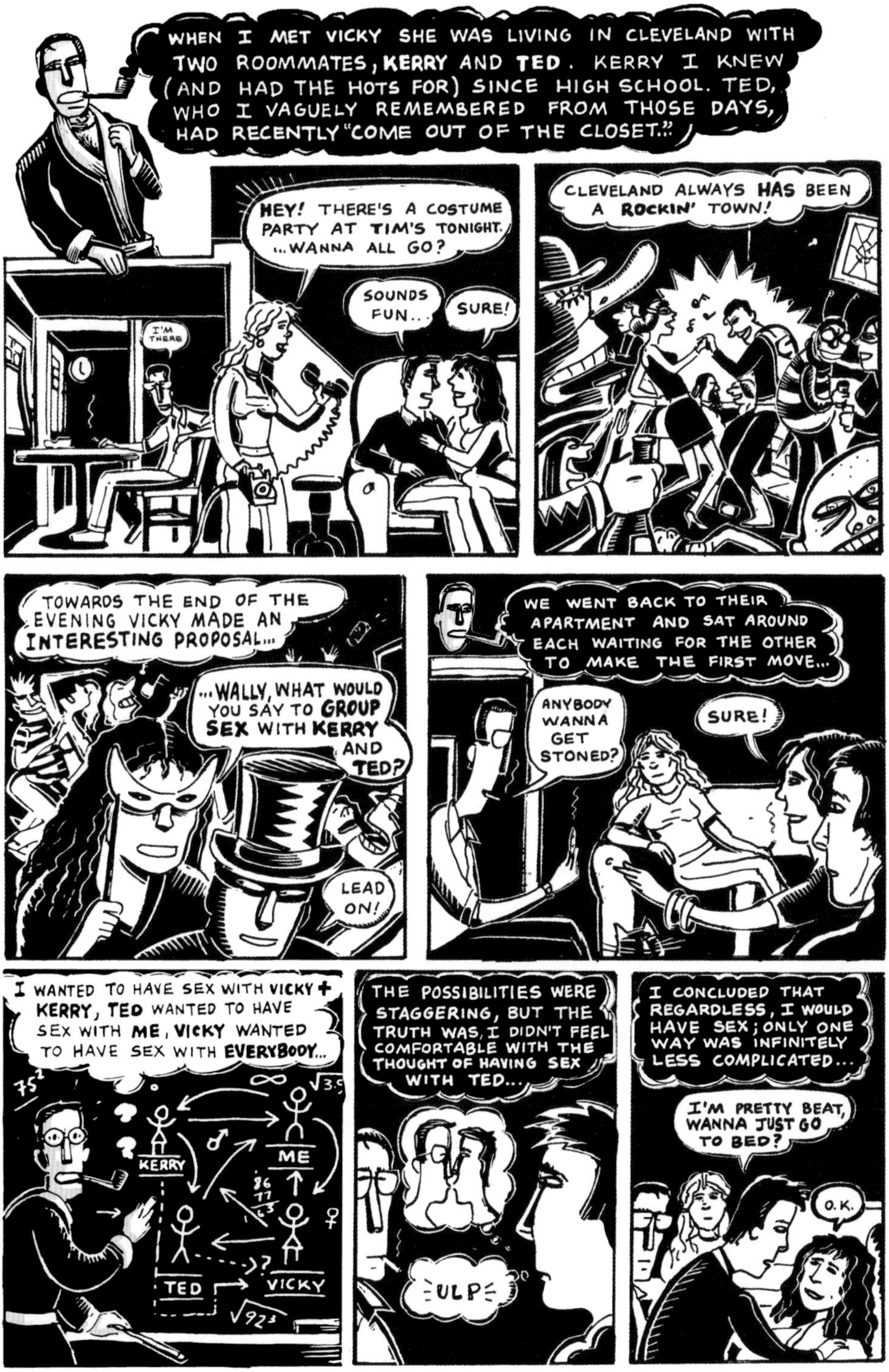
WHEN I MET VICKY SHE WAS LIVING IN CLEVELAND WITH TWO ROOMMATES, KERRY AND TED. KERRY I KNEW (AND HAD THE HOTS FOR) SINCE HIGH SCHOOL. TED, WHO I VAGUELY REMEMBERED FROM THOSE DAYS, HAD RECENTLY "COME OUT OF THE CLOSET."
I'M THERE
HEY! THERE'S A COSTUME PARTY AT TIM'S TONIGHT. ...WANNA ALL GO?
SOUNDS FUN...
SURE!
CLEVELAND ALWAYS HAS BEEN A ROCKIN' TOWN!
TOWARDS THE END OF THE EVENING VICKY MADE AN INTERESTING PROPOSAL...
...WALLY, WHAT WOULD YOU SAY TO GROUP SEX WITH KERRY AND TED?
LEAD ON!
WE WENT BACK TO THEIR APARTMENT AND SAT AROUND EACH WAITING FOR THE OTHER TO MAKE THE FIRST MOVE...
ANYBODY WANNA GET STONED?
SURE!
I WANTED TO HAVE SEX WITH VICKY + KERRY, TED WANTED TO HAVE SEX WITH ME, VICKY WANTED TO HAVE SEX WITH EVERYBODY...
KERRY
ME
TED
VICKY
THE POSSIBILITIES WERE STAGGERING, BUT THE TRUTH WAS, I DIDN'T FEEL COMFORTABLE WITH THE THOUGHT OF HAVING SEX WITH TED...
ULP
I CONCLUDED THAT REGARDLESS, I WOULD HAVE SEX; ONLY ONE WAY WAS INFINITELY LESS COMPLICATED...
I'M PRETTY BEAT, WANNA JUST GO TO BED?
O.K.

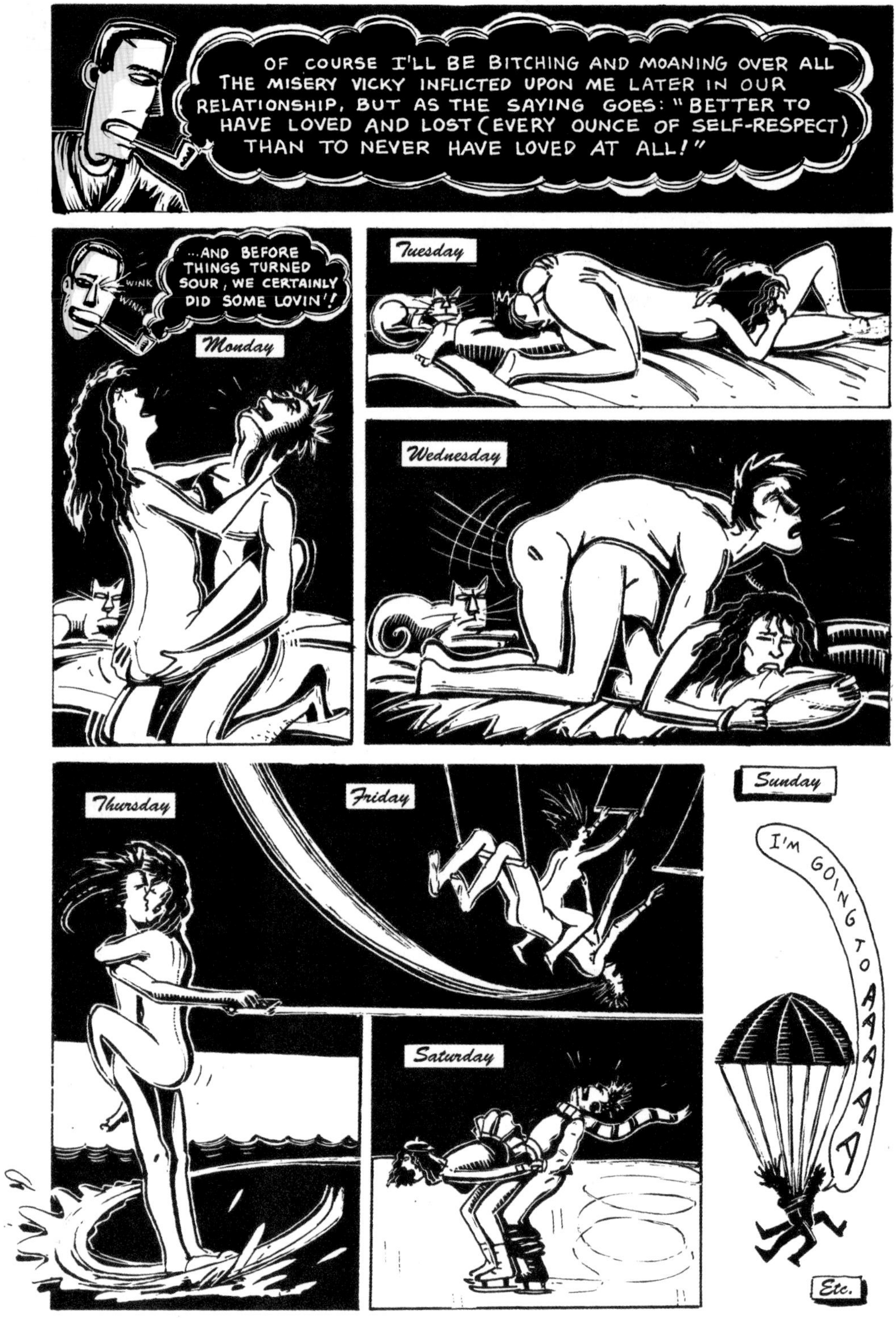
OF COURSE I'LL BE BITCHING AND MOANING OVER ALL THE MISERY VICKY INFLICTED UPON ME LATER IN OUR RELATIONSHIP, BUT AS THE SAYING GOES: "BETTER TO HAVE LOVED AND LOST (EVERY OUNCE OF SELF-RESPECT) THAN TO NEVER HAVE LOVED AT ALL!"
WINK
WINK
...AND BEFORE THINGS TURNED SOUR, WE CERTAINLY DID SOME LOVIN'!
Monday
Tuesday
Wednesday
Thursday
Friday
Saturday
Sunday
I'M GOING TO AAAAAA
Etc.

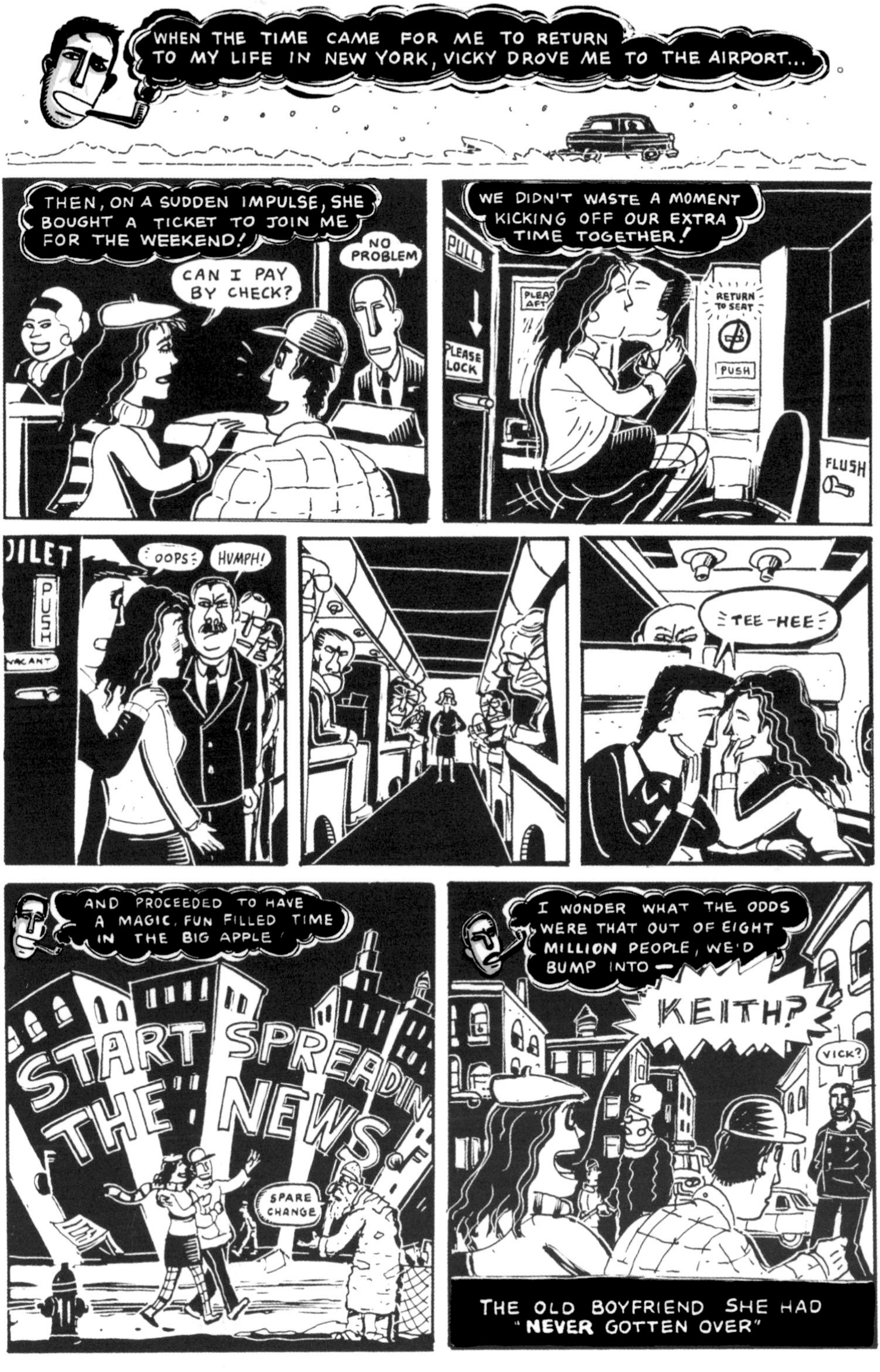

WHEN THE TIME CAME FOR ME TO RETURN TO MY LIFE IN NEW YORK, VICKY DROVE ME TO THE AIRPORT...
THEN, ON A SUDDEN IMPULSE, SHE BOUGHT A TICKET TO JOIN ME FOR THE WEEKEND!
CAN I PAY BY CHECK?
NO PROBLEM
WE DIDN'T WASTE A MOMENT KICKING OFF OUR EXTRA TIME TOGETHER!
PULL
PLEASE LOCK
RETURN TO SEAT
PUSH
FLUSH
OILET
PUSH
VACANT
OOPS
HUMPH!
TEE-HEE
AND PROCEEDED TO HAVE A MAGIC, FUN FILLED TIME IN THE BIG APPLE
START SPREADIN' THE NEWS
SPARE CHANGE
I WONDER WHAT THE ODDS WERE THAT OUT OF EIGHT MILLION PEOPLE, WE'D BUMP INTO—
KEITH?
VICK?
THE OLD BOYFRIEND SHE HAD "NEVER GOTTEN OVER"

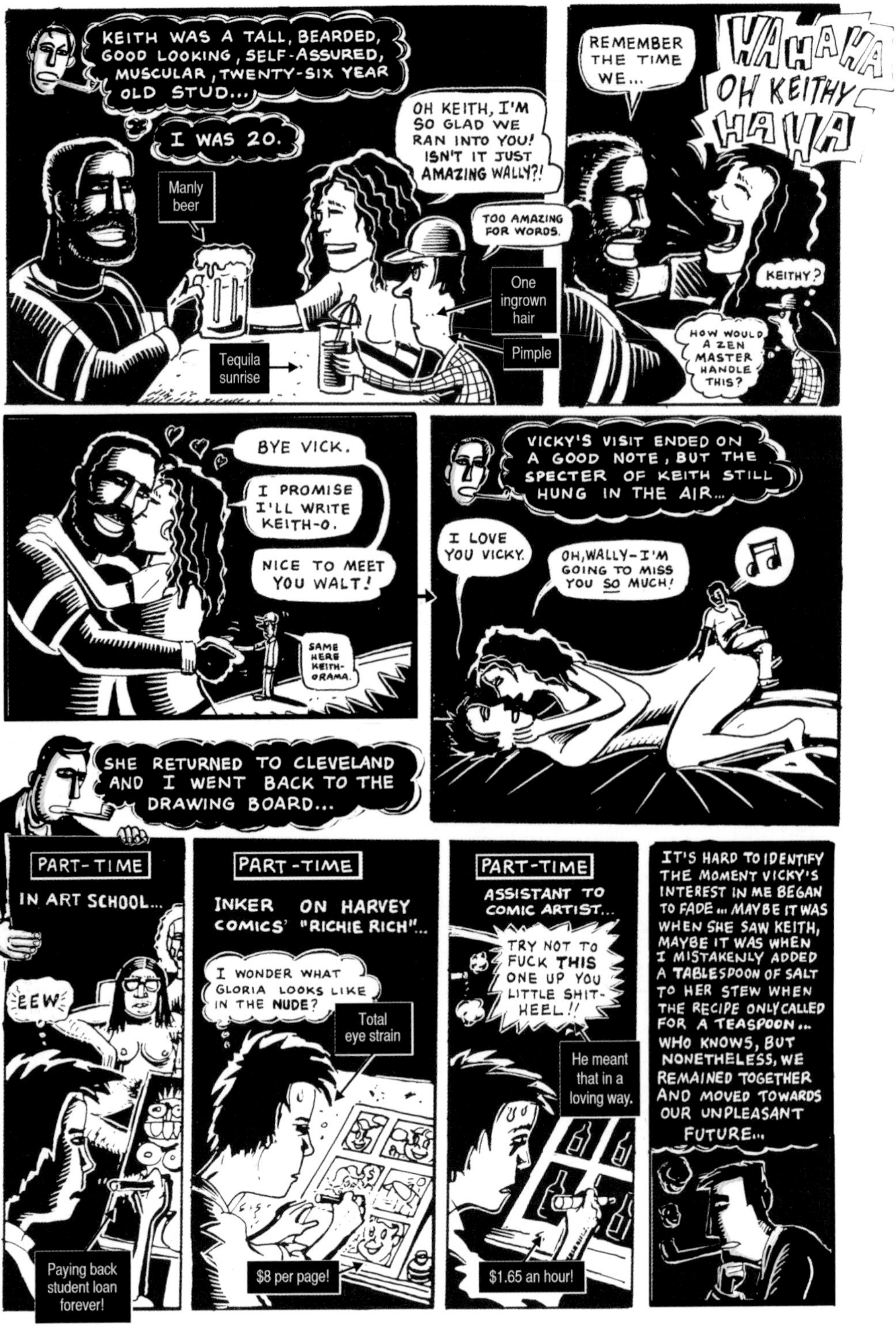

KEITH WAS A TALL, BEARDED, GOOD LOOKING, SELF-ASSURED, MUSCULAR, TWENTY-SIX YEAR OLD STUD...
I WAS 20.
Manly beer
OH KEITH, I'M SO GLAD WE RAN INTO YOU! ISN'T IT JUST AMAZING WALLY?!
TOO AMAZING FOR WORDS.
One ingrown hair
Pimple
Tequila sunrise
REMEMBER THE TIME WE...
HAHAHA OH KEITHY HAHA
KEITHY?
HOW WOULD A ZEN MASTER HANDLE THIS?
BYE VICK.
I PROMISE I'LL WRITE KEITH-O.
NICE TO MEET YOU WALT!
SAME HERE KEITH-ORAMA.
VICKY'S VISIT ENDED ON A GOOD NOTE, BUT THE SPECTER OF KEITH STILL HUNG IN THE AIR...
I LOVE YOU VICKY.
OH, WALLY-I'M GOING TO MISS YOU SO MUCH!
SHE RETURNED TO CLEVELAND AND I WENT BACK TO THE DRAWING BOARD...
PART-TIME
IN ART SCHOOL...
EEW
Paying back student loan forever!
PART-TIME
INKER ON HARVEY COMICS' "RICHIE RICH"...
I WONDER WHAT GLORIA LOOKS LIKE IN THE NUDE?
Total eye strain
$8 per page!
PART-TIME
ASSISTANT TO COMIC ARTIST...
TRY NOT TO FUCK THIS ONE UP YOU LITTLE SHIT-HEEL!!
He meant that in a loving way.
$1.65 an hour!
IT'S HARD TO IDENTIFY THE MOMENT VICKY'S INTEREST IN ME BEGAN TO FADE... MAYBE IT WAS WHEN SHE SAW KEITH, MAYBE IT WAS WHEN I MISTAKENLY ADDED A TABLESPOON OF SALT TO HER STEW WHEN THE RECIPE ONLY CALLED FOR A TEASPOON... WHO KNOWS, BUT NONETHELESS, WE REMAINED TOGETHER AND MOVED TOWARDS OUR UNPLEASANT FUTURE...

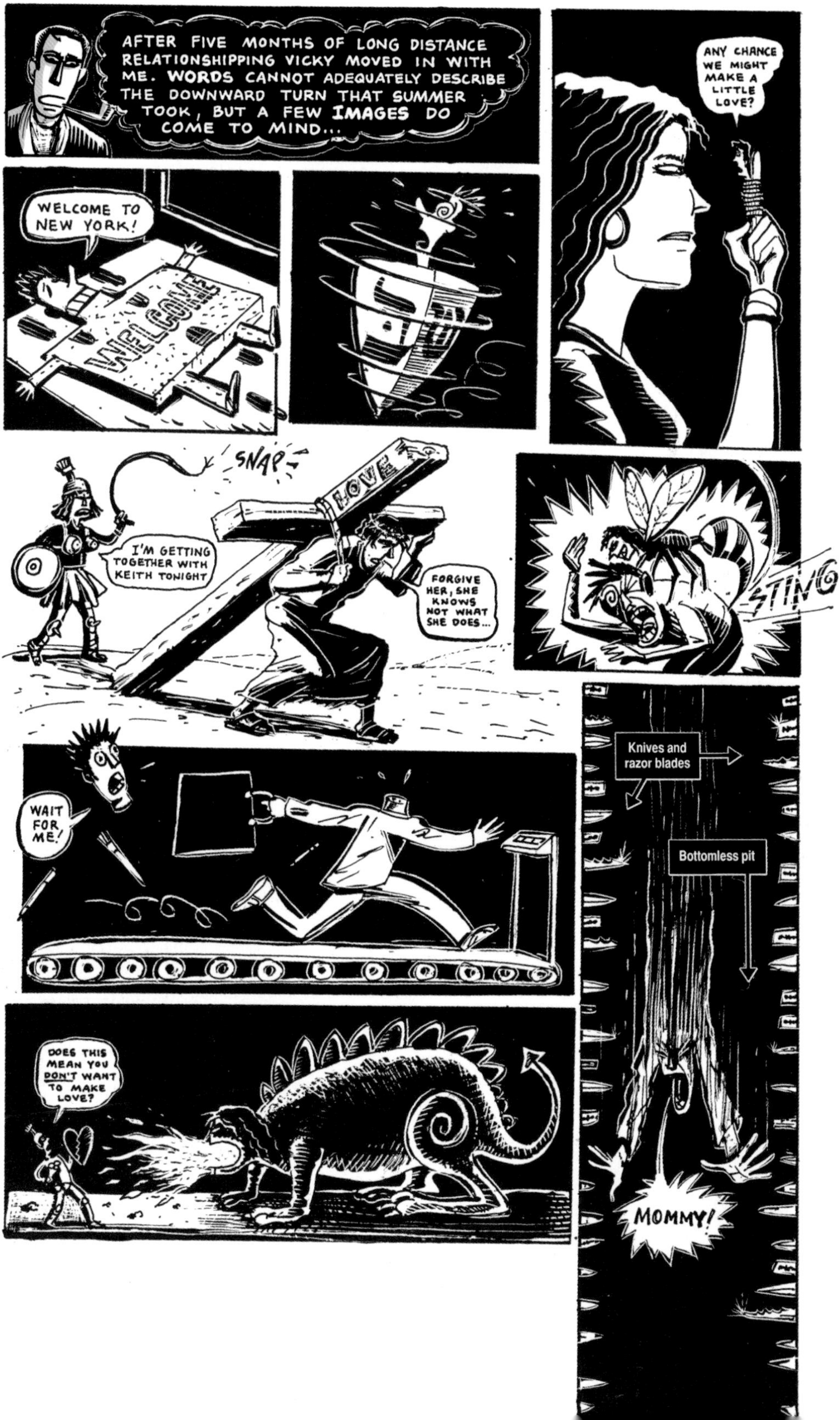

AFTER FIVE MONTHS OF LONG DISTANCE RELATIONSHIPPING VICKY MOVED IN WITH ME. WORDS CANNOT ADEQUATELY DESCRIBE THE DOWNWARD TURN THAT SUMMER TOOK, BUT A FEW IMAGES DO COME TO MIND...
ANY CHANCE WE MIGHT MAKE A LITTLE LOVE?
WELCOME TO NEW YORK!
WELCOME
SNAP!
LOVE
I'M GETTING TOGETHER WITH KEITH TONIGHT
FORGIVE HER, SHE KNOWS NOT WHAT SHE DOES...
STING
Knives and razor blades
Bottomless pit
WAIT FOR ME!
MOMMY!
DOES THIS MEAN YOU DON'T WANT TO MAKE LOVE?

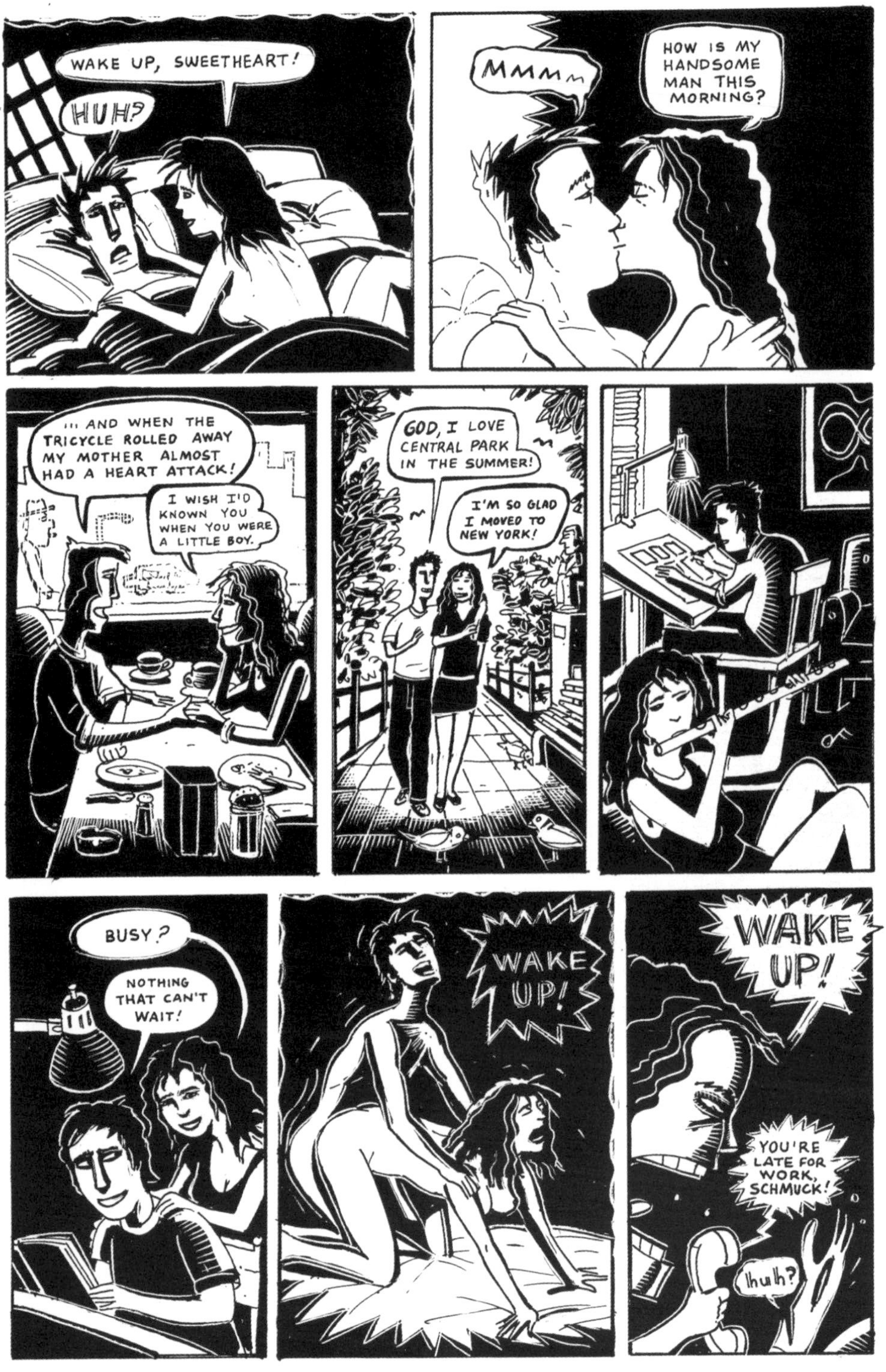
WAKE UP, SWEETHEART!
HUH?
MMMm
HOW IS MY HANDSOME MAN THIS MORNING?
... AND WHEN THE TRICYCLE ROLLED AWAY MY MOTHER ALMOST HAD A HEART ATTACK!
I WISH I'D KNOWN YOU WHEN YOU WERE A LITTLE BOY.
GOD, I LOVE CENTRAL PARK IN THE SUMMER!
I'M SO GLAD I MOVED TO NEW YORK!
BUSY?
NOTHING THAT CAN'T WAIT!
WAKE UP!
WAKE UP!
YOU'RE LATE FOR WORK, SCHMUCK!
huh?

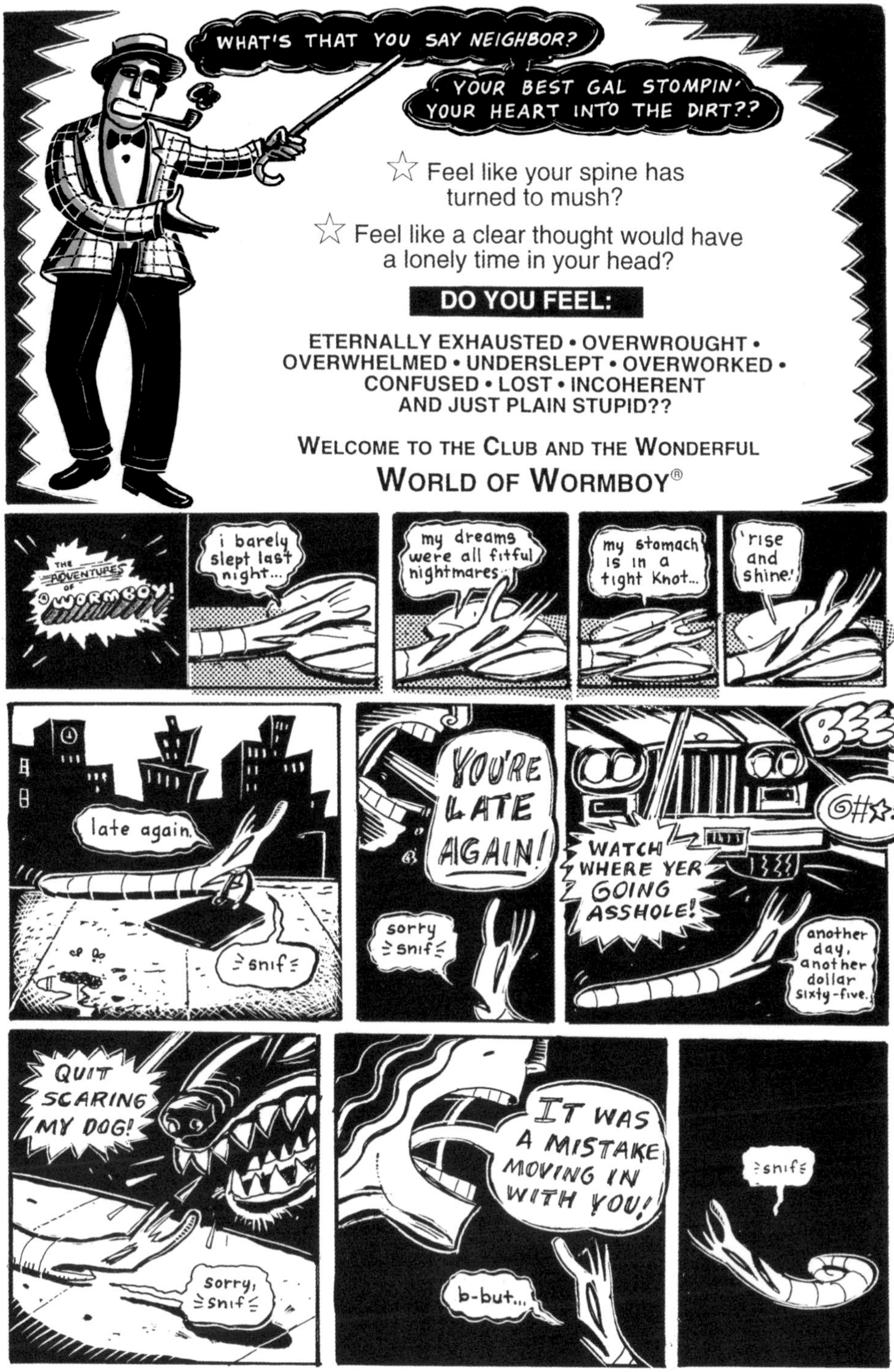
WHAT'S THAT YOU SAY NEIGHBOR?
YOUR BEST GAL STOMPIN' YOUR HEART INTO THE DIRT??
☆ Feel like your spine has turned to mush?
☆ Feel like a clear thought would have a lonely time in your head?
DO YOU FEEL:
ETERNALLY EXHAUSTED • OVERWROUGHT • OVERWHELMED • UNDERSLEPT • OVERWORKED • CONFUSED • LOST • INCOHERENT AND JUST PLAIN STUPID??
WELCOME TO THE CLUB AND THE WONDERFUL
WORLD OF WORMBOY®
THE ADVENTURES OF WORMBOY!
i barely slept last night...
my dreams were all fitful nightmares...
my stomach is in a tight knot...
'rise and shine!
late again.
snif
YOU'RE LATE AGAIN!
sorry snif
BEEP!
@#☆!!
WATCH WHERE YER GOING ASSHOLE!
another day, another dollar sixty-five.
QUIT SCARING MY DOG!
sorry, snif
IT WAS A MISTAKE MOVING IN WITH YOU!
b-but...
snif

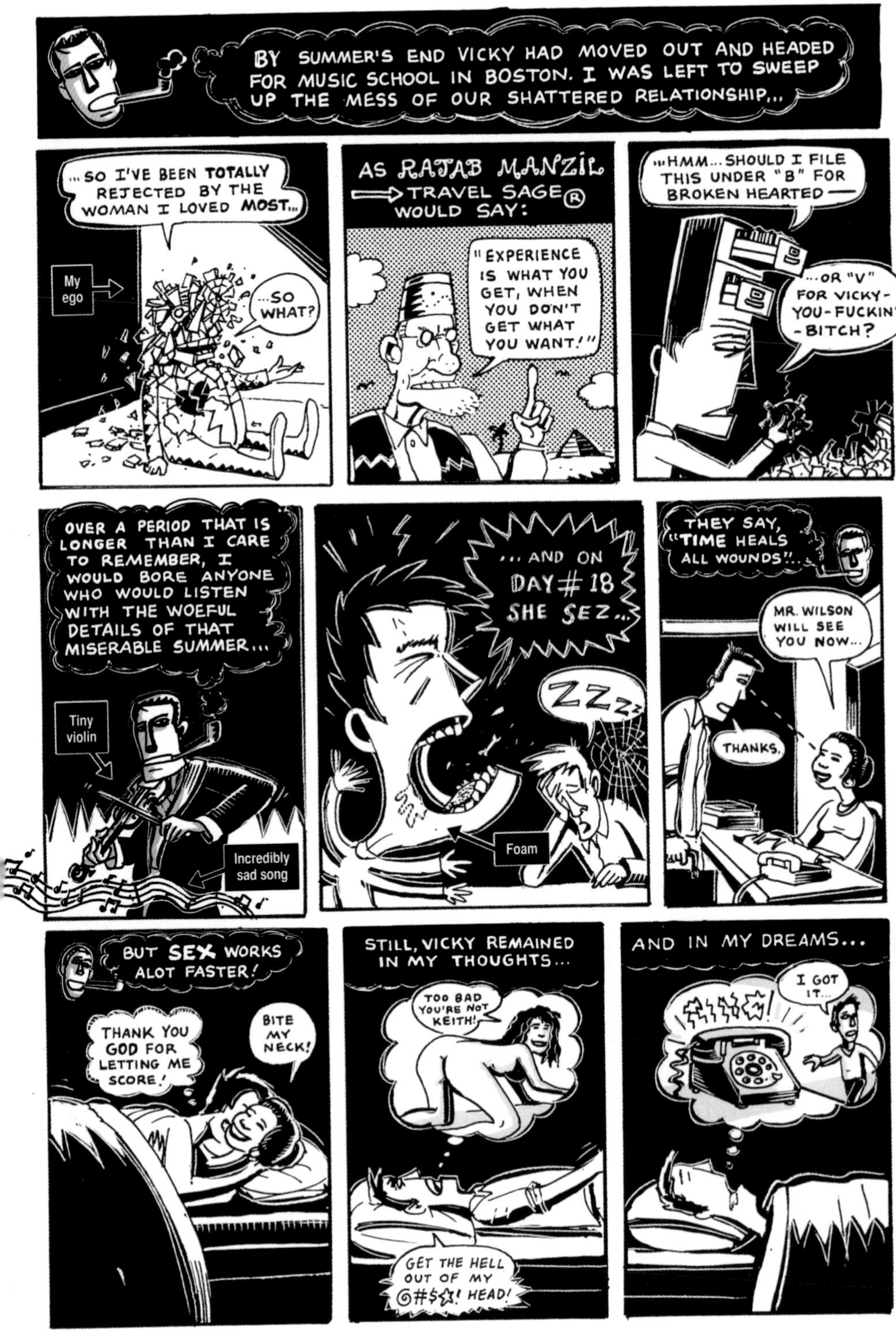

BY SUMMER'S END VICKY HAD MOVED OUT AND HEADED FOR MUSIC SCHOOL IN BOSTON. I WAS LEFT TO SWEEP UP THE MESS OF OUR SHATTERED RELATIONSHIP...
...SO I'VE BEEN TOTALLY REJECTED BY THE WOMAN I LOVED MOST...
My ego
...SO WHAT?
AS RAJAB MANZIL TRAVEL SAGE® WOULD SAY:
"EXPERIENCE IS WHAT YOU GET, WHEN YOU DON'T GET WHAT YOU WANT!"
...HMM... SHOULD I FILE THIS UNDER "B" FOR BROKEN HEARTED —
...OR "V" FOR VICKY-YOU-FUCKIN'-BITCH?
OVER A PERIOD THAT IS LONGER THAN I CARE TO REMEMBER, I WOULD BORE ANYONE WHO WOULD LISTEN WITH THE WOEFUL DETAILS OF THAT MISERABLE SUMMER...
Tiny violin
Incredibly sad song
...AND ON DAY #18 SHE SEZ...
ZZZzz
Foam
THEY SAY, "TIME HEALS ALL WOUNDS"...
MR. WILSON WILL SEE YOU NOW...
THANKS.
BUT SEX WORKS ALOT FASTER!
THANK YOU GOD FOR LETTING ME SCORE!
BITE MY NECK!
STILL, VICKY REMAINED IN MY THOUGHTS...
TOO BAD YOU'RE NOT KEITH!
GET THE HELL OUT OF MY @#$☆! HEAD!
AND IN MY DREAMS...
I GOT IT...

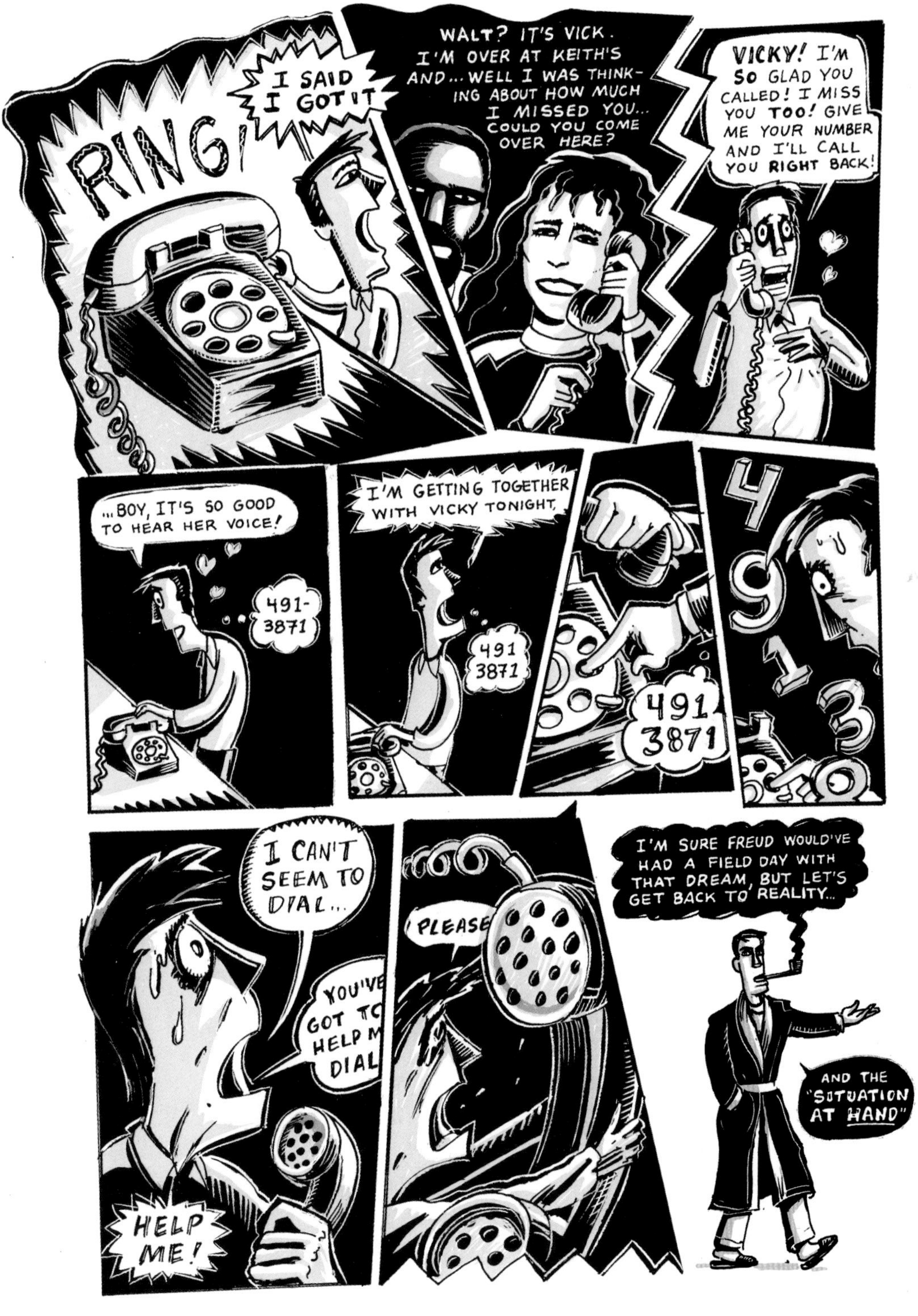
RING!
I SAID I GOT IT
WALT? IT'S VICK. I'M OVER AT KEITH'S AND... WELL I WAS THINKING ABOUT HOW MUCH I MISSED YOU... COULD YOU COME OVER HERE?
VICKY! I'M SO GLAD YOU CALLED! I MISS YOU TOO! GIVE ME YOUR NUMBER AND I'LL CALL YOU RIGHT BACK!
...BOY, IT'S SO GOOD TO HEAR HER VOICE!
491-3871
I'M GETTING TOGETHER WITH VICKY TONIGHT
491 3871
491 3871
4 9 1 3 0
I CAN'T SEEM TO DIAL...
YOU'VE GOT TO HELP ME DIAL
HELP ME!
PLEASE
I'M SURE FREUD WOULD'VE HAD A FIELD DAY WITH THAT DREAM, BUT LET'S GET BACK TO REALITY...
AND THE "SITUATION AT HAND"

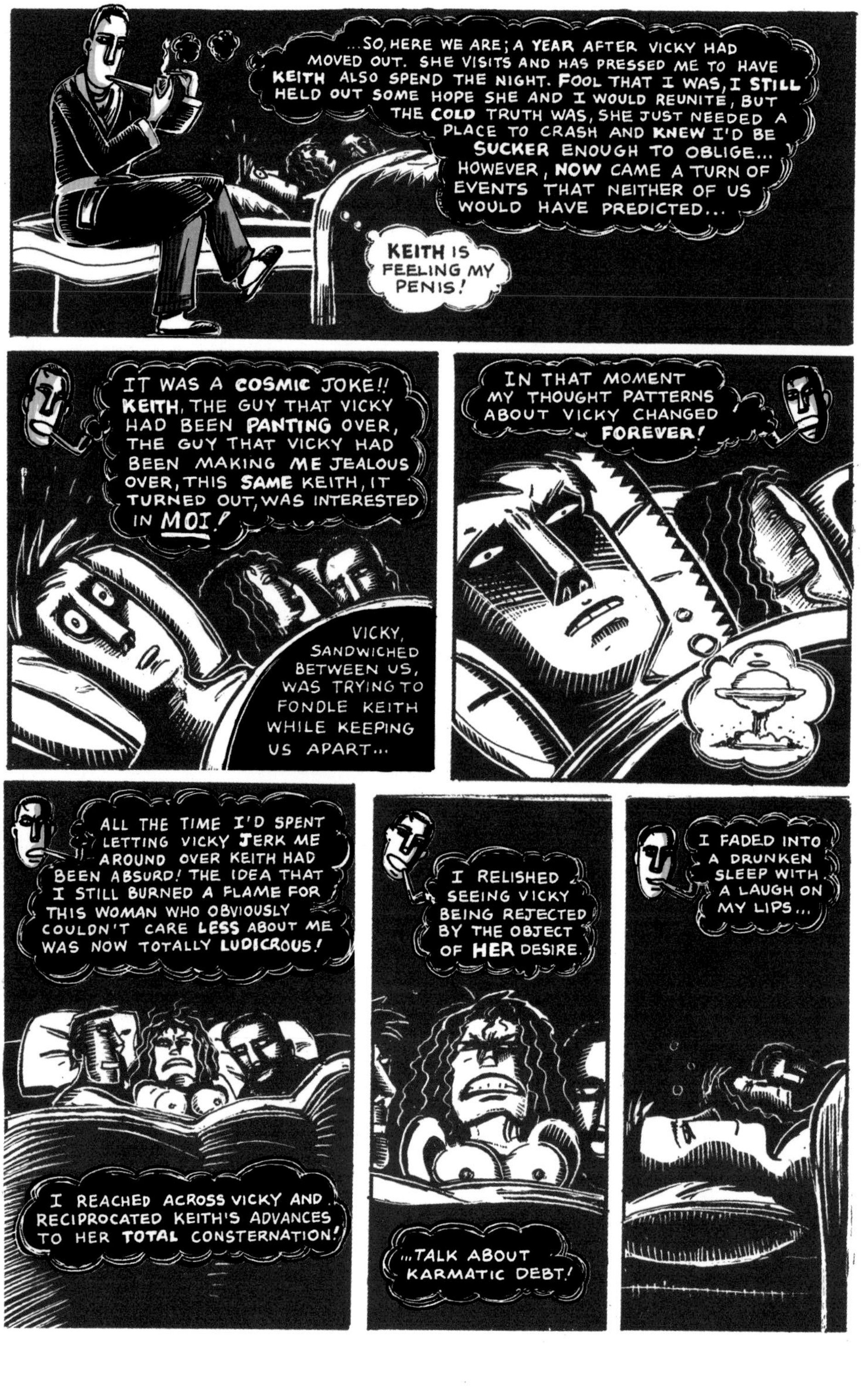
...SO, HERE WE ARE; A YEAR AFTER VICKY HAD MOVED OUT. SHE VISITS AND HAS PRESSED ME TO HAVE KEITH ALSO SPEND THE NIGHT. FOOL THAT I WAS, I STILL HELD OUT SOME HOPE SHE AND I WOULD REUNITE, BUT THE COLD TRUTH WAS, SHE JUST NEEDED A PLACE TO CRASH AND KNEW I'D BE SUCKER ENOUGH TO OBLIGE... HOWEVER, NOW CAME A TURN OF EVENTS THAT NEITHER OF US WOULD HAVE PREDICTED...
KEITH IS FEELING MY PENIS!
IT WAS A COSMIC JOKE!! KEITH, THE GUY THAT VICKY HAD BEEN PANTING OVER, THE GUY THAT VICKY HAD BEEN MAKING ME JEALOUS OVER, THIS SAME KEITH, IT TURNED OUT, WAS INTERESTED IN MOI!
VICKY, SANDWICHED BETWEEN US, WAS TRYING TO FONDLE KEITH WHILE KEEPING US APART...
IN THAT MOMENT MY THOUGHT PATTERNS ABOUT VICKY CHANGED FOREVER!
ALL THE TIME I'D SPENT LETTING VICKY JERK ME AROUND OVER KEITH HAD BEEN ABSURD! THE IDEA THAT I STILL BURNED A FLAME FOR THIS WOMAN WHO OBVIOUSLY COULDN'T CARE LESS ABOUT ME WAS NOW TOTALLY LUDICROUS!
I REACHED ACROSS VICKY AND RECIPROCATED KEITH'S ADVANCES TO HER TOTAL CONSTERNATION!
I RELISHED SEEING VICKY BEING REJECTED BY THE OBJECT OF HER DESIRE.
...TALK ABOUT KARMATIC DEBT!
I FADED INTO A DRUNKEN SLEEP WITH A LAUGH ON MY LIPS...

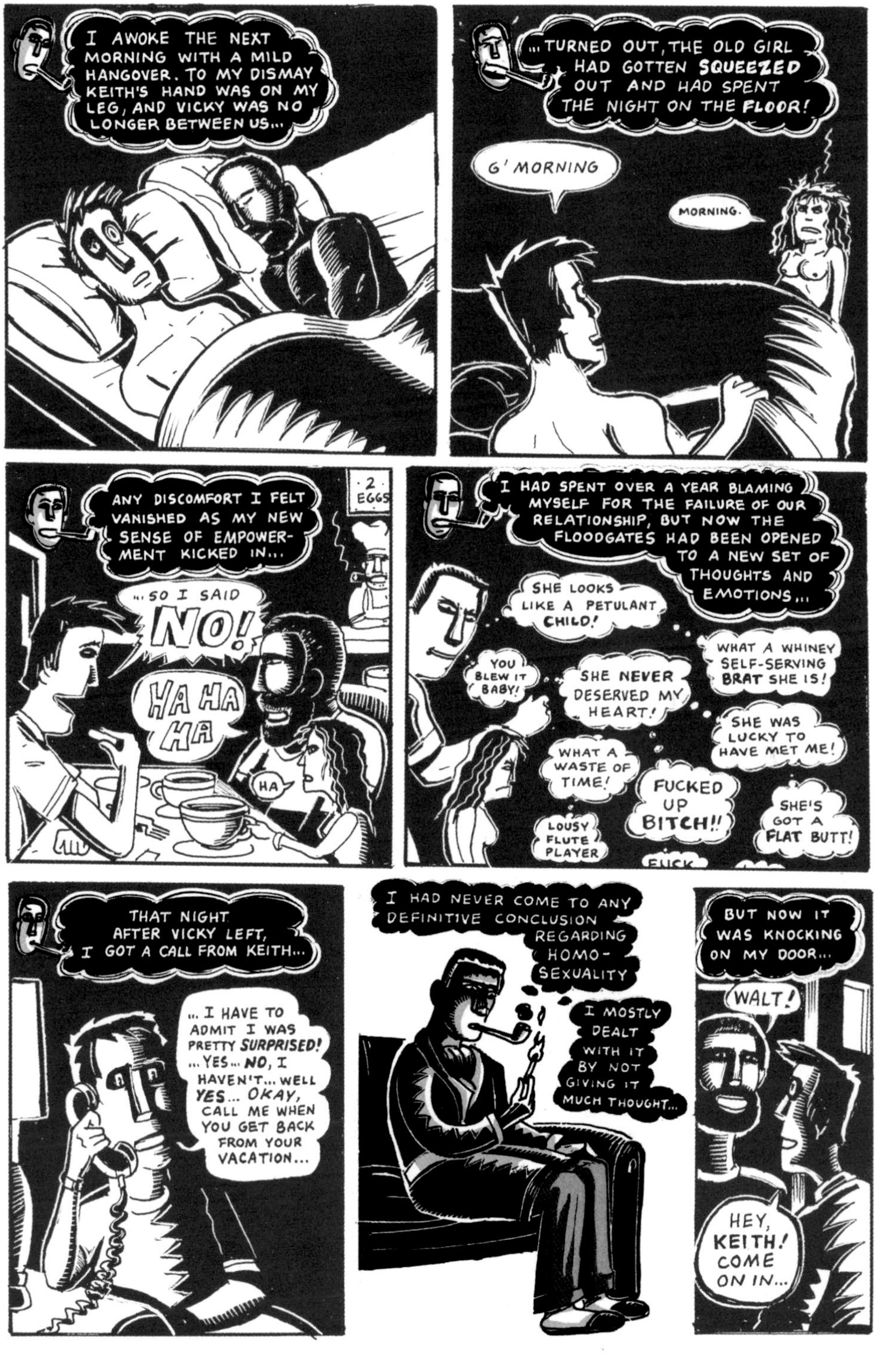
I AWOKE THE NEXT MORNING WITH A MILD HANGOVER. TO MY DISMAY KEITH'S HAND WAS ON MY LEG, AND VICKY WAS NO LONGER BETWEEN US...
...TURNED OUT, THE OLD GIRL HAD GOTTEN SQUEEZED OUT AND HAD SPENT THE NIGHT ON THE FLOOR!
G' MORNING
MORNING.
ANY DISCOMFORT I FELT VANISHED AS MY NEW SENSE OF EMPOWERMENT KICKED IN...
2 EGGS
...SO I SAID NO!
HA HA HA
HA
I HAD SPENT OVER A YEAR BLAMING MYSELF FOR THE FAILURE OF OUR RELATIONSHIP, BUT NOW THE FLOODGATES HAD BEEN OPENED TO A NEW SET OF THOUGHTS AND EMOTIONS...
SHE LOOKS LIKE A PETULANT CHILD!
WHAT A WHINEY SELF-SERVING BRAT SHE IS!
YOU BLEW IT BABY!
SHE NEVER DESERVED MY HEART!
SHE WAS LUCKY TO HAVE MET ME!
WHAT A WASTE OF TIME!
FUCKED UP BITCH!!
SHE'S GOT A FLAT BUTT!
LOUSY FLUTE PLAYER
THAT NIGHT AFTER VICKY LEFT, I GOT A CALL FROM KEITH...
... I HAVE TO ADMIT I WAS PRETTY SURPRISED! ...YES... NO, I HAVEN'T... WELL YES... OKAY, CALL ME WHEN YOU GET BACK FROM YOUR VACATION...
I HAD NEVER COME TO ANY DEFINITIVE CONCLUSION REGARDING HOMO-SEXUALITY
I MOSTLY DEALT WITH IT BY NOT GIVING IT MUCH THOUGHT...
BUT NOW IT WAS KNOCKING ON MY DOOR...
WALT!
HEY, KEITH! COME ON IN...

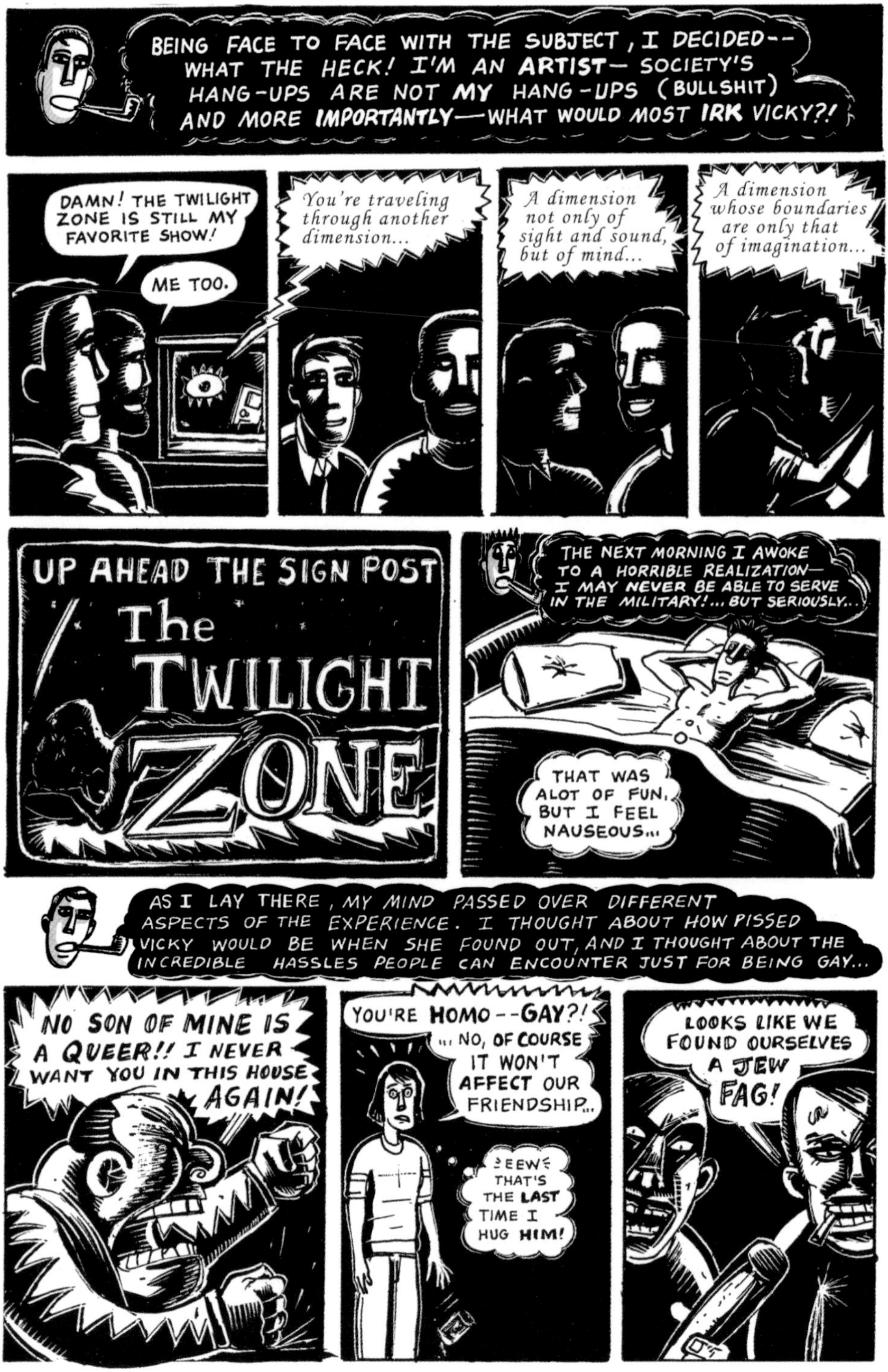
BEING FACE TO FACE WITH THE SUBJECT, I DECIDED-- WHAT THE HECK! I'M AN ARTIST— SOCIETY'S HANG-UPS ARE NOT MY HANG-UPS (BULLSHIT) AND MORE IMPORTANTLY—WHAT WOULD MOST IRK VICKY?!
DAMN! THE TWILIGHT ZONE IS STILL MY FAVORITE SHOW!
ME TOO.
You're traveling through another dimension...
A dimension not only of sight and sound, but of mind...
A dimension whose boundaries are only that of imagination...
UP AHEAD THE SIGN POST
The TWILIGHT ZONE
THE NEXT MORNING I AWOKE TO A HORRIBLE REALIZATION— I MAY NEVER BE ABLE TO SERVE IN THE MILITARY!... BUT SERIOUSLY...
THAT WAS ALOT OF FUN, BUT I FEEL NAUSEOUS...
AS I LAY THERE, MY MIND PASSED OVER DIFFERENT ASPECTS OF THE EXPERIENCE. I THOUGHT ABOUT HOW PISSED VICKY WOULD BE WHEN SHE FOUND OUT, AND I THOUGHT ABOUT THE INCREDIBLE HASSLES PEOPLE CAN ENCOUNTER JUST FOR BEING GAY...
NO SON OF MINE IS A QUEER!! I NEVER WANT YOU IN THIS HOUSE AGAIN!
YOU'RE HOMO--GAY?!
... NO, OF COURSE IT WON'T AFFECT OUR FRIENDSHIP...
EEW THAT'S THE LAST TIME I HUG HIM!
LOOKS LIKE WE FOUND OURSELVES A JEW FAG!

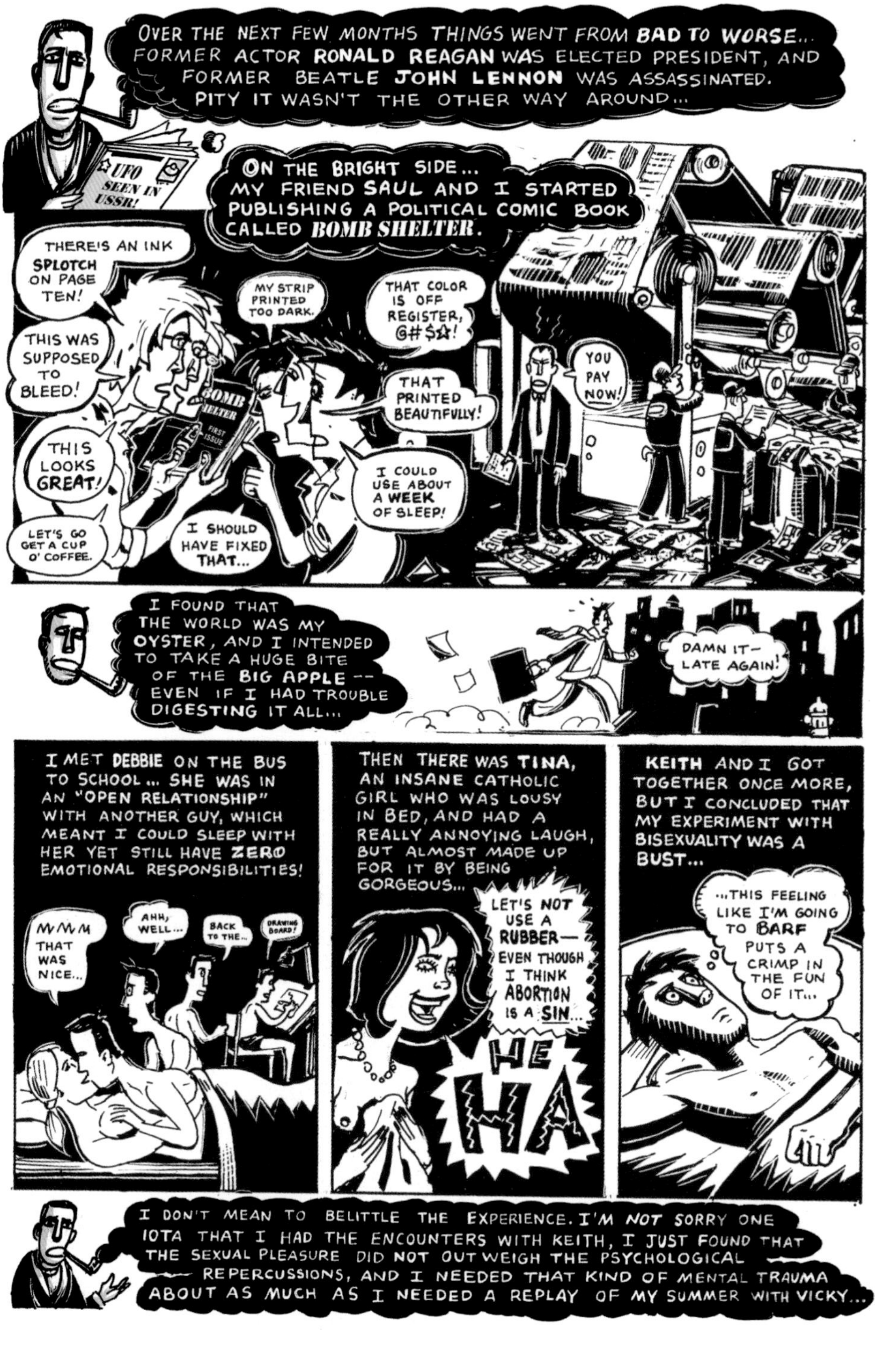
OVER THE NEXT FEW MONTHS THINGS WENT FROM BAD TO WORSE... FORMER ACTOR RONALD REAGAN WAS ELECTED PRESIDENT, AND FORMER BEATLE JOHN LENNON WAS ASSASSINATED. PITY IT WASN'T THE OTHER WAY AROUND...
UFO SEEN IN USSR!
ON THE BRIGHT SIDE... MY FRIEND SAUL AND I STARTED PUBLISHING A POLITICAL COMIC BOOK CALLED BOMB SHELTER.
THERE'S AN INK SPLOTCH ON PAGE TEN!
MY STRIP PRINTED TOO DARK.
THAT COLOR IS OFF REGISTER, @#$☆!
THIS WAS SUPPOSED TO BLEED!
BOMB SHELTER FIRST ISSUE
YOU PAY NOW!
THAT PRINTED BEAUTIFULLY!
THIS LOOKS GREAT!
I COULD USE ABOUT A WEEK OF SLEEP!
LET'S GO GET A CUP O' COFFEE.
I SHOULD HAVE FIXED THAT...
I FOUND THAT THE WORLD WAS MY OYSTER, AND I INTENDED TO TAKE A HUGE BITE OF THE BIG APPLE -- EVEN IF I HAD TROUBLE DIGESTING IT ALL...
DAMN IT- LATE AGAIN!
I MET DEBBIE ON THE BUS TO SCHOOL... SHE WAS IN AN "OPEN RELATIONSHIP" WITH ANOTHER GUY, WHICH MEANT I COULD SLEEP WITH HER YET STILL HAVE ZERO EMOTIONAL RESPONSIBILITIES!
MMM THAT WAS NICE...
AHH, WELL...
BACK TO THE...
DRAWING BOARD!
THEN THERE WAS TINA, AN INSANE CATHOLIC GIRL WHO WAS LOUSY IN BED, AND HAD A REALLY ANNOYING LAUGH, BUT ALMOST MADE UP FOR IT BY BEING GORGEOUS...
LET'S NOT USE A RUBBER— EVEN THOUGH I THINK ABORTION IS A SIN...
HE HA
KEITH AND I GOT TOGETHER ONCE MORE, BUT I CONCLUDED THAT MY EXPERIMENT WITH BISEXUALITY WAS A BUST...
...THIS FEELING LIKE I'M GOING TO BARF PUTS A CRIMP IN THE FUN OF IT...
I DON'T MEAN TO BELITTLE THE EXPERIENCE. I'M NOT SORRY ONE IOTA THAT I HAD THE ENCOUNTERS WITH KEITH, I JUST FOUND THAT THE SEXUAL PLEASURE DID NOT OUTWEIGH THE PSYCHOLOGICAL REPERCUSSIONS, AND I NEEDED THAT KIND OF MENTAL TRAUMA ABOUT AS MUCH AS I NEEDED A REPLAY OF MY SUMMER WITH VICKY...

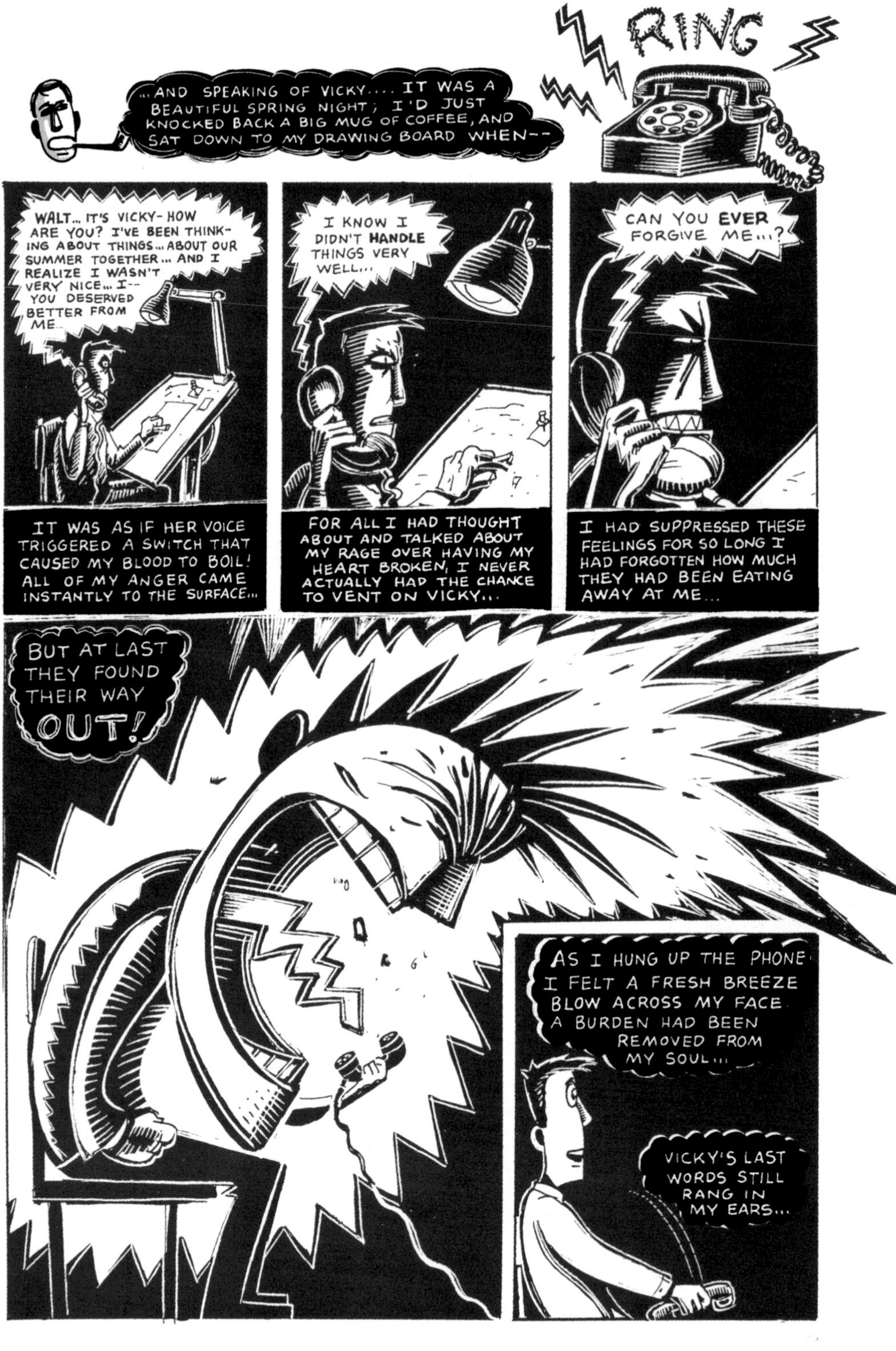
...AND SPEAKING OF VICKY.... IT WAS A BEAUTIFUL SPRING NIGHT; I'D JUST KNOCKED BACK A BIG MUG OF COFFEE, AND SAT DOWN TO MY DRAWING BOARD WHEN--
RING
WALT... IT'S VICKY- HOW ARE YOU? I'VE BEEN THINKING ABOUT THINGS... ABOUT OUR SUMMER TOGETHER... AND I REALIZE I WASN'T VERY NICE... I-- YOU DESERVED BETTER FROM ME...
IT WAS AS IF HER VOICE TRIGGERED A SWITCH THAT CAUSED MY BLOOD TO BOIL! ALL OF MY ANGER CAME INSTANTLY TO THE SURFACE...
I KNOW I DIDN'T HANDLE THINGS VERY WELL...
FOR ALL I HAD THOUGHT ABOUT AND TALKED ABOUT MY RAGE OVER HAVING MY HEART BROKEN, I NEVER ACTUALLY HAD THE CHANCE TO VENT ON VICKY...
CAN YOU EVER FORGIVE ME...?
I HAD SUPPRESSED THESE FEELINGS FOR SO LONG I HAD FORGOTTEN HOW MUCH THEY HAD BEEN EATING AWAY AT ME...
BUT AT LAST THEY FOUND THEIR WAY OUT!
AS I HUNG UP THE PHONE I FELT A FRESH BREEZE BLOW ACROSS MY FACE. A BURDEN HAD BEEN REMOVED FROM MY SOUL...
VICKY'S LAST WORDS STILL RANG IN MY EARS...

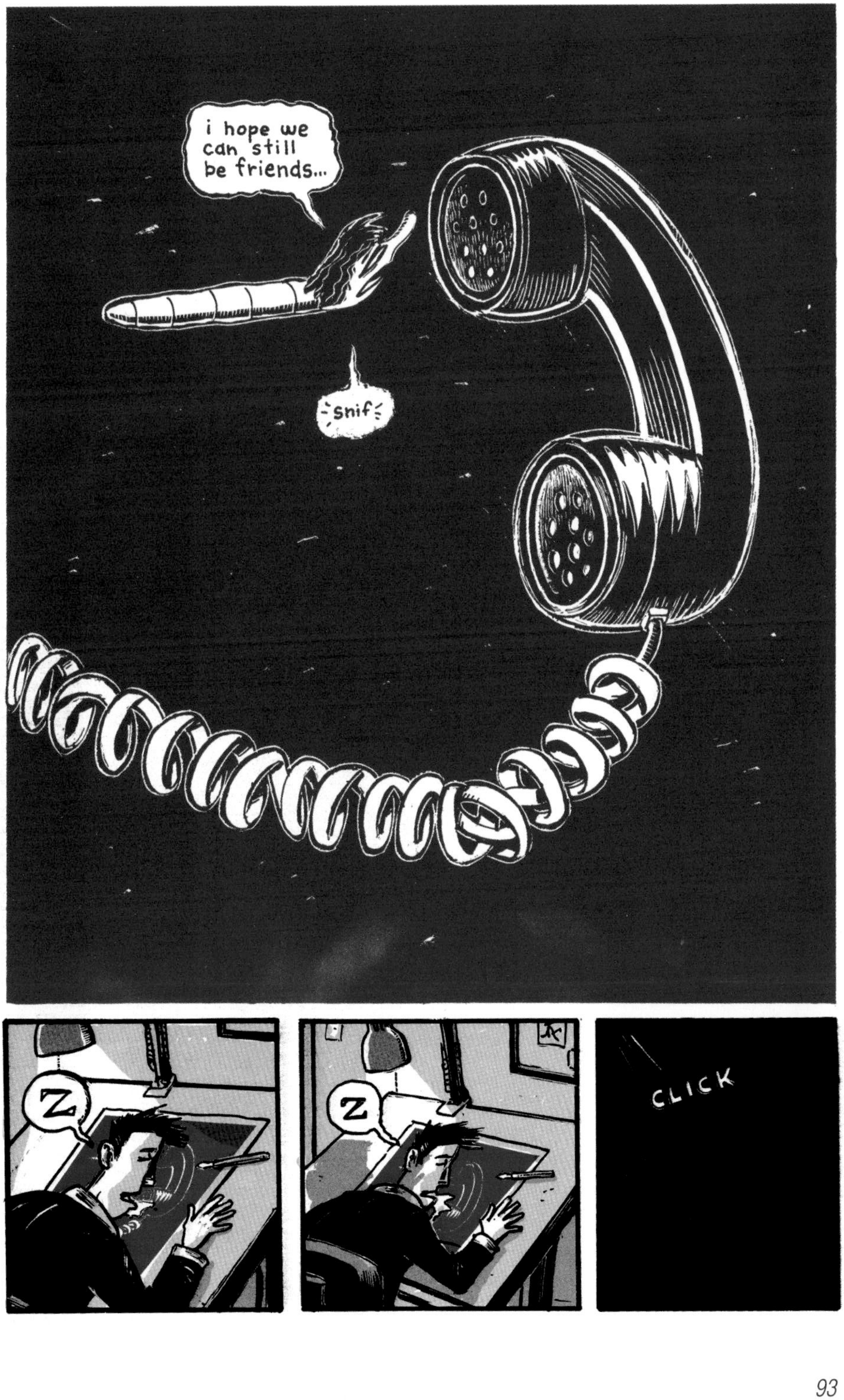
i hope we can still be friends...
snif
Z
Z
CLICK

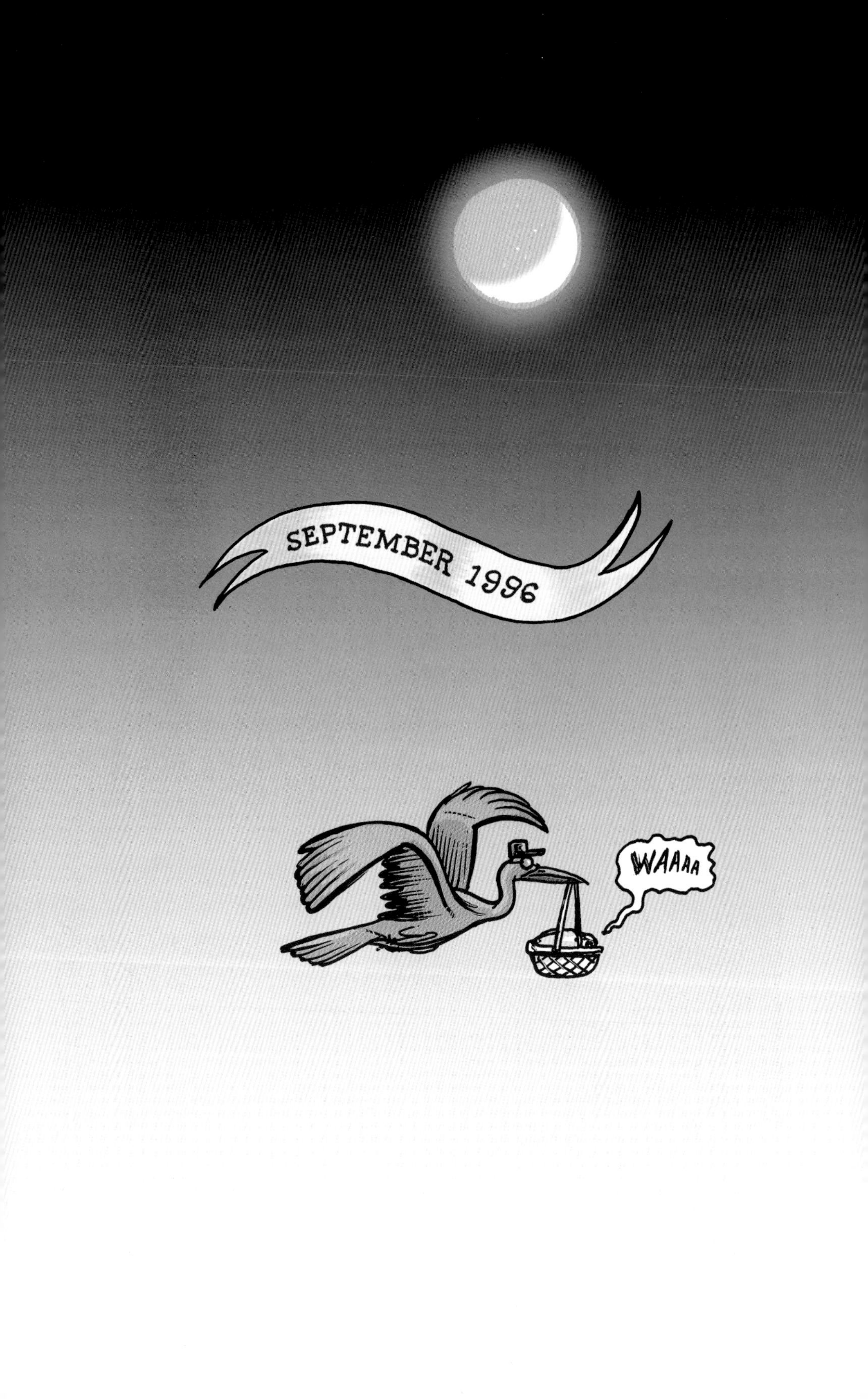
SEPTEMBER 1996
WAAAA

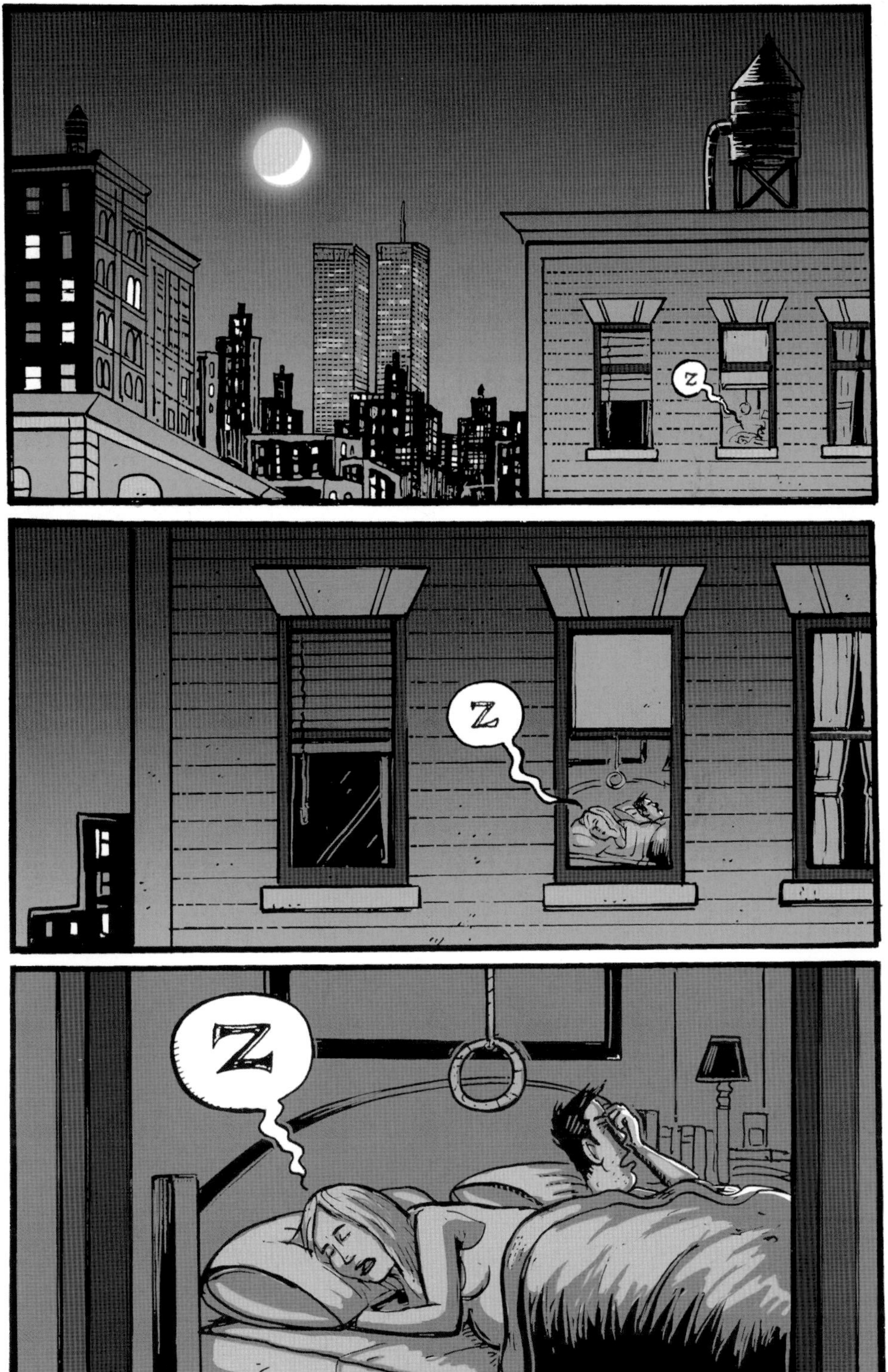
Z
Z
Z

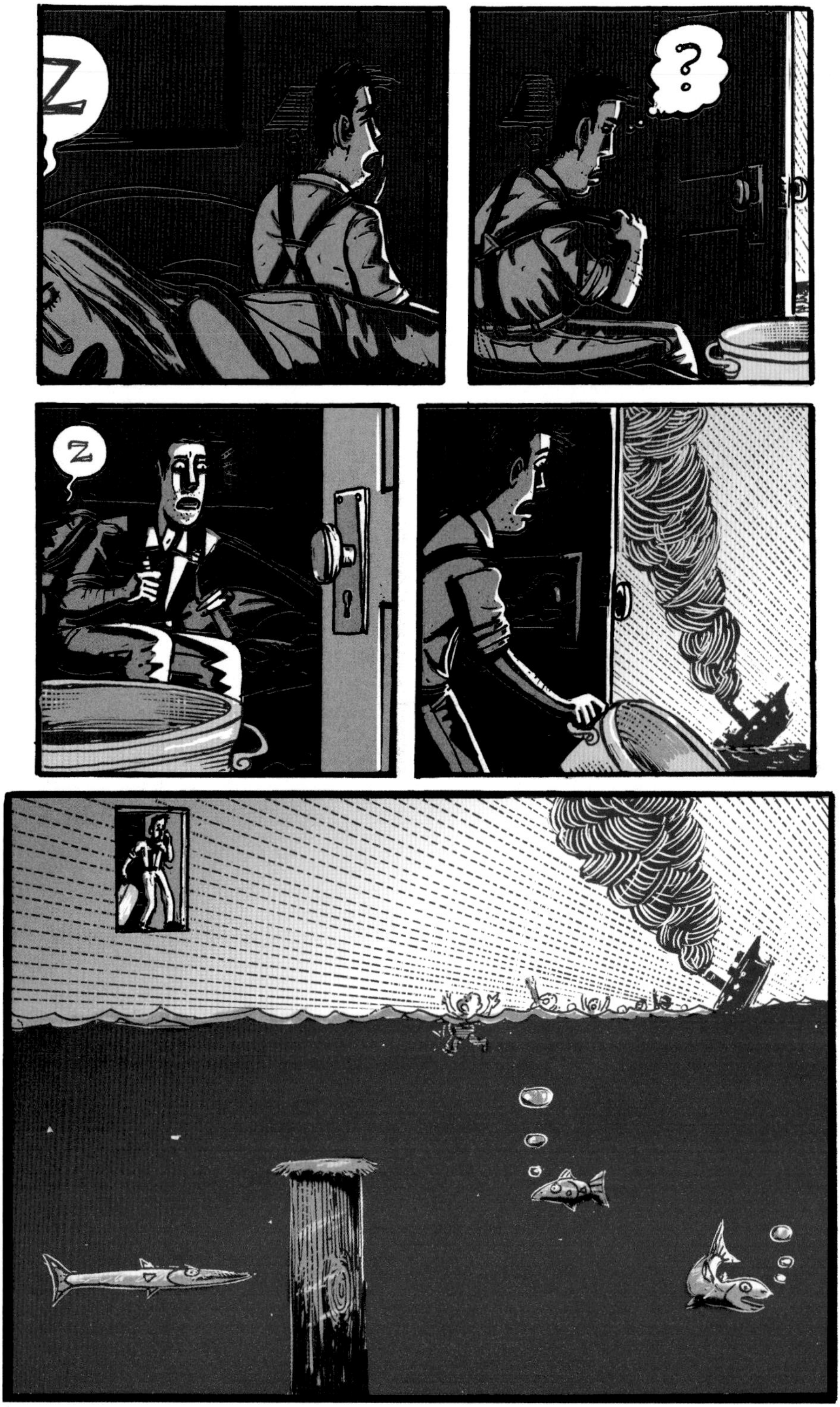
Z
?
Z

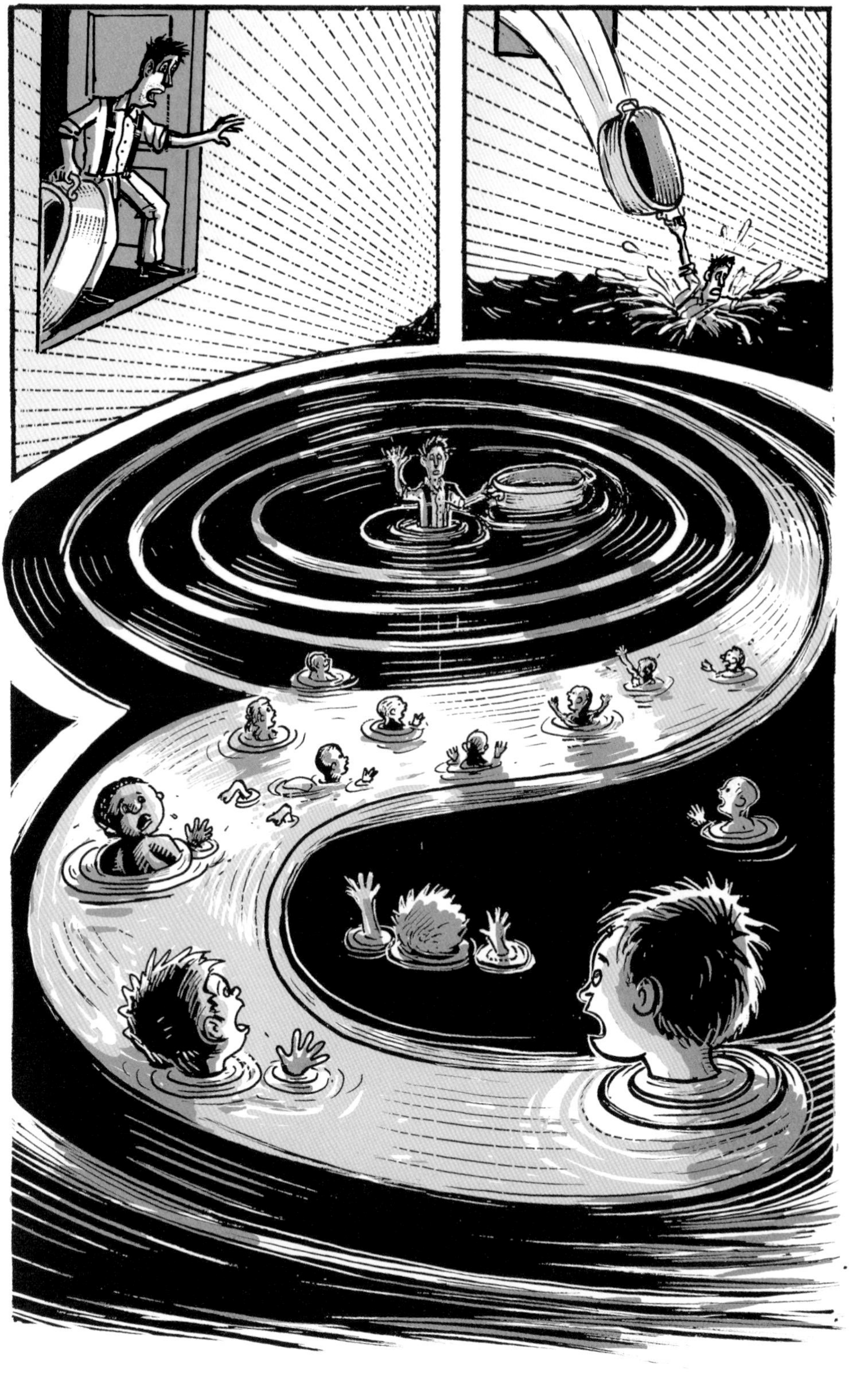

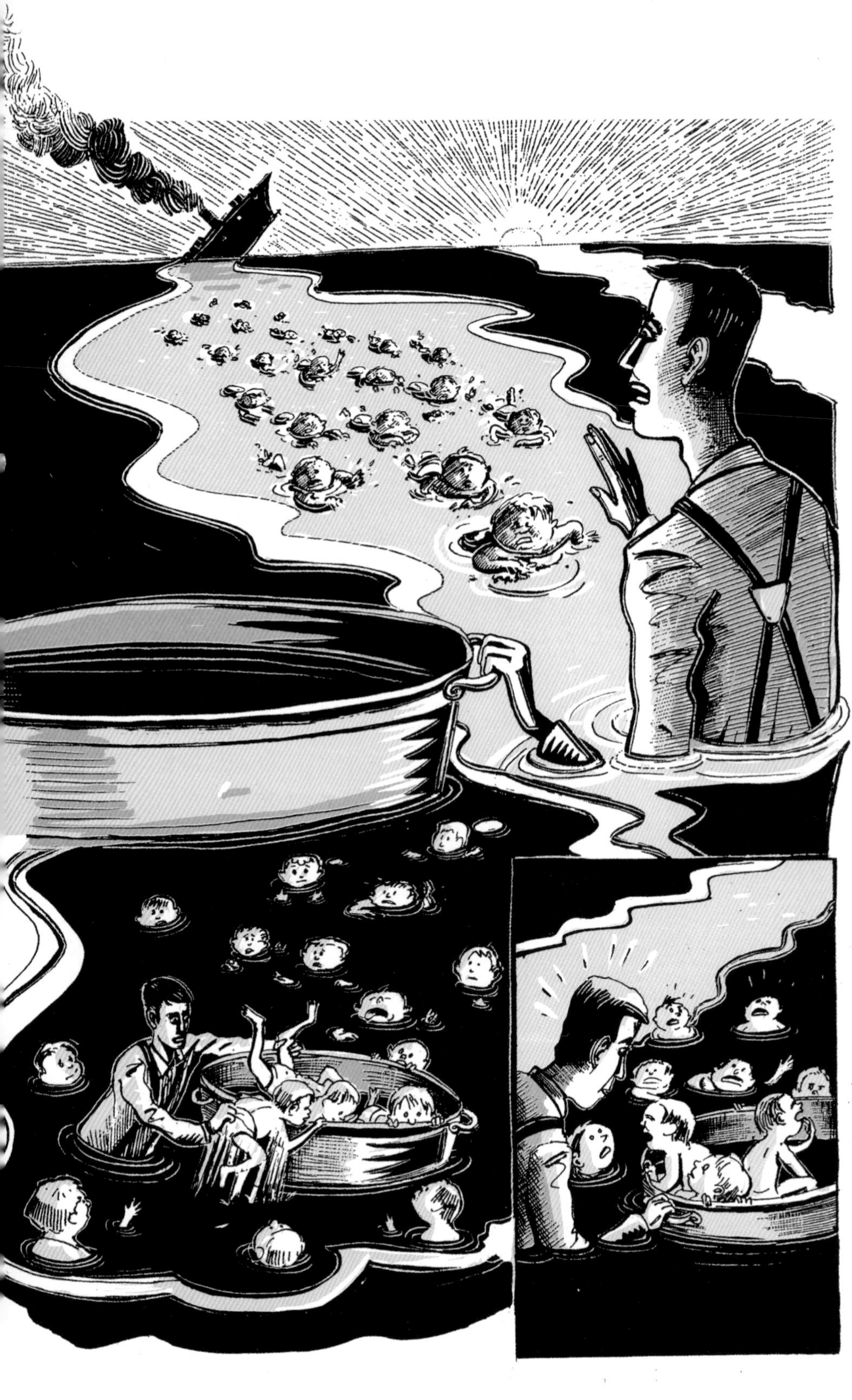

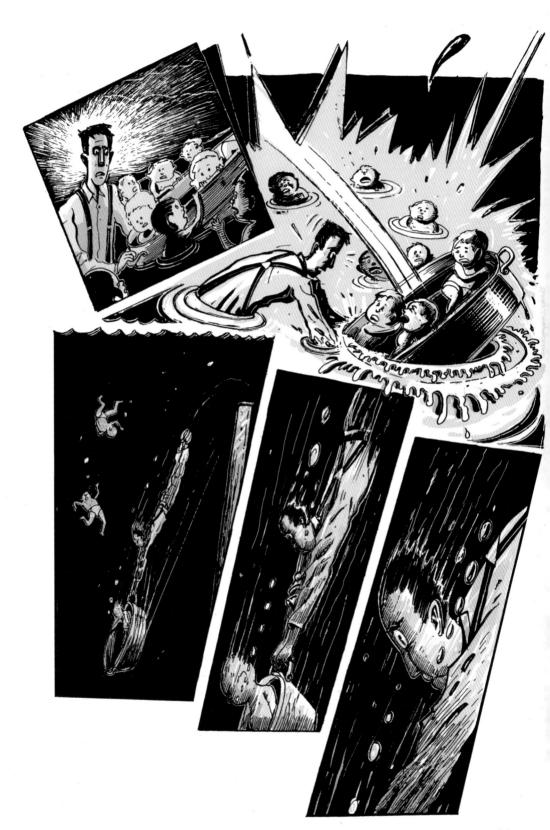

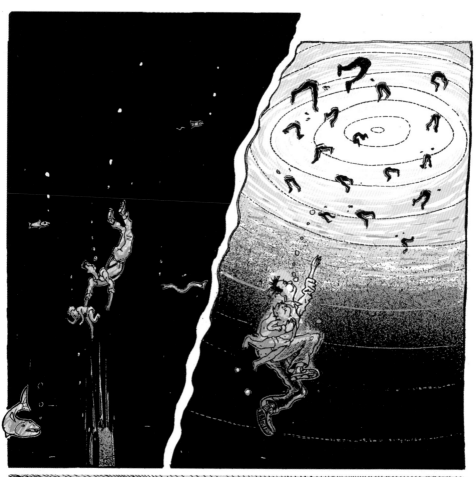

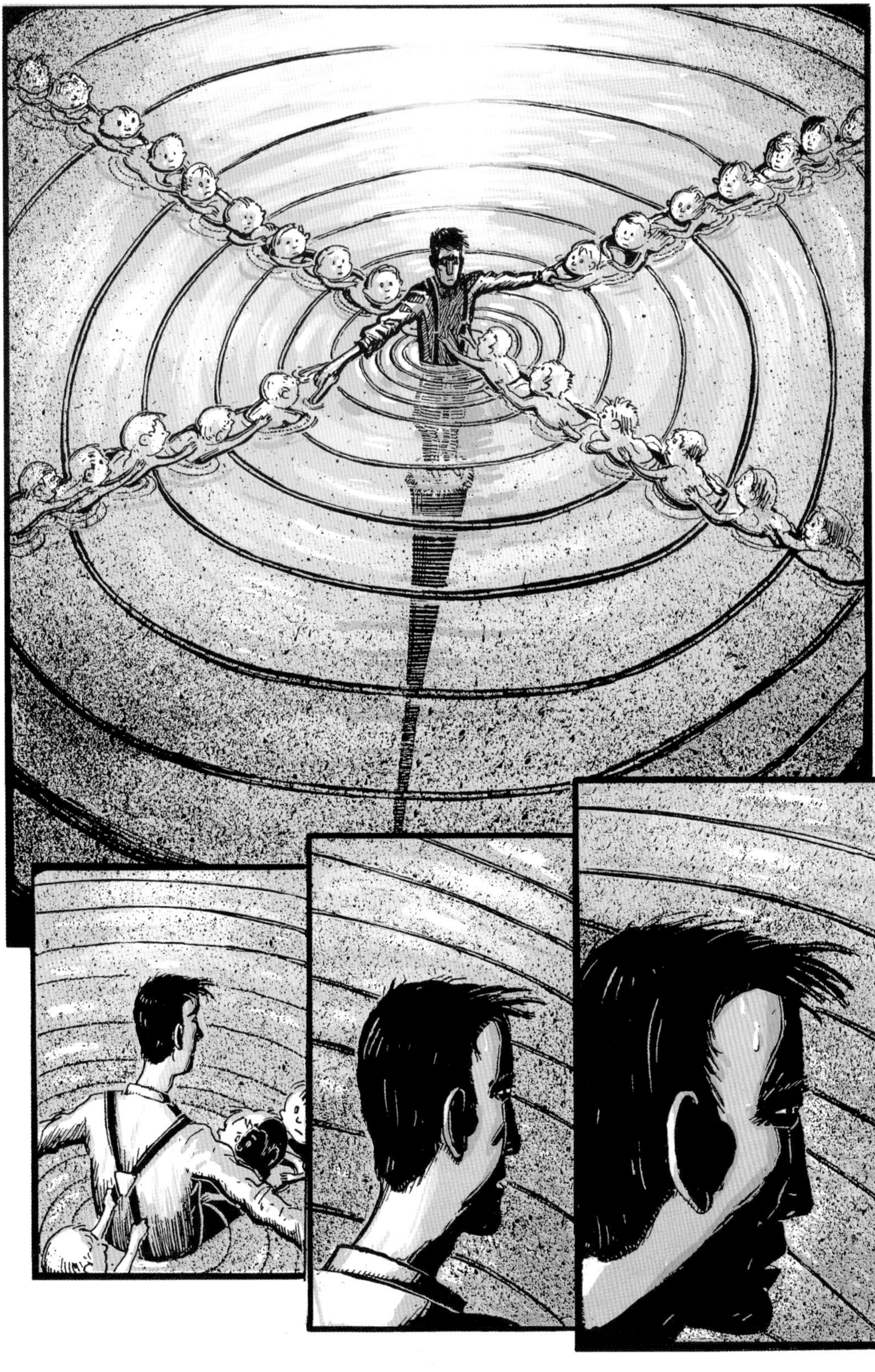

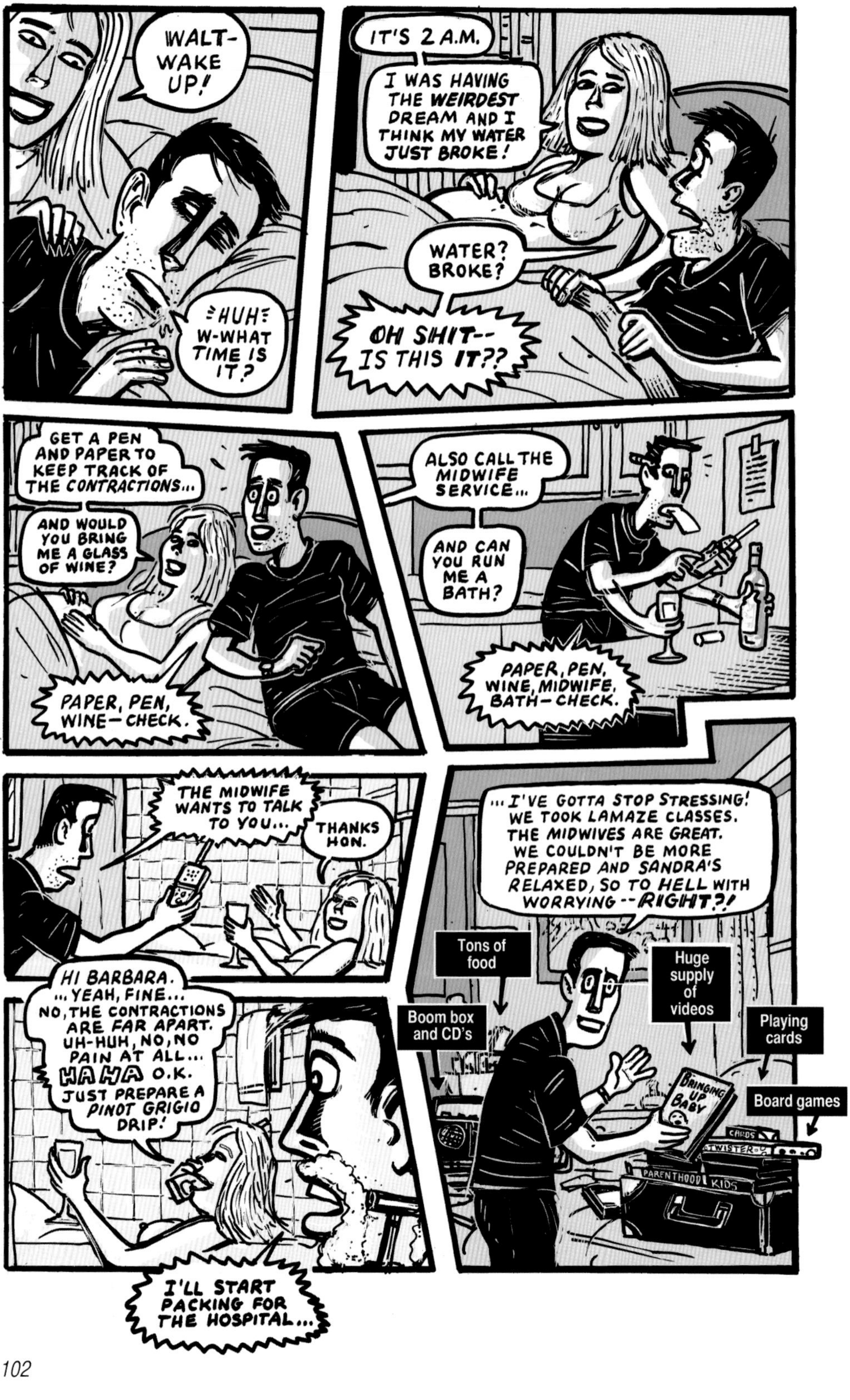
WALT- WAKE UP!
HUH W-WHAT TIME IS IT?
IT'S 2 A.M.
I WAS HAVING THE WEIRDEST DREAM AND I THINK MY WATER JUST BROKE!
WATER? BROKE?
OH SHIT-- IS THIS IT??
GET A PEN AND PAPER TO KEEP TRACK OF THE CONTRACTIONS...
AND WOULD YOU BRING ME A GLASS OF WINE?
PAPER, PEN, WINE—CHECK.
ALSO CALL THE MIDWIFE SERVICE...
AND CAN YOU RUN ME A BATH?
PAPER, PEN, WINE, MIDWIFE, BATH—CHECK.
THE MIDWIFE WANTS TO TALK TO YOU...
THANKS HON.
HI BARBARA. ...YEAH, FINE... NO, THE CONTRACTIONS ARE FAR APART. UH-HUH, NO, NO PAIN AT ALL... HAHA O.K. JUST PREPARE A PINOT GRIGIO DRIP!
I'LL START PACKING FOR THE HOSPITAL...
...I'VE GOTTA STOP STRESSING! WE TOOK LAMAZE CLASSES. THE MIDWIVES ARE GREAT. WE COULDN'T BE MORE PREPARED AND SANDRA'S RELAXED, SO TO HELL WITH WORRYING --RIGHT?!
Tons of food
Boom box and CD's
Huge supply of videos
Playing cards
Board games
BRINGING UP BABY
CARDS
TWISTER
PARENTHOOD
KIDS

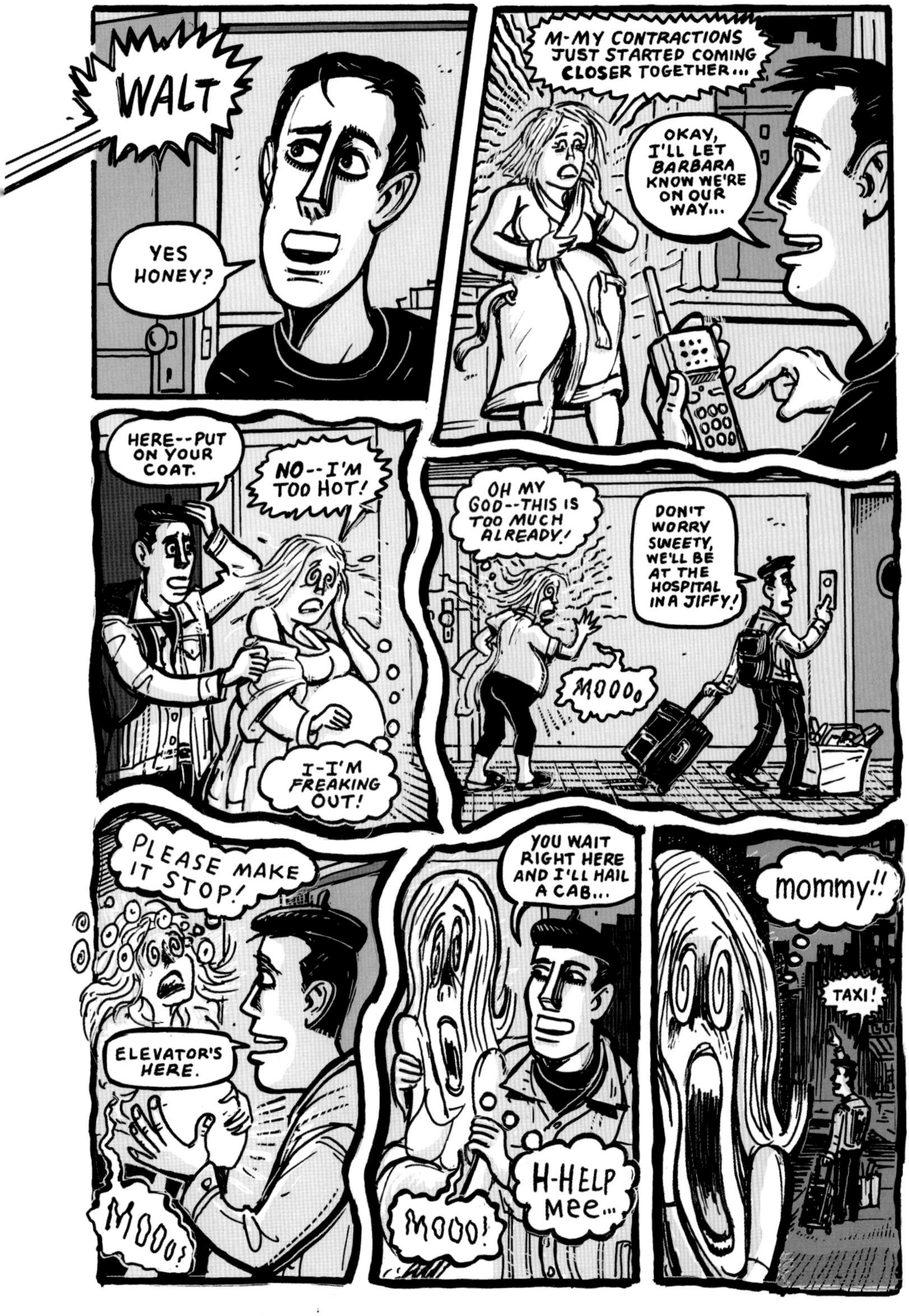
WALT
YES HONEY?
M-MY CONTRACTIONS JUST STARTED COMING CLOSER TOGETHER...
OKAY, I'LL LET BARBARA KNOW WE'RE ON OUR WAY...
HERE--PUT ON YOUR COAT.
NO--I'M TOO HOT!
I-I'M FREAKING OUT!
OH MY GOD--THIS IS TOO MUCH ALREADY!
DON'T WORRY SWEETY, WE'LL BE AT THE HOSPITAL IN A JIFFY!
MOOOo
PLEASE MAKE IT STOP!
ELEVATOR'S HERE.
MOOo!
YOU WAIT RIGHT HERE AND I'LL HAIL A CAB...
H-HELP mee...
MOOO!
mommy!!
TAXI!

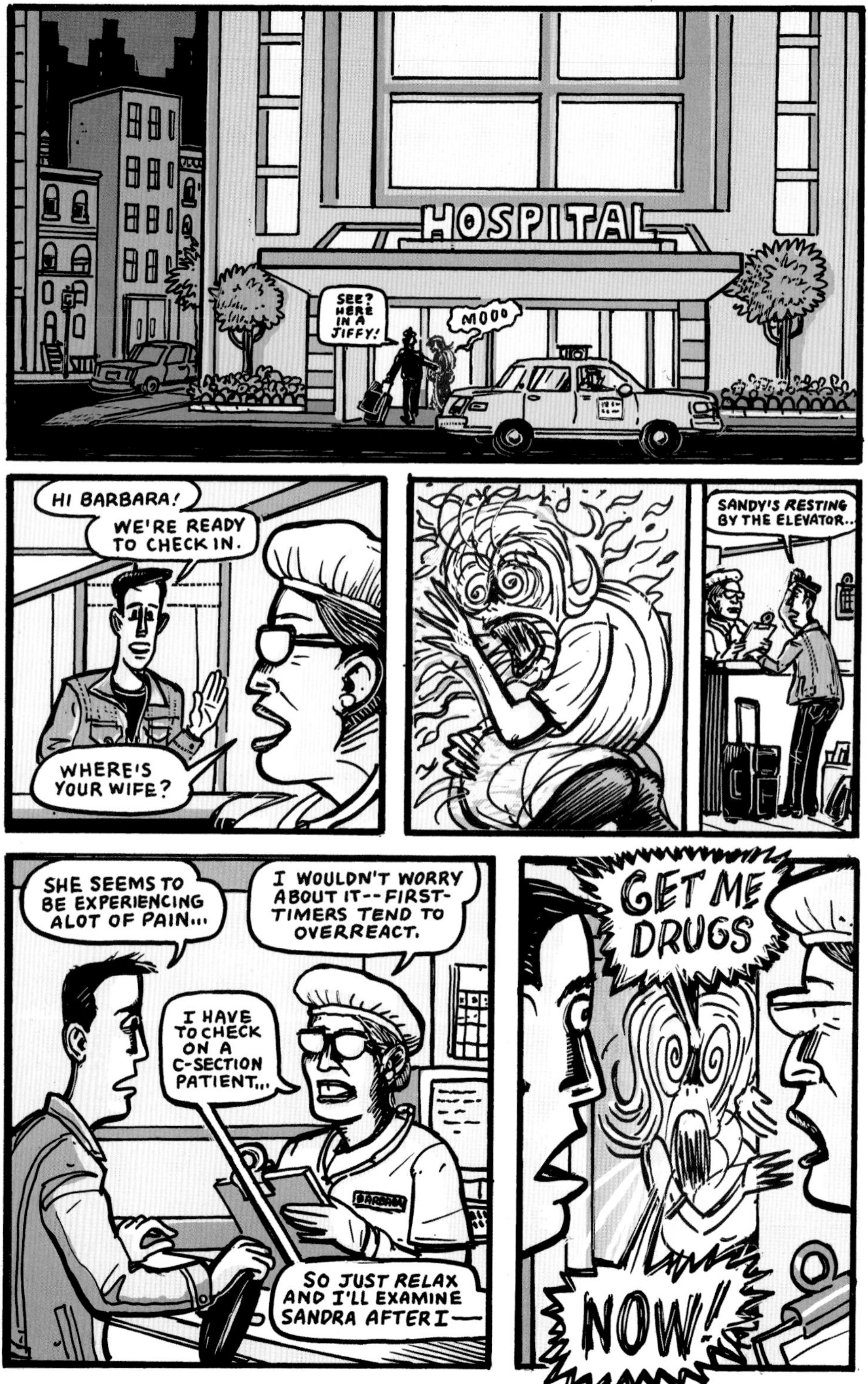
HOSPITAL
SEE? HERE IN A JIFFY!
MOOO
HI BARBARA!
WE'RE READY TO CHECK IN.
WHERE'S YOUR WIFE?
SANDY'S RESTING BY THE ELEVATOR...
SHE SEEMS TO BE EXPERIENCING ALOT OF PAIN...
I WOULDN'T WORRY ABOUT IT--FIRST-TIMERS TEND TO OVERREACT.
I HAVE TO CHECK ON A C-SECTION PATIENT...
SO JUST RELAX AND I'LL EXAMINE SANDRA AFTER I—
BARBARA
GET ME DRUGS
NOW!

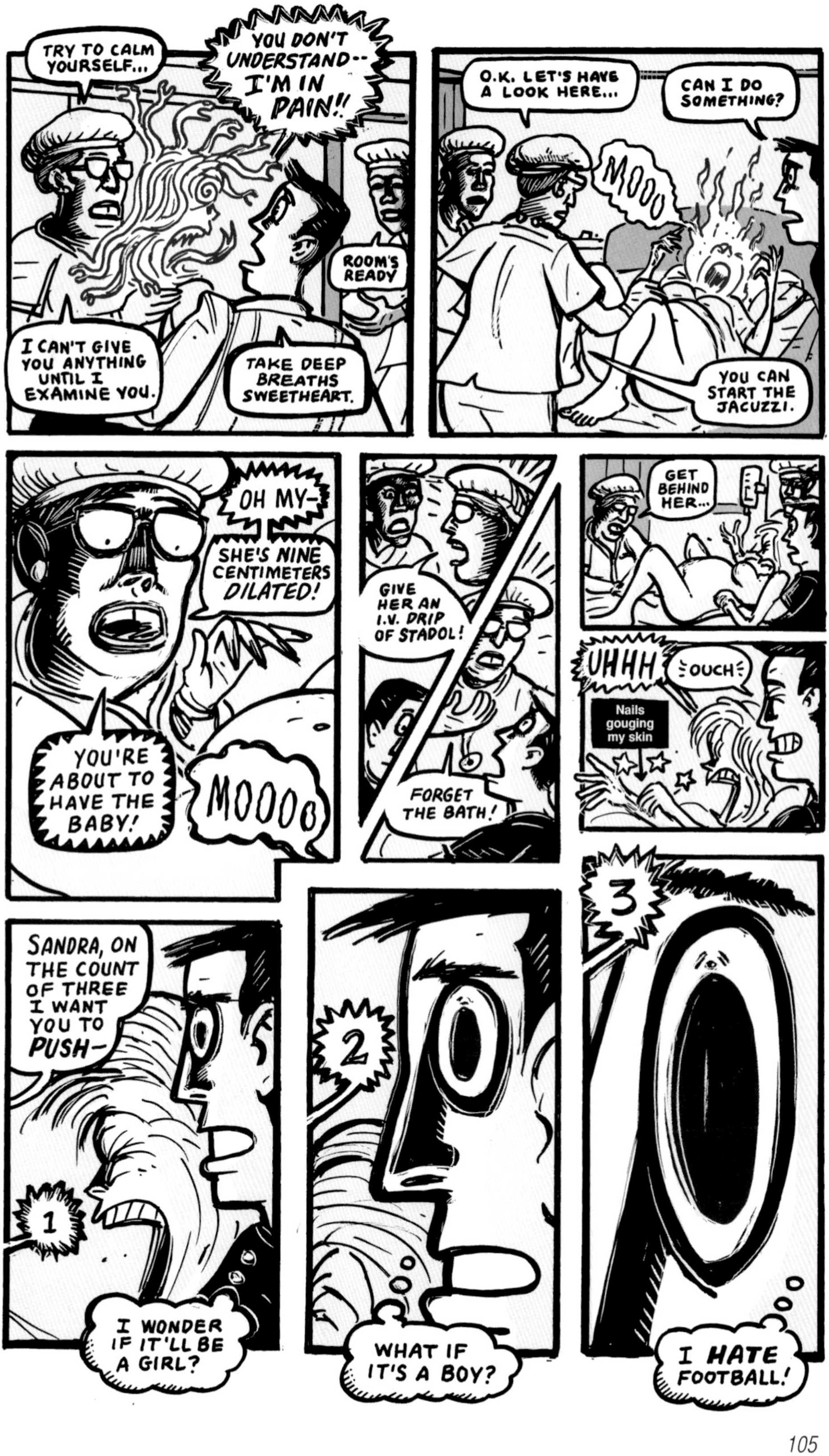
TRY TO CALM YOURSELF...
YOU DON'T UNDERSTAND-- I'M IN PAIN!!
ROOM'S READY
I CAN'T GIVE YOU ANYTHING UNTIL I EXAMINE YOU.
TAKE DEEP BREATHS SWEETHEART.
O.K. LET'S HAVE A LOOK HERE...
CAN I DO SOMETHING?
MOOO
YOU CAN START THE JACUZZI.
OH MY-
SHE'S NINE CENTIMETERS DILATED!
YOU'RE ABOUT TO HAVE THE BABY!
MOOOO
GIVE HER AN I.V. DRIP OF STADOL!
FORGET THE BATH!
GET BEHIND HER...
UHHH
OUCH
Nails gouging my skin
SANDRA, ON THE COUNT OF THREE I WANT YOU TO PUSH-
1
I WONDER IF IT'LL BE A GIRL?
2
WHAT IF IT'S A BOY?
3
I HATE FOOTBALL!

umph w-what's happening?
what's that--? oooh too bright!
OW! some-thing's pulling me towards it!
must... fight... pull!
UUH
maybe if i hold this rope...
oof can't resist...
must go to light!
Gasp can't breathe!!
getting crushed!!
must escape!!
PUSH!
EEEAHA

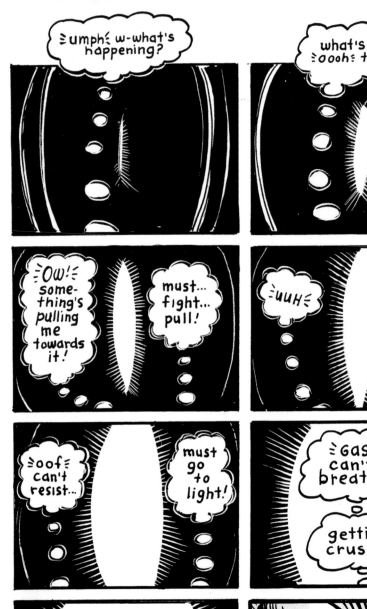

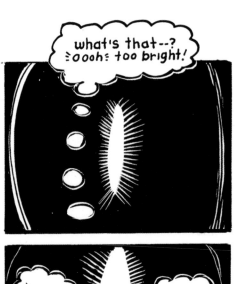

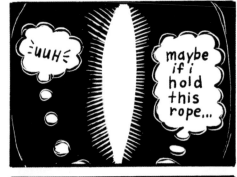

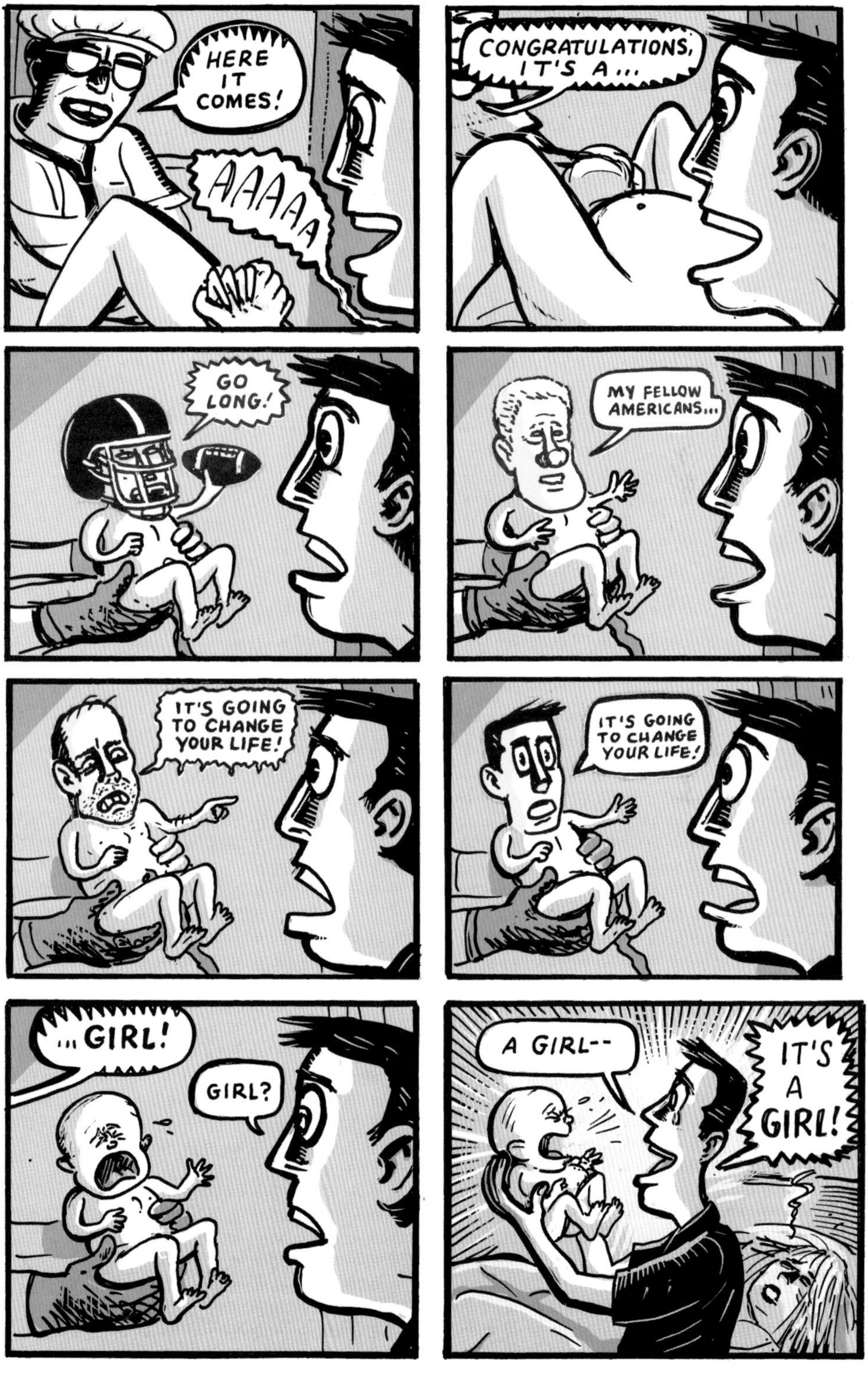
HERE IT COMES!
AAAAA
CONGRATULATIONS, IT'S A...
GO LONG!
MY FELLOW AMERICANS...
IT'S GOING TO CHANGE YOUR LIFE!
IT'S GOING TO CHANGE YOUR LIFE!
...GIRL!
GIRL?
A GIRL--
IT'S A GIRL!

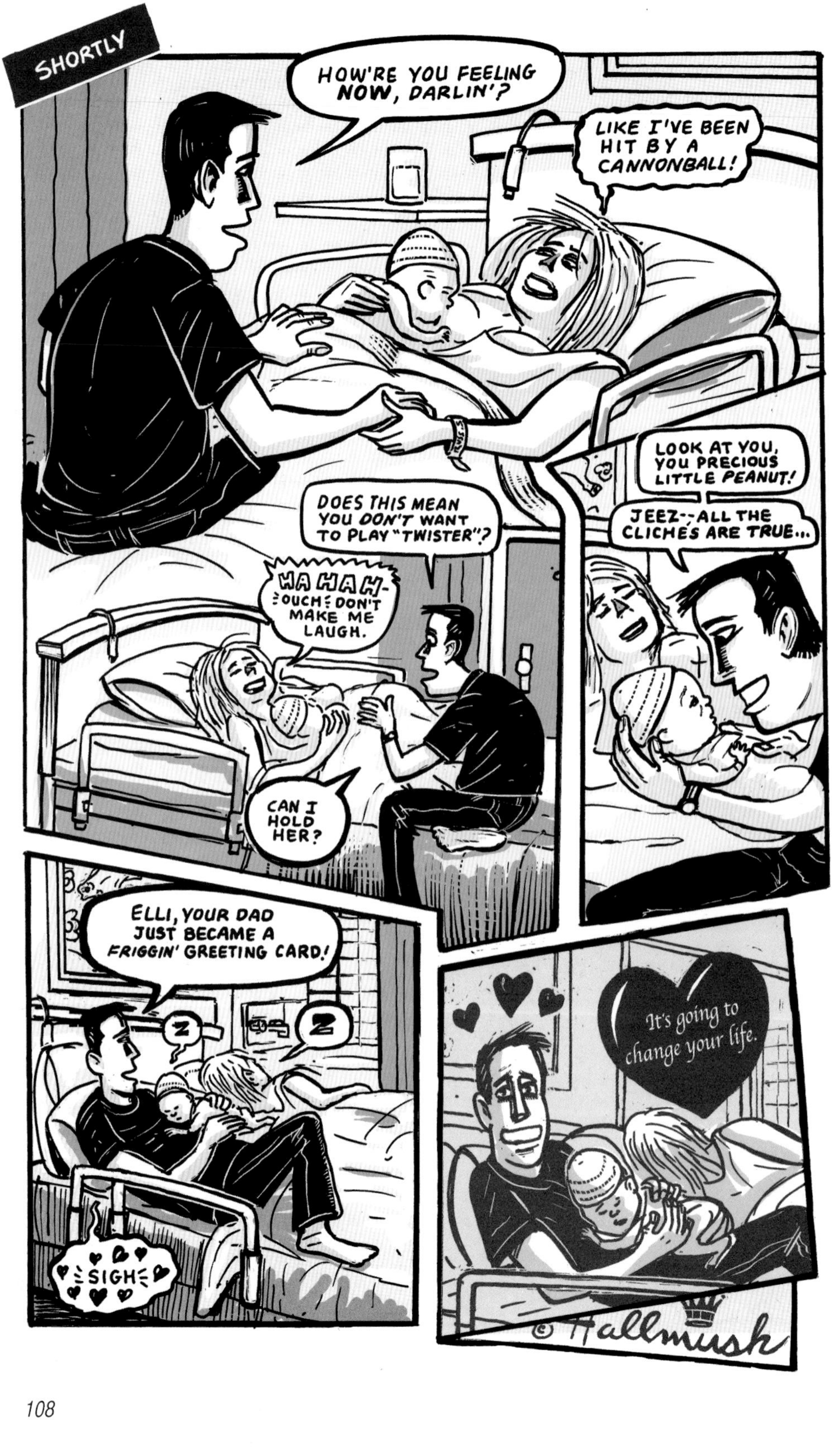
SHORTLY
HOW'RE YOU FEELING NOW, DARLIN'?
LIKE I'VE BEEN HIT BY A CANNONBALL!
DOES THIS MEAN YOU DON'T WANT TO PLAY "TWISTER"?
HA HAH- OUCH- DON'T MAKE ME LAUGH.
CAN I HOLD HER?
LOOK AT YOU, YOU PRECIOUS LITTLE PEANUT!
JEEZ--ALL THE CLICHÉS ARE TRUE...
ELLI, YOUR DAD JUST BECAME A FRIGGIN' GREETING CARD!
Z
Z
SIGH
It's going to change your life.
© Hallmush

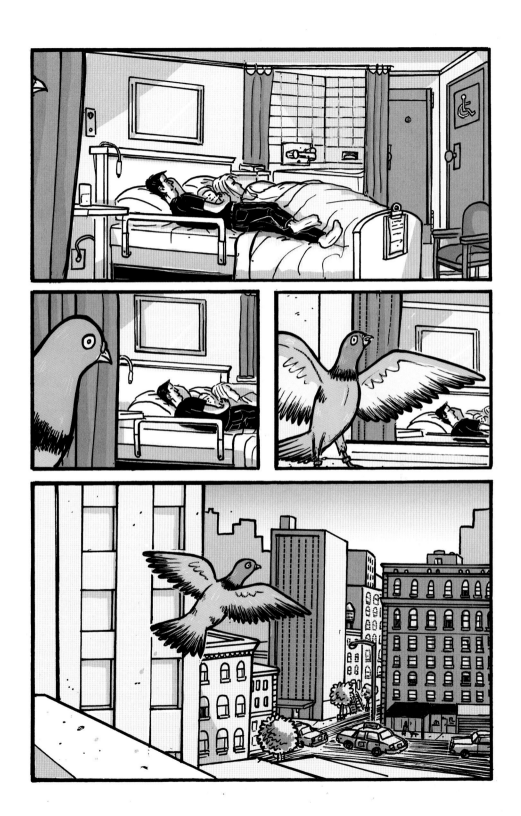

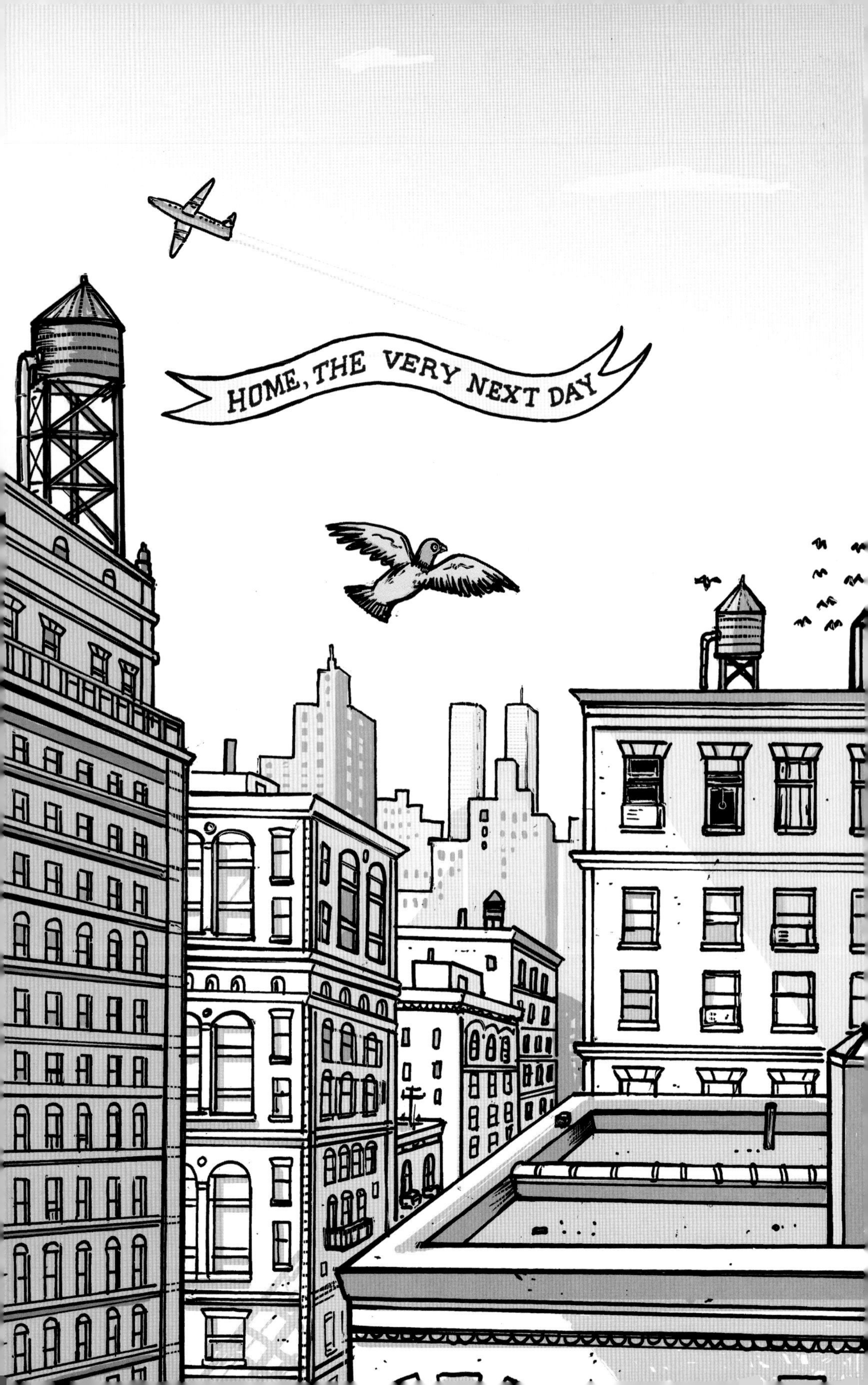
HOME, THE VERY NEXT DAY

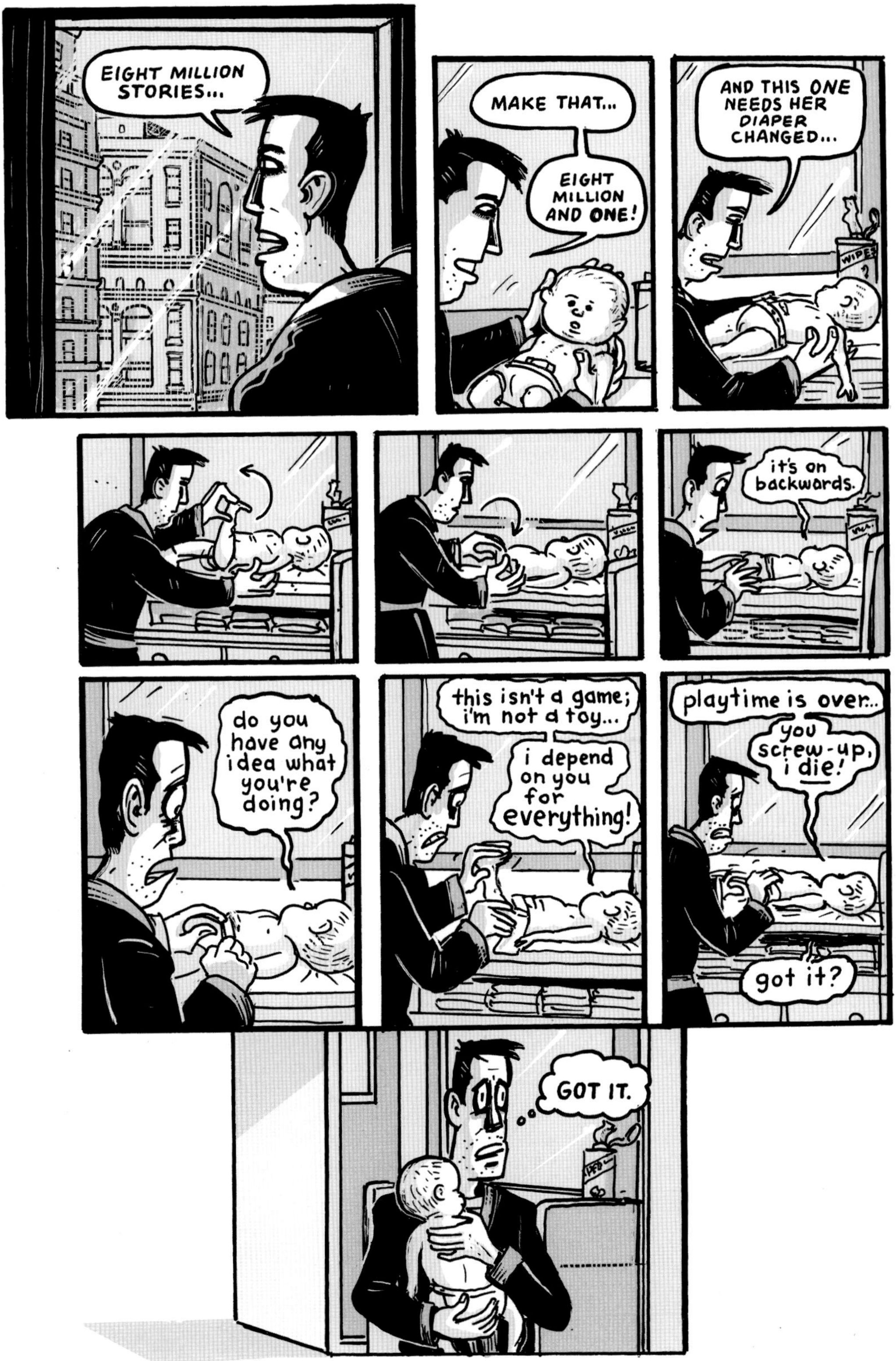
EIGHT MILLION STORIES...
MAKE THAT...
EIGHT MILLION AND ONE!
AND THIS ONE NEEDS HER DIAPER CHANGED...
. . .
WIPES
it's on backwards.
do you have any idea what you're doing?
this isn't a game; i'm not a toy...
i depend on you for everything!
playtime is over...
you screw-up, i die!
got it?
GOT IT.

PLOP!

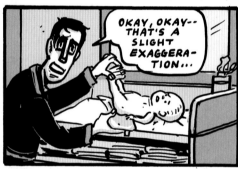

OKAY, OKAY-- THAT'S A SLIGHT EXAGGERA- TION...

BUT I'VE GOTTEN PRETTY GOOD AT THIS...

HAVEN'T I, MISS PEANUT?

wa, wa, wa...

WHAT YOU NEED NOW THOUGH, I CAN'T GIVE YOU...

wa, wa, wa.

SANDRA?

SANDRA-- ARE YOU ALRIGHT?

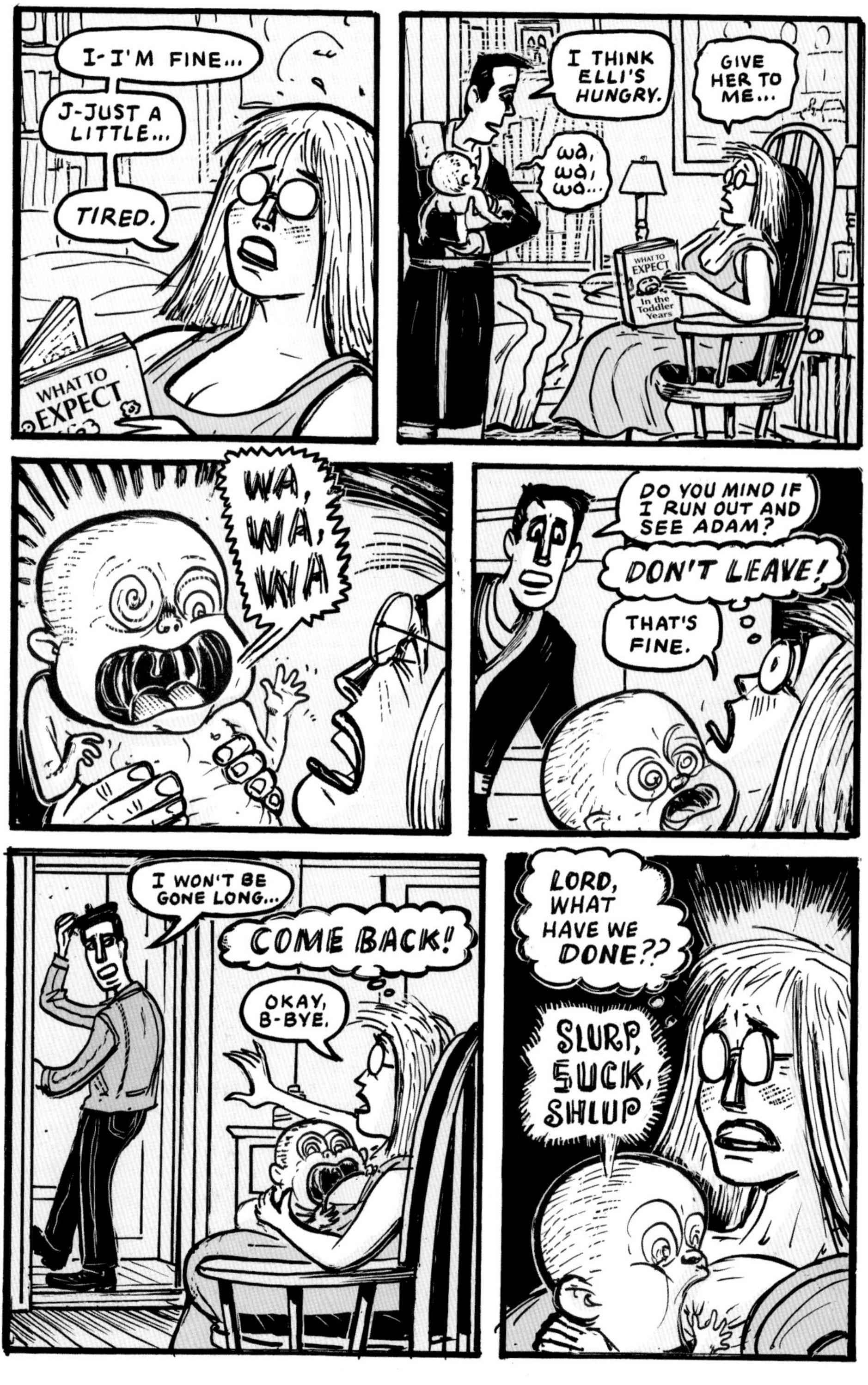
I-I'M FINE...
J-JUST A LITTLE...
TIRED.
WHAT TO EXPECT
I THINK ELLI'S HUNGRY.
WA, WA, WA...
GIVE HER TO ME...
WHAT TO EXPECT In the Toddler Years
WA, WA, WA
DO YOU MIND IF I RUN OUT AND SEE ADAM?
DON'T LEAVE!
THAT'S FINE.
I WON'T BE GONE LONG...
COME BACK!
OKAY, B-BYE.
LORD, WHAT HAVE WE DONE??
SLURP, SUCK, SHLUP

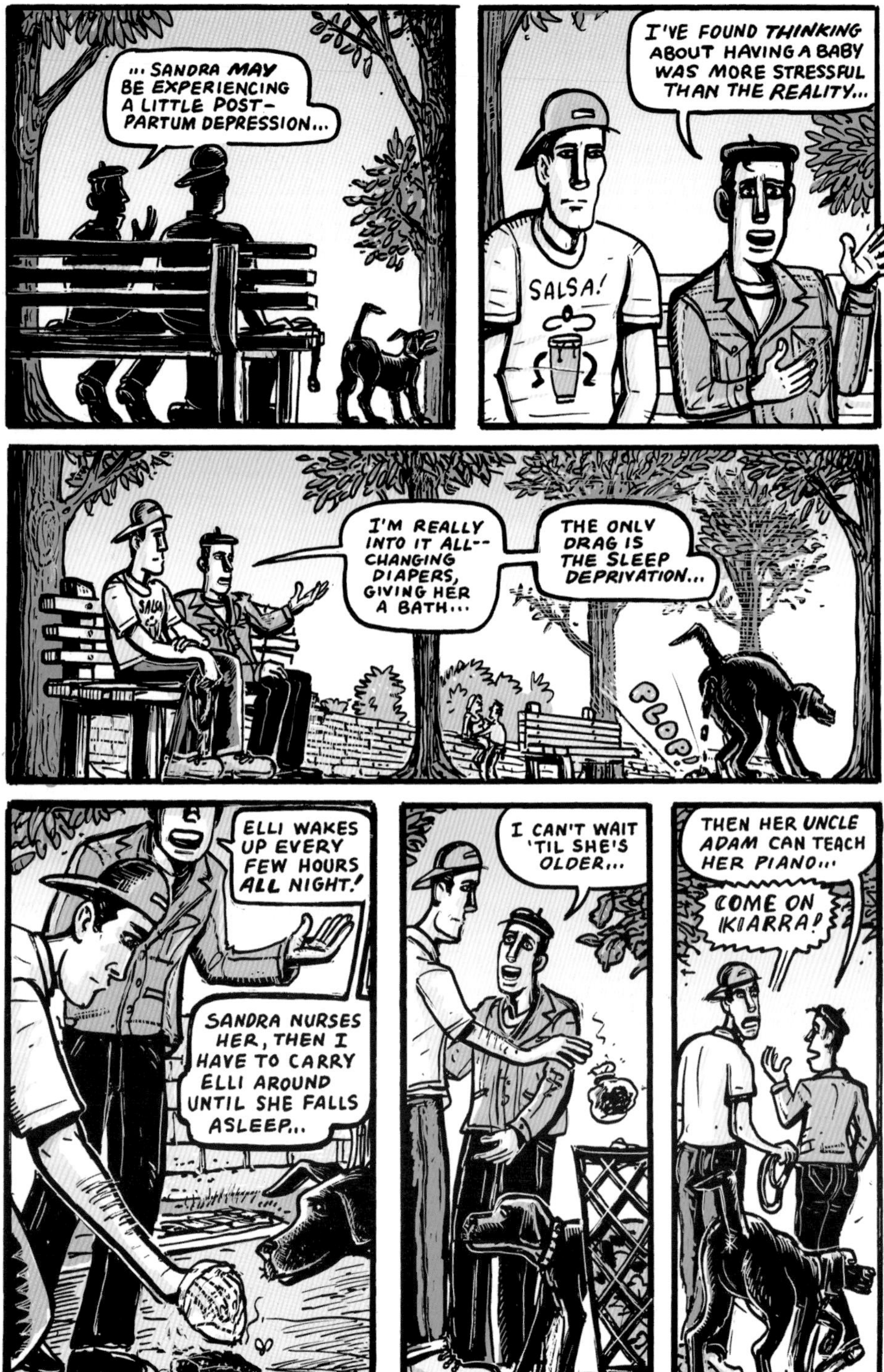
...SANDRA MAY BE EXPERIENCING A LITTLE POST-PARTUM DEPRESSION...
I'VE FOUND THINKING ABOUT HAVING A BABY WAS MORE STRESSFUL THAN THE REALITY...
SALSA!
I'M REALLY INTO IT ALL-- CHANGING DIAPERS, GIVING HER A BATH...
THE ONLY DRAG IS THE SLEEP DEPRIVATION...
PLOP!
ELLI WAKES UP EVERY FEW HOURS ALL NIGHT!
SANDRA NURSES HER, THEN I HAVE TO CARRY ELLI AROUND UNTIL SHE FALLS ASLEEP...
I CAN'T WAIT 'TIL SHE'S OLDER...
THEN HER UNCLE ADAM CAN TEACH HER PIANO...
COME ON KIARRA!

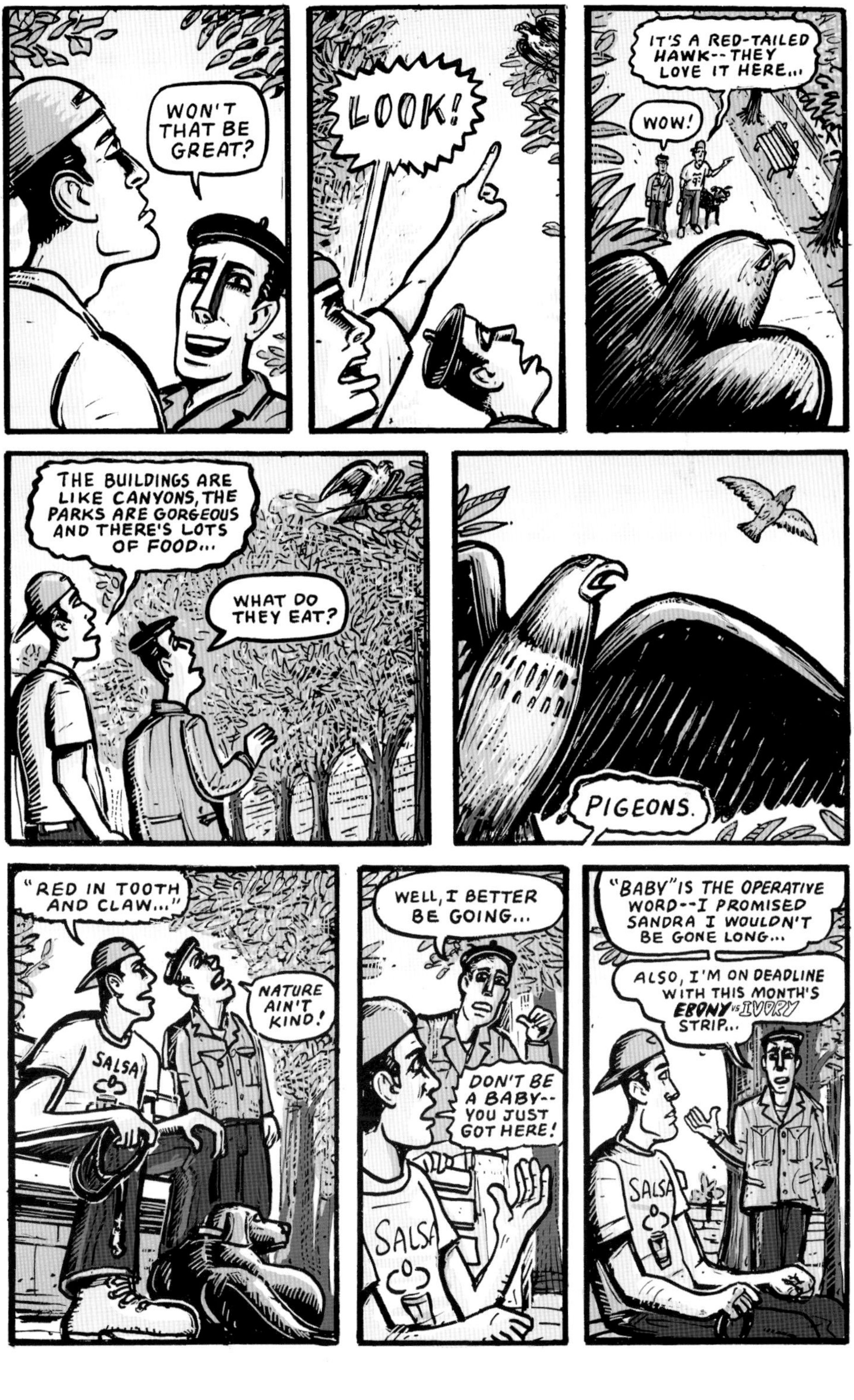
WON'T THAT BE GREAT?
LOOK!
IT'S A RED-TAILED HAWK--THEY LOVE IT HERE...
WOW!
THE BUILDINGS ARE LIKE CANYONS, THE PARKS ARE GORGEOUS AND THERE'S LOTS OF FOOD...
WHAT DO THEY EAT?
PIGEONS.
"RED IN TOOTH AND CLAW..."
NATURE AIN'T KIND!
SALSA
WELL, I BETTER BE GOING...
DON'T BE A BABY--YOU JUST GOT HERE!
SALSA
"BABY" IS THE OPERATIVE WORD--I PROMISED SANDRA I WOULDN'T BE GONE LONG...
ALSO, I'M ON DEADLINE WITH THIS MONTH'S EBONY VS IVORY STRIP...
SALSA

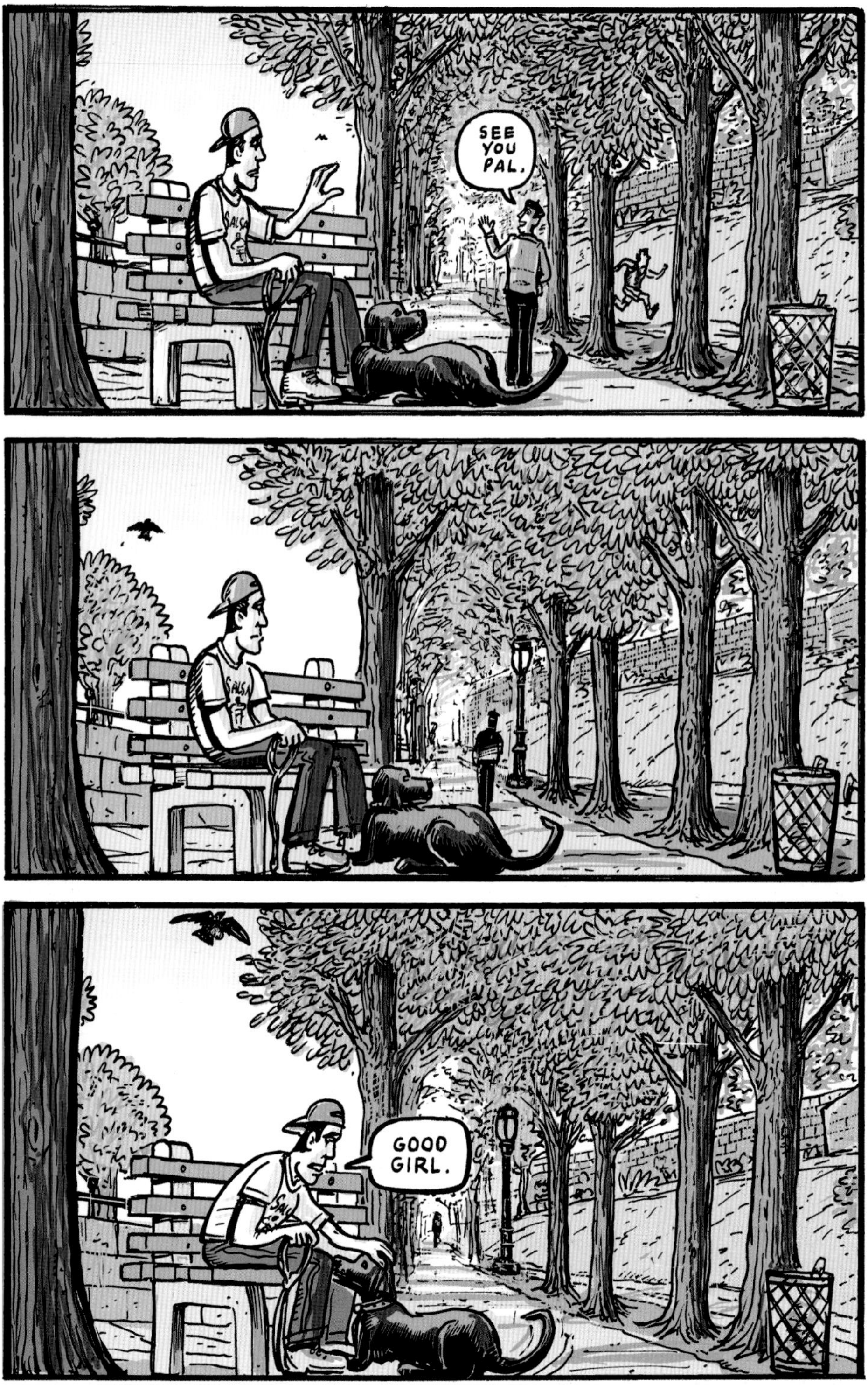
SEE YOU PAL.
GOOD GIRL.

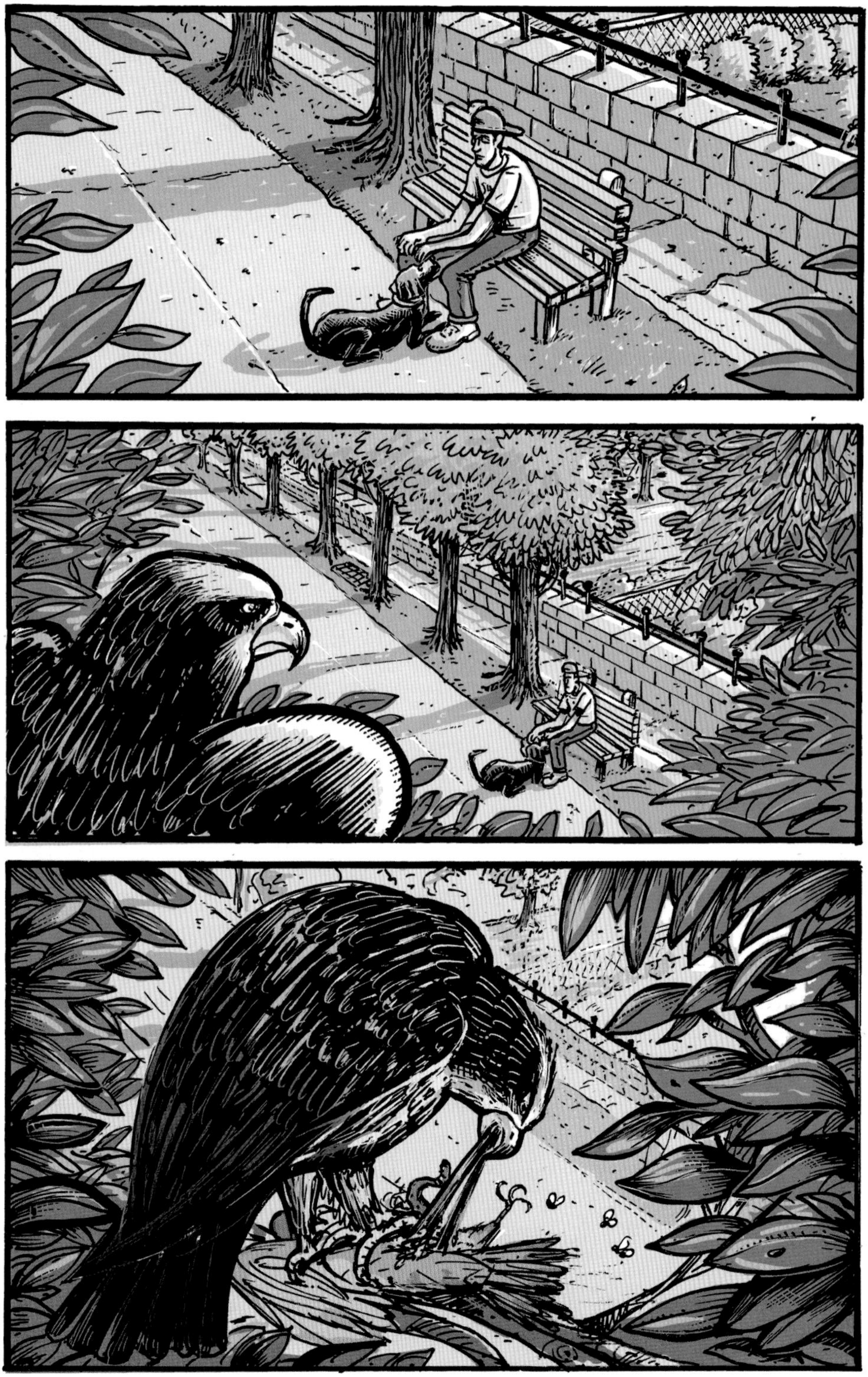

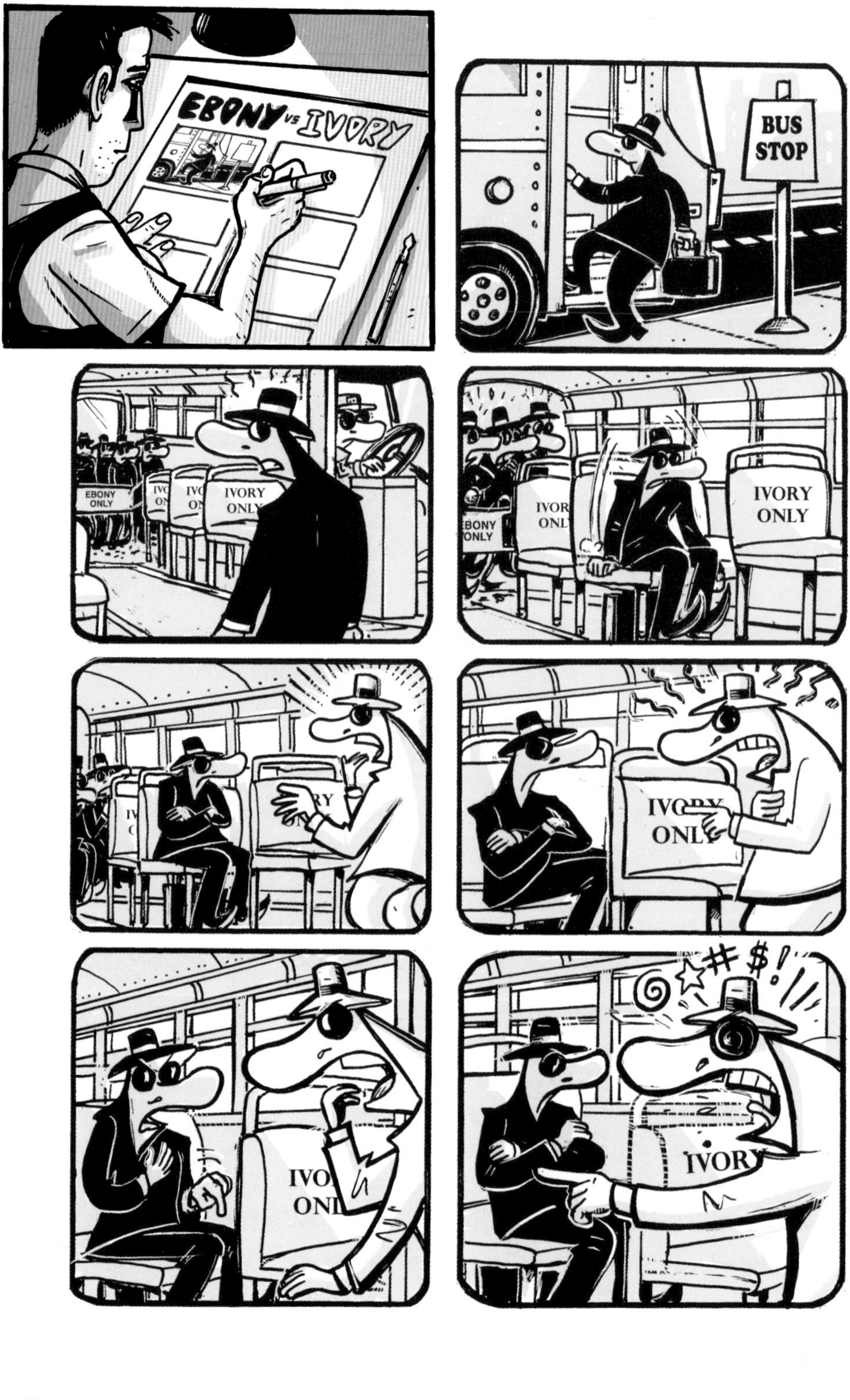
EBONY vs IVORY
BUS STOP
EBONY ONLY
IVORY ONLY
IVORY ONLY

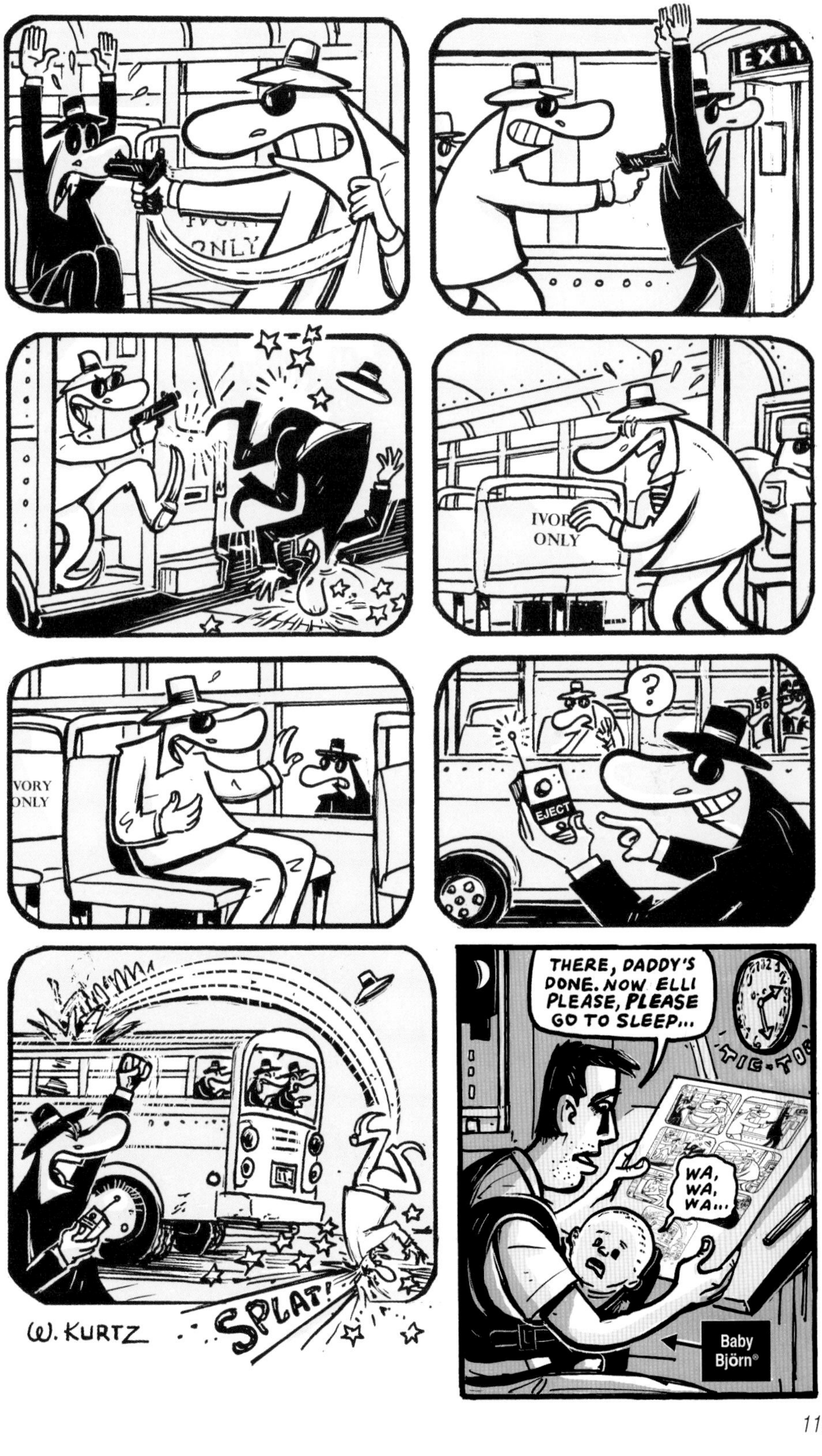
EXIT
IVORY
ONLY
EJECT
SPLAT!
W. KURTZ
THERE, DADDY'S DONE. NOW ELLI PLEASE, PLEASE GO TO SLEEP...
WA, WA, WA...
Baby Björn®

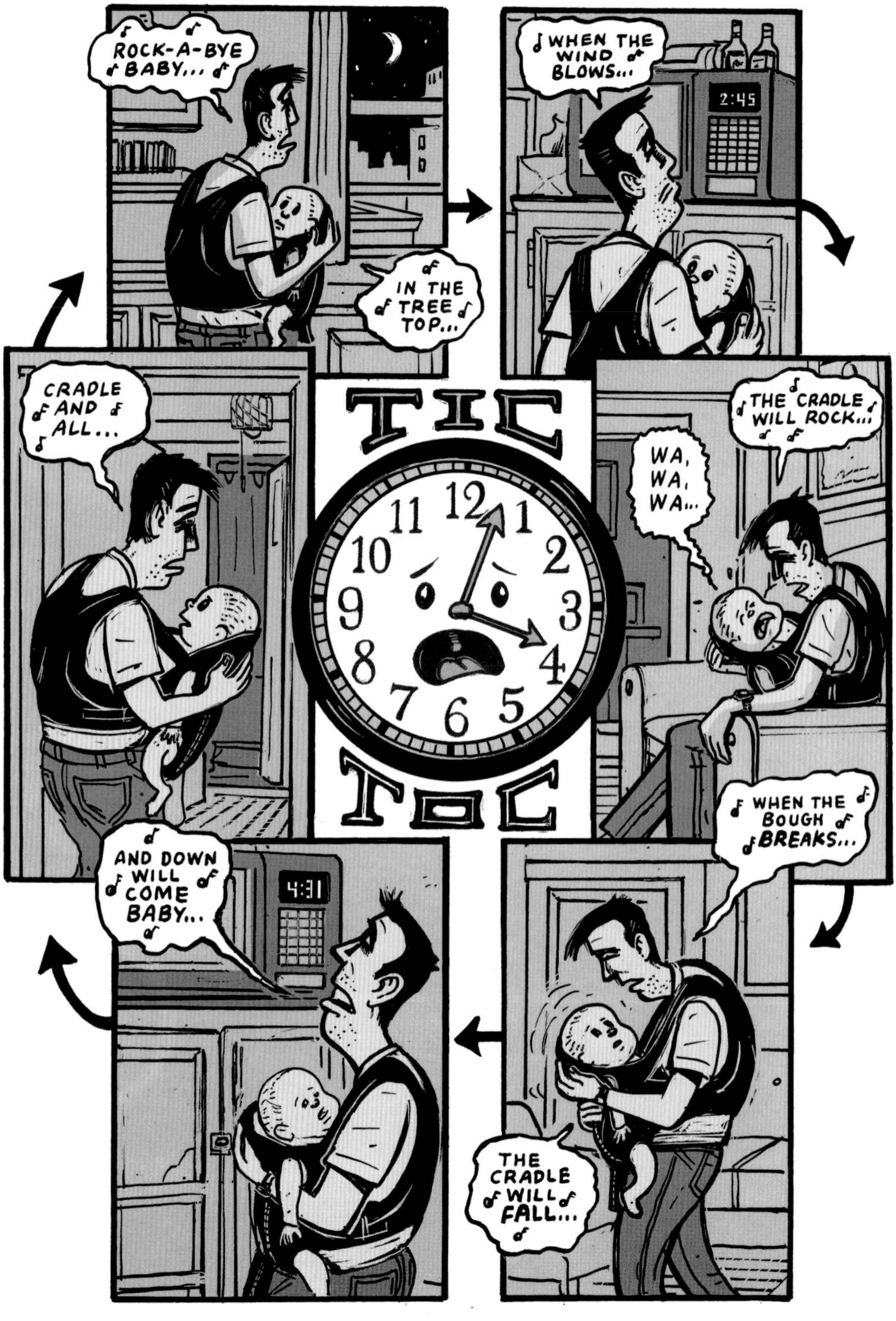
ROCK-A-BYE BABY...
IN THE TREE TOP...
WHEN THE WIND BLOWS...
2:45
THE CRADLE WILL ROCK...
WA, WA, WA...
TIC
TOC
WHEN THE BOUGH BREAKS...
THE CRADLE WILL FALL...
AND DOWN WILL COME BABY...
4:31
CRADLE AND ALL...

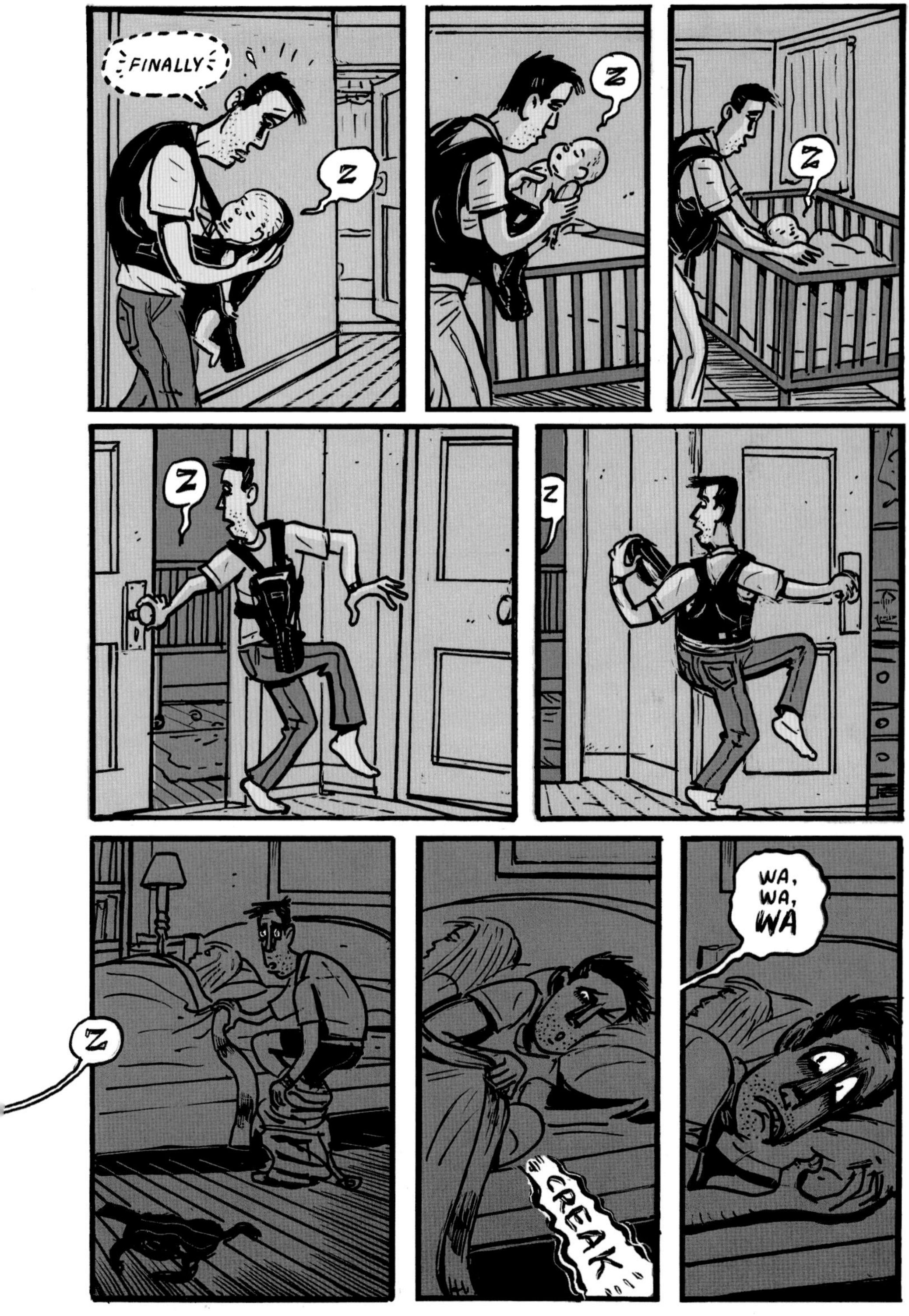
FINALLY
Z
Z
Z
Z
Z
Z
CREAK
WA, WA, WA

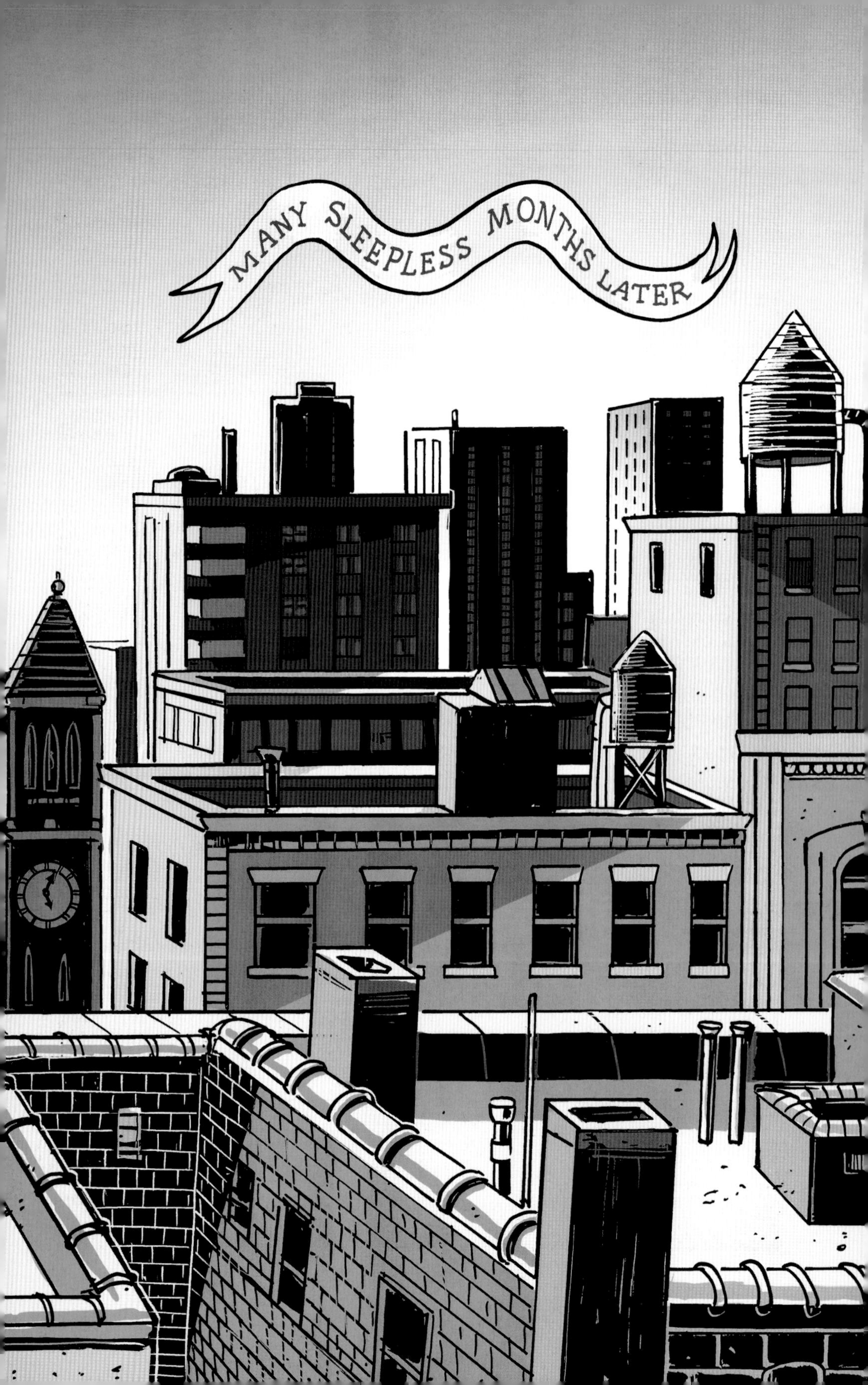
MANY SLEEPLESS MONTHS LATER

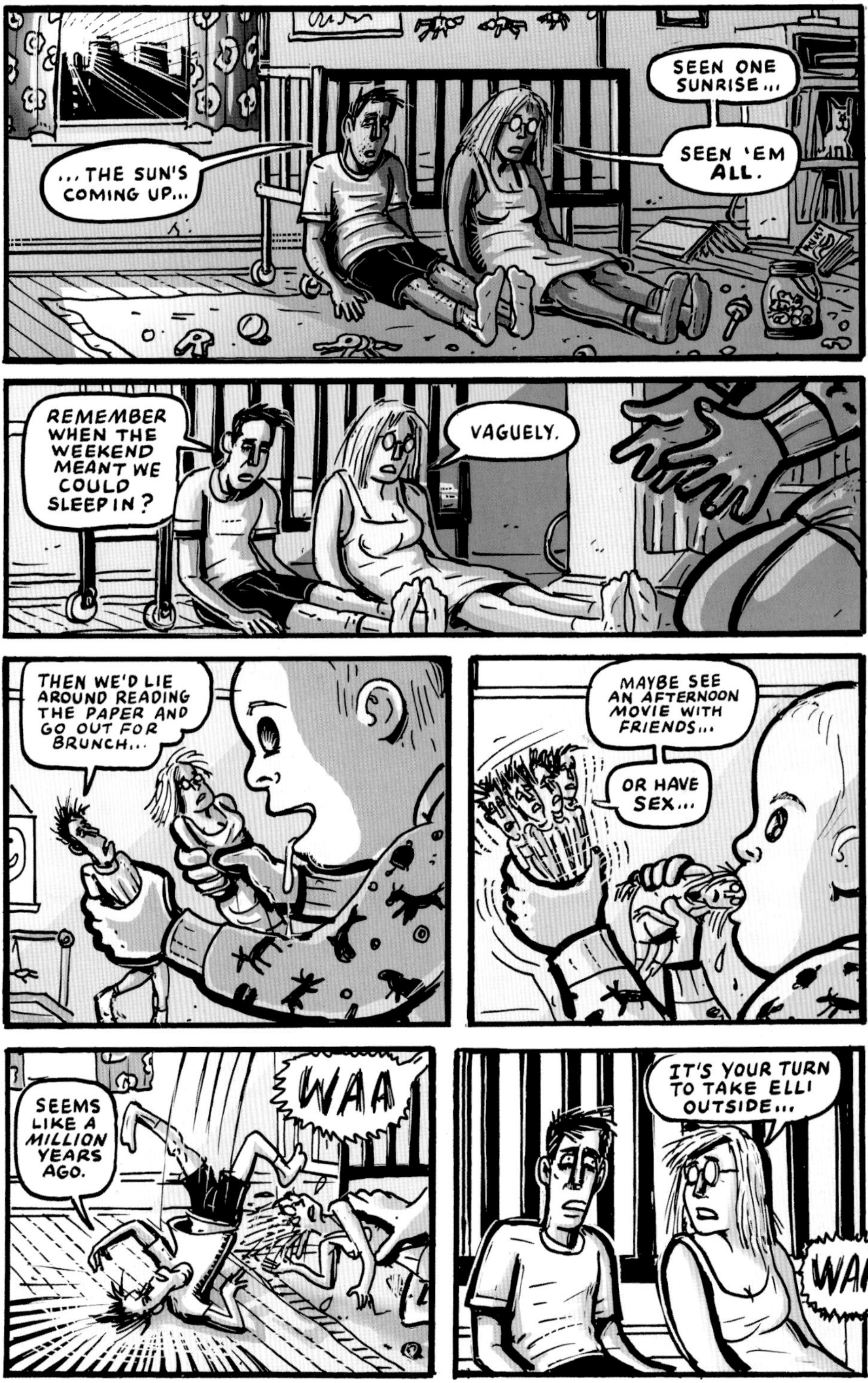
...THE SUN'S COMING UP...
SEEN ONE SUNRISE...
SEEN 'EM ALL.
REMEMBER WHEN THE WEEKEND MEANT WE COULD SLEEP IN?
VAGUELY.
THEN WE'D LIE AROUND READING THE PAPER AND GO OUT FOR BRUNCH...
MAYBE SEE AN AFTERNOON MOVIE WITH FRIENDS...
OR HAVE SEX...
SEEMS LIKE A MILLION YEARS AGO.
WAA
IT'S YOUR TURN TO TAKE ELLI OUTSIDE...
WAA

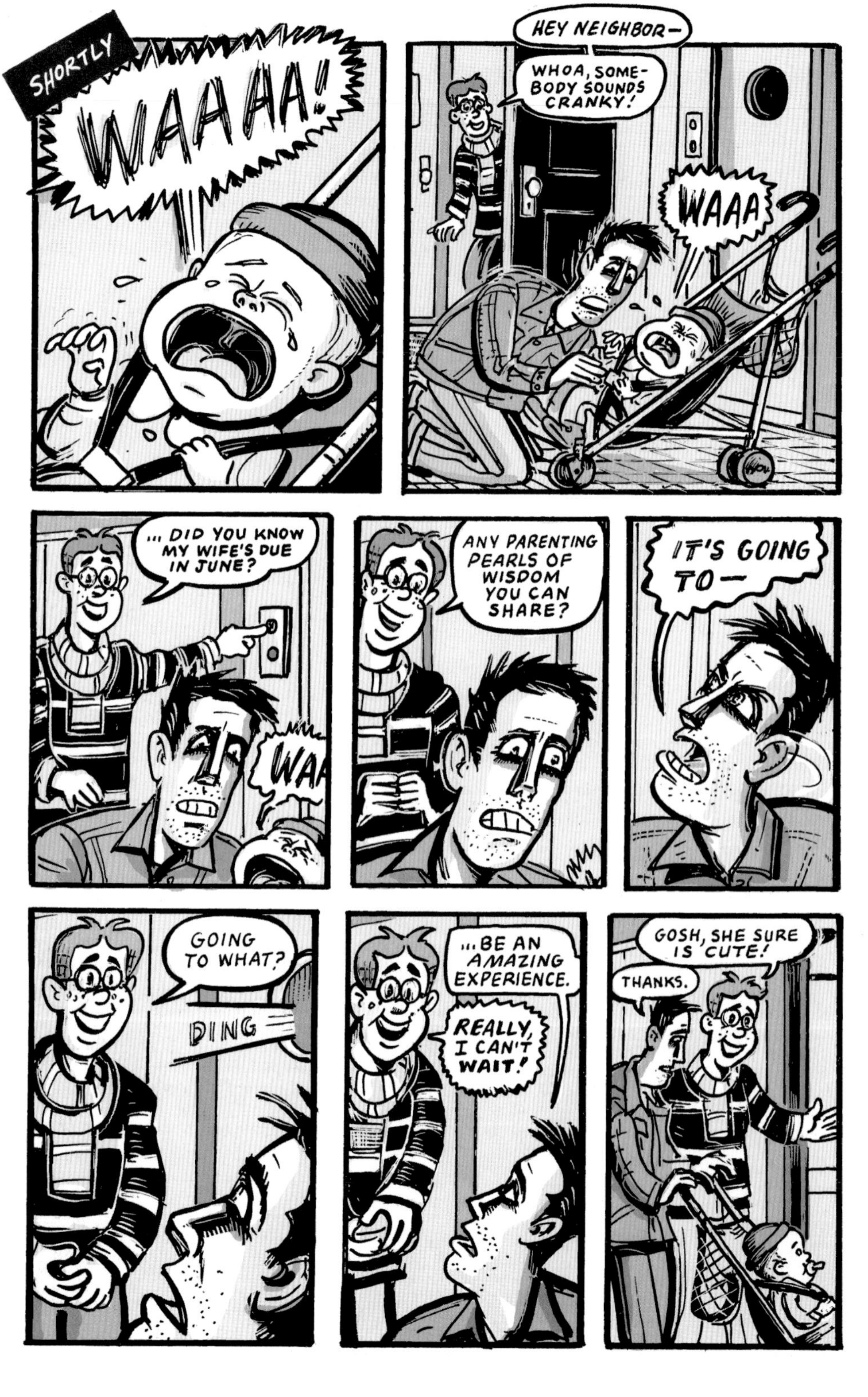
SHORTLY
WAAAAA!
HEY NEIGHBOR—
WHOA, SOME-BODY SOUNDS CRANKY!
WAAA
...DID YOU KNOW MY WIFE'S DUE IN JUNE?
WAA
ANY PARENTING PEARLS OF WISDOM YOU CAN SHARE?
IT'S GOING TO—
GOING TO WHAT?
DING
...BE AN AMAZING EXPERIENCE.
REALLY, I CAN'T WAIT!
GOSH, SHE SURE IS CUTE!
THANKS.

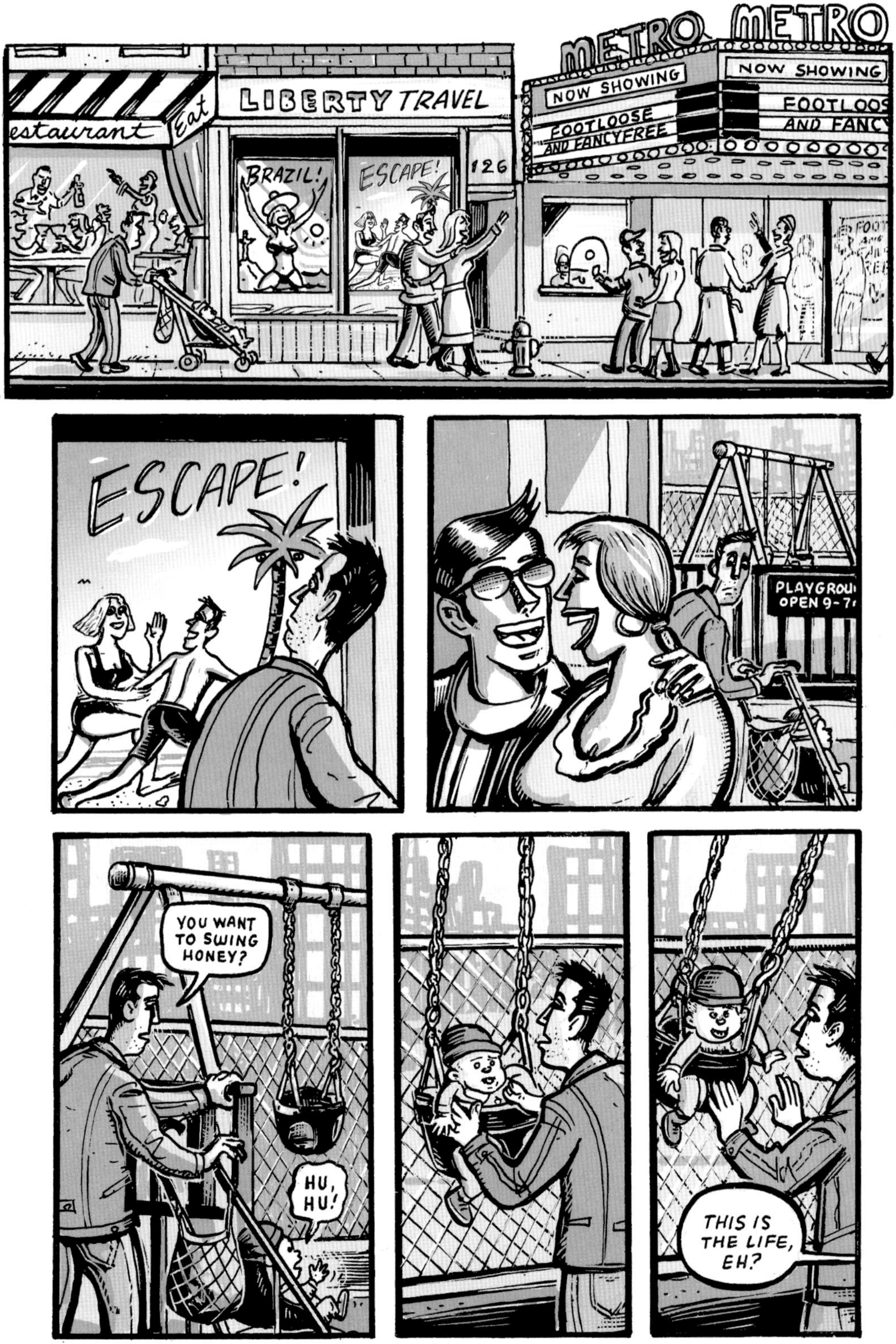
METRO METRO
NOW SHOWING
FOOTLOOSE AND FANCYFREE
LIBERTY TRAVEL
Eat
estaurant
BRAZIL!
ESCAPE!
126
ESCAPE!
PLAYGROU
OPEN 9-7
YOU WANT TO SWING HONEY?
HU, HU!
THIS IS THE LIFE, EH?

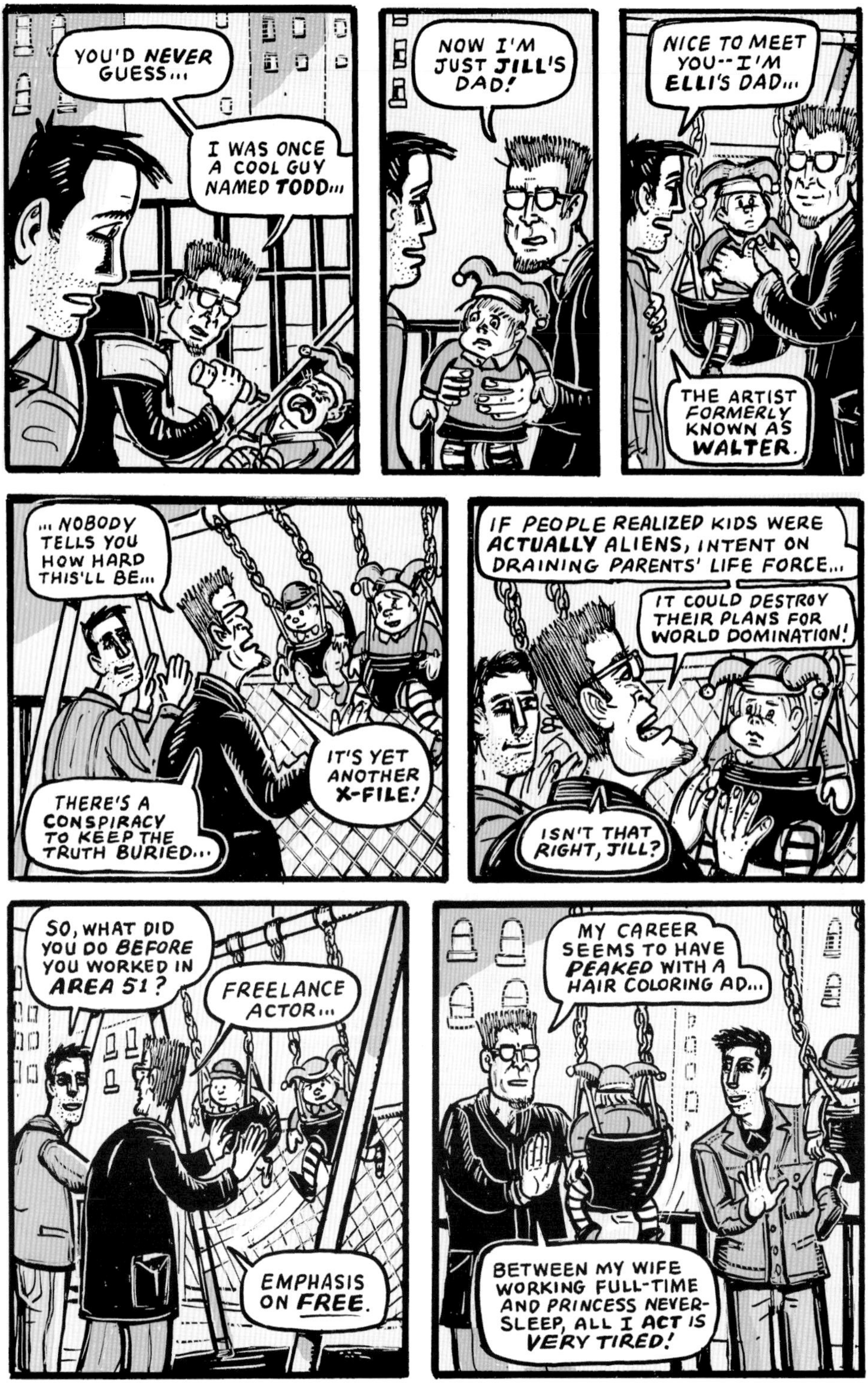
YOU'D NEVER GUESS...
I WAS ONCE A COOL GUY NAMED TODD...
NOW I'M JUST JILL'S DAD!
NICE TO MEET YOU--I'M ELLI'S DAD...
THE ARTIST FORMERLY KNOWN AS WALTER.
...NOBODY TELLS YOU HOW HARD THIS'LL BE...
THERE'S A CONSPIRACY TO KEEP THE TRUTH BURIED...
IT'S YET ANOTHER X-FILE!
IF PEOPLE REALIZED KIDS WERE ACTUALLY ALIENS, INTENT ON DRAINING PARENTS' LIFE FORCE...
IT COULD DESTROY THEIR PLANS FOR WORLD DOMINATION!
ISN'T THAT RIGHT, JILL?
SO, WHAT DID YOU DO BEFORE YOU WORKED IN AREA 51?
FREELANCE ACTOR...
EMPHASIS ON FREE.
MY CAREER SEEMS TO HAVE PEAKED WITH A HAIR COLORING AD...
BETWEEN MY WIFE WORKING FULL-TIME AND PRINCESS NEVER-SLEEP, ALL I ACT IS VERY TIRED!

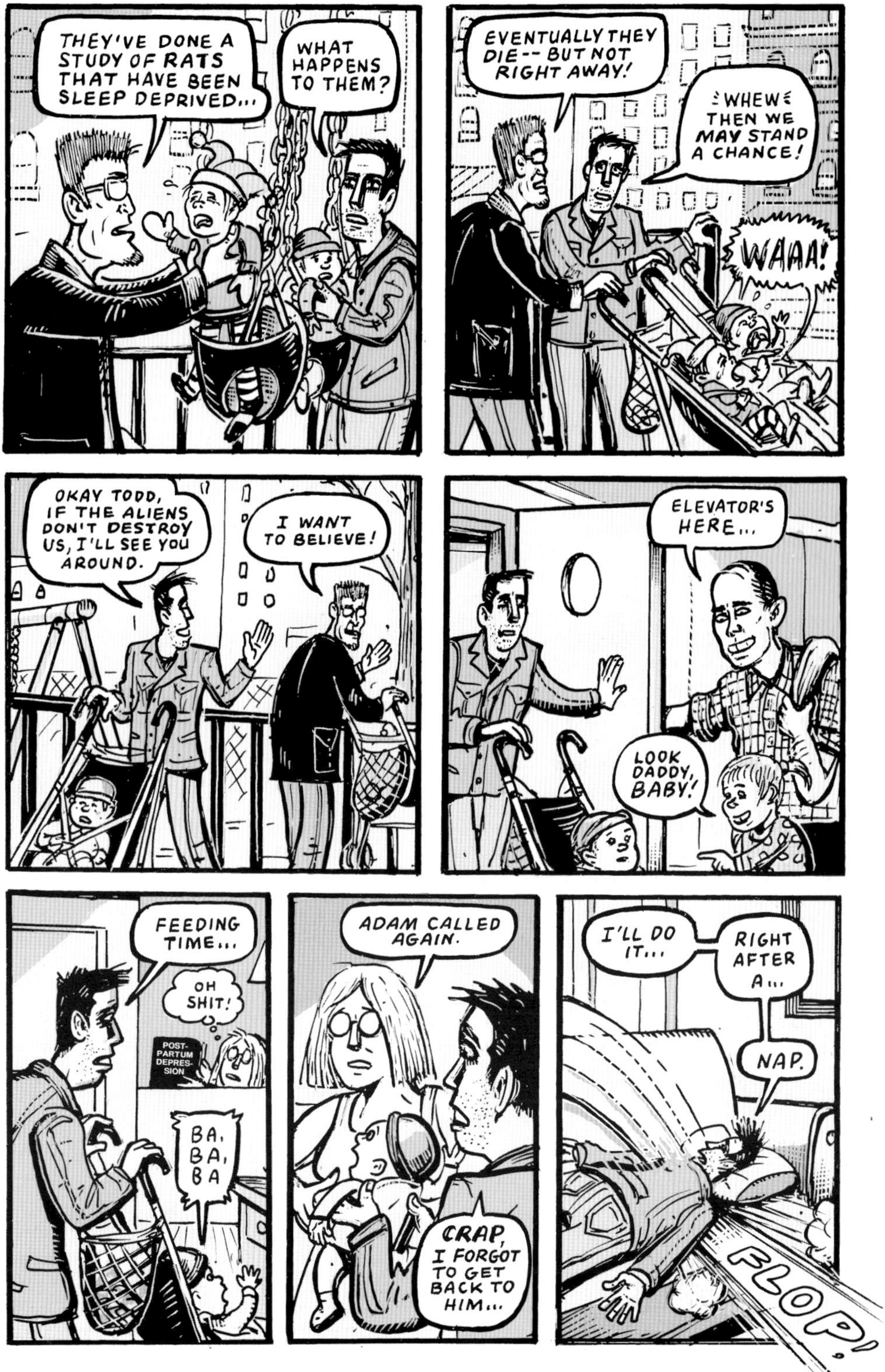
THEY'VE DONE A STUDY OF RATS THAT HAVE BEEN SLEEP DEPRIVED...
WHAT HAPPENS TO THEM?
EVENTUALLY THEY DIE-- BUT NOT RIGHT AWAY!
WHEW THEN WE MAY STAND A CHANCE!
WAAA!
OKAY TODD, IF THE ALIENS DON'T DESTROY US, I'LL SEE YOU AROUND.
I WANT TO BELIEVE!
ELEVATOR'S HERE...
LOOK DADDY, BABY!
FEEDING TIME...
OH SHIT!
POST-PARTUM DEPRES-SION
BA, BA, BA
ADAM CALLED AGAIN.
CRAP, I FORGOT TO GET BACK TO HIM...
I'LL DO IT...
RIGHT AFTER A...
NAP.
FLOP!

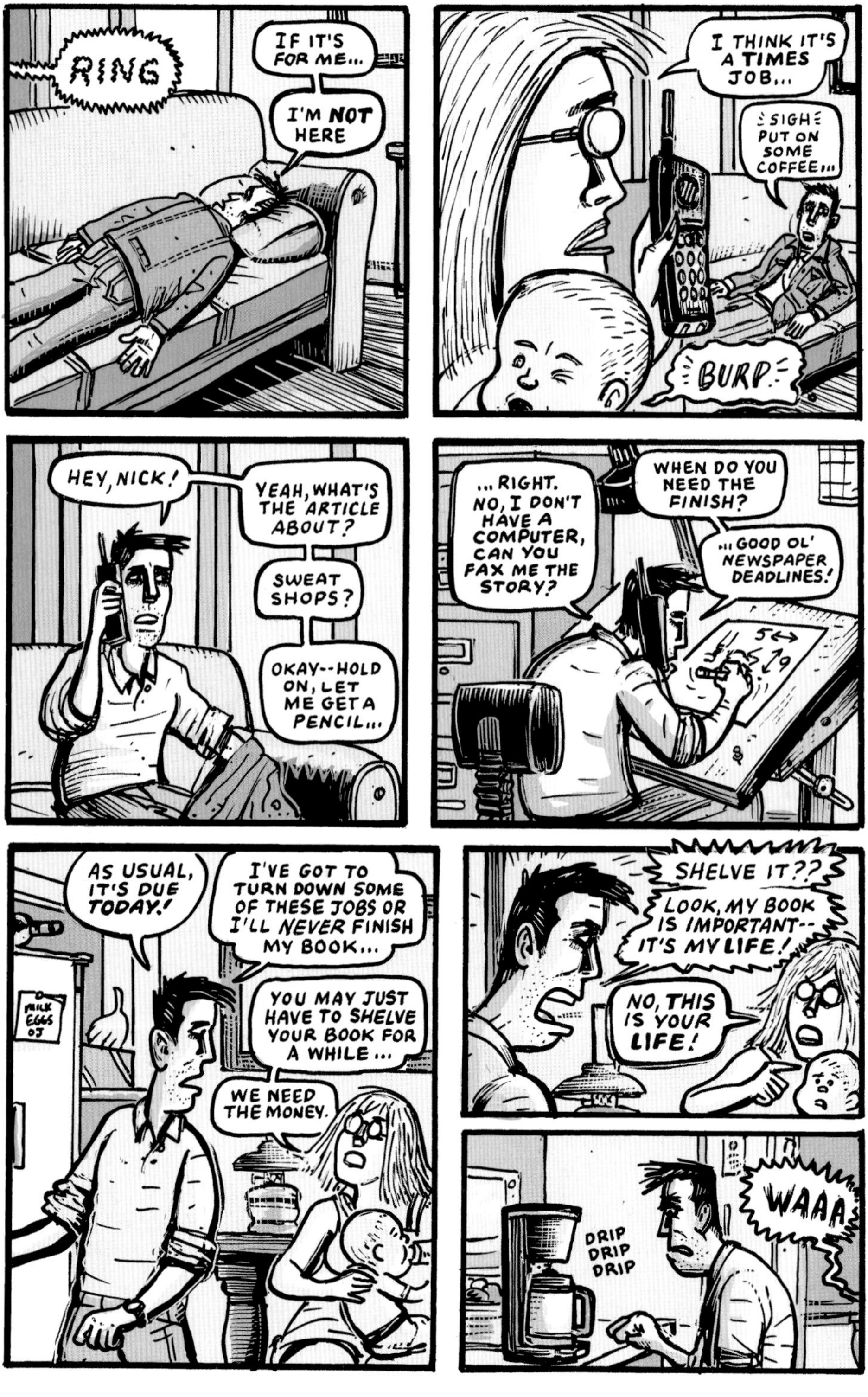

RING
IF IT'S FOR ME...
I'M NOT HERE
I THINK IT'S A TIMES JOB...
SIGH PUT ON SOME COFFEE...
BURP
HEY, NICK!
YEAH, WHAT'S THE ARTICLE ABOUT?
SWEAT SHOPS?
OKAY--HOLD ON, LET ME GET A PENCIL...
...RIGHT. NO, I DON'T HAVE A COMPUTER, CAN YOU FAX ME THE STORY?
WHEN DO YOU NEED THE FINISH?
...GOOD OL' NEWSPAPER DEADLINES!
AS USUAL, IT'S DUE TODAY!
I'VE GOT TO TURN DOWN SOME OF THESE JOBS OR I'LL NEVER FINISH MY BOOK...
YOU MAY JUST HAVE TO SHELVE YOUR BOOK FOR A WHILE...
WE NEED THE MONEY.
MILK EGGS OJ
SHELVE IT??
LOOK, MY BOOK IS IMPORTANT-- IT'S MY LIFE!
NO, THIS IS YOUR LIFE!
DRIP DRIP DRIP
WAAA

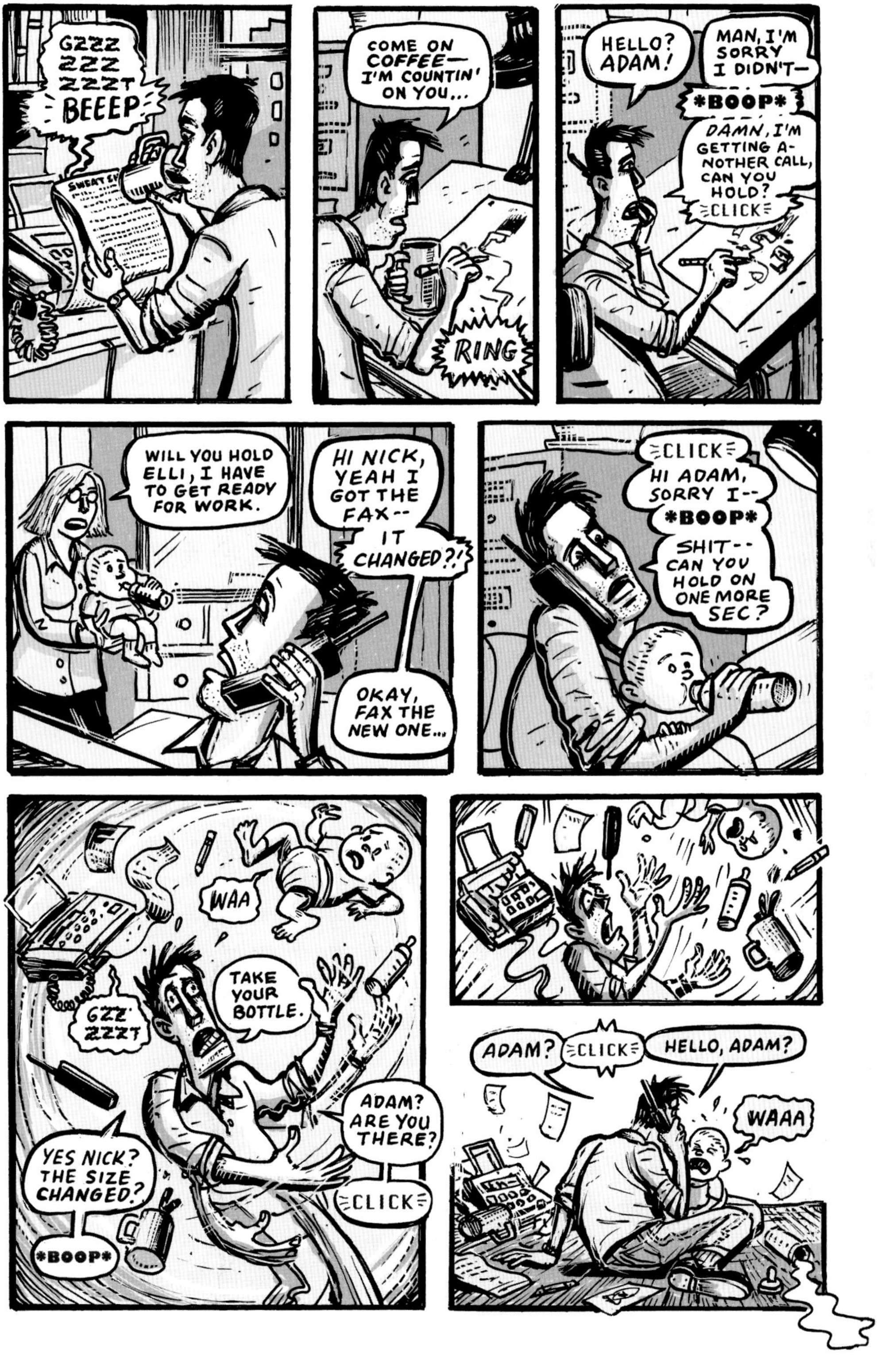
GZZZ ZZZ ZZZT BEEEP
COME ON COFFEE— I'M COUNTIN' ON YOU...
RING
HELLO? ADAM!
MAN, I'M SORRY I DIDN'T—
BOOP
DAMN, I'M GETTING ANOTHER CALL, CAN YOU HOLD?
CLICK
WILL YOU HOLD ELLI, I HAVE TO GET READY FOR WORK.
HI NICK, YEAH I GOT THE FAX--
IT CHANGED?!
OKAY, FAX THE NEW ONE...
CLICK
HI ADAM, SORRY I--
BOOP
SHIT-- CAN YOU HOLD ON ONE MORE SEC?
WAA
TAKE YOUR BOTTLE.
GZZ ZZZT
ADAM? ARE YOU THERE?
CLICK
YES NICK? THE SIZE CHANGED?
BOOP
ADAM?
CLICK
HELLO, ADAM?
WAAA

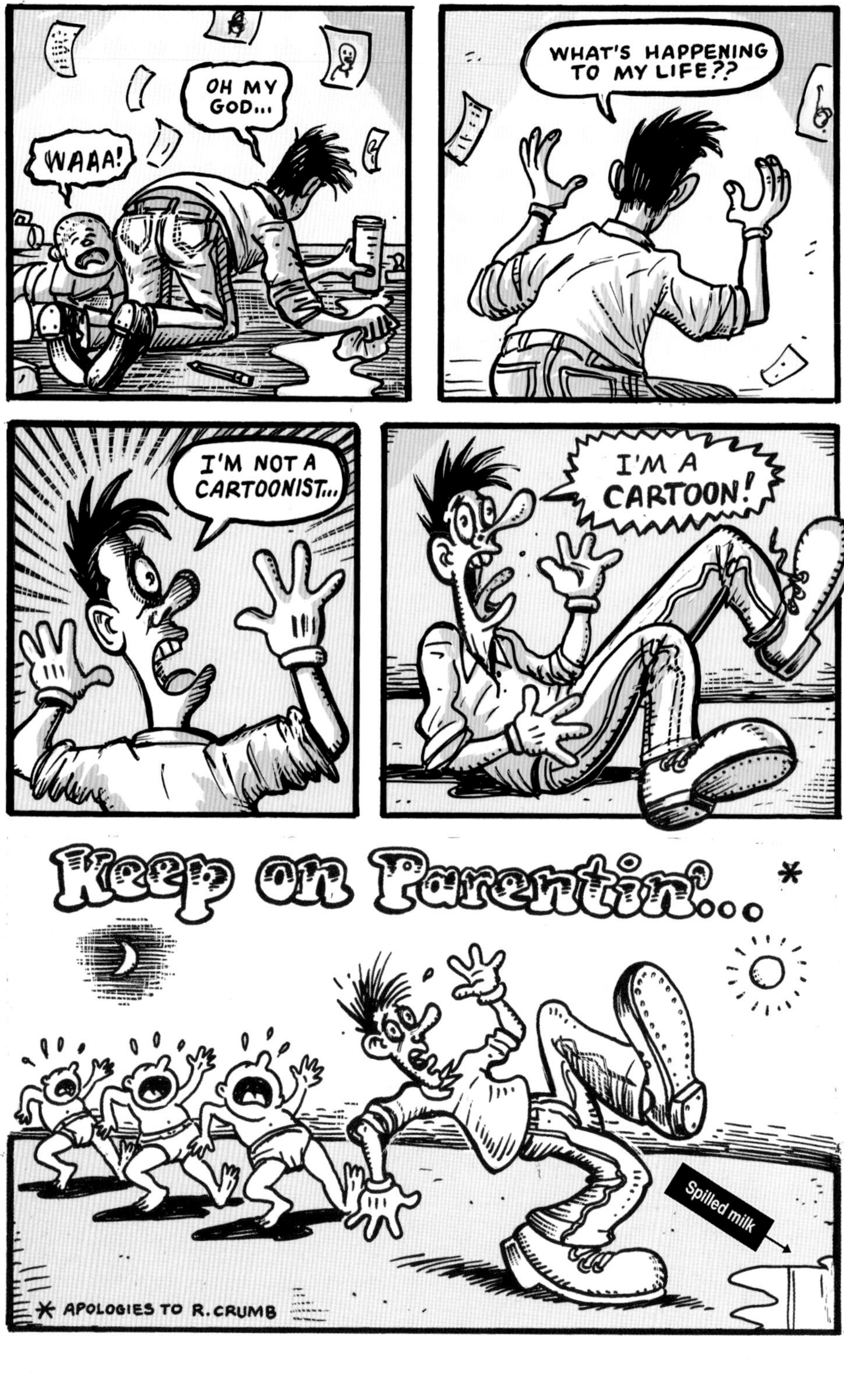
WAAA!
OH MY GOD...
WHAT'S HAPPENING TO MY LIFE??
I'M NOT A CARTOONIST...
I'M A CARTOON!
Keep on Parentin'...*
Spilled milk
* APOLOGIES TO R. CRUMB

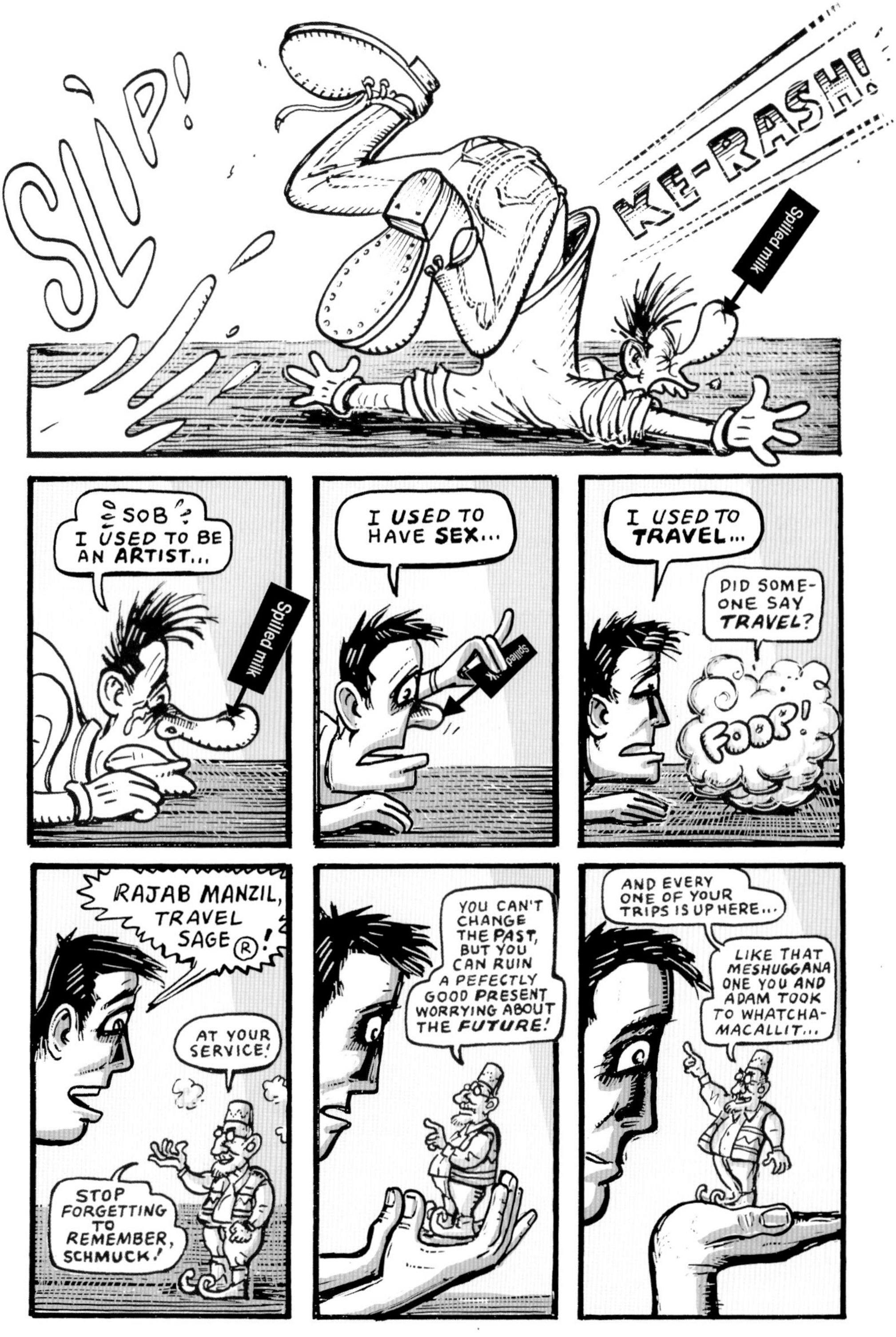
SLIP!
KE-RASH!
Spilled milk
SOB I USED TO BE AN ARTIST...
Spilled milk
I USED TO HAVE SEX...
I USED TO TRAVEL...
DID SOME-ONE SAY TRAVEL?
FOOP!
RAJAB MANZIL, TRAVEL SAGE®!
AT YOUR SERVICE!
STOP FORGETTING TO REMEMBER, SCHMUCK!
YOU CAN'T CHANGE THE PAST, BUT YOU CAN RUIN A PEFECTLY GOOD PRESENT WORRYING ABOUT THE FUTURE!
AND EVERY ONE OF YOUR TRIPS IS UP HERE...
LIKE THAT MESHUGGANA ONE YOU AND ADAM TOOK TO WHATCHA-MACALLIT...

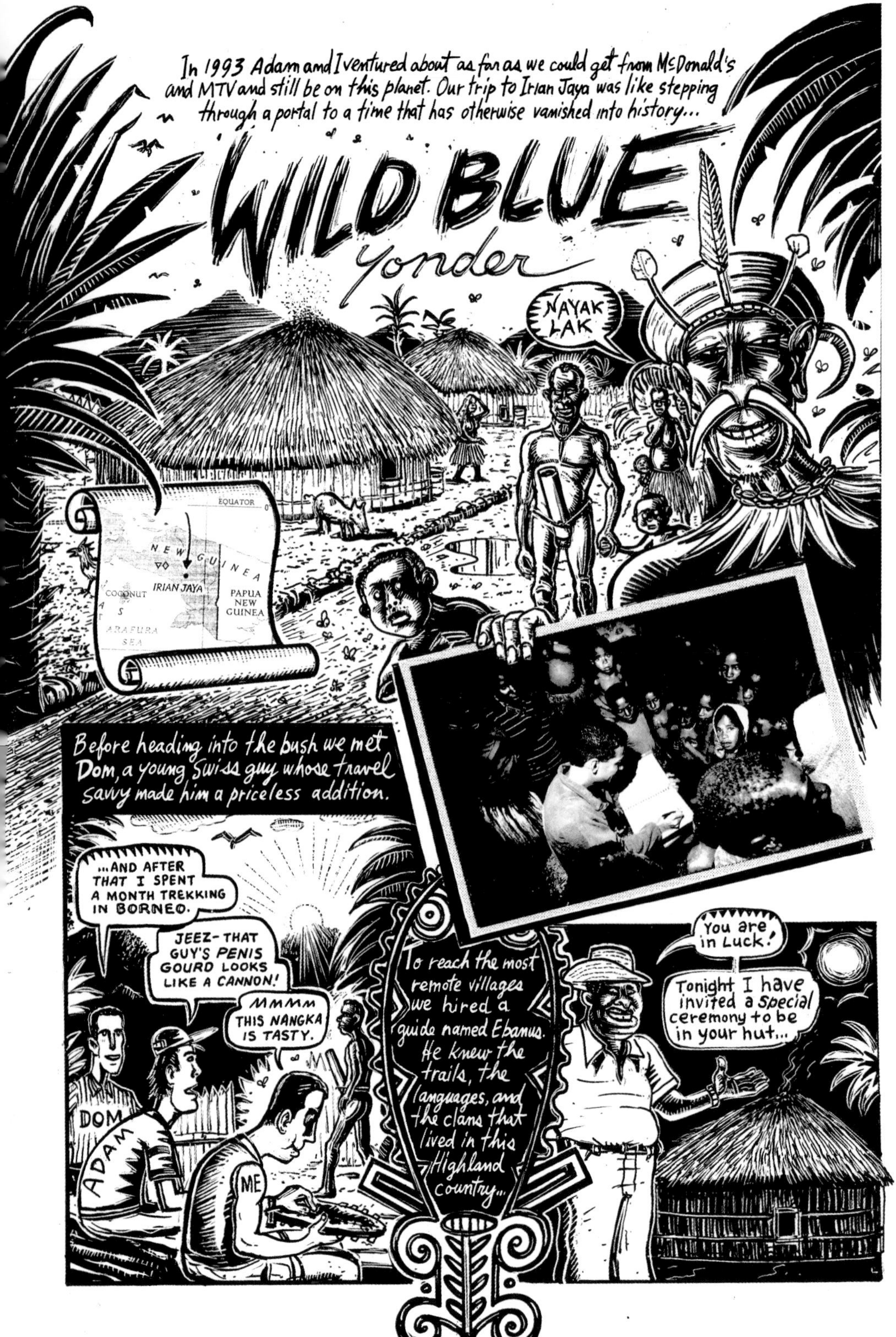

In 1993 Adam and I ventured about as far as we could get from McDonald's and MTV and still be on this planet. Our trip to Irian Jaya was like stepping through a portal to a time that has otherwise vanished into history...
WILD BLUE yonder
NAYAK LAK
EQUATOR
NEW GUINEA
IRIAN JAYA
PAPUA NEW GUINEA
COCONUT
ARAFURA SEA
Before heading into the bush we met Dom, a young Swiss guy whose travel savvy made him a priceless addition.
...AND AFTER THAT I SPENT A MONTH TREKKING IN BORNEO.
JEEZ- THAT GUY'S PENIS GOURD LOOKS LIKE A CANNON!
MMMM THIS NANGKA IS TASTY.
DOM
ADAM
ME
To reach the most remote villages we hired a guide named Ebanus. He knew the trails, the languages, and the clans that lived in this Highland country...
You are in Luck!
Tonight I have invited a special ceremony to be in your hut...

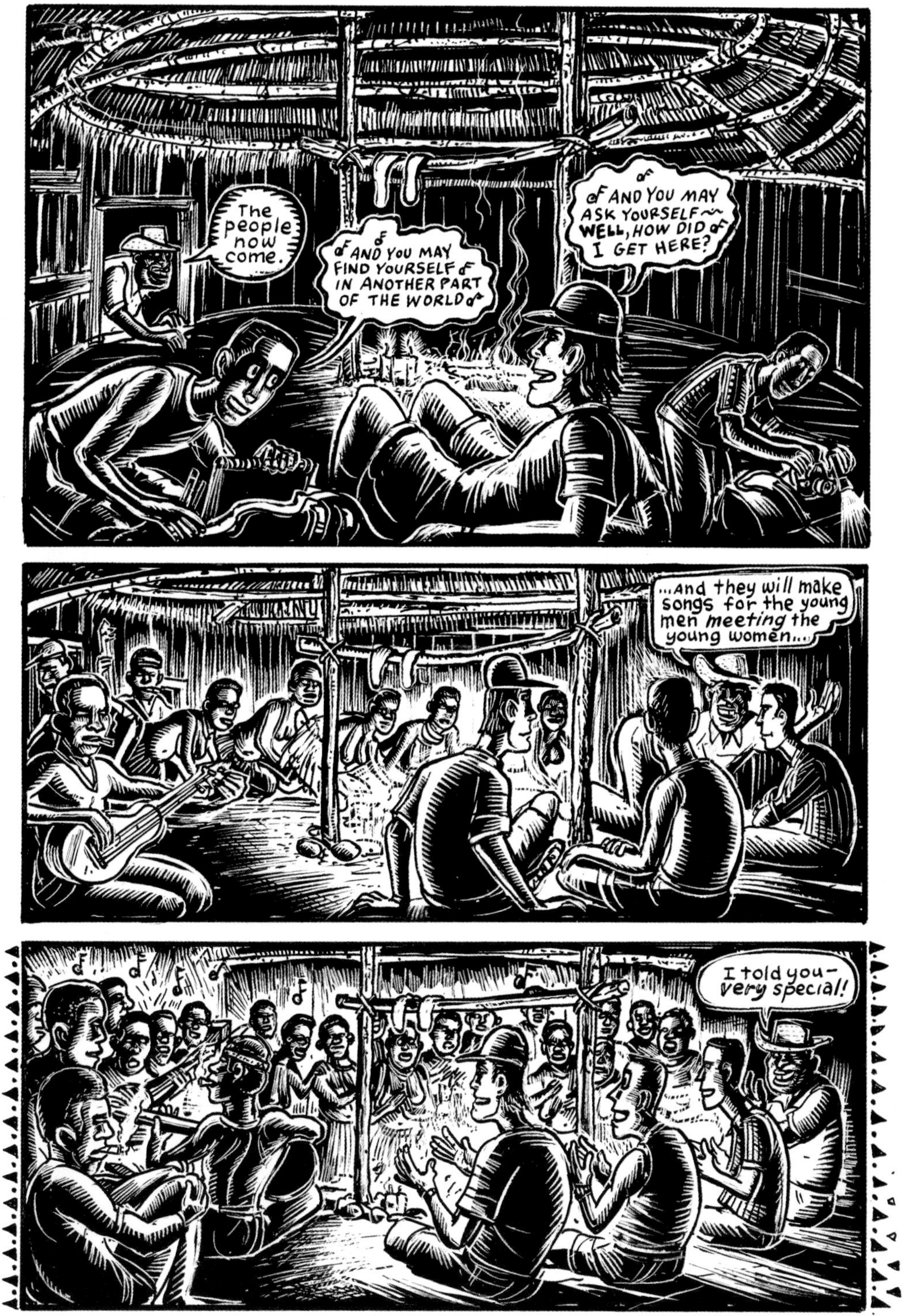
The people now come.
AND YOU MAY FIND YOURSELF IN ANOTHER PART OF THE WORLD
AND YOU MAY ASK YOURSELF~~ WELL, HOW DID I GET HERE?
...And they will make songs for the young men meeting the young women...
I told you-very special!

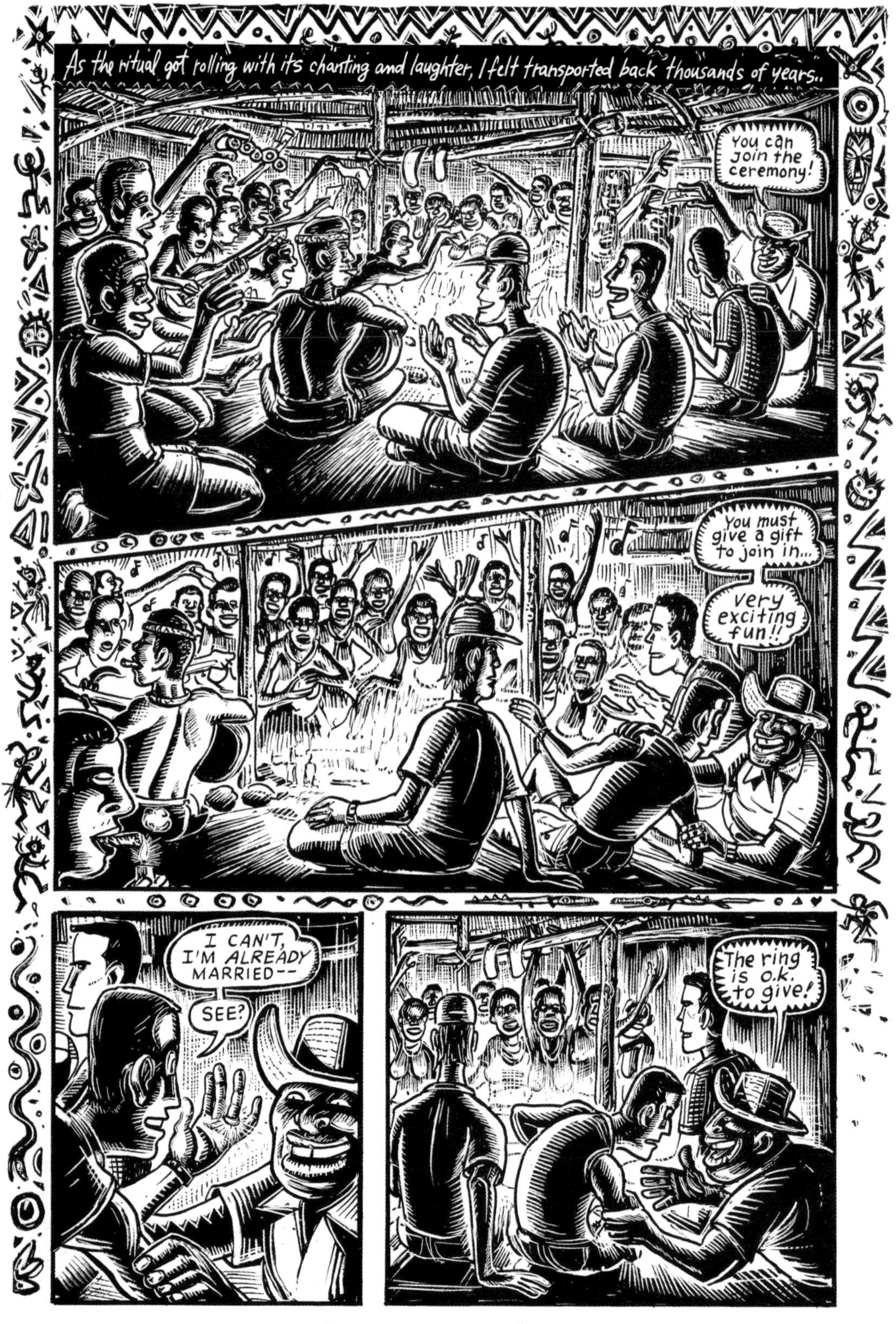
As the ritual got rolling with its chanting and laughter, I felt transported back thousands of years..
You can join the ceremony!
You must give a gift to join in...
very exciting fun!!
I CAN'T, I'M ALREADY MARRIED--
SEE?
The ring is o.k. to give!

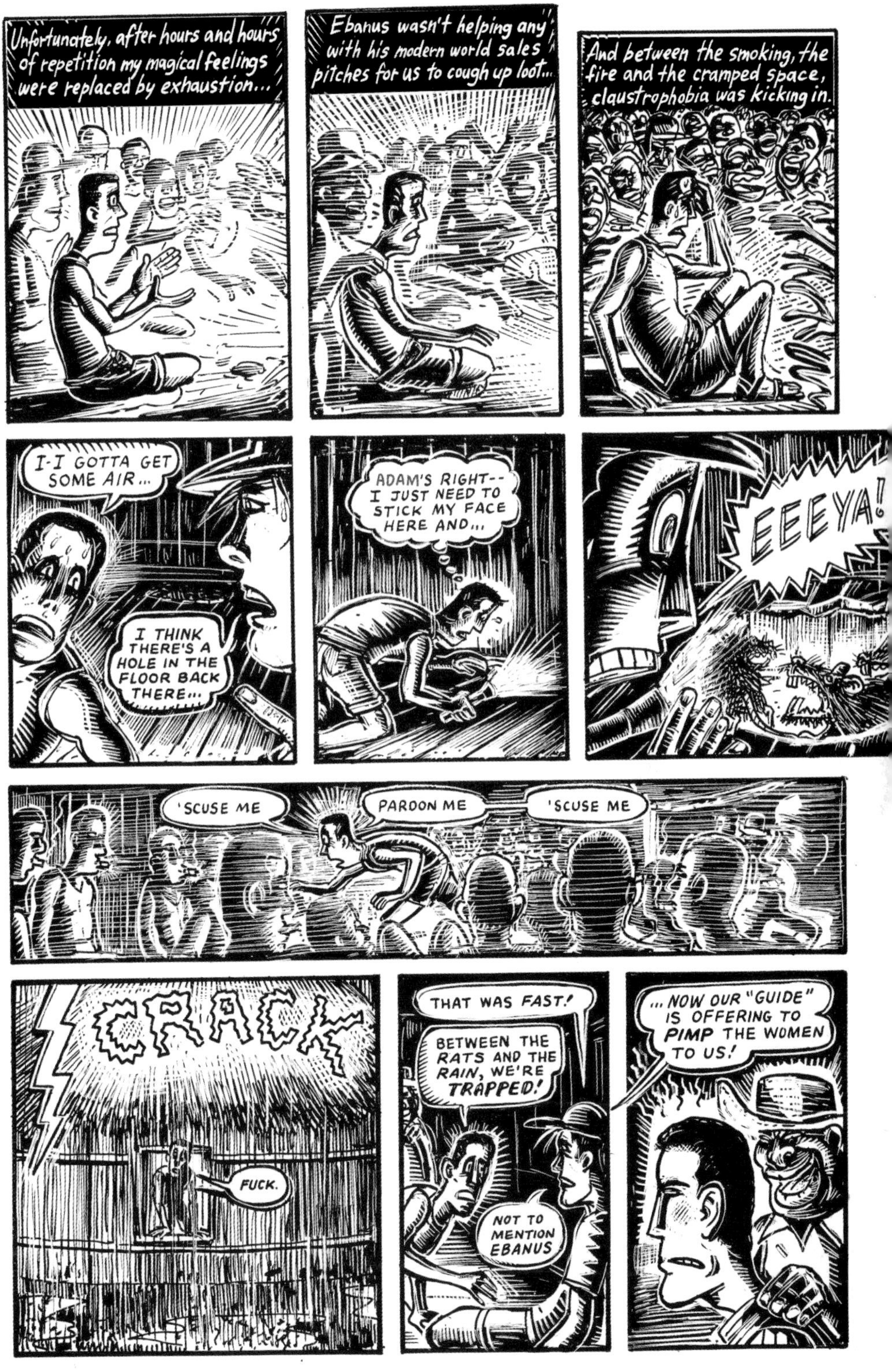
Unfortunately, after hours and hours of repetition my magical feelings were replaced by exhaustion...
Ebanus wasn't helping any with his modern world sales pitches for us to cough up loot...
And between the smoking, the fire and the cramped space, claustrophobia was kicking in.
I-I GOTTA GET SOME AIR...
I THINK THERE'S A HOLE IN THE FLOOR BACK THERE...
ADAM'S RIGHT-- I JUST NEED TO STICK MY FACE HERE AND...
EEEYA!
'SCUSE ME
PARDON ME
'SCUSE ME
CRACK
FUCK.
THAT WAS FAST!
BETWEEN THE RATS AND THE RAIN, WE'RE TRAPPED!
NOT TO MENTION EBANUS
...NOW OUR "GUIDE" IS OFFERING TO PIMP THE WOMEN TO US!

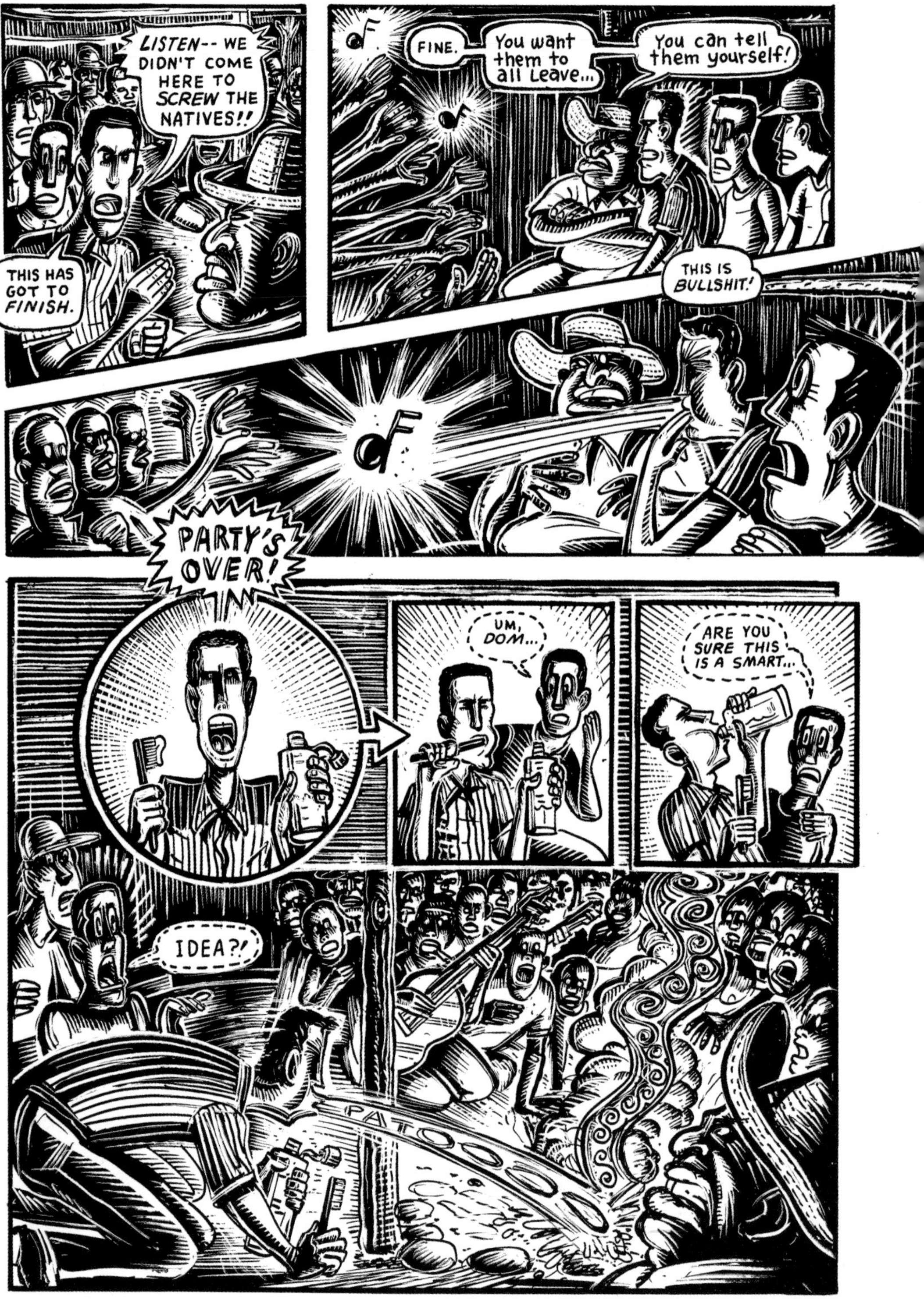
LISTEN-- WE DIDN'T COME HERE TO SCREW THE NATIVES!!
THIS HAS GOT TO FINISH.
FINE.
You want them to all Leave...
You can tell them yourself!
THIS IS BULLSHIT!
PARTY'S OVER!
UM, DOM...
ARE YOU SURE THIS IS A SMART...
IDEA?!
PATOOOOO

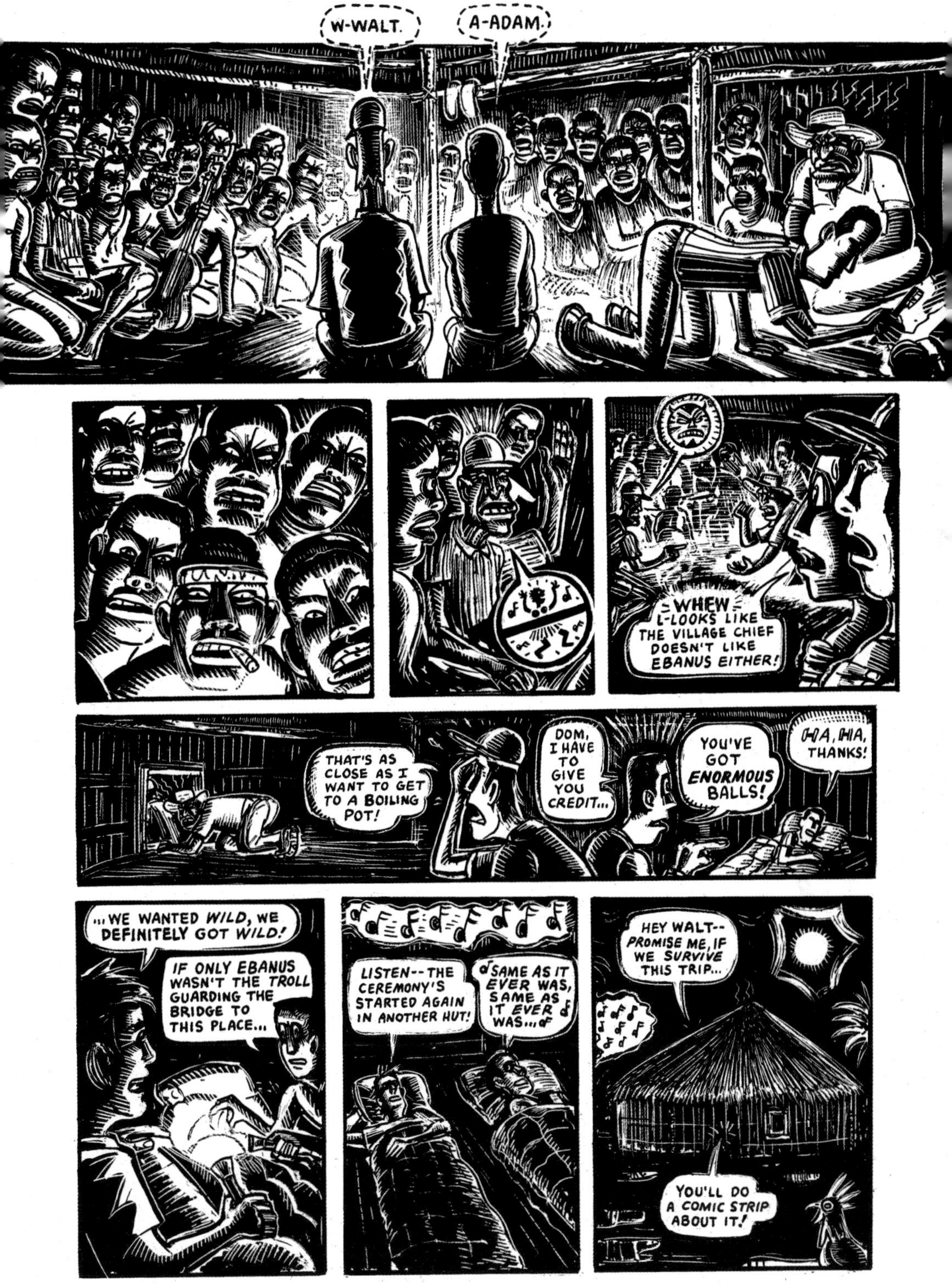
W-WALT.
A-ADAM.
WHEW
L-LOOKS LIKE THE VILLAGE CHIEF DOESN'T LIKE EBANUS EITHER!
THAT'S AS CLOSE AS I WANT TO GET TO A BOILING POT!
DOM, I HAVE TO GIVE YOU CREDIT...
YOU'VE GOT ENORMOUS BALLS!
HA, HA, THANKS!
...WE WANTED WILD, WE DEFINITELY GOT WILD!
IF ONLY EBANUS WASN'T THE TROLL GUARDING THE BRIDGE TO THIS PLACE...
LISTEN--THE CEREMONY'S STARTED AGAIN IN ANOTHER HUT!
SAME AS IT EVER WAS, SAME AS IT EVER WAS...
HEY WALT-- PROMISE ME, IF WE SURVIVE THIS TRIP...
YOU'LL DO A COMIC STRIP ABOUT IT!

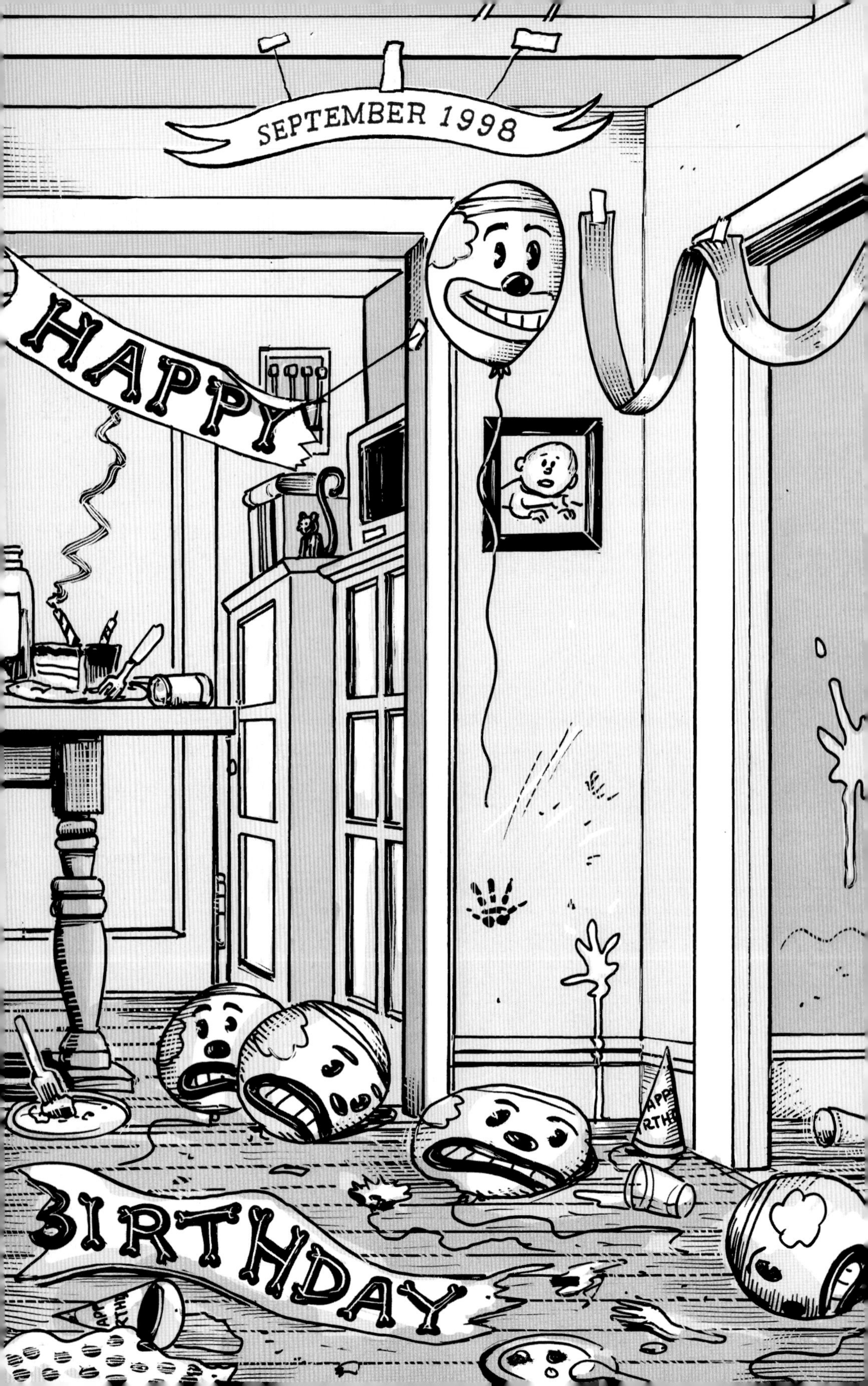
SEPTEMBER 1998
HAPPY
BIRTHDAY

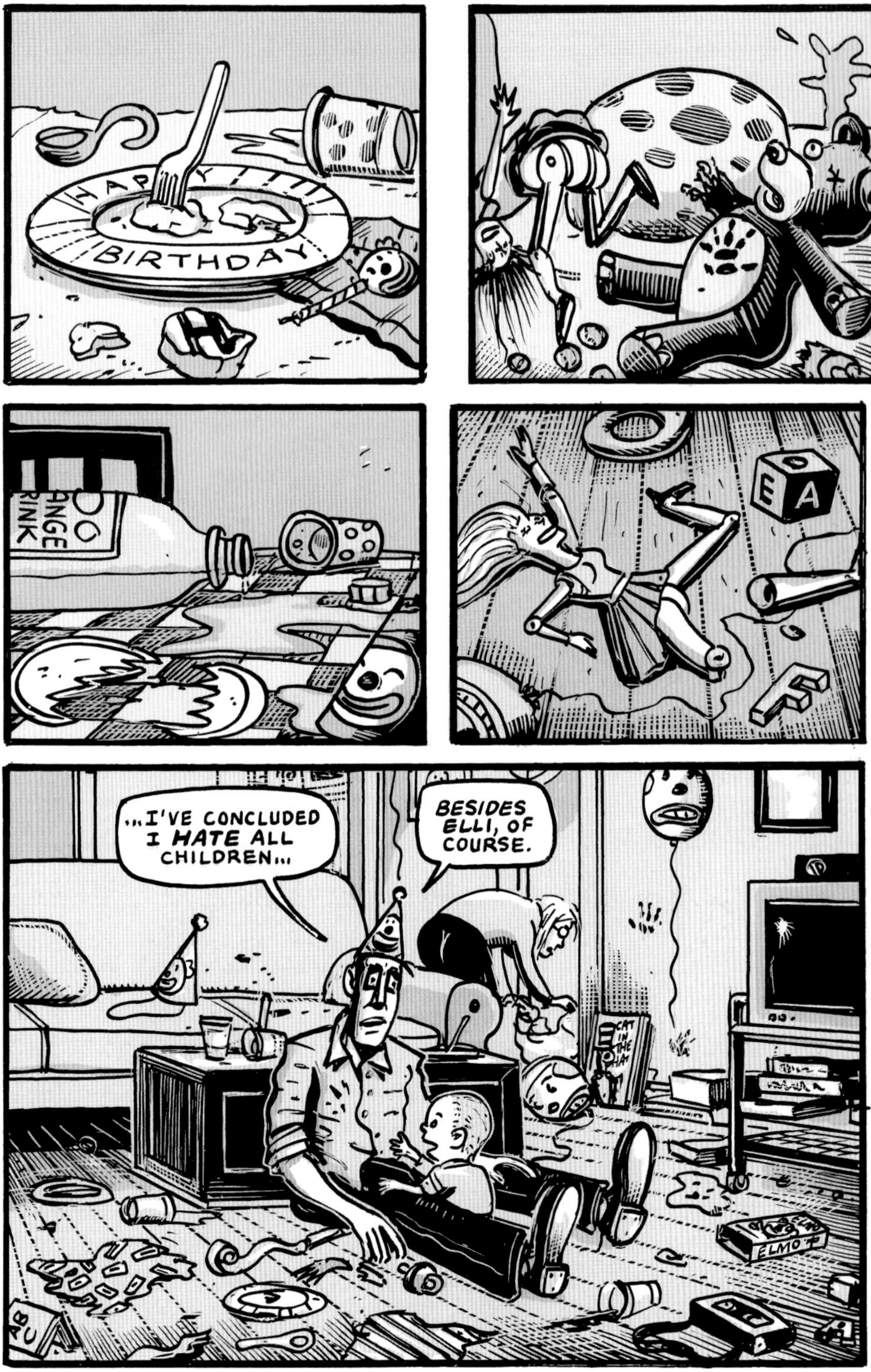
BIRTHDAY
...I'VE CONCLUDED I HATE ALL CHILDREN...
BESIDES ELLI, OF COURSE.
CAT IN THE HAT
ELMO

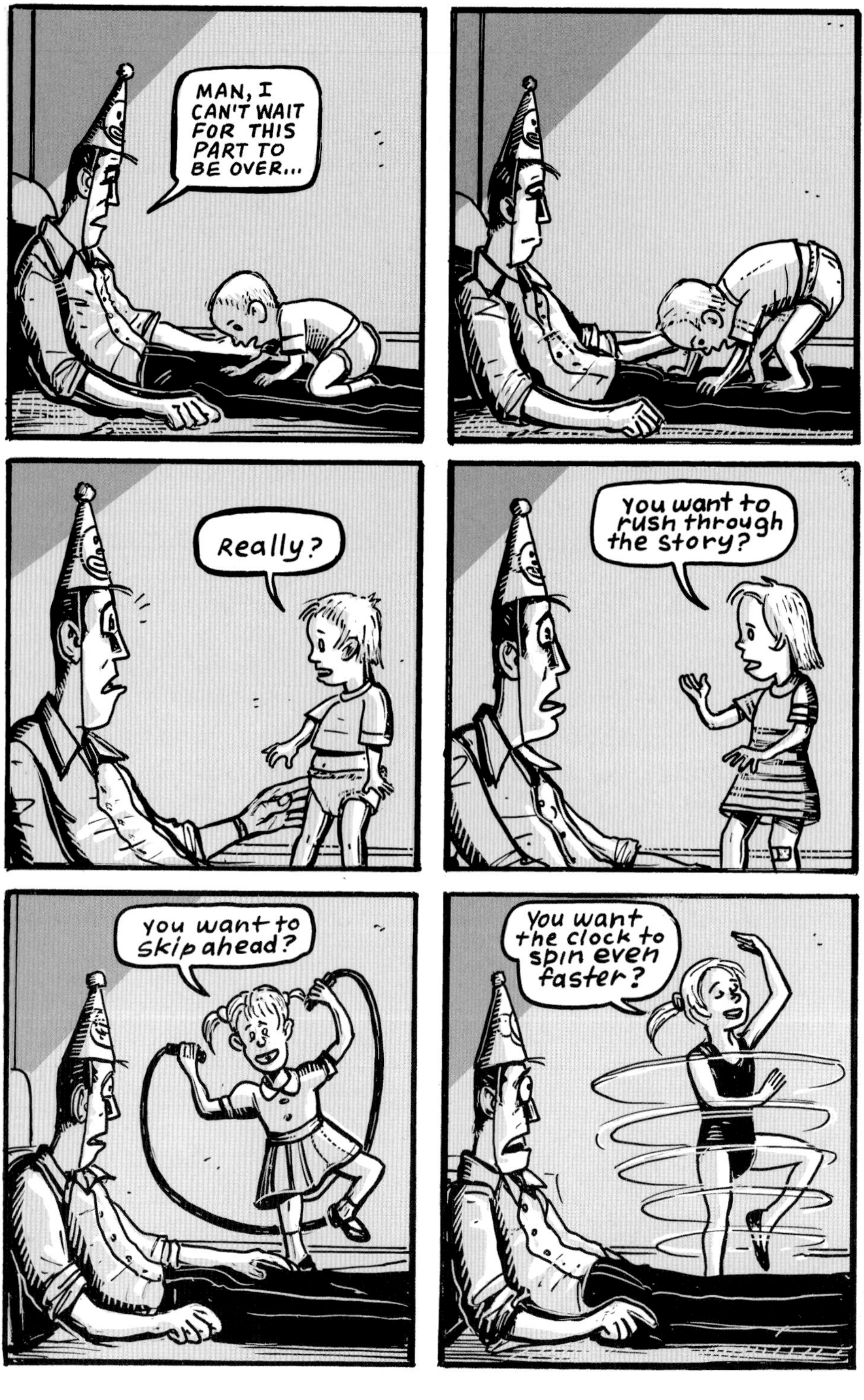
MAN, I CAN'T WAIT FOR THIS PART TO BE OVER...
Really?
You want to rush through the story?
You want to skip ahead?
You want the clock to spin even faster?

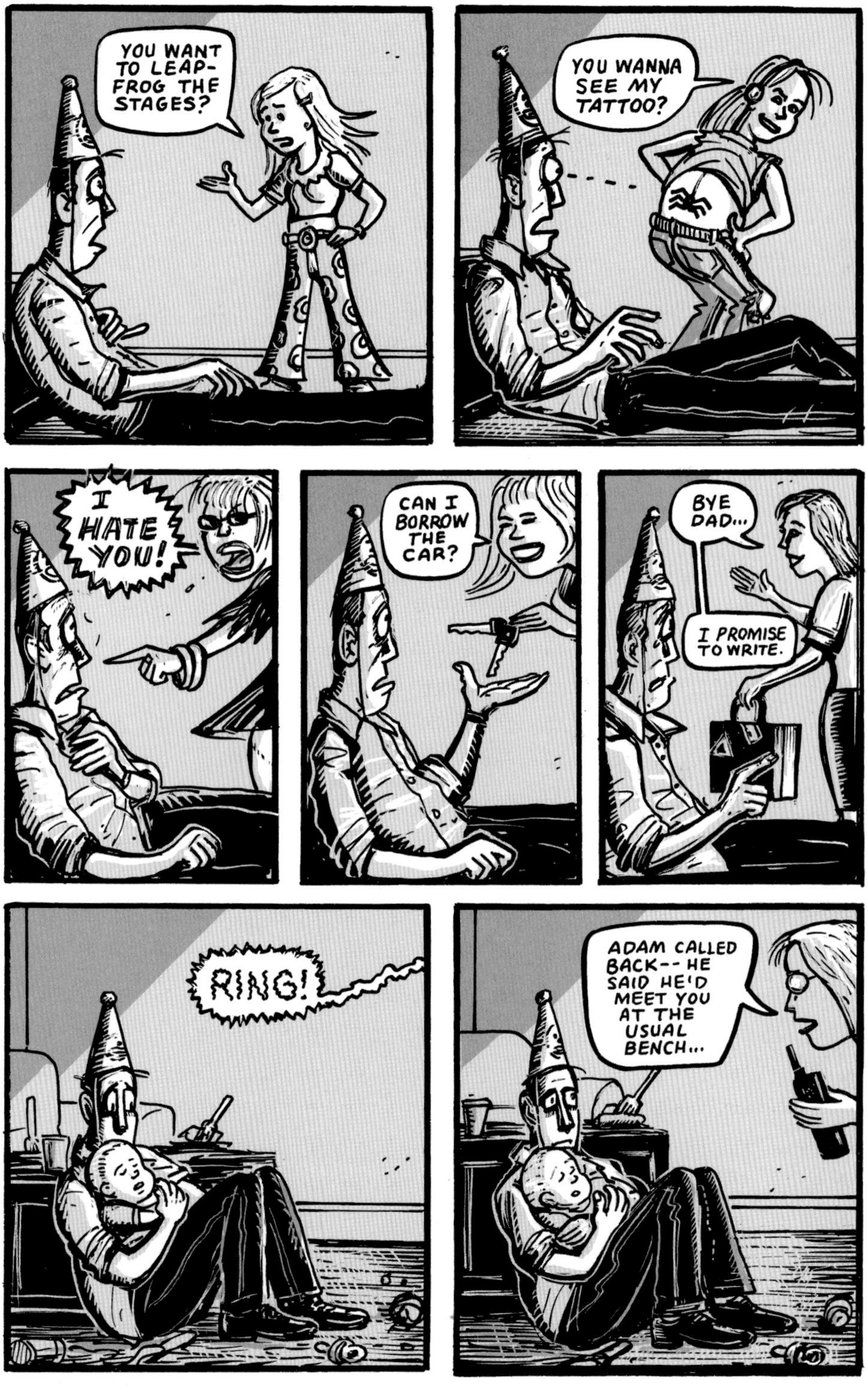
YOU WANT TO LEAP-FROG THE STAGES?
YOU WANNA SEE MY TATTOO?
I HATE YOU!
CAN I BORROW THE CAR?
BYE DAD...
I PROMISE TO WRITE.
RING!
ADAM CALLED BACK-- HE SAID HE'D MEET YOU AT THE USUAL BENCH...

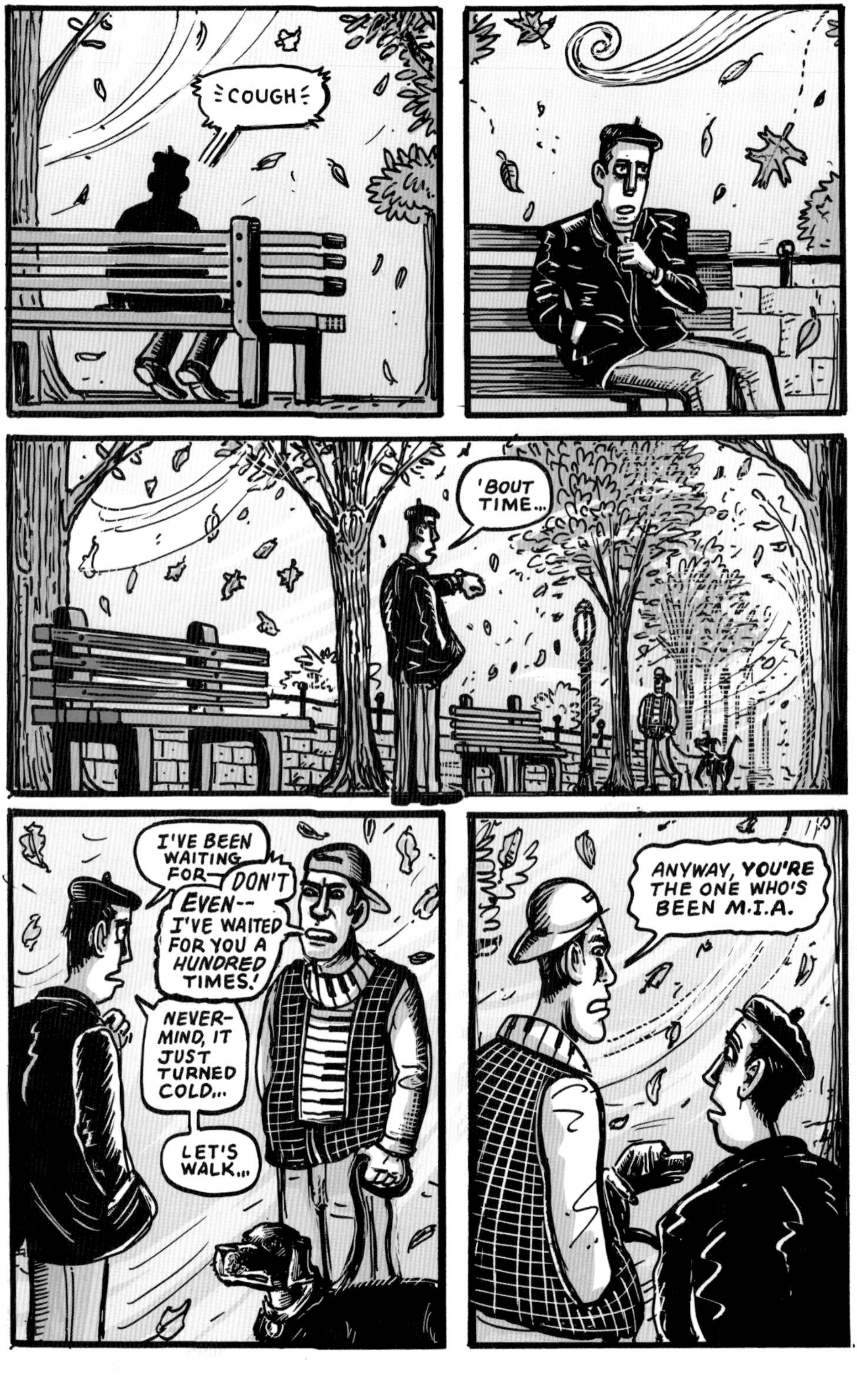
COUGH
'BOUT TIME...
I'VE BEEN WAITING FOR—
DON'T EVEN-- I'VE WAITED FOR YOU A HUNDRED TIMES!
NEVER-MIND, IT JUST TURNED COLD...
LET'S WALK...
ANYWAY, YOU'RE THE ONE WHO'S BEEN M.I.A.

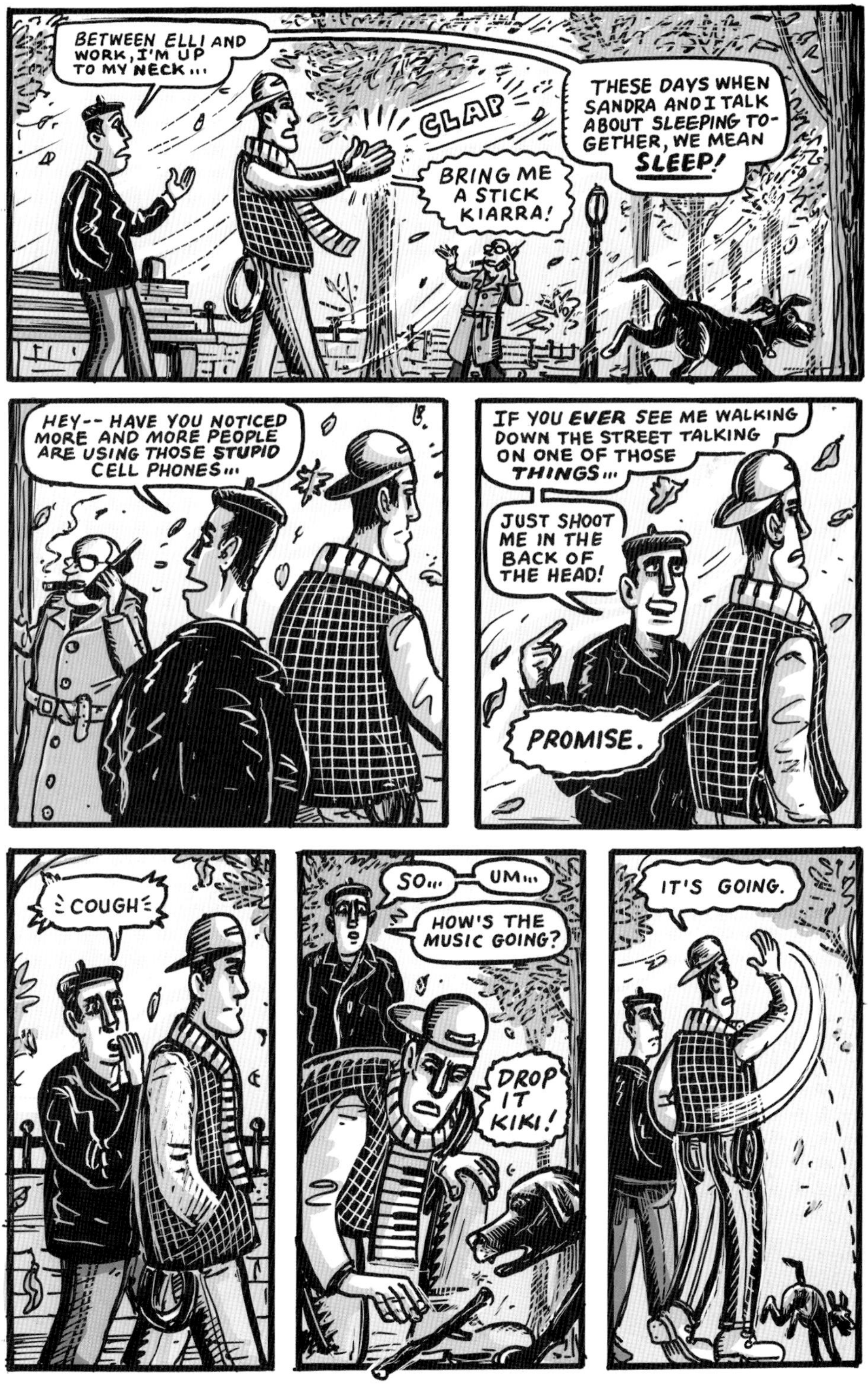
BETWEEN ELLI AND WORK, I'M UP TO MY NECK...
CLAP
THESE DAYS WHEN SANDRA AND I TALK ABOUT SLEEPING TOGETHER, WE MEAN SLEEP!
BRING ME A STICK KIARRA!
HEY-- HAVE YOU NOTICED MORE AND MORE PEOPLE ARE USING THOSE STUPID CELL PHONES...
IF YOU EVER SEE ME WALKING DOWN THE STREET TALKING ON ONE OF THOSE THINGS...
JUST SHOOT ME IN THE BACK OF THE HEAD!
PROMISE.
COUGH
SO...
UM...
HOW'S THE MUSIC GOING?
DROP IT KIKI!
IT'S GOING.

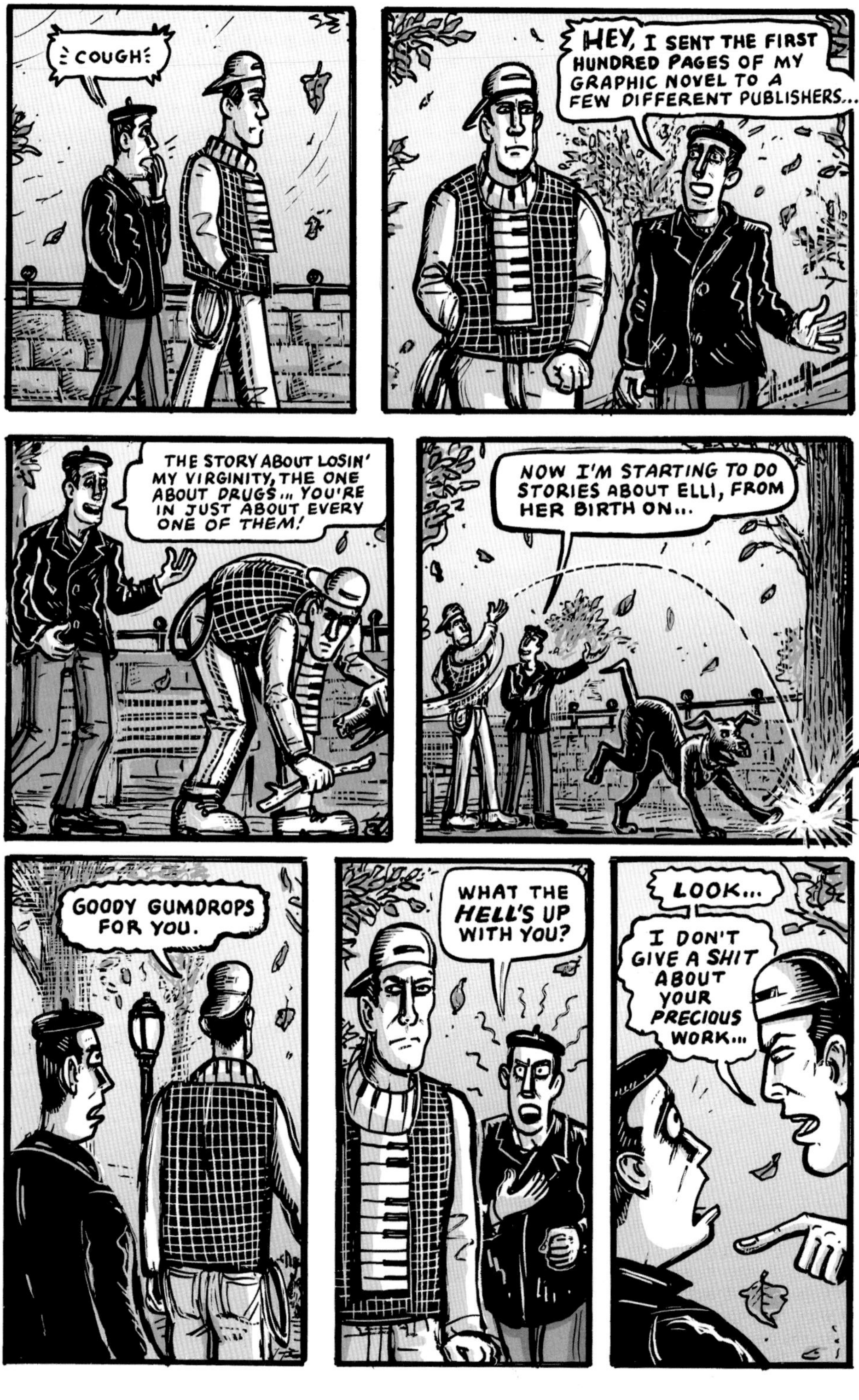
COUGH
HEY, I SENT THE FIRST HUNDRED PAGES OF MY GRAPHIC NOVEL TO A FEW DIFFERENT PUBLISHERS...
THE STORY ABOUT LOSIN' MY VIRGINITY, THE ONE ABOUT DRUGS... YOU'RE IN JUST ABOUT EVERY ONE OF THEM!
NOW I'M STARTING TO DO STORIES ABOUT ELLI, FROM HER BIRTH ON...
GOODY GUMDROPS FOR YOU.
WHAT THE HELL'S UP WITH YOU?
LOOK...
I DON'T GIVE A SHIT ABOUT YOUR PRECIOUS WORK...

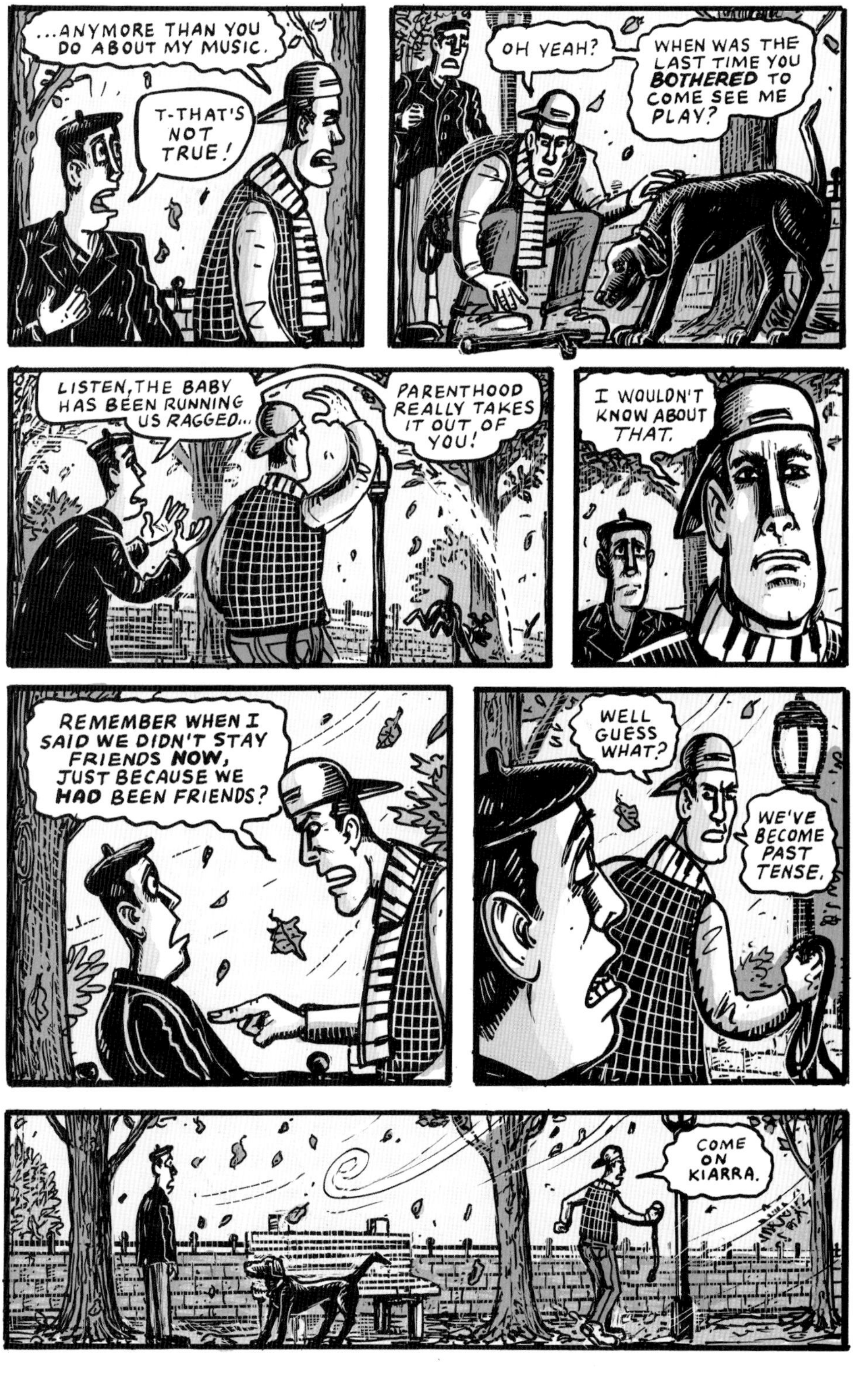
...ANYMORE THAN YOU DO ABOUT MY MUSIC.
T-THAT'S NOT TRUE!
OH YEAH?
WHEN WAS THE LAST TIME YOU **BOTHERED** TO COME SEE ME PLAY?
LISTEN, THE BABY HAS BEEN RUNNING US RAGGED...
PARENTHOOD REALLY TAKES IT OUT OF YOU!
I WOULDN'T KNOW ABOUT *THAT.*
REMEMBER WHEN I SAID WE DIDN'T STAY FRIENDS **NOW,** JUST BECAUSE WE **HAD** BEEN FRIENDS?
WELL GUESS WHAT?
WE'VE BECOME PAST TENSE.
COME ON KIARRA.

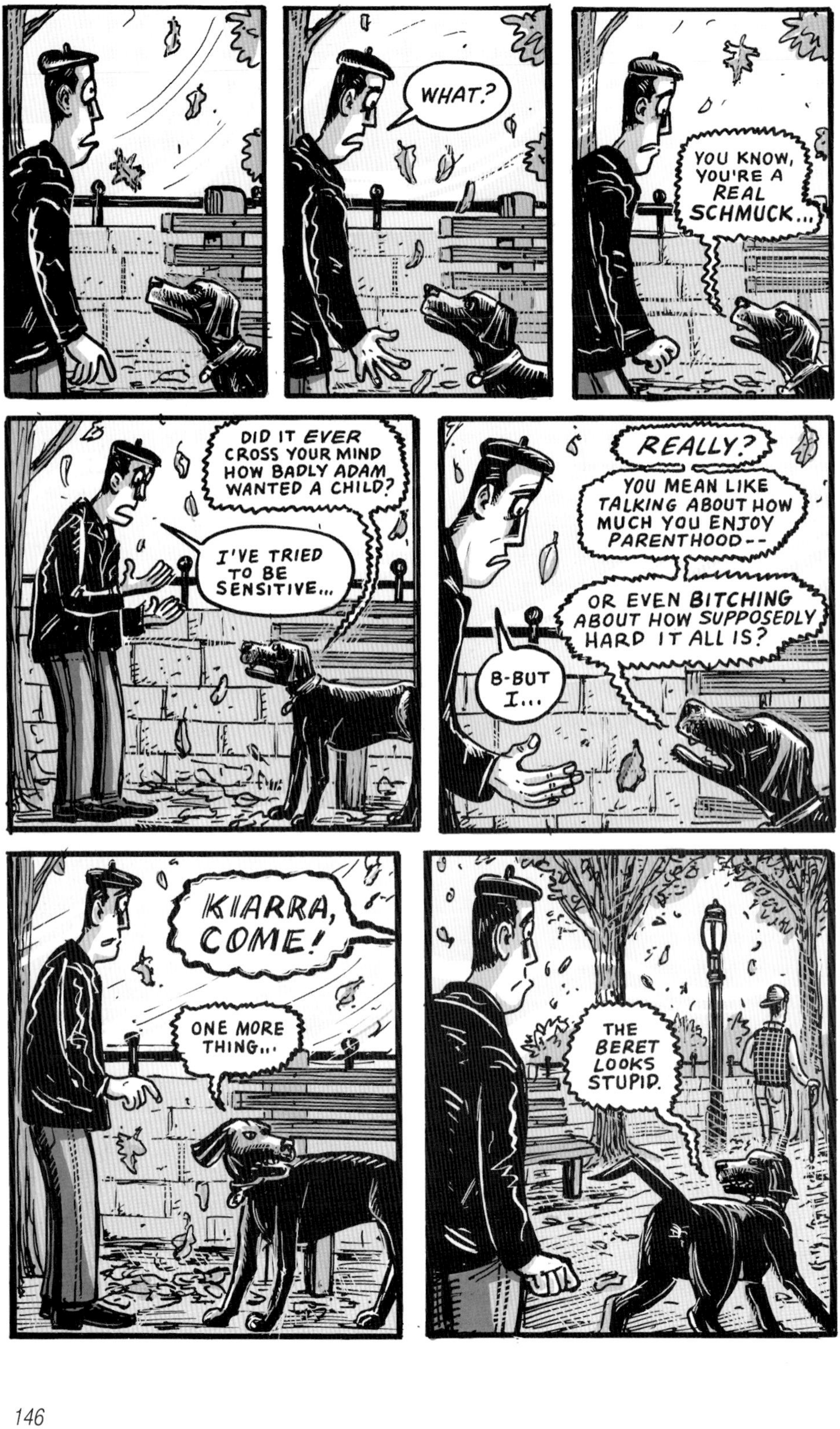
WHAT?
YOU KNOW, YOU'RE A REAL SCHMUCK...
DID IT EVER CROSS YOUR MIND HOW BADLY ADAM WANTED A CHILD?
I'VE TRIED TO BE SENSITIVE...
REALLY?
YOU MEAN LIKE TALKING ABOUT HOW MUCH YOU ENJOY PARENTHOOD--
OR EVEN BITCHING ABOUT HOW SUPPOSEDLY HARD IT ALL IS?
B-BUT I...
KIARRA, COME!
ONE MORE THING...
THE BERET LOOKS STUPID.

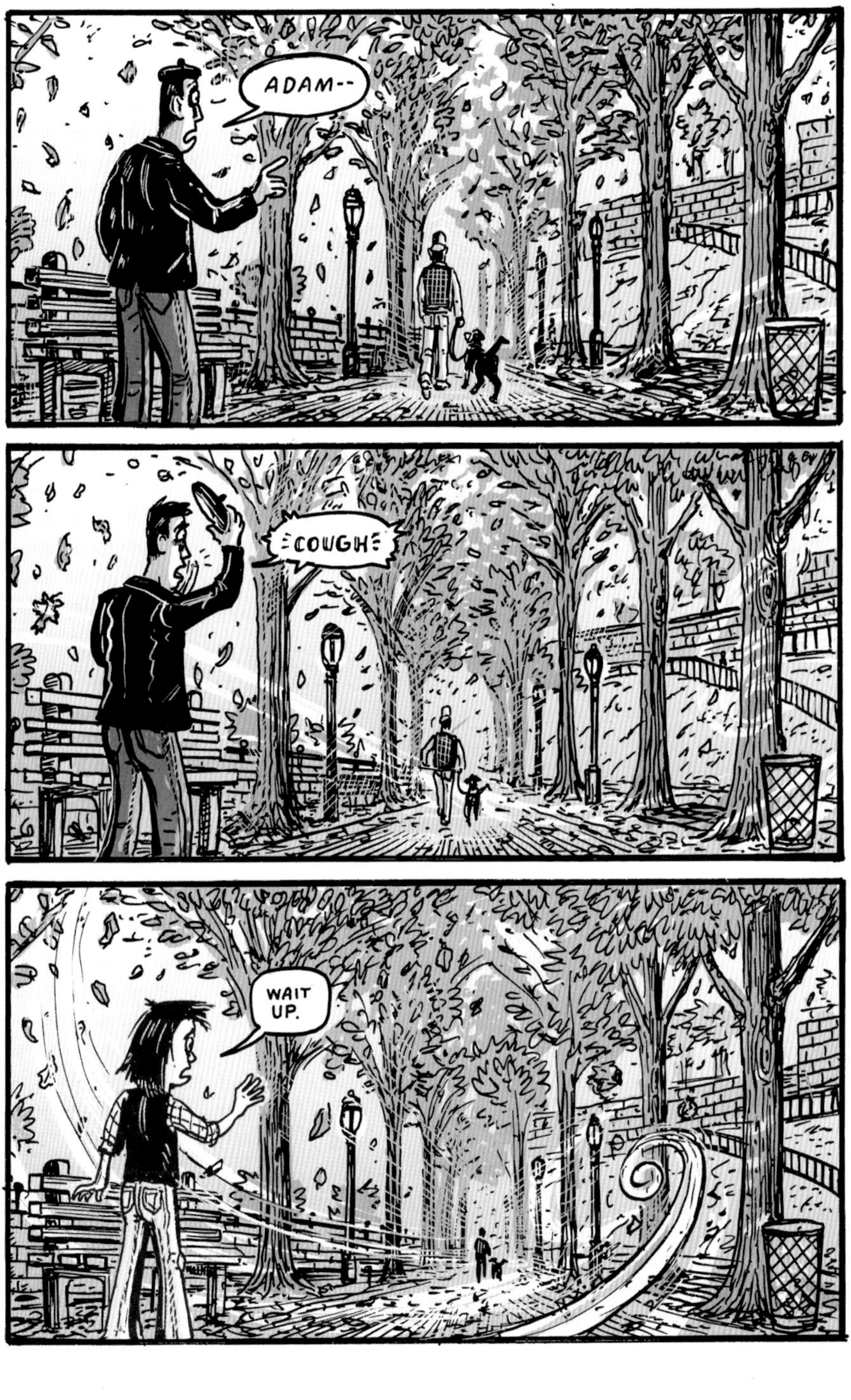
ADAM--
COUGH
WAIT UP.

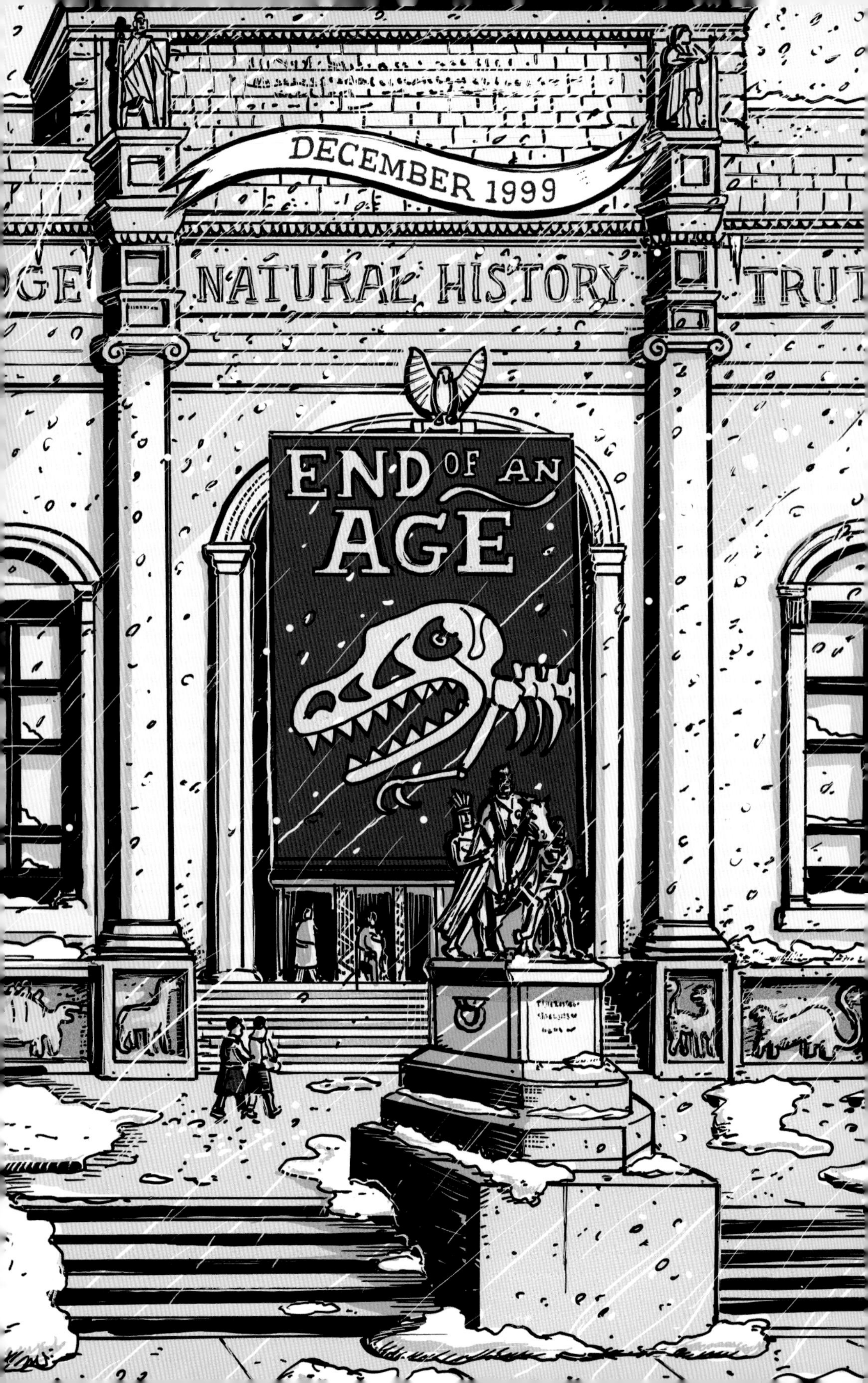
DECEMBER 1999
GE
NATURAL HISTORY
TRU
END OF AN
AGE

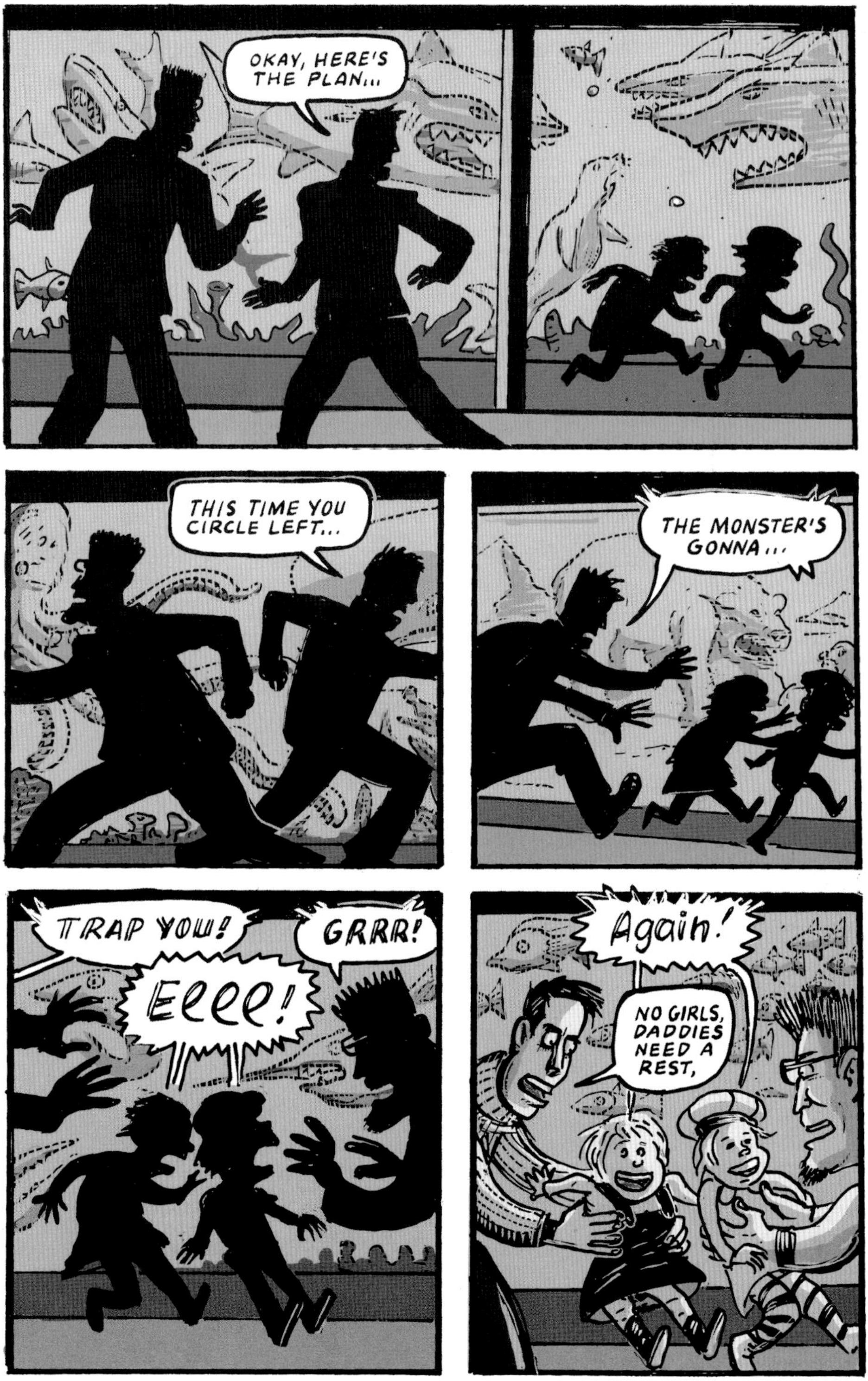
OKAY, HERE'S THE PLAN...
THIS TIME YOU CIRCLE LEFT...
THE MONSTER'S GONNA...
TRAP YOU!
GRRR!
EEEE!
Again!
NO GIRLS, DADDIES NEED A REST,

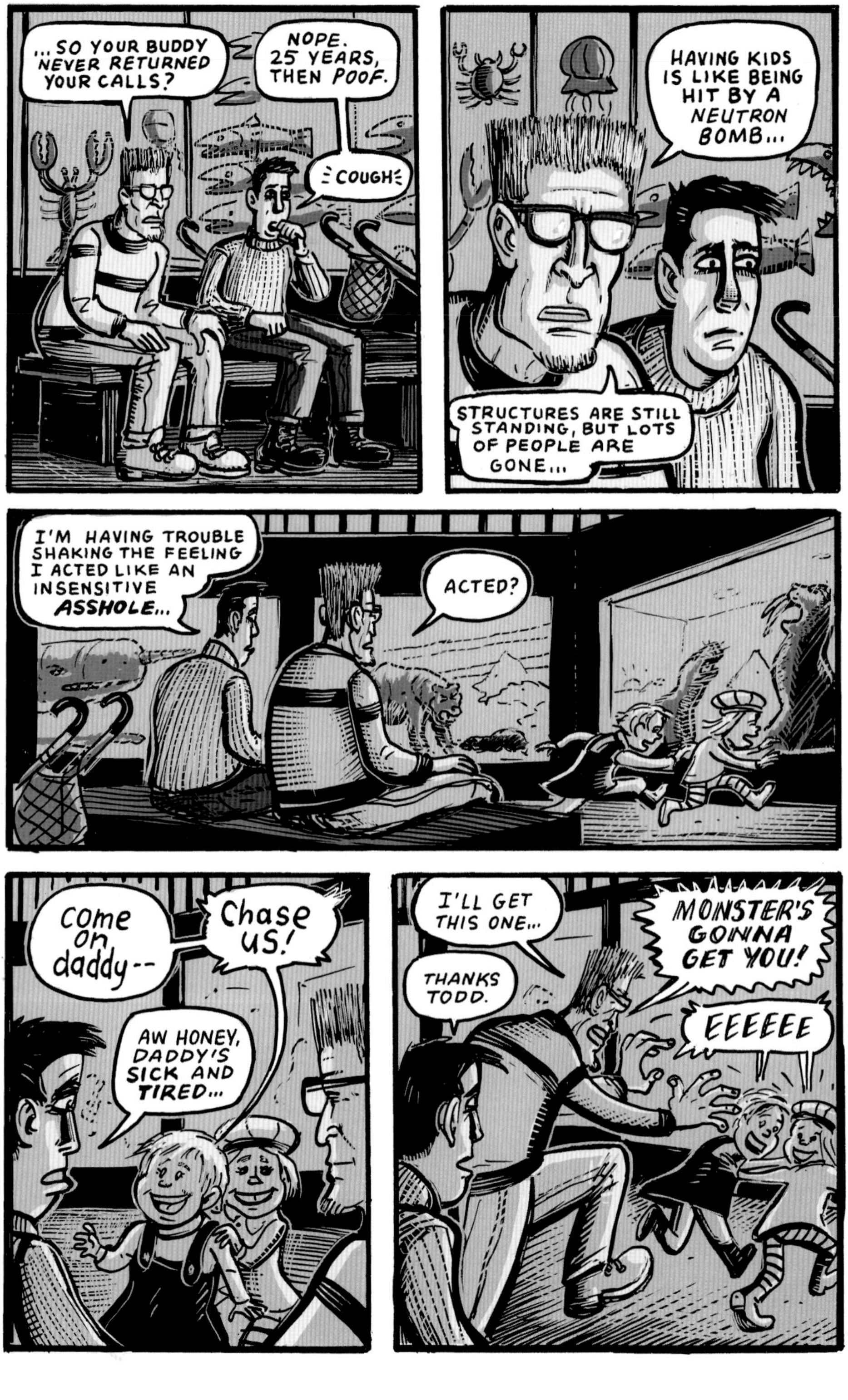
...SO YOUR BUDDY NEVER RETURNED YOUR CALLS?
NOPE. 25 YEARS, THEN POOF.
COUGH
HAVING KIDS IS LIKE BEING HIT BY A NEUTRON BOMB...
STRUCTURES ARE STILL STANDING, BUT LOTS OF PEOPLE ARE GONE...
I'M HAVING TROUBLE SHAKING THE FEELING I ACTED LIKE AN INSENSITIVE ASSHOLE...
ACTED?
come on daddy--
Chase us!
AW HONEY, DADDY'S SICK AND TIRED...
I'LL GET THIS ONE...
THANKS TODD.
MONSTER'S GONNA GET YOU!
EEEEEE

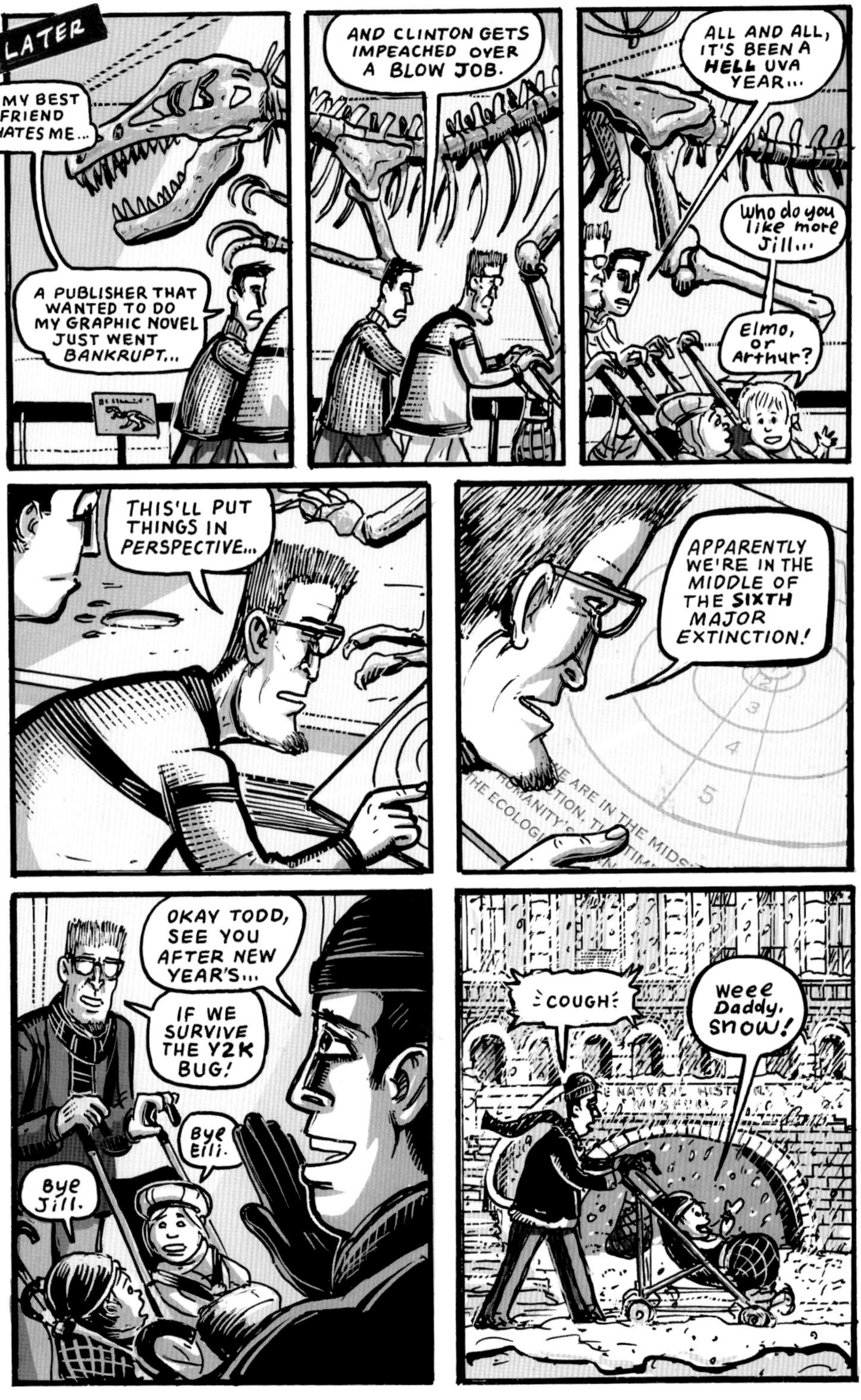
LATER
...MY BEST FRIEND HATES ME...
A PUBLISHER THAT WANTED TO DO MY GRAPHIC NOVEL JUST WENT BANKRUPT...
AND CLINTON GETS IMPEACHED OVER A BLOW JOB.
ALL AND ALL, IT'S BEEN A HELL UVA YEAR...
Who do you like more Jill...
Elmo, or Arthur?
THIS'LL PUT THINGS IN PERSPECTIVE...
APPARENTLY WE'RE IN THE MIDDLE OF THE SIXTH MAJOR EXTINCTION!
OKAY TODD, SEE YOU AFTER NEW YEAR'S...
IF WE SURVIVE THE Y2K BUG!
Bye Eli.
Bye Jill.
COUGH
Weee Daddy, snow!

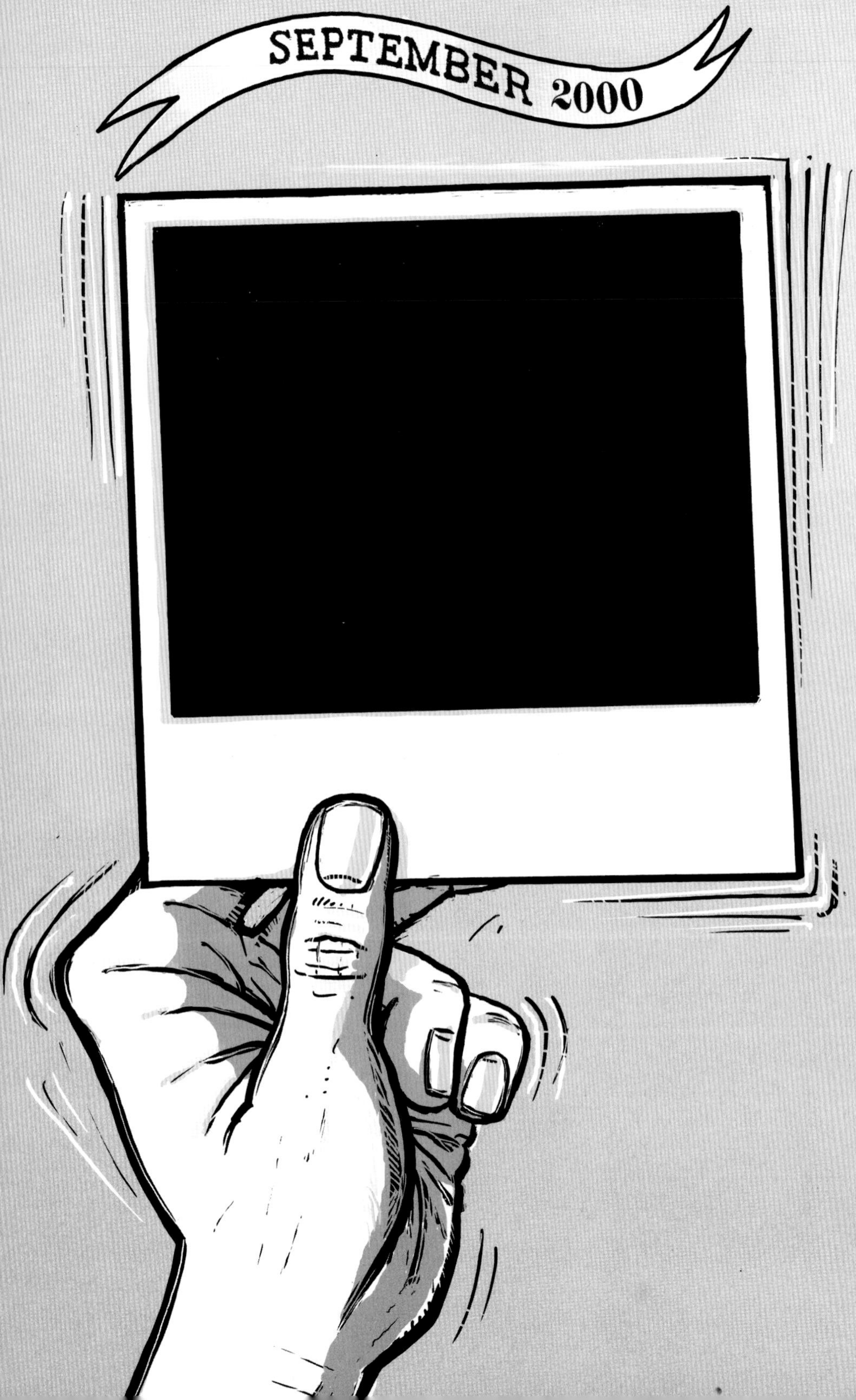
SEPTEMBER 2000

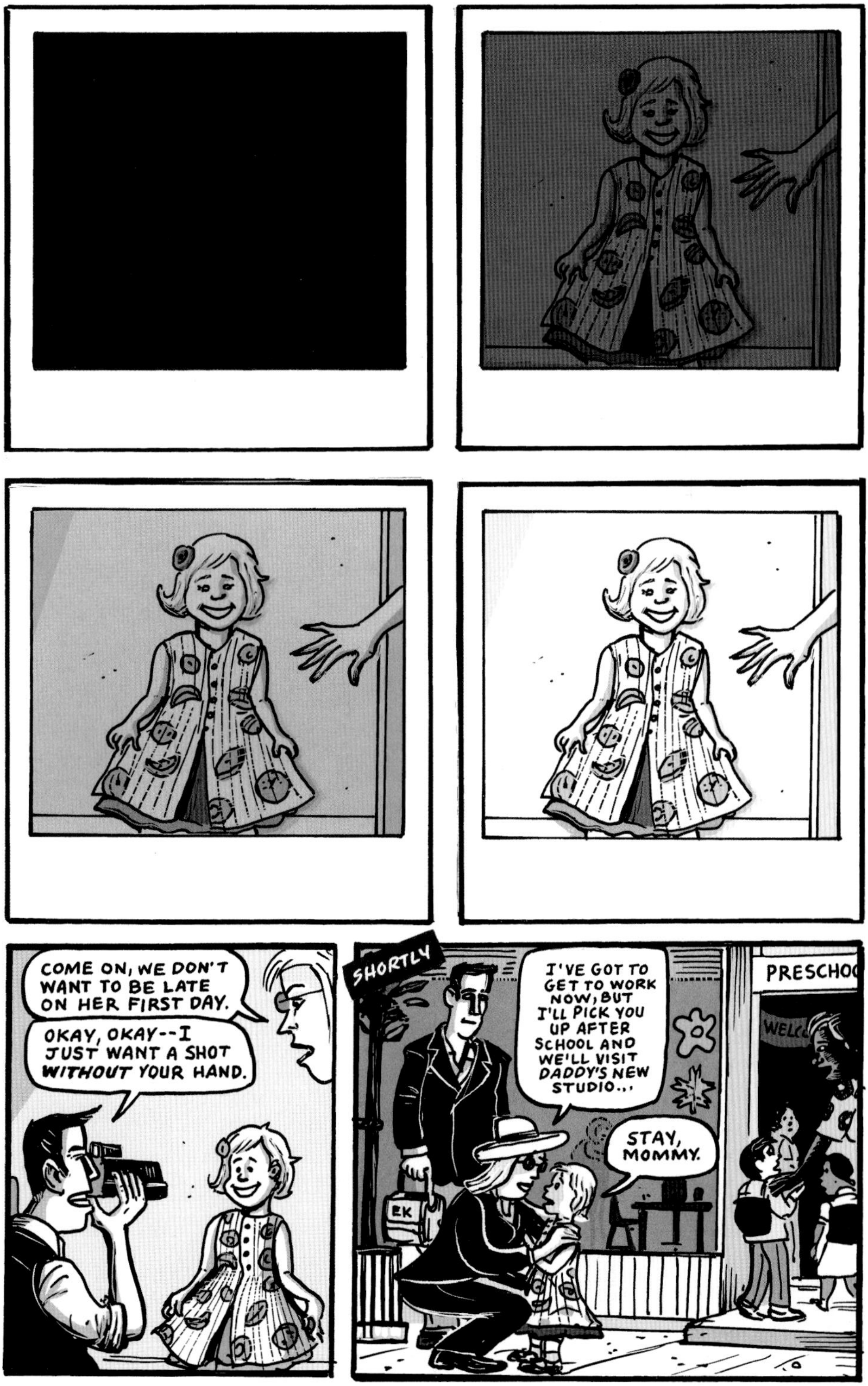
COME ON, WE DON'T WANT TO BE LATE ON HER FIRST DAY.
OKAY, OKAY--I JUST WANT A SHOT *WITHOUT* YOUR HAND.
SHORTLY
I'VE GOT TO GET TO WORK NOW, BUT I'LL PICK YOU UP AFTER SCHOOL AND WE'LL VISIT DADDY'S NEW STUDIO...
STAY, MOMMY.
PRESCHOO
EK

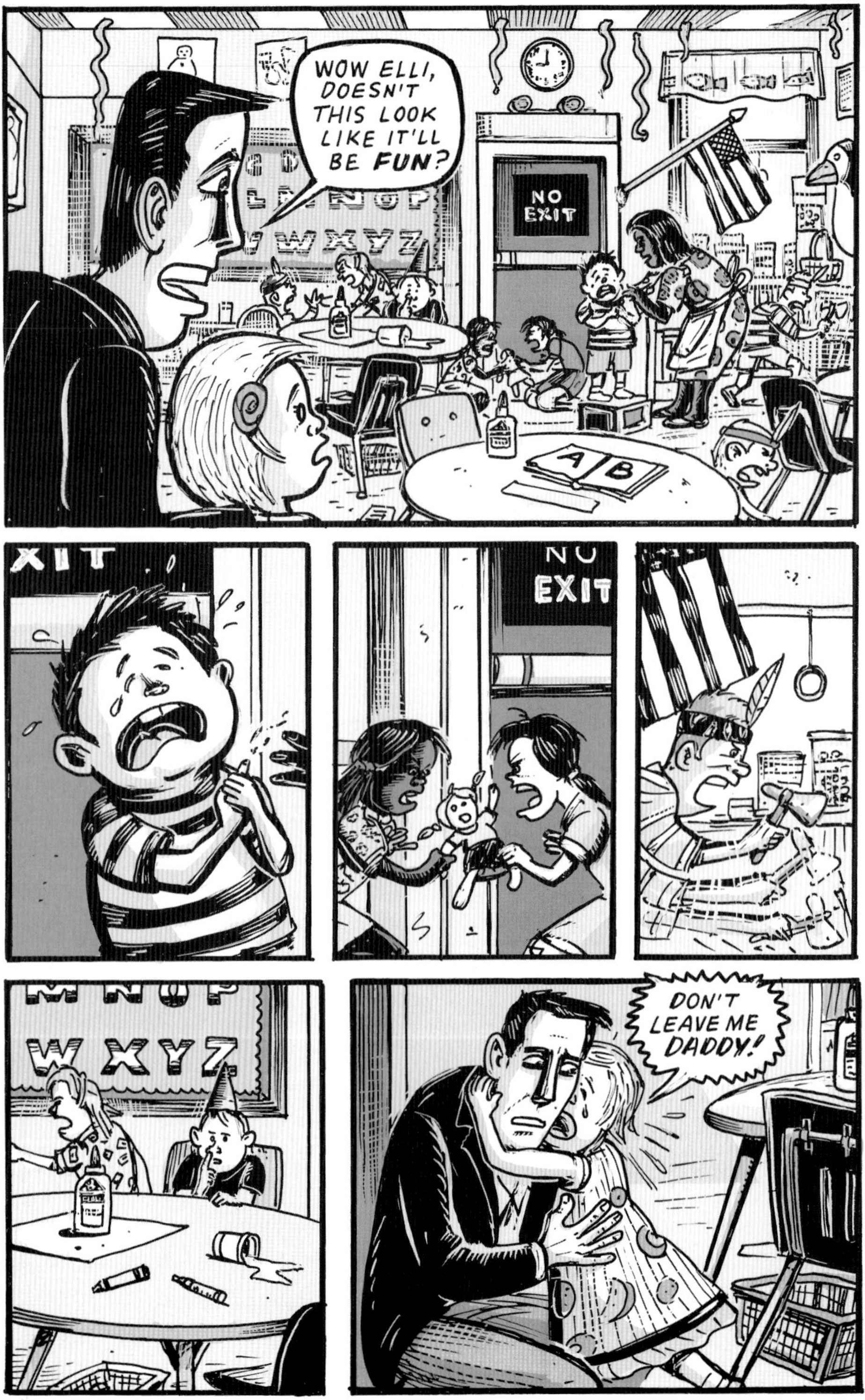
WOW ELLI, DOESN'T THIS LOOK LIKE IT'LL BE FUN?
NO EXIT
NO EXIT
DON'T LEAVE ME DADDY!

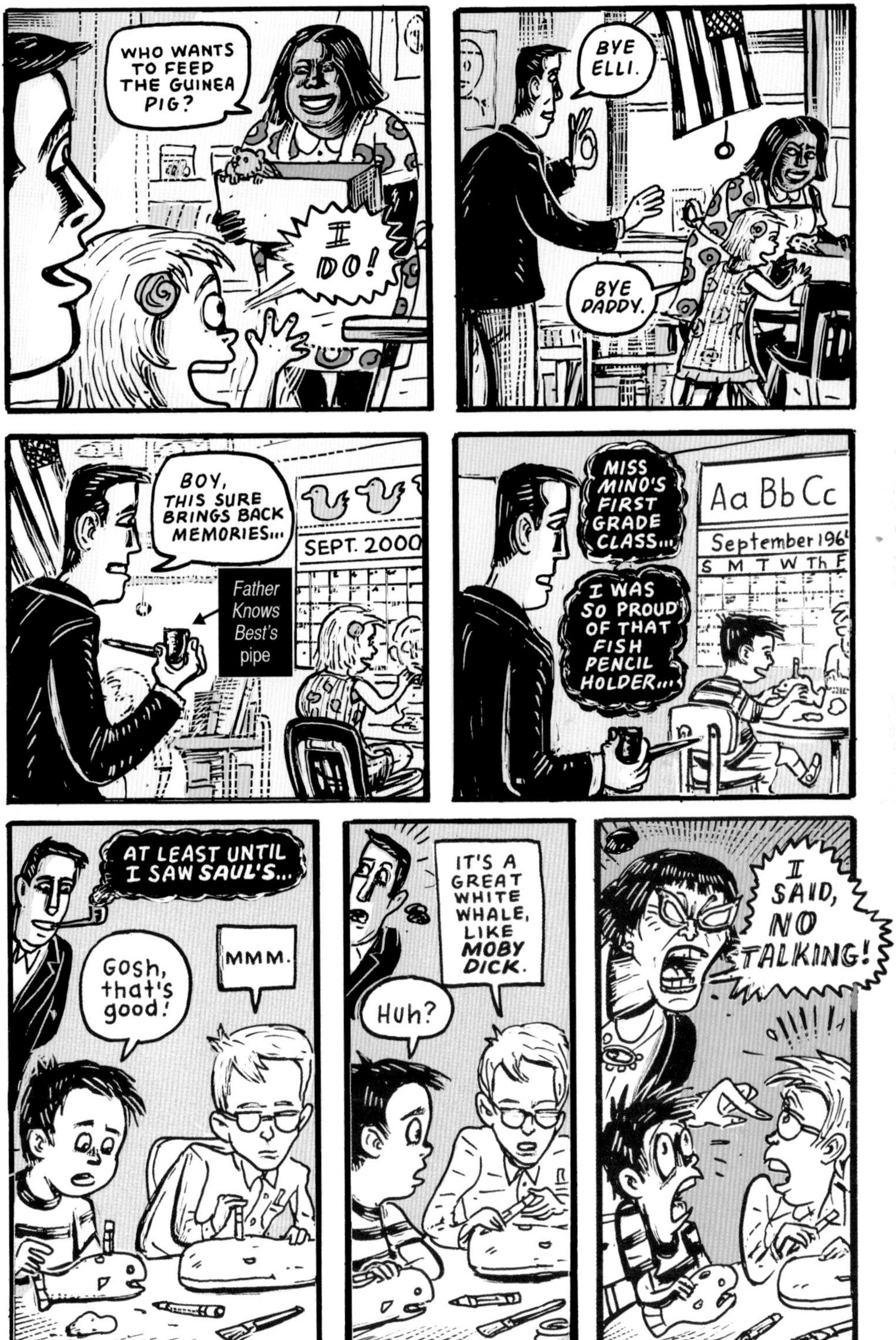
WHO WANTS TO FEED THE GUINEA PIG?
I DO!
BYE ELLI.
BYE DADDY.
BOY, THIS SURE BRINGS BACK MEMORIES...
SEPT. 2000
Father Knows Best's pipe
MISS MINO'S FIRST GRADE CLASS...
I WAS SO PROUD OF THAT FISH PENCIL HOLDER...
Aa Bb Cc
September 1964
S M T W Th F
AT LEAST UNTIL I SAW SAUL'S...
Gosh, that's good!
MMM.
IT'S A GREAT WHITE WHALE, LIKE MOBY DICK.
Huh?
I SAID, NO TALKING!

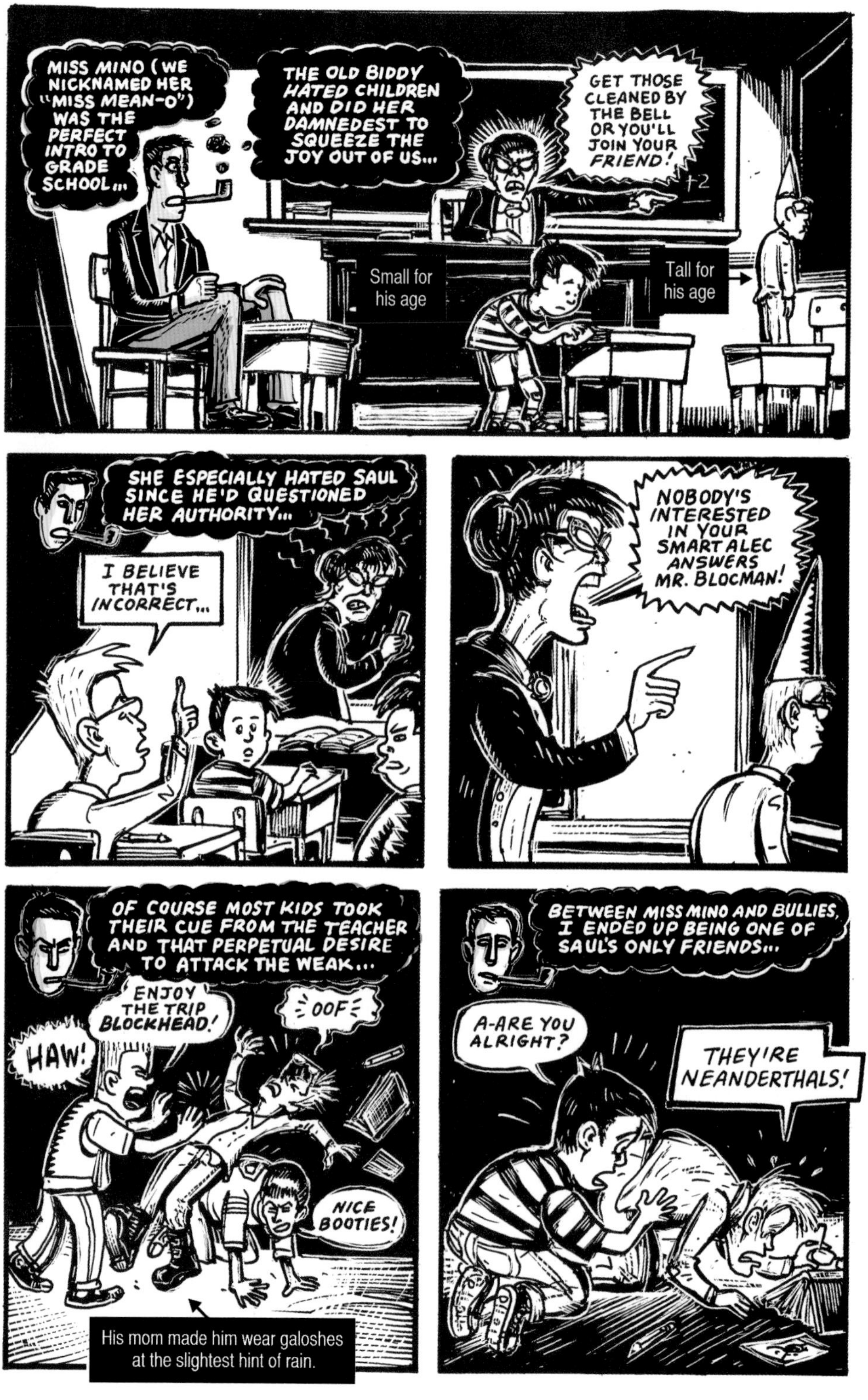
MISS MINO (WE NICKNAMED HER "MISS MEAN-O") WAS THE PERFECT INTRO TO GRADE SCHOOL...
THE OLD BIDDY HATED CHILDREN AND DID HER DAMNEDEST TO SQUEEZE THE JOY OUT OF US...
GET THOSE CLEANED BY THE BELL OR YOU'LL JOIN YOUR FRIEND!
+2
Small for his age
Tall for his age
SHE ESPECIALLY HATED SAUL SINCE HE'D QUESTIONED HER AUTHORITY...
I BELIEVE THAT'S INCORRECT...
NOBODY'S INTERESTED IN YOUR SMART ALEC ANSWERS MR. BLOCMAN!
OF COURSE MOST KIDS TOOK THEIR CUE FROM THE TEACHER AND THAT PERPETUAL DESIRE TO ATTACK THE WEAK...
HAW!
ENJOY THE TRIP BLOCKHEAD!
OOF
NICE BOOTIES!
His mom made him wear galoshes at the slightest hint of rain.
BETWEEN MISS MINO AND BULLIES, I ENDED UP BEING ONE OF SAUL'S ONLY FRIENDS...
A-ARE YOU ALRIGHT?
THEY'RE NEANDERTHALS!

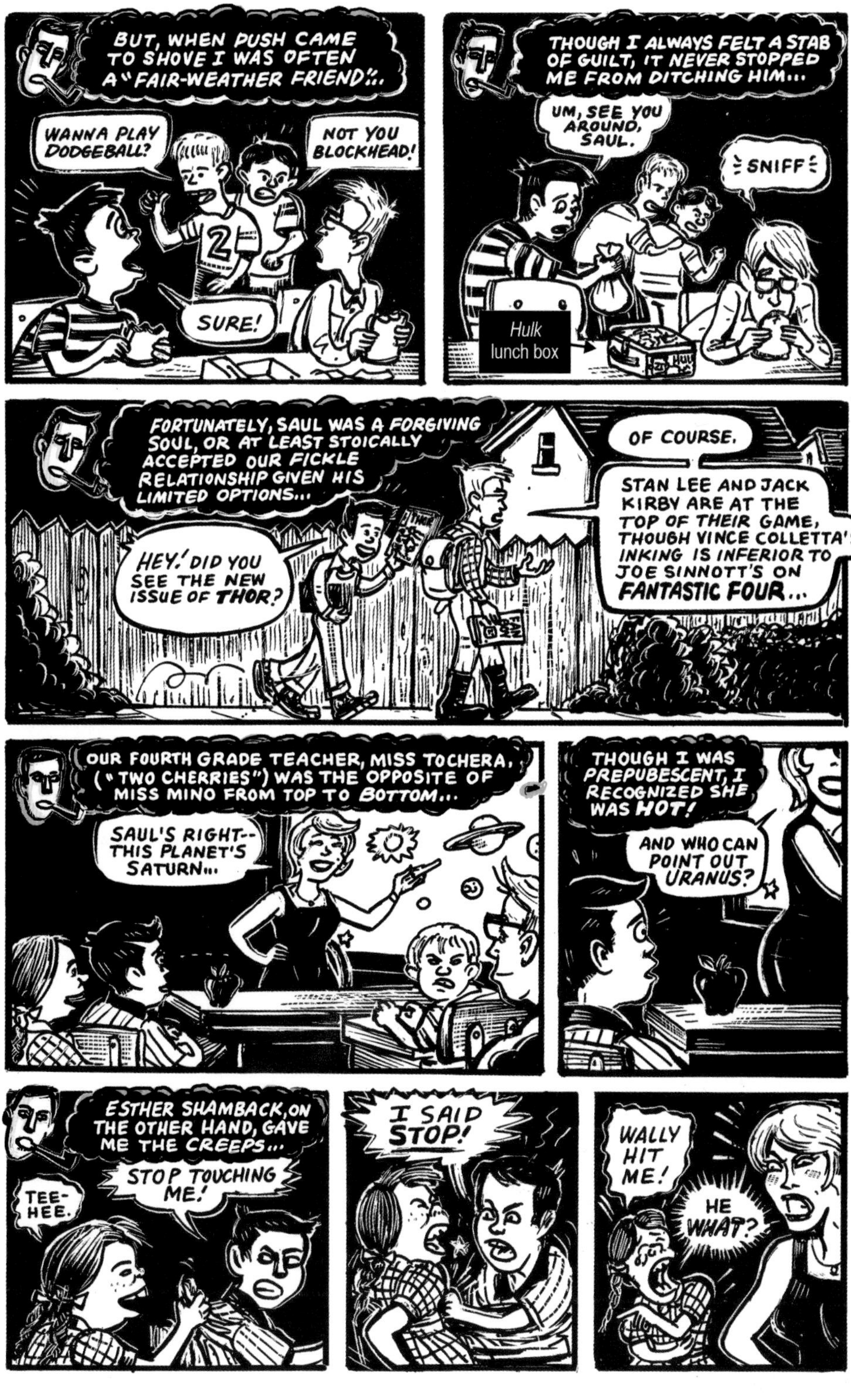
BUT, WHEN PUSH CAME TO SHOVE I WAS OFTEN A "FAIR-WEATHER FRIEND"...
WANNA PLAY DODGEBALL?
NOT YOU BLOCKHEAD!
SURE!
THOUGH I ALWAYS FELT A STAB OF GUILT, IT NEVER STOPPED ME FROM DITCHING HIM...
UM, SEE YOU AROUND, SAUL.
SNIFF
Hulk lunch box
FORTUNATELY, SAUL WAS A FORGIVING SOUL, OR AT LEAST STOICALLY ACCEPTED OUR FICKLE RELATIONSHIP GIVEN HIS LIMITED OPTIONS...
HEY! DID YOU SEE THE NEW ISSUE OF THOR?
OF COURSE.
STAN LEE AND JACK KIRBY ARE AT THE TOP OF THEIR GAME, THOUGH VINCE COLLETTA'S INKING IS INFERIOR TO JOE SINNOTT'S ON FANTASTIC FOUR...
OUR FOURTH GRADE TEACHER, MISS TOCHERA, ("TWO CHERRIES") WAS THE OPPOSITE OF MISS MINO FROM TOP TO BOTTOM...
SAUL'S RIGHT-- THIS PLANET'S SATURN...
THOUGH I WAS PREPUBESCENT, I RECOGNIZED SHE WAS HOT!
AND WHO CAN POINT OUT URANUS?
ESTHER SHAMBACK, ON THE OTHER HAND, GAVE ME THE CREEPS...
TEE-HEE.
STOP TOUCHING ME!
I SAID STOP!
WALLY HIT ME!
HE WHAT?

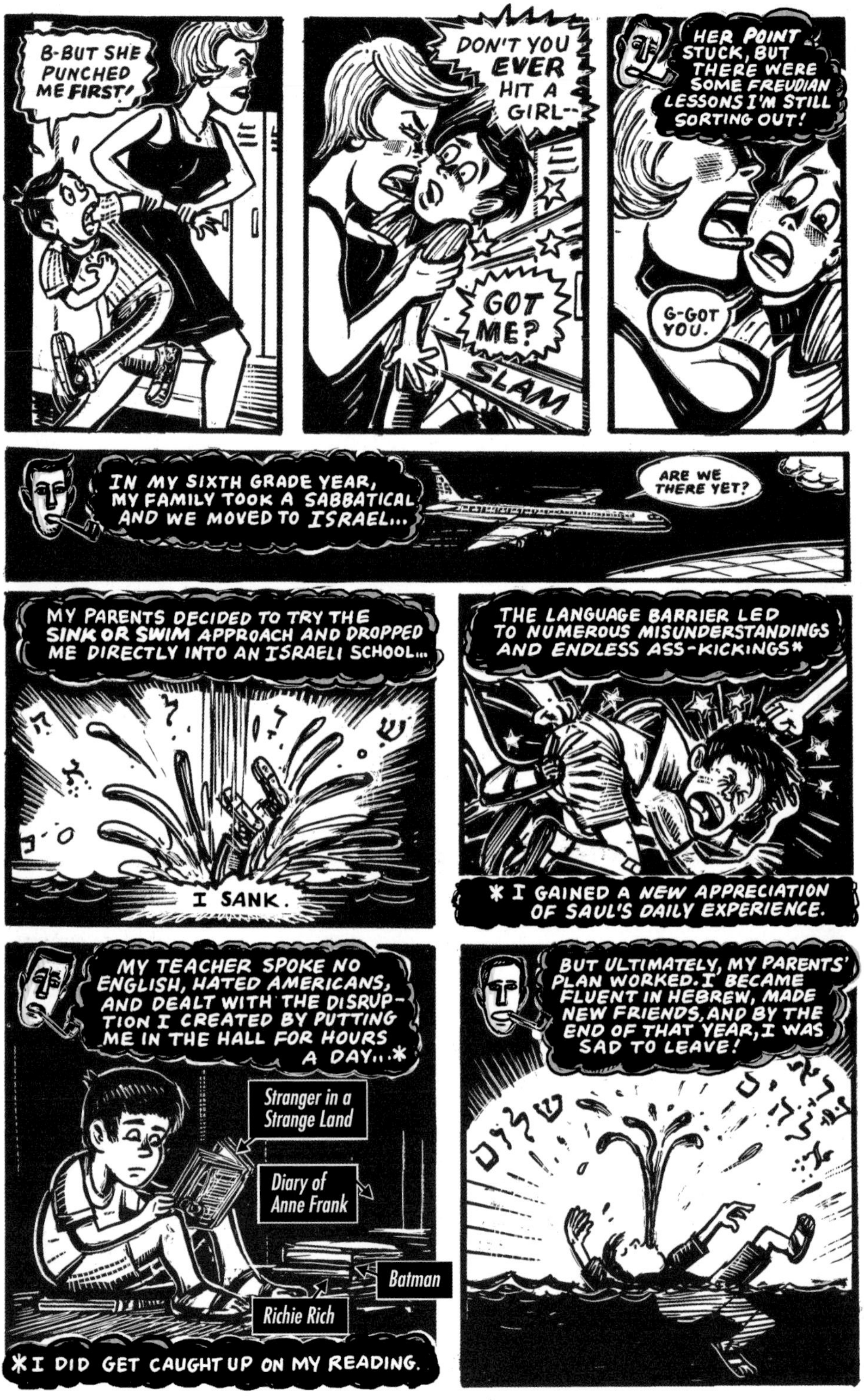
B-BUT SHE PUNCHED ME FIRST!
DON'T YOU EVER HIT A GIRL--
GOT ME?
SLAM
HER POINT STUCK, BUT THERE WERE SOME FREUDIAN LESSONS I'M STILL SORTING OUT!
G-GOT YOU.
IN MY SIXTH GRADE YEAR, MY FAMILY TOOK A SABBATICAL AND WE MOVED TO ISRAEL...
ARE WE THERE YET?
MY PARENTS DECIDED TO TRY THE SINK OR SWIM APPROACH AND DROPPED ME DIRECTLY INTO AN ISRAELI SCHOOL...
I SANK.
THE LANGUAGE BARRIER LED TO NUMEROUS MISUNDERSTANDINGS AND ENDLESS ASS-KICKINGS*
* I GAINED A NEW APPRECIATION OF SAUL'S DAILY EXPERIENCE.
MY TEACHER SPOKE NO ENGLISH, HATED AMERICANS, AND DEALT WITH THE DISRUPTION I CREATED BY PUTTING ME IN THE HALL FOR HOURS A DAY...*
Stranger in a Strange Land
Diary of Anne Frank
Batman
Richie Rich
*I DID GET CAUGHT UP ON MY READING.
BUT ULTIMATELY, MY PARENTS' PLAN WORKED. I BECAME FLUENT IN HEBREW, MADE NEW FRIENDS, AND BY THE END OF THAT YEAR, I WAS SAD TO LEAVE!
שלום

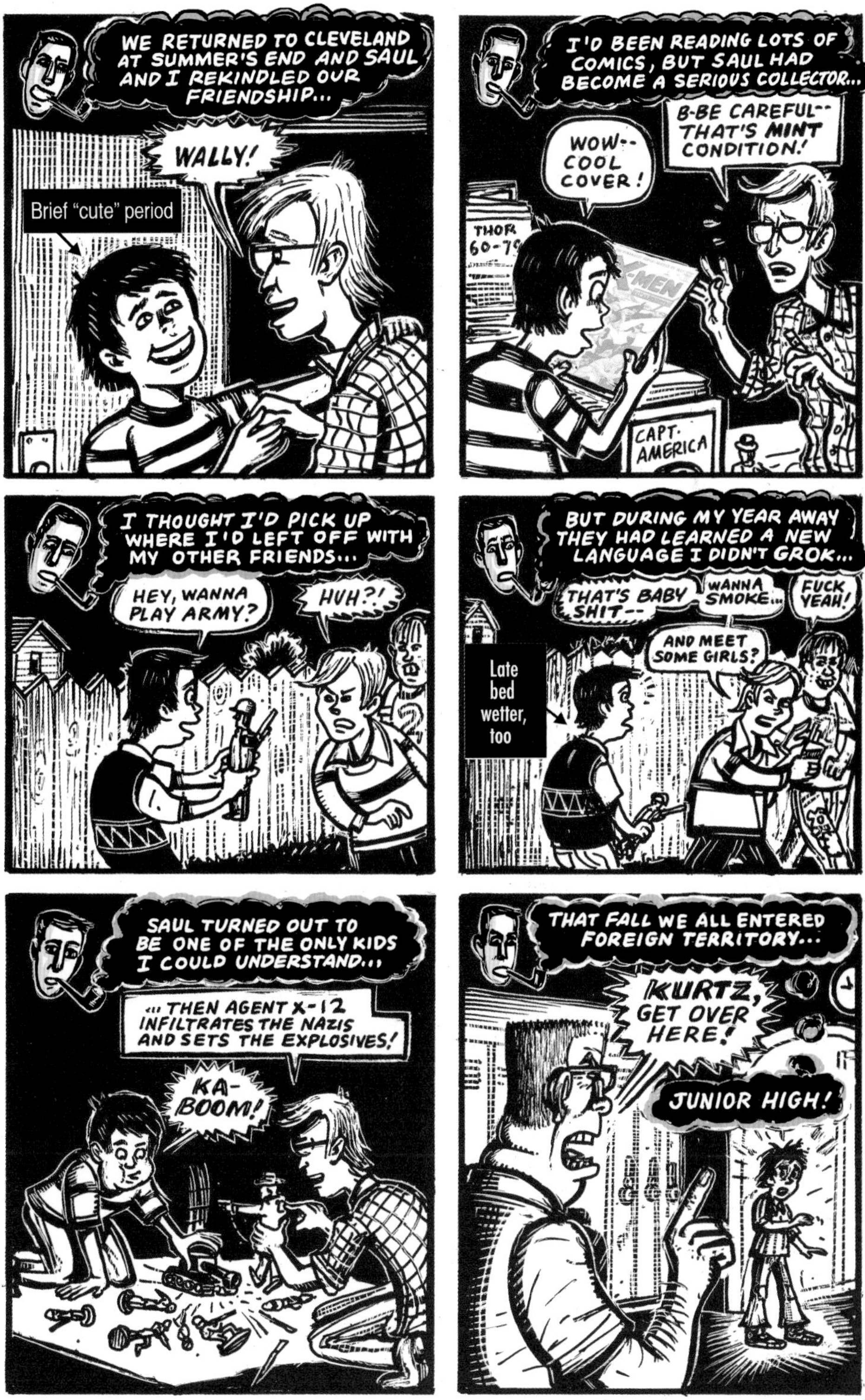
WE RETURNED TO CLEVELAND AT SUMMER'S END AND SAUL AND I REKINDLED OUR FRIENDSHIP...
WALLY!
Brief "cute" period
I'D BEEN READING LOTS OF COMICS, BUT SAUL HAD BECOME A SERIOUS COLLECTOR...
WOW-- COOL COVER!
B-BE CAREFUL-- THAT'S MINT CONDITION!
THOR 60-79
X-MEN
CAPT. AMERICA
I THOUGHT I'D PICK UP WHERE I'D LEFT OFF WITH MY OTHER FRIENDS...
HEY, WANNA PLAY ARMY?
HUH?!
BUT DURING MY YEAR AWAY THEY HAD LEARNED A NEW LANGUAGE I DIDN'T GROK...
THAT'S BABY SHIT--
WANNA SMOKE...
FUCK YEAH!
AND MEET SOME GIRLS?
Late bed wetter, too
SAUL TURNED OUT TO BE ONE OF THE ONLY KIDS I COULD UNDERSTAND...
...THEN AGENT X-12 INFILTRATES THE NAZIS AND SETS THE EXPLOSIVES!
KA-BOOM!
THAT FALL WE ALL ENTERED FOREIGN TERRITORY...
KURTZ, GET OVER HERE!
JUNIOR HIGH!

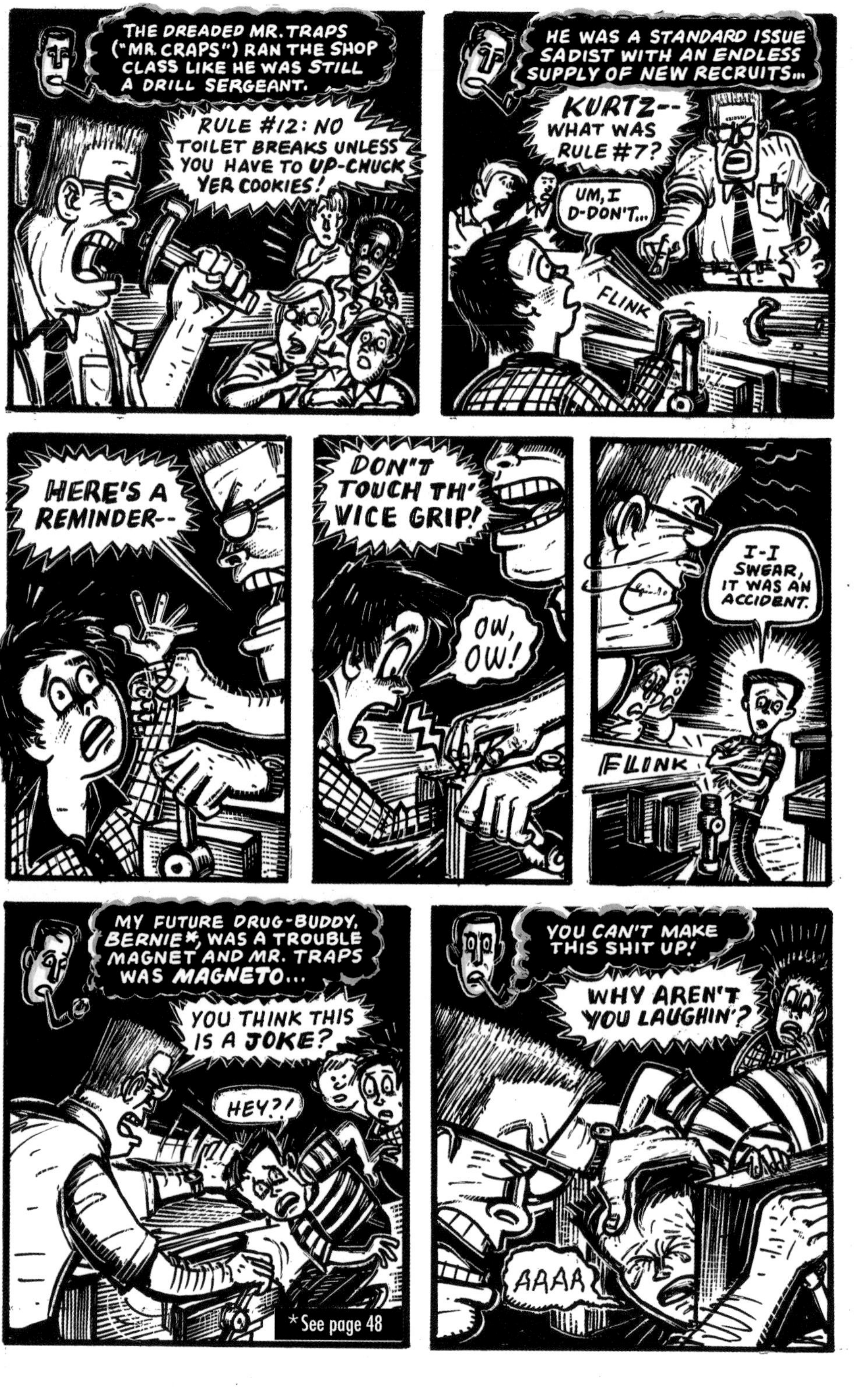
THE DREADED MR. TRAPS ("MR. CRAPS") RAN THE SHOP CLASS LIKE HE WAS STILL A DRILL SERGEANT.
RULE #12: NO TOILET BREAKS UNLESS YOU HAVE TO UP-CHUCK YER COOKIES!
HE WAS A STANDARD ISSUE SADIST WITH AN ENDLESS SUPPLY OF NEW RECRUITS...
KURTZ-- WHAT WAS RULE #7?
UM, I D-DON'T...
FLINK
HERE'S A REMINDER--
DON'T TOUCH TH' VICE GRIP!
OW, OW!
I-I SWEAR, IT WAS AN ACCIDENT.
FLINK
MY FUTURE DRUG-BUDDY, BERNIE*, WAS A TROUBLE MAGNET AND MR. TRAPS WAS MAGNETO...
YOU THINK THIS IS A JOKE?
HEY?!
*See page 48
YOU CAN'T MAKE THIS SHIT UP!
WHY AREN'T YOU LAUGHIN'?
AAAA

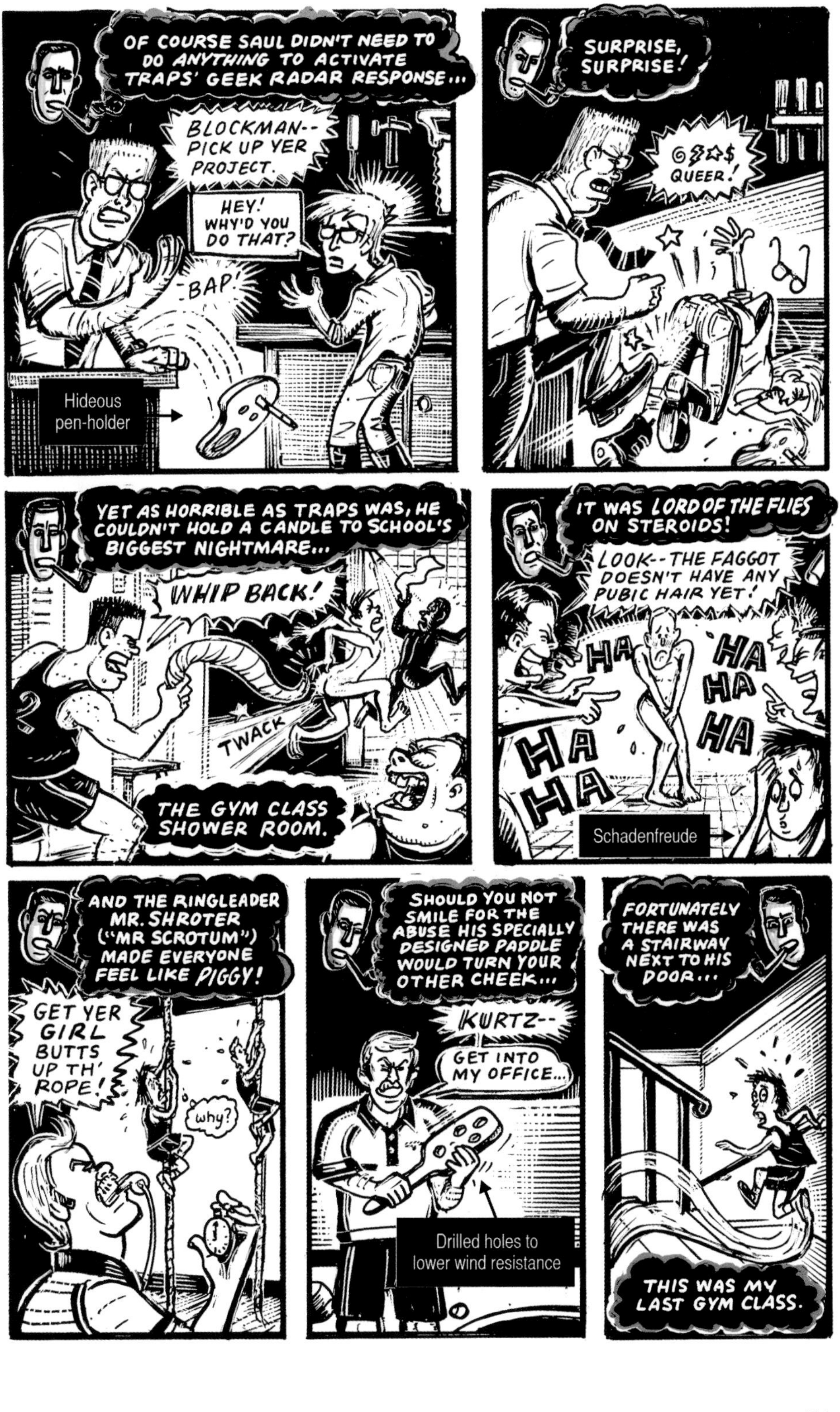
OF COURSE SAUL DIDN'T NEED TO DO ANYTHING TO ACTIVATE TRAPS' GEEK RADAR RESPONSE...
BLOCKMAN-- PICK UP YER PROJECT.
HEY! WHY'D YOU DO THAT?
BAP!
Hideous pen-holder
SURPRISE, SURPRISE!
QUEER!
YET AS HORRIBLE AS TRAPS WAS, HE COULDN'T HOLD A CANDLE TO SCHOOL'S BIGGEST NIGHTMARE...
WHIP BACK!
TWACK
THE GYM CLASS SHOWER ROOM.
IT WAS LORD OF THE FLIES ON STEROIDS!
LOOK--THE FAGGOT DOESN'T HAVE ANY PUBIC HAIR YET!
HA HA HA HA HA HA HA
Schadenfreude
AND THE RINGLEADER MR. SHROTER ("MR SCROTUM") MADE EVERYONE FEEL LIKE PIGGY!
GET YER GIRL BUTTS UP TH' ROPE!
why?
SHOULD YOU NOT SMILE FOR THE ABUSE HIS SPECIALLY DESIGNED PADDLE WOULD TURN YOUR OTHER CHEEK...
KURTZ--
GET INTO MY OFFICE...
Drilled holes to lower wind resistance
FORTUNATELY THERE WAS A STAIRWAY NEXT TO HIS DOOR...
THIS WAS MY LAST GYM CLASS.

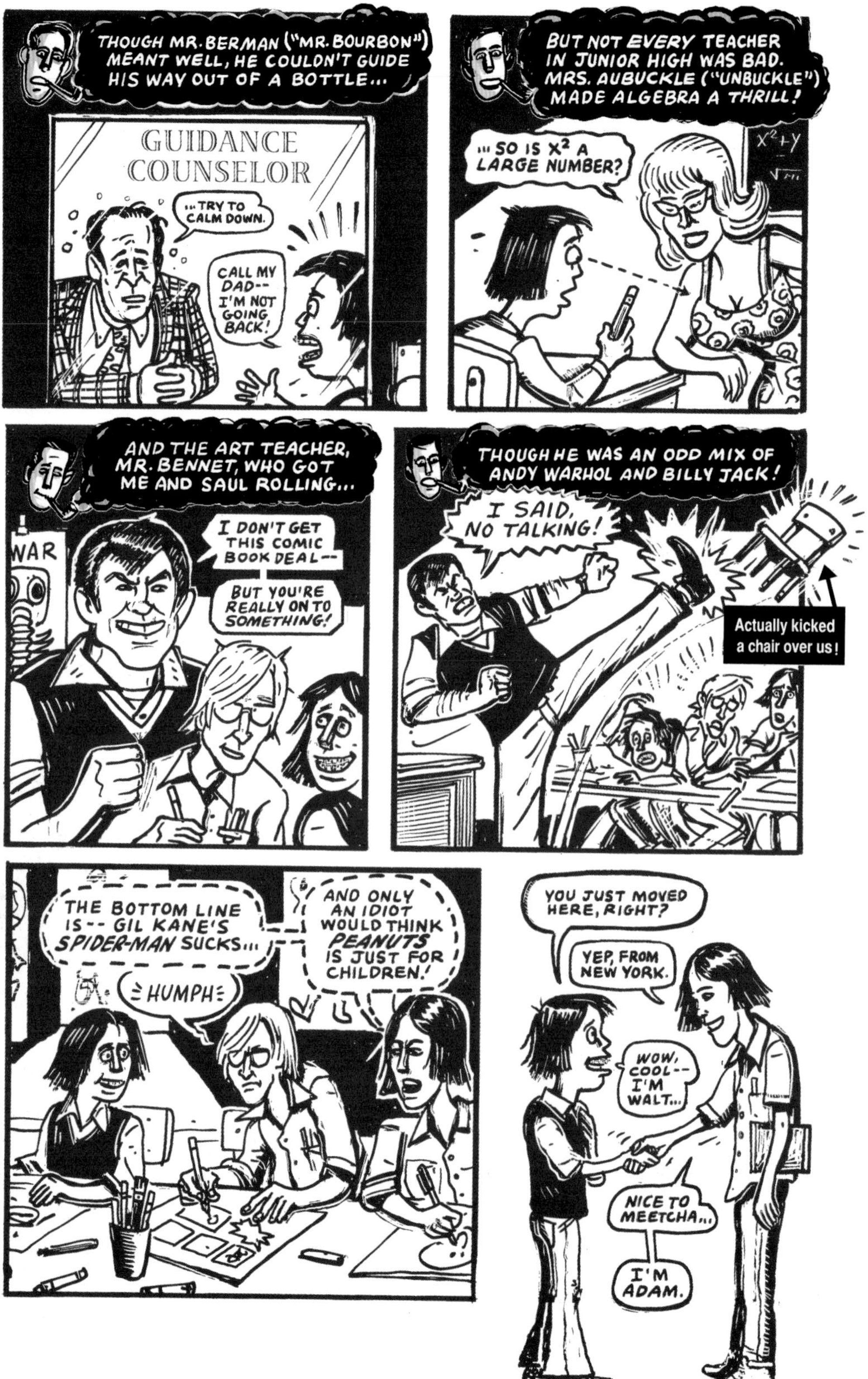
THOUGH MR. BERMAN ("MR. BOURBON") MEANT WELL, HE COULDN'T GUIDE HIS WAY OUT OF A BOTTLE...
GUIDANCE COUNSELOR
...TRY TO CALM DOWN.
CALL MY DAD-- I'M NOT GOING BACK!
BUT NOT EVERY TEACHER IN JUNIOR HIGH WAS BAD. MRS. AUBUCKLE ("UNBUCKLE") MADE ALGEBRA A THRILL!
...SO IS X² A LARGE NUMBER?
AND THE ART TEACHER, MR. BENNET, WHO GOT ME AND SAUL ROLLING...
WAR
I DON'T GET THIS COMIC BOOK DEAL--
BUT YOU'RE REALLY ON TO SOMETHING!
THOUGH HE WAS AN ODD MIX OF ANDY WARHOL AND BILLY JACK!
I SAID, NO TALKING!
Actually kicked a chair over us!
THE BOTTOM LINE IS-- GIL KANE'S SPIDER-MAN SUCKS...
AND ONLY AN IDIOT WOULD THINK PEANUTS IS JUST FOR CHILDREN!
HUMPH
YOU JUST MOVED HERE, RIGHT?
YEP, FROM NEW YORK.
WOW, COOL-- I'M WALT...
NICE TO MEETCHA...
I'M ADAM.

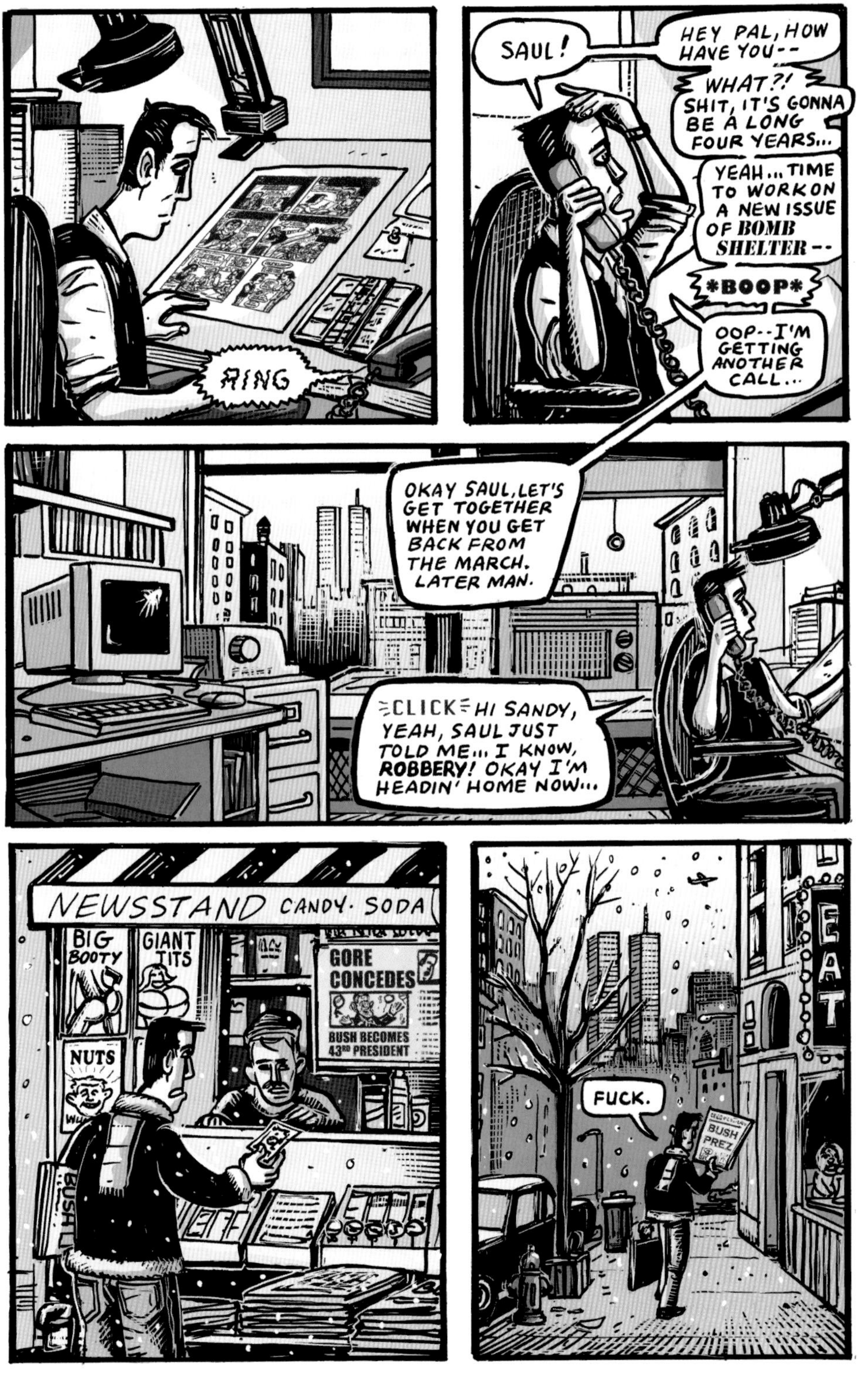
RING
SAUL!
HEY PAL, HOW HAVE YOU--
WHAT?! SHIT, IT'S GONNA BE A LONG FOUR YEARS...
YEAH... TIME TO WORK ON A NEW ISSUE OF BOMB SHELTER--
BOOP
OOP--I'M GETTING ANOTHER CALL...
OKAY SAUL, LET'S GET TOGETHER WHEN YOU GET BACK FROM THE MARCH. LATER MAN.
CLICK HI SANDY, YEAH, SAUL JUST TOLD ME... I KNOW, ROBBERY! OKAY I'M HEADIN' HOME NOW...
NEWSSTAND CANDY · SODA
BIG BOOTY
GIANT TITS
NUTS
GORE CONCEDES
BUSH BECOMES 43RD PRESIDENT
EAT
FUCK.
BUSH PREZ

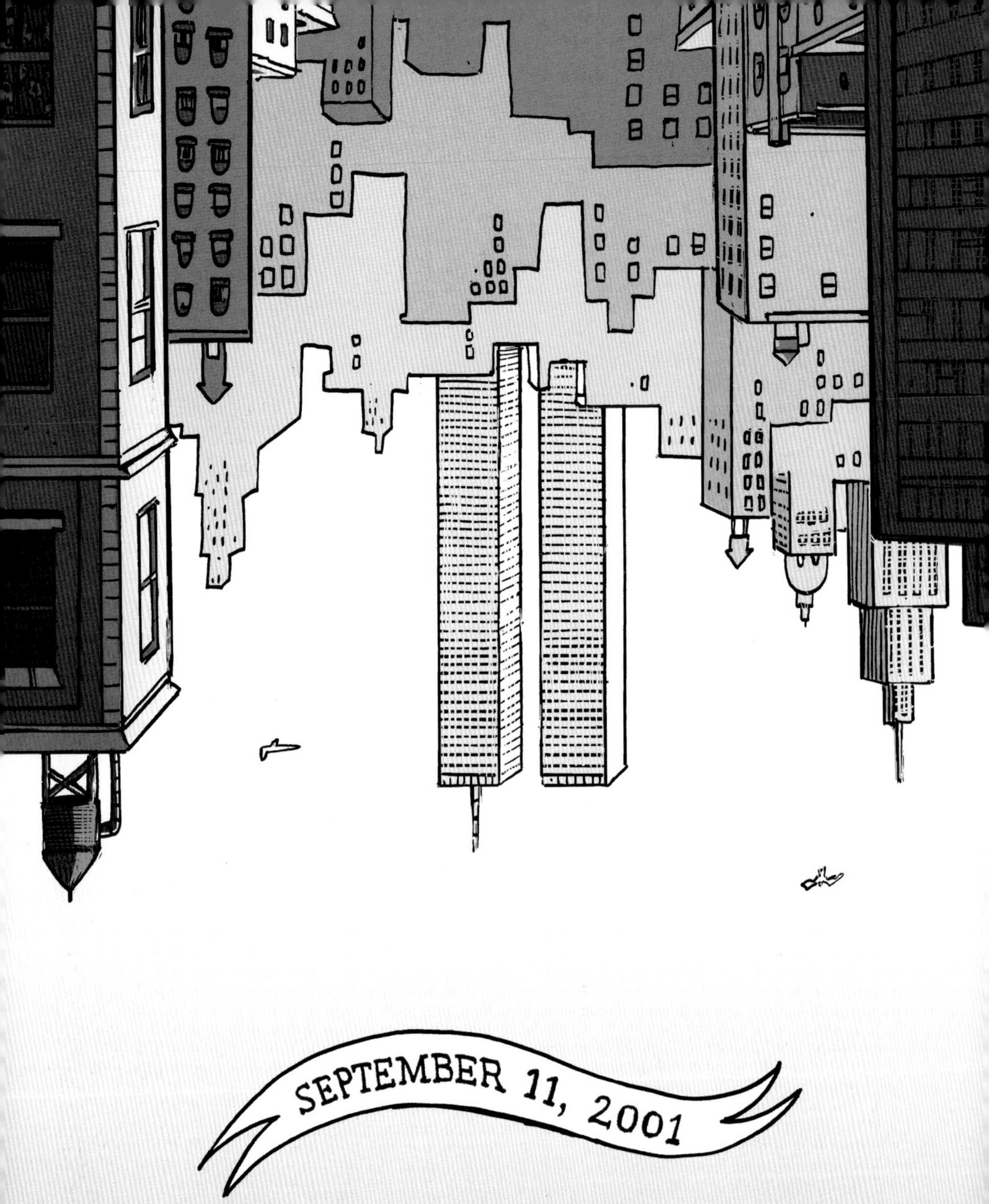
SEPTEMBER 11, 2001

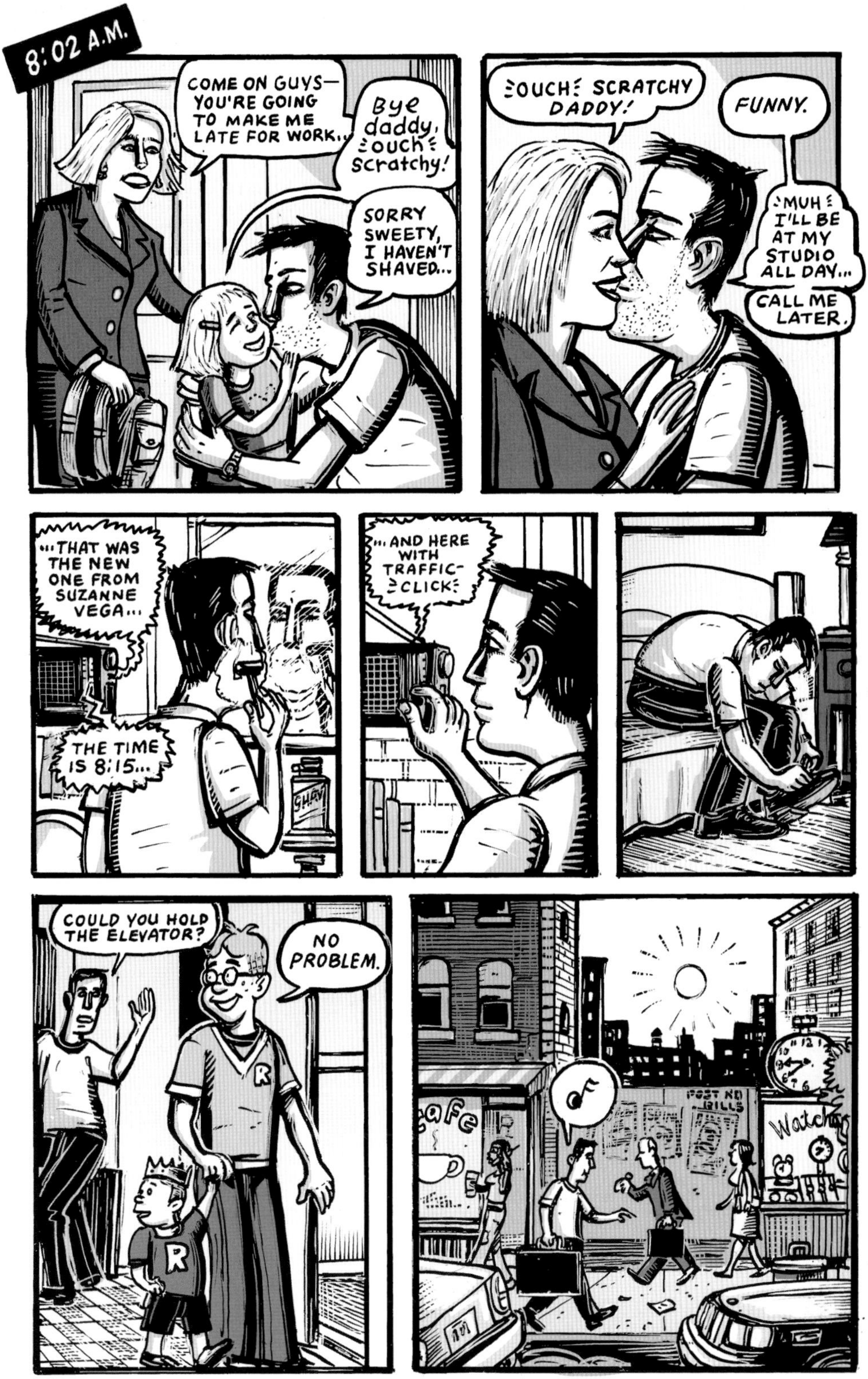
8:02 A.M.
COME ON GUYS— YOU'RE GOING TO MAKE ME LATE FOR WORK...
Bye daddy, ouch scratchy!
SORRY SWEETY, I HAVEN'T SHAVED...
OUCH SCRATCHY DADDY!
FUNNY.
MUH I'LL BE AT MY STUDIO ALL DAY...
CALL ME LATER.
...THAT WAS THE NEW ONE FROM SUZANNE VEGA...
THE TIME IS 8:15...
...AND HERE WITH TRAFFIC- CLICK
COULD YOU HOLD THE ELEVATOR?
NO PROBLEM.
POST NO BILLS
Cafe
Watch

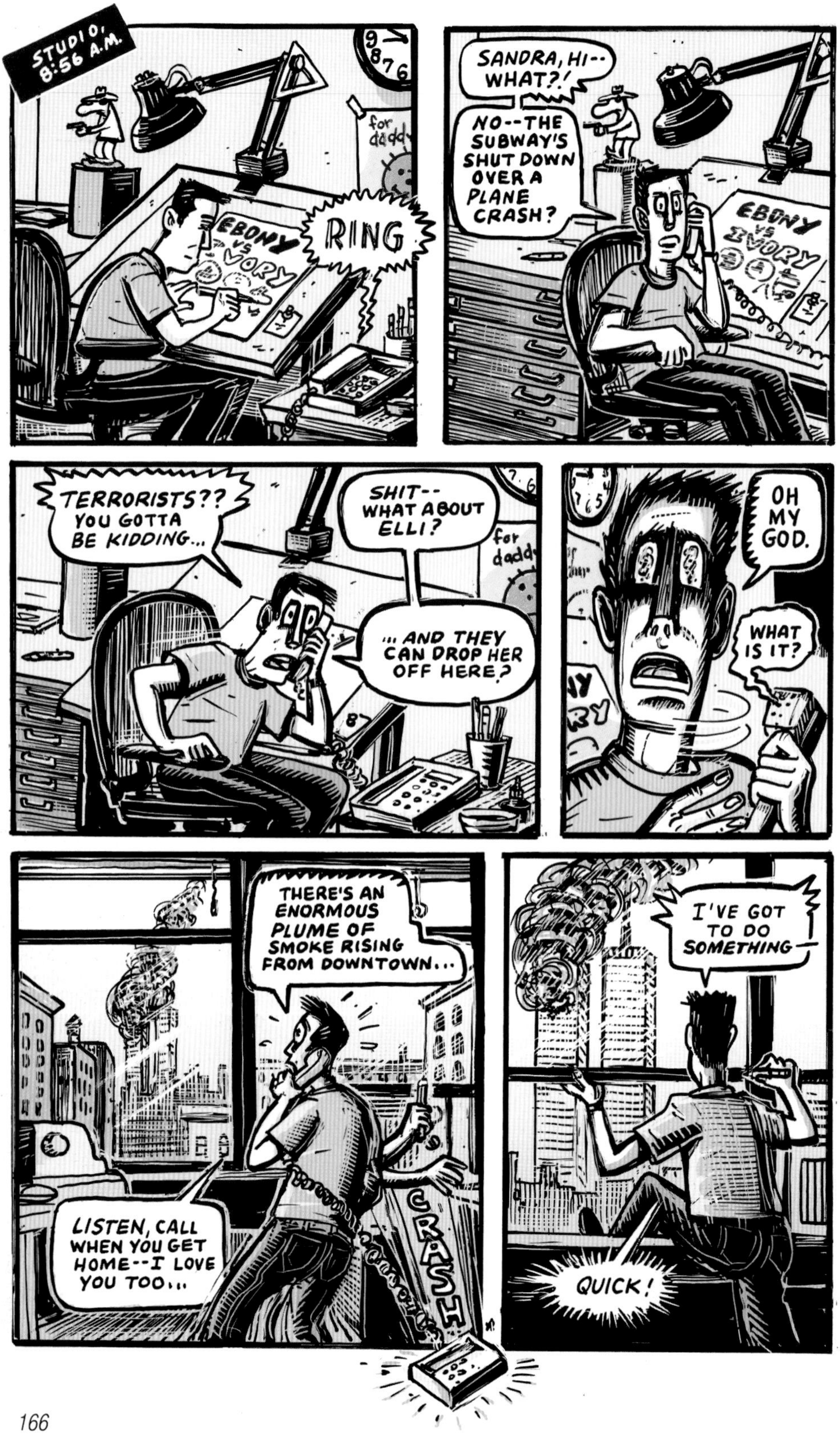
STUDIO, 8:56 A.M.
for daddy
EBONY VS IVORY
RING
SANDRA, HI-- WHAT?!
NO--THE SUBWAY'S SHUT DOWN OVER A PLANE CRASH?
TERRORISTS?? YOU GOTTA BE KIDDING...
SHIT-- WHAT ABOUT ELLI?
...AND THEY CAN DROP HER OFF HERE?
OH MY GOD.
WHAT IS IT?
THERE'S AN ENORMOUS PLUME OF SMOKE RISING FROM DOWNTOWN...
LISTEN, CALL WHEN YOU GET HOME--I LOVE YOU TOO...
CRASH
I'VE GOT TO DO SOMETHING--
QUICK!

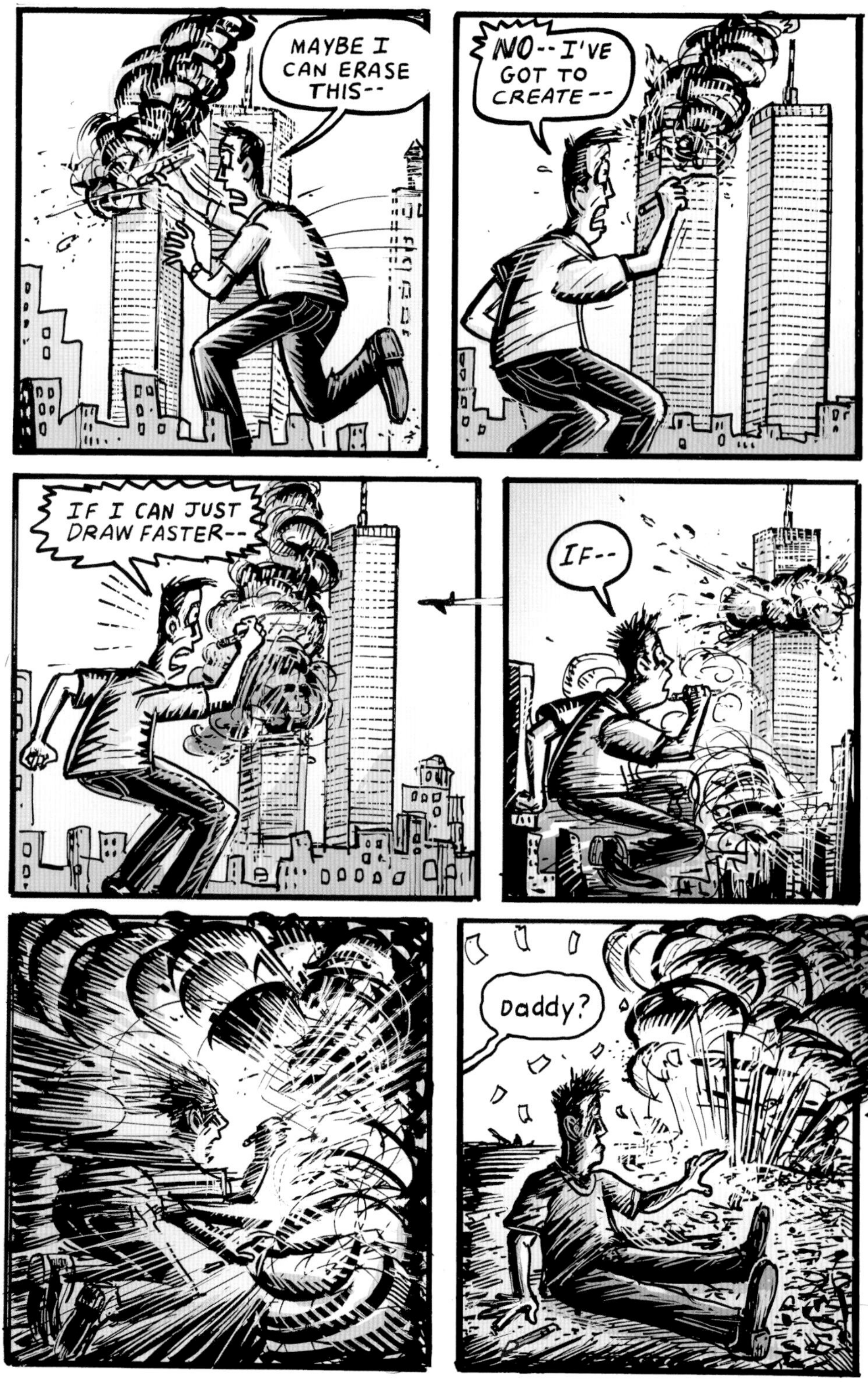
MAYBE I CAN ERASE THIS--
NO--I'VE GOT TO CREATE--
IF I CAN JUST DRAW FASTER--
IF--
Daddy?

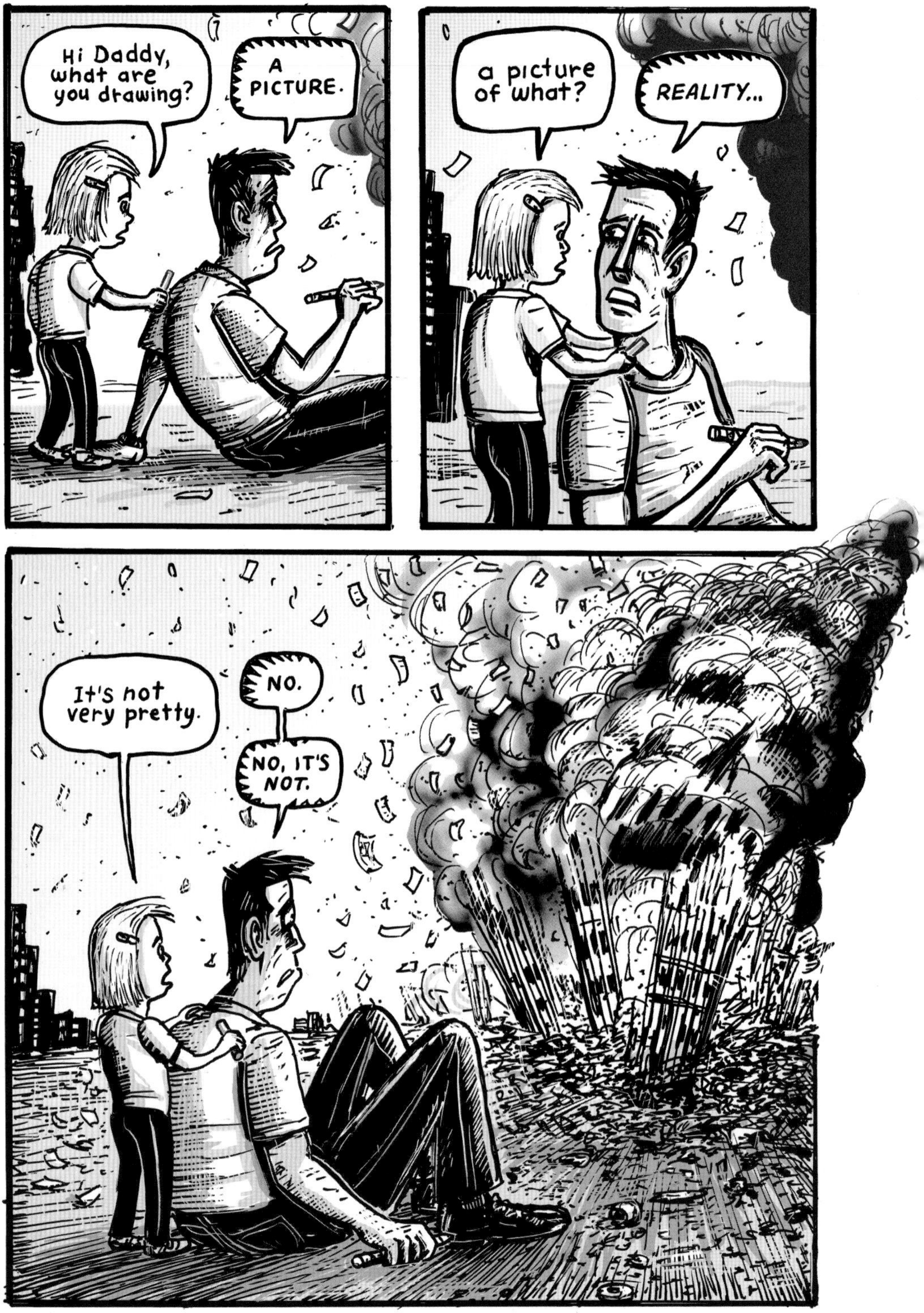
Hi Daddy, what are you drawing?
A PICTURE.
a picture of what?
REALITY...
It's not very pretty.
NO.
NO, IT'S NOT.

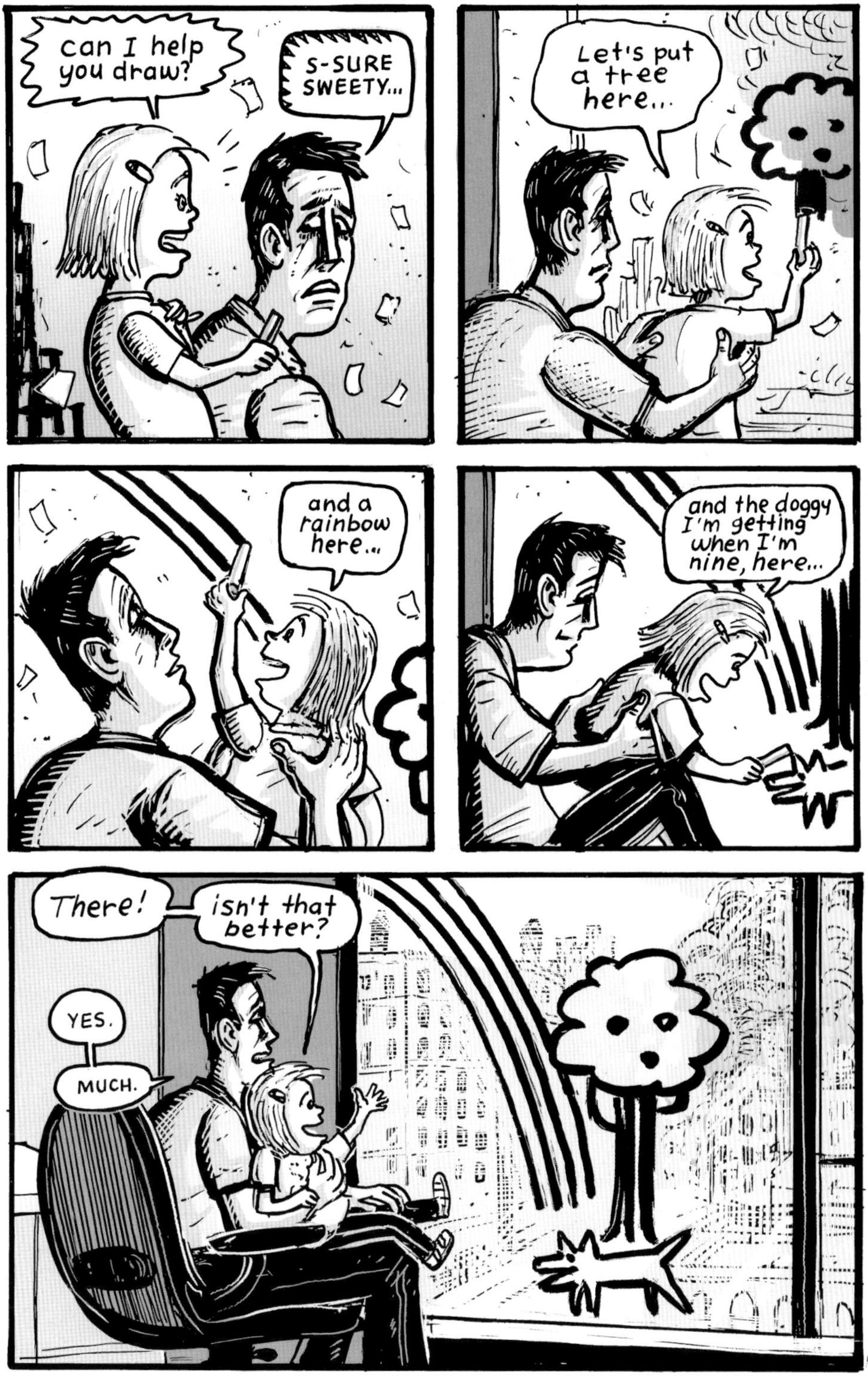
can I help you draw?
S-SURE SWEETY...
Let's put a tree here...
and a rainbow here...
and the doggy I'm getting when I'm nine, here...
There!
isn't that better?
YES.
MUCH.

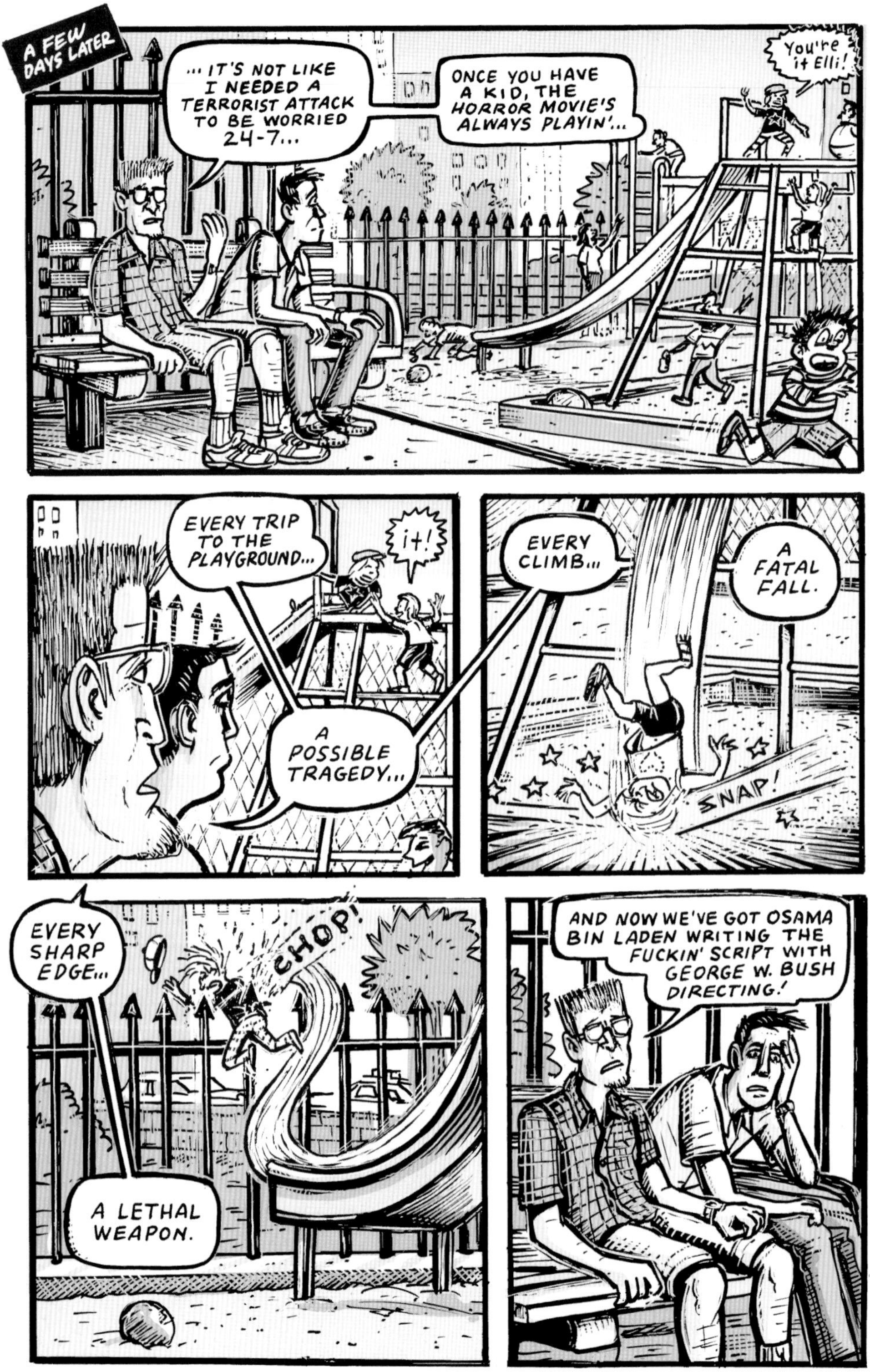
A FEW DAYS LATER
...IT'S NOT LIKE I NEEDED A TERRORIST ATTACK TO BE WORRIED 24-7...
ONCE YOU HAVE A KID, THE HORROR MOVIE'S ALWAYS PLAYIN'...
You're it Elli!
EVERY TRIP TO THE PLAYGROUND...
it!
A POSSIBLE TRAGEDY...
EVERY CLIMB...
A FATAL FALL.
SNAP!
EVERY SHARP EDGE...
CHOP!
A LETHAL WEAPON.
AND NOW WE'VE GOT OSAMA BIN LADEN WRITING THE FUCKIN' SCRIPT WITH GEORGE W. BUSH DIRECTING!

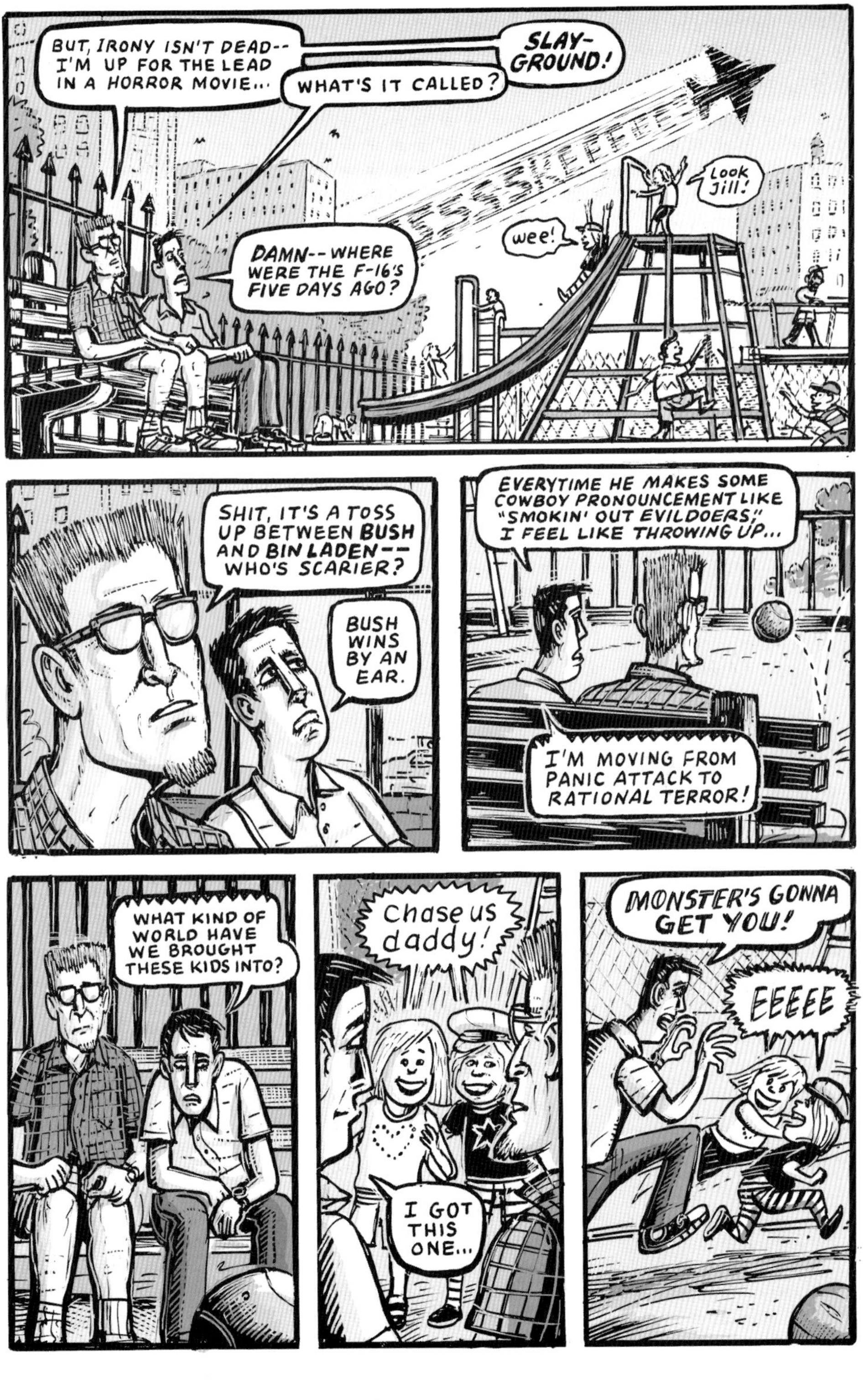

BUT, IRONY ISN'T DEAD-- I'M UP FOR THE LEAD IN A HORROR MOVIE...
WHAT'S IT CALLED?
SLAY-GROUND!
SSSSKEEEEEE
Look Jill!
wee!
DAMN-- WHERE WERE THE F-16'S FIVE DAYS AGO?
SHIT, IT'S A TOSS UP BETWEEN BUSH AND BIN LADEN-- WHO'S SCARIER?
BUSH WINS BY AN EAR.
EVERYTIME HE MAKES SOME COWBOY PRONOUNCEMENT LIKE "SMOKIN' OUT EVILDOERS," I FEEL LIKE THROWING UP...
I'M MOVING FROM PANIC ATTACK TO RATIONAL TERROR!
WHAT KIND OF WORLD HAVE WE BROUGHT THESE KIDS INTO?
Chase us daddy!
I GOT THIS ONE...
MONSTER'S GONNA GET YOU!
EEEEE

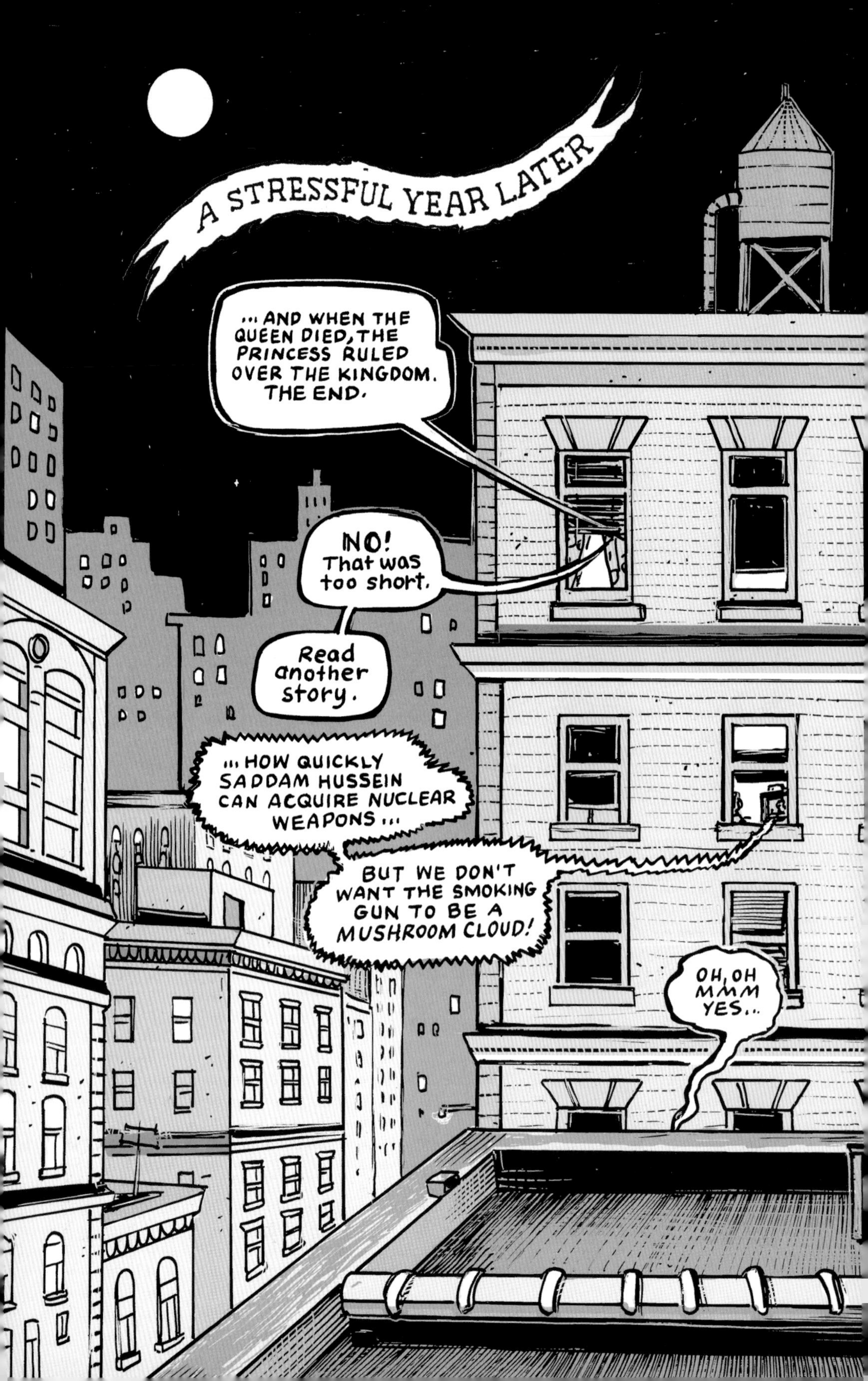
A STRESSFUL YEAR LATER
...AND WHEN THE QUEEN DIED, THE PRINCESS RULED OVER THE KINGDOM. THE END.
NO! That was too short.
Read another story.
...HOW QUICKLY SADDAM HUSSEIN CAN ACQUIRE NUCLEAR WEAPONS...
BUT WE DON'T WANT THE SMOKING GUN TO BE A MUSHROOM CLOUD!
OH, OH MMM YES...

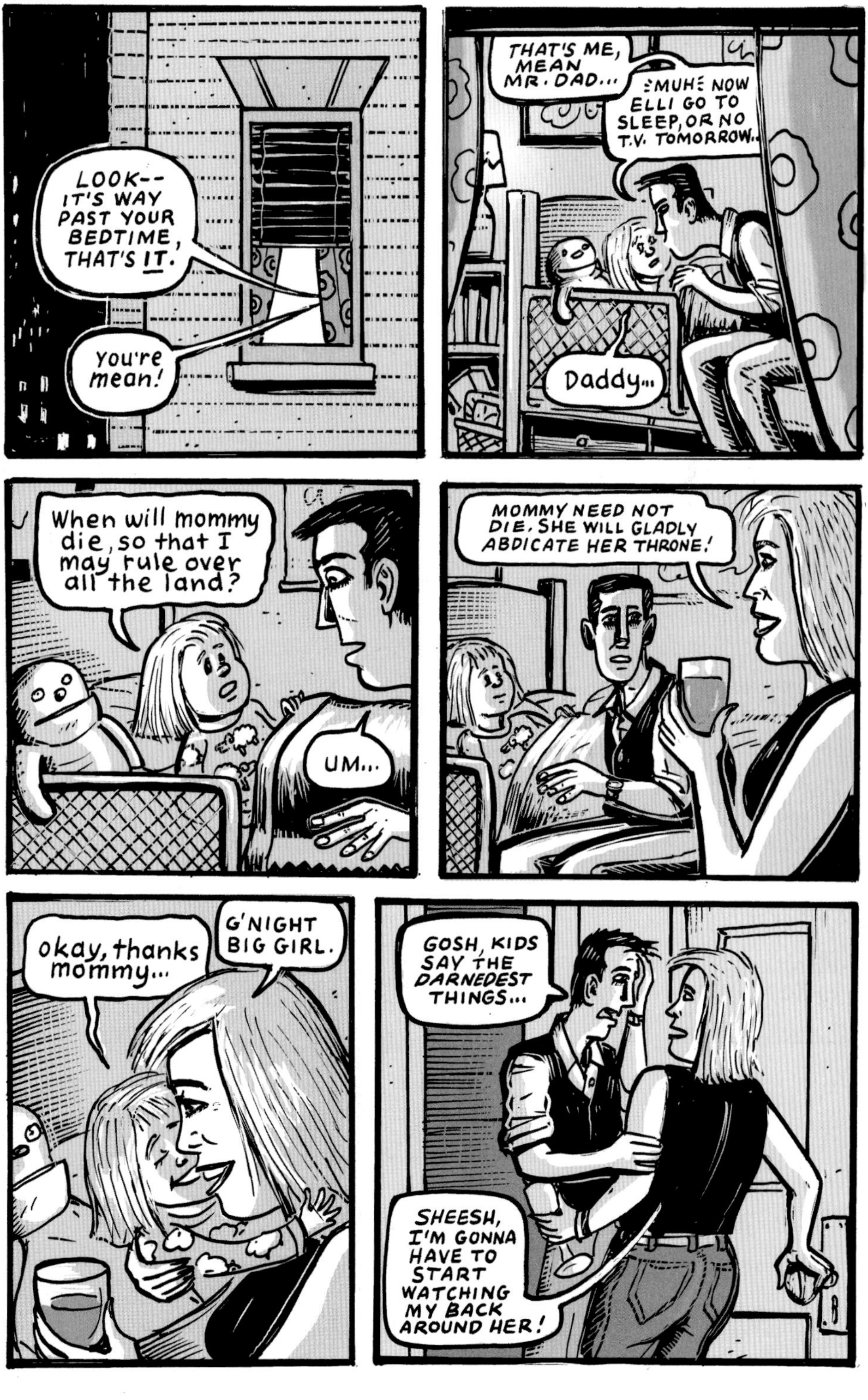
LOOK--
IT'S WAY PAST YOUR BEDTIME, THAT'S IT.
you're mean!
THAT'S ME, MEAN MR. DAD...
MUH NOW ELLI GO TO SLEEP, OR NO T.V. TOMORROW..
Daddy...
When will mommy die, so that I may rule over all the land?
UM...
MOMMY NEED NOT DIE. SHE WILL GLADLY ABDICATE HER THRONE!
okay, thanks mommy...
G'NIGHT BIG GIRL.
GOSH, KIDS SAY THE DARNEDEST THINGS...
SHEESH, I'M GONNA HAVE TO START WATCHING MY BACK AROUND HER!

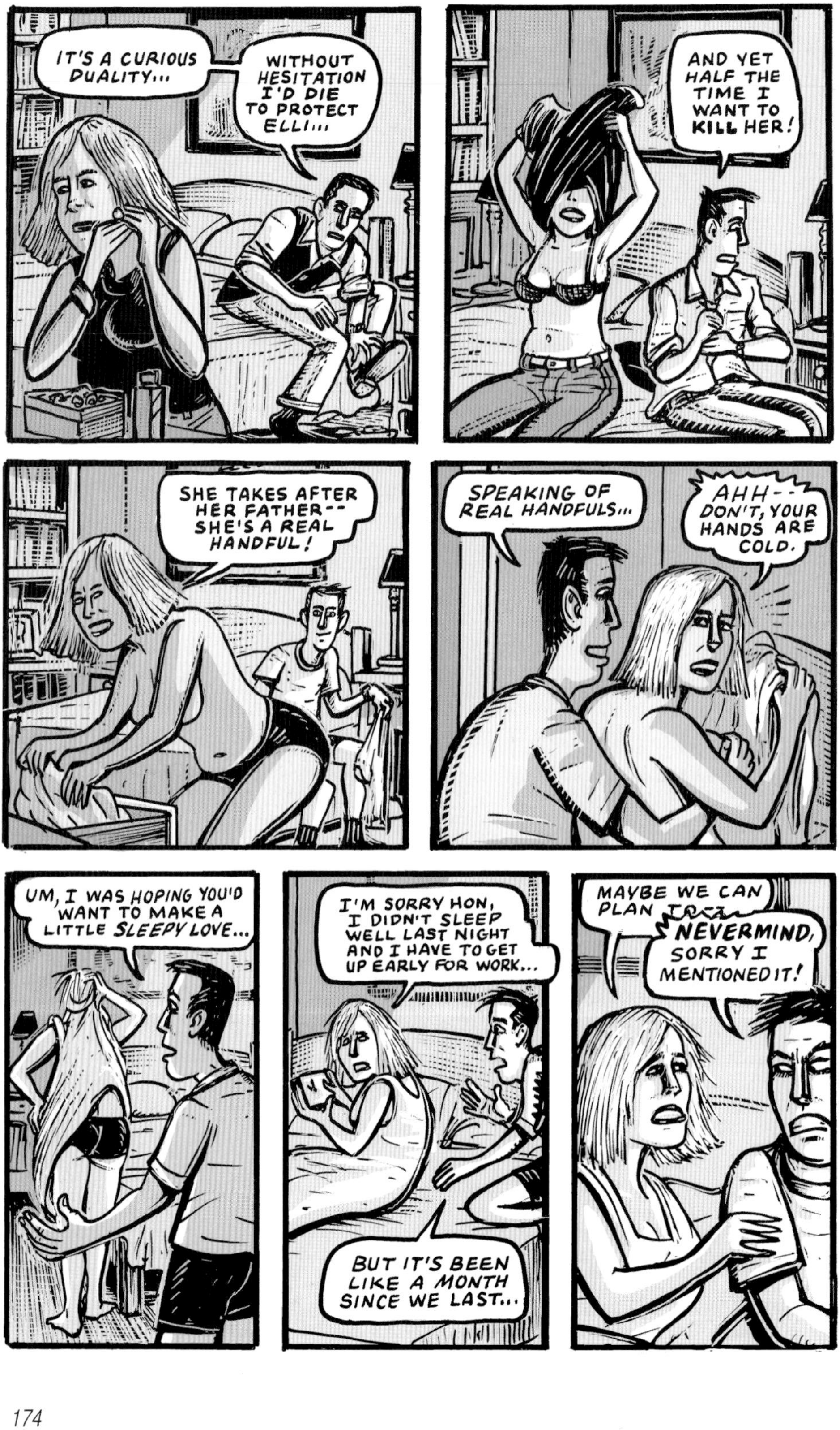
IT'S A CURIOUS DUALITY...
WITHOUT HESITATION I'D DIE TO PROTECT ELLI...
AND YET HALF THE TIME I WANT TO KILL HER!
SHE TAKES AFTER HER FATHER-- SHE'S A REAL HANDFUL!
SPEAKING OF REAL HANDFULS...
AHH-- DON'T, YOUR HANDS ARE COLD.
UM, I WAS HOPING YOU'D WANT TO MAKE A LITTLE SLEEPY LOVE...
I'M SORRY HON, I DIDN'T SLEEP WELL LAST NIGHT AND I HAVE TO GET UP EARLY FOR WORK...
BUT IT'S BEEN LIKE A MONTH SINCE WE LAST...
MAYBE WE CAN PLAN TO--
NEVERMIND, SORRY I MENTIONED IT!

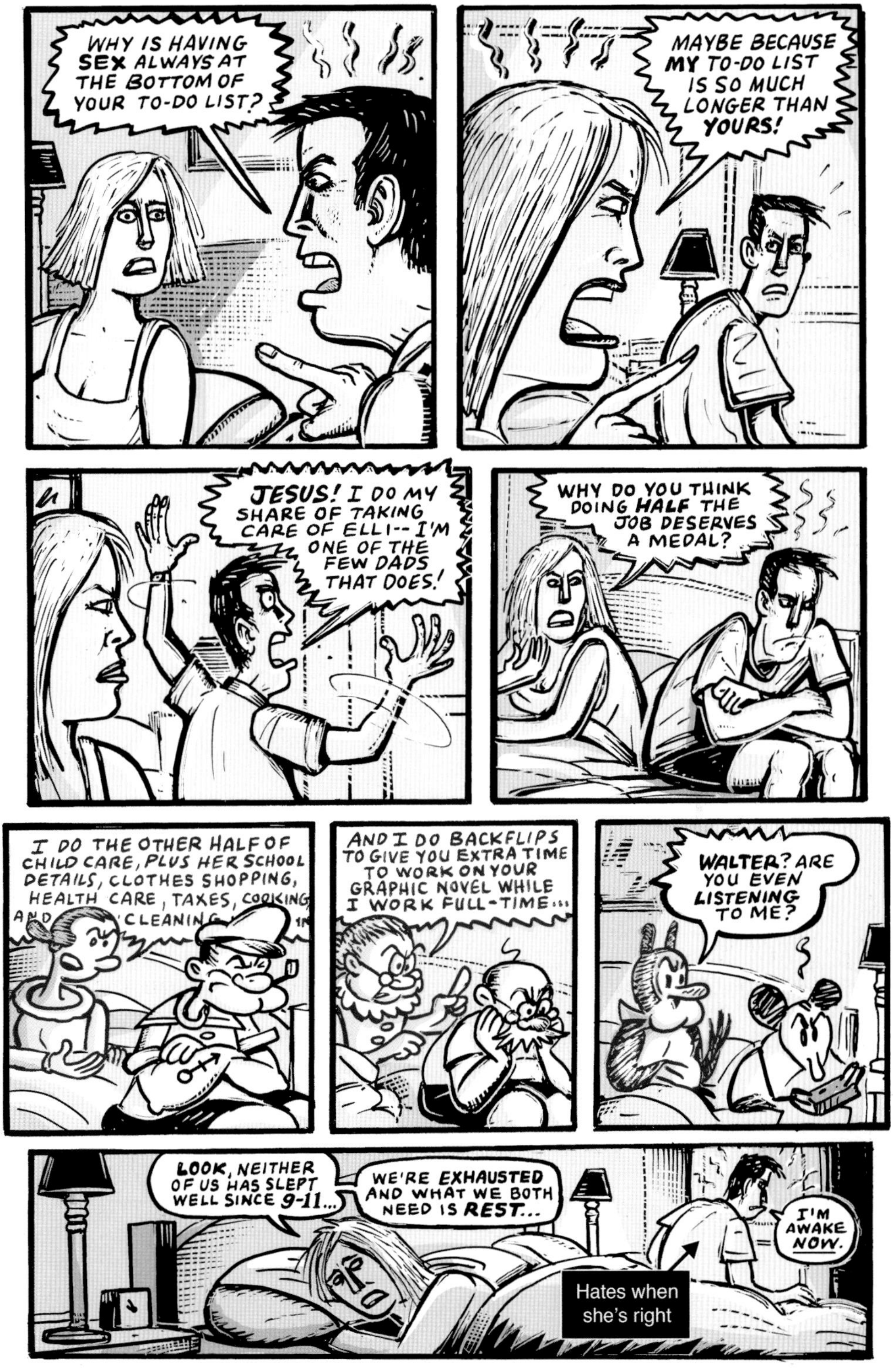

WHY IS HAVING SEX ALWAYS AT THE BOTTOM OF YOUR TO-DO LIST?
MAYBE BECAUSE MY TO-DO LIST IS SO MUCH LONGER THAN YOURS!
JESUS! I DO MY SHARE OF TAKING CARE OF ELLI-- I'M ONE OF THE FEW DADS THAT DOES!
WHY DO YOU THINK DOING HALF THE JOB DESERVES A MEDAL?
I DO THE OTHER HALF OF CHILD CARE, PLUS HER SCHOOL DETAILS, CLOTHES SHOPPING, HEALTH CARE, TAXES, COOKING AND
CLEANING
AND I DO BACKFLIPS TO GIVE YOU EXTRA TIME TO WORK ON YOUR GRAPHIC NOVEL WHILE I WORK FULL-TIME...
WALTER? ARE YOU EVEN LISTENING TO ME?
LOOK, NEITHER OF US HAS SLEPT WELL SINCE 9-11...
WE'RE EXHAUSTED AND WHAT WE BOTH NEED IS REST...
Hates when she's right
I'M AWAKE NOW.

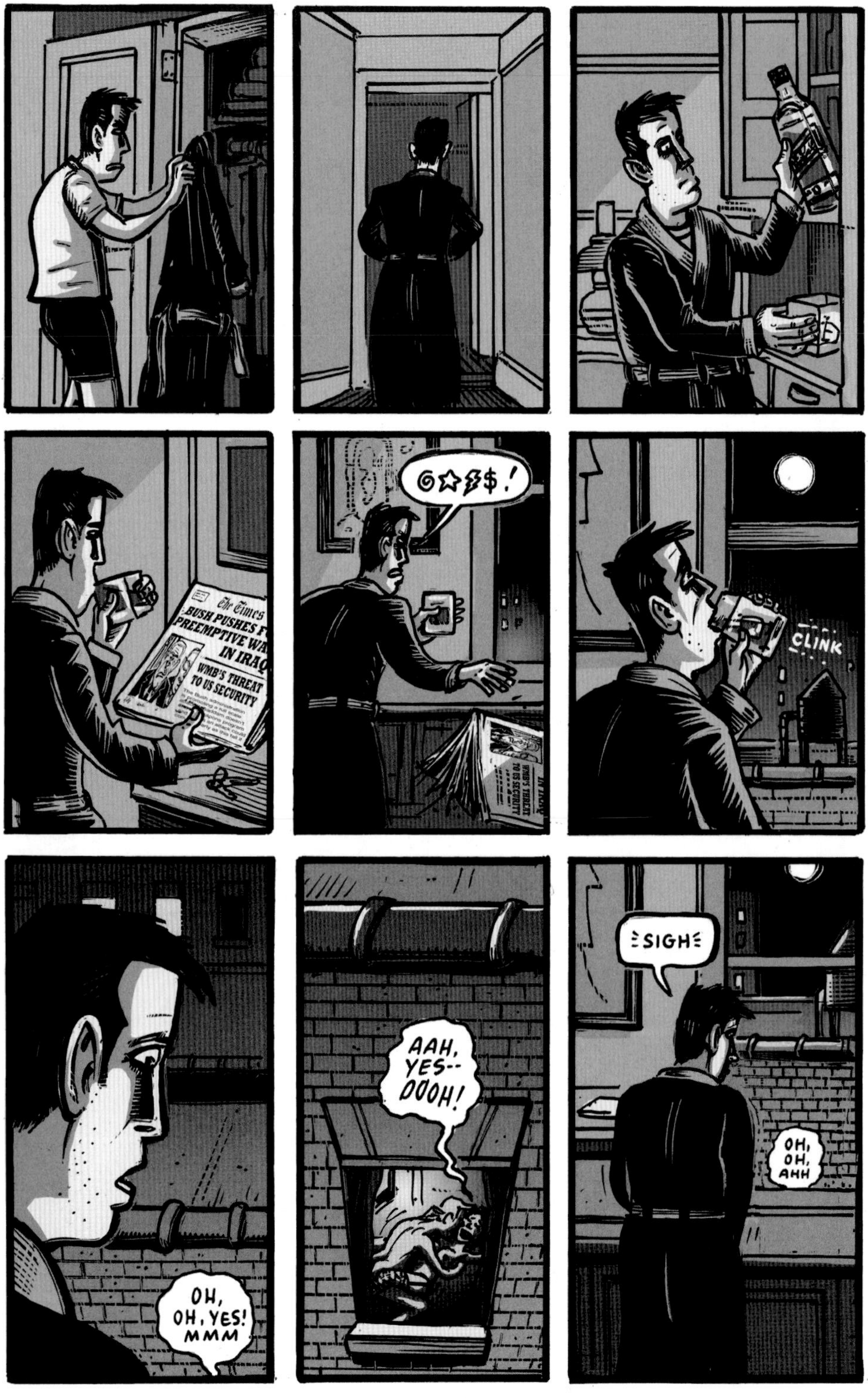
The Times
BUSH PUSHES F
PREEMPTIVE WA
IN IRAQ
WMB'S THREAT
TO US SECURITY
CLINK
OH,
OH, YES!
MMM
AAH,
YES--
OOOH!
SIGH
OH,
OH,
AHH

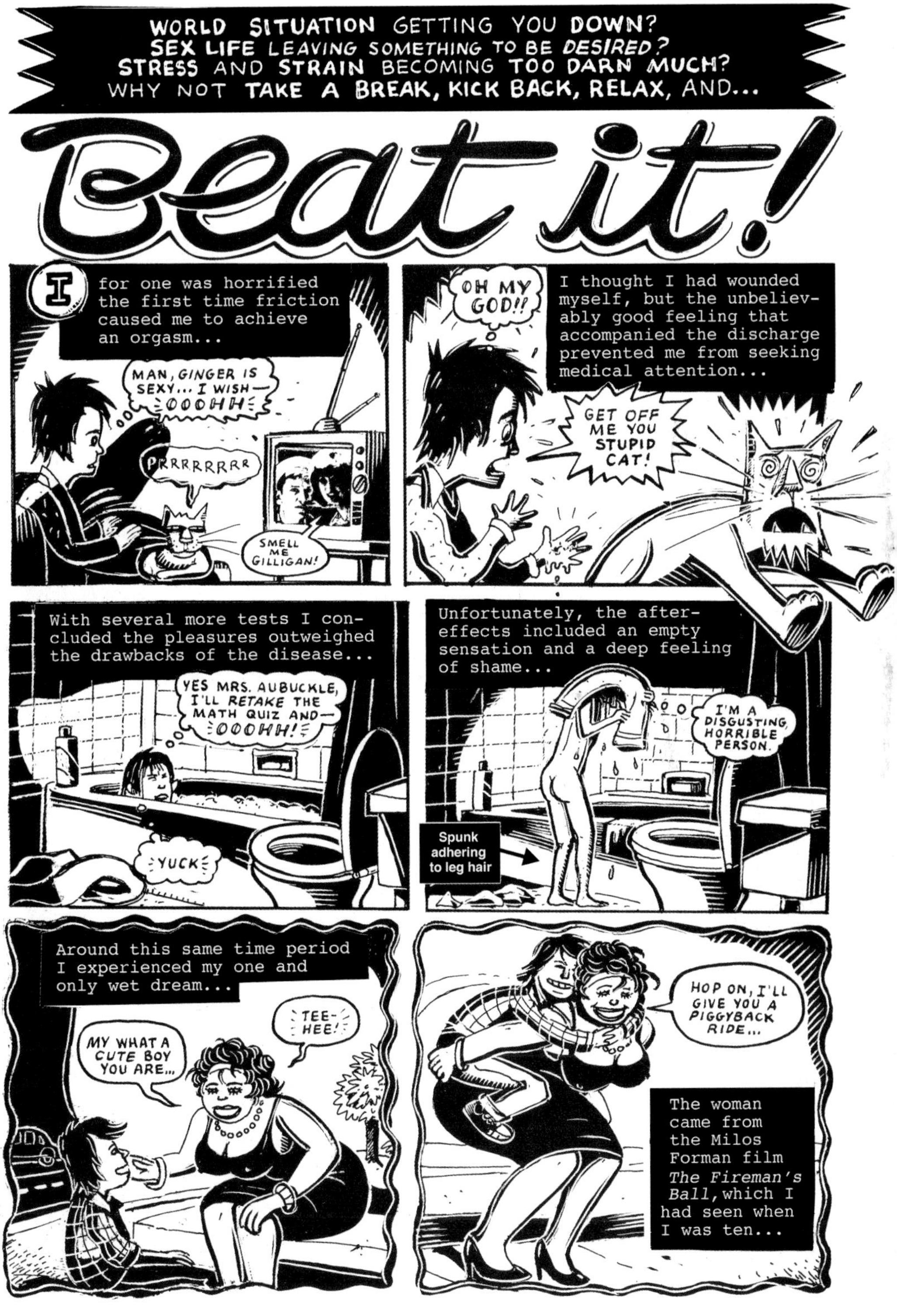
WORLD SITUATION GETTING YOU DOWN?
SEX LIFE LEAVING SOMETHING TO BE DESIRED?
STRESS AND STRAIN BECOMING TOO DARN MUCH?
WHY NOT TAKE A BREAK, KICK BACK, RELAX, AND...
Beat it!
I for one was horrified the first time friction caused me to achieve an orgasm...
MAN, GINGER IS SEXY... I WISH— OOOHH
PRRRRRRRR
SMELL ME GILLIGAN!
OH MY GOD!!
I thought I had wounded myself, but the unbelievably good feeling that accompanied the discharge prevented me from seeking medical attention...
GET OFF ME YOU STUPID CAT!
With several more tests I concluded the pleasures outweighed the drawbacks of the disease...
YES MRS. AUBUCKLE, I'LL RETAKE THE MATH QUIZ AND— OOOHH!
YUCK
Unfortunately, the aftereffects included an empty sensation and a deep feeling of shame...
I'M A DISGUSTING, HORRIBLE PERSON.
Spunk adhering to leg hair
Around this same time period I experienced my one and only wet dream...
MY WHAT A CUTE BOY YOU ARE...
TEE-HEE!
HOP ON, I'LL GIVE YOU A PIGGYBACK RIDE...
The woman came from the Milos Forman film The Fireman's Ball, which I had seen when I was ten...

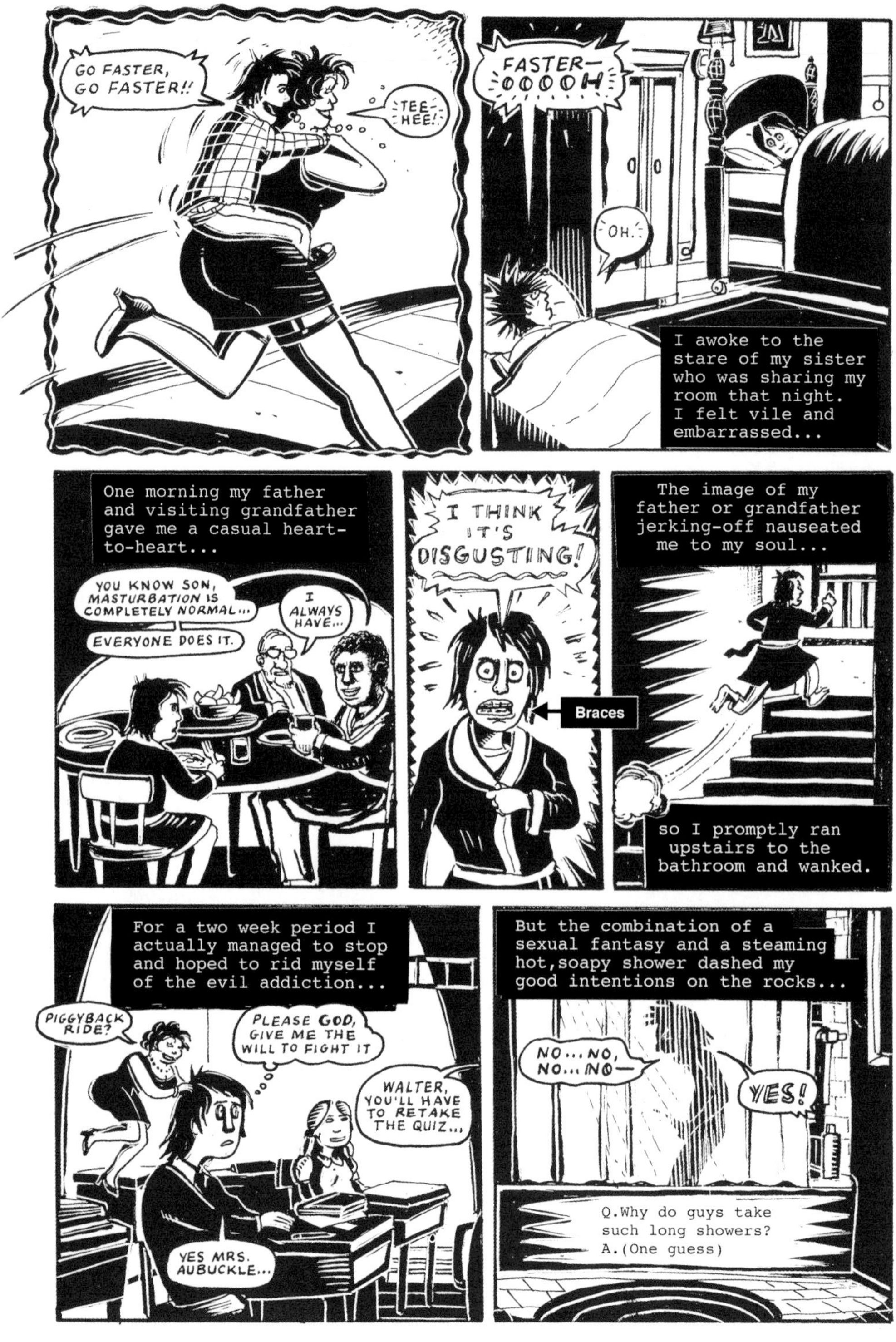
GO FASTER, GO FASTER!!
TEE HEE!
FASTER—OOOOH
OH.
I awoke to the stare of my sister who was sharing my room that night. I felt vile and embarrassed...
One morning my father and visiting grandfather gave me a casual heart-to-heart...
YOU KNOW SON, MASTURBATION IS COMPLETELY NORMAL...
EVERYONE DOES IT.
I ALWAYS HAVE...
I THINK IT'S DISGUSTING!
Braces
The image of my father or grandfather jerking-off nauseated me to my soul...
so I promptly ran upstairs to the bathroom and wanked.
For a two week period I actually managed to stop and hoped to rid myself of the evil addiction...
PIGGYBACK RIDE?
PLEASE GOD, GIVE ME THE WILL TO FIGHT IT
WALTER, YOU'LL HAVE TO RETAKE THE QUIZ...
YES MRS. AUBUCKLE...
But the combination of a sexual fantasy and a steaming hot,soapy shower dashed my good intentions on the rocks...
NO...NO, NO...NO—
YES!
Q.Why do guys take such long showers?
A.(One guess)

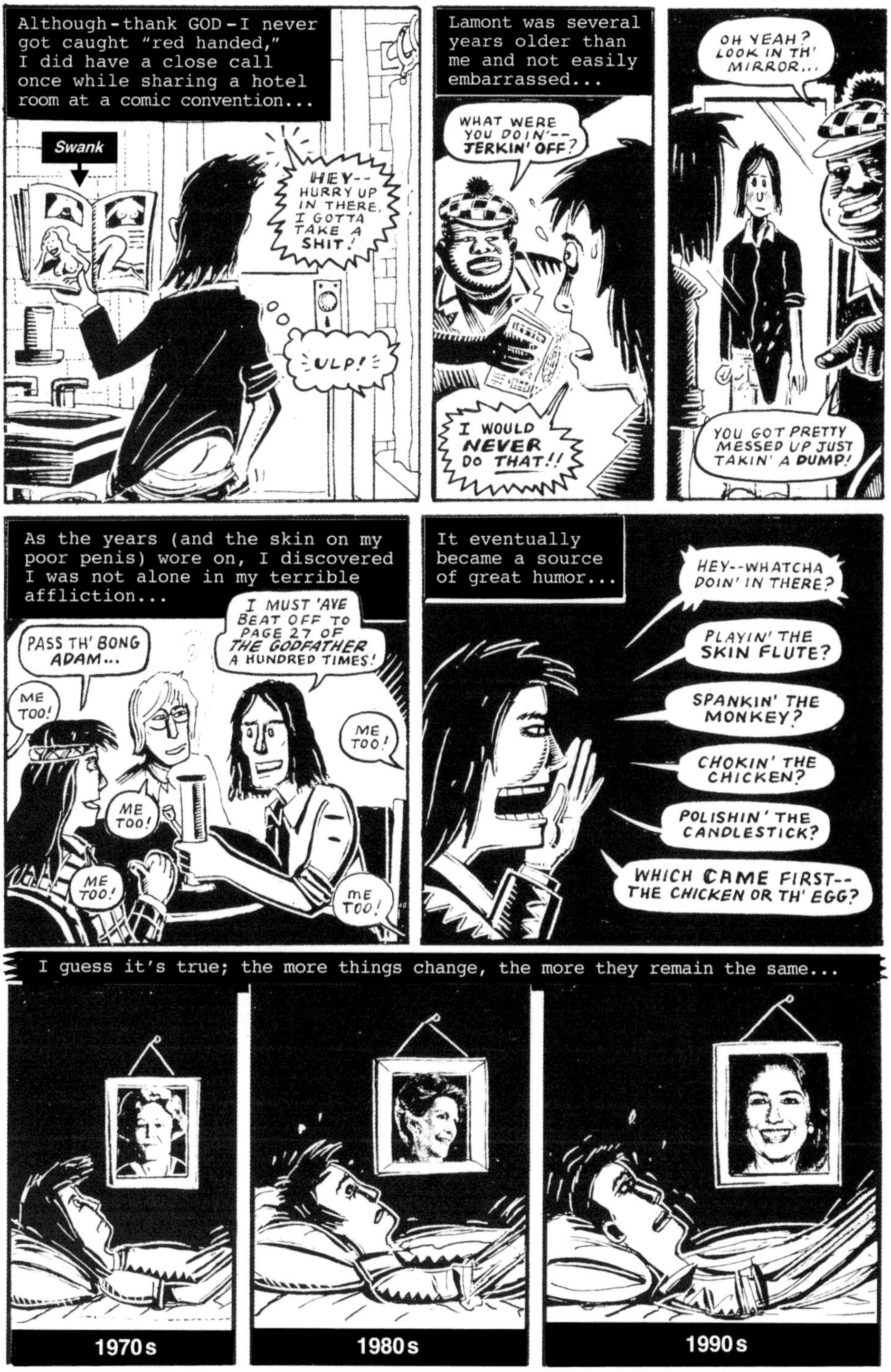
Although-thank GOD-I never got caught "red handed," I did have a close call once while sharing a hotel room at a comic convention...
Swank
HEY--HURRY UP IN THERE, I GOTTA TAKE A SHIT!
ULP!
Lamont was several years older than me and not easily embarrassed...
WHAT WERE YOU DOIN'--JERKIN' OFF?
I WOULD NEVER DO THAT!!
OH YEAH? LOOK IN TH' MIRROR...
YOU GOT PRETTY MESSED UP JUST TAKIN' A DUMP!
As the years (and the skin on my poor penis) wore on, I discovered I was not alone in my terrible affliction...
PASS TH' BONG ADAM...
I MUST 'AVE BEAT OFF TO PAGE 27 OF THE GODFATHER A HUNDRED TIMES!
ME TOO!
ME TOO!
ME TOO!
ME TOO!
ME TOO!
It eventually became a source of great humor...
HEY--WHATCHA DOIN' IN THERE?
PLAYIN' THE SKIN FLUTE?
SPANKIN' THE MONKEY?
CHOKIN' THE CHICKEN?
POLISHIN' THE CANDLESTICK?
WHICH CAME FIRST--THE CHICKEN OR TH' EGG?
I guess it's true; the more things change, the more they remain the same...
1970s
1980s
1990s

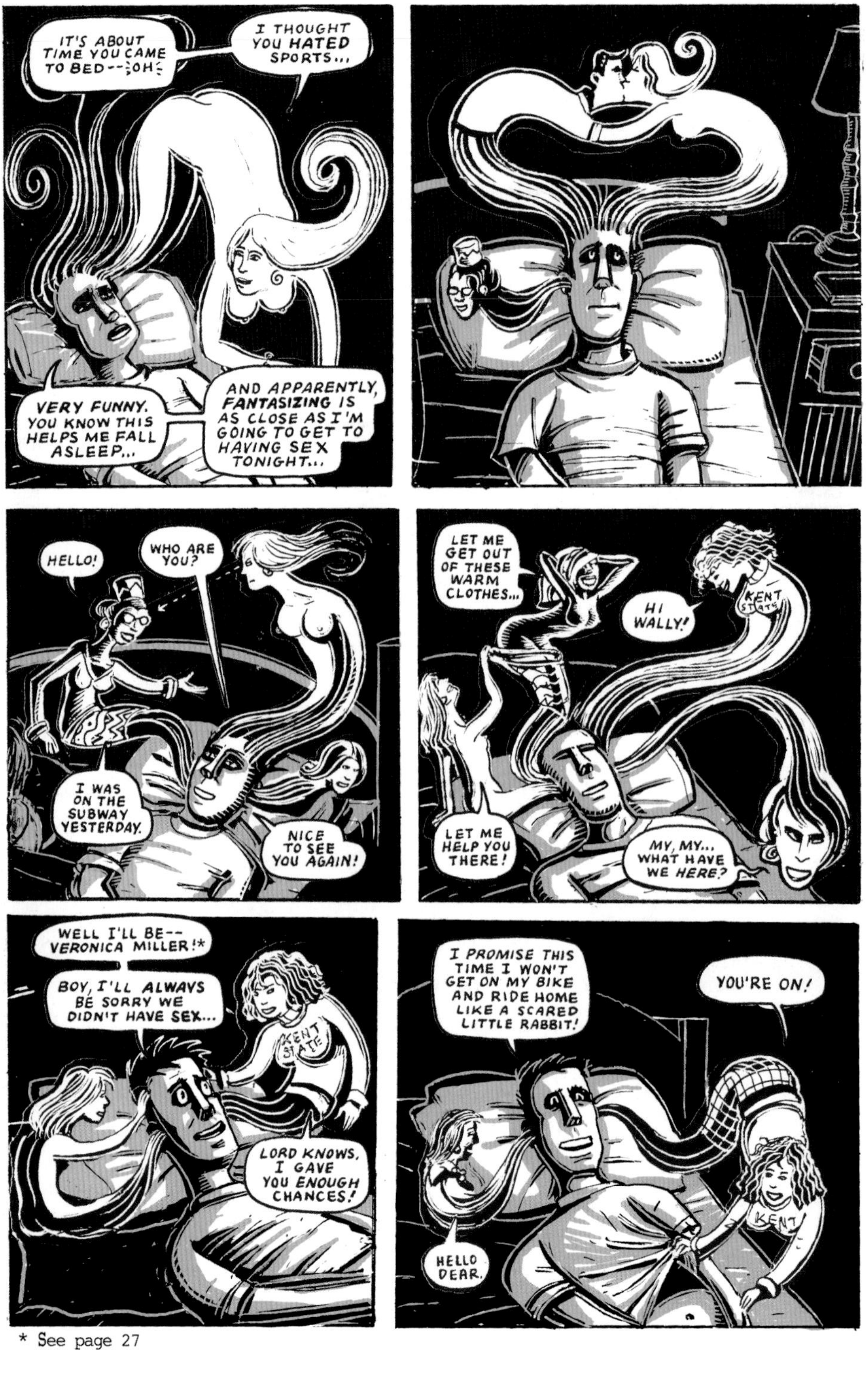
IT'S ABOUT TIME YOU CAME TO BED--¡OH!
I THOUGHT YOU HATED SPORTS...
VERY FUNNY. YOU KNOW THIS HELPS ME FALL ASLEEP...
AND APPARENTLY, FANTASIZING IS AS CLOSE AS I'M GOING TO GET TO HAVING SEX TONIGHT...
HELLO!
WHO ARE YOU?
I WAS ON THE SUBWAY YESTERDAY.
NICE TO SEE YOU AGAIN!
LET ME GET OUT OF THESE WARM CLOTHES...
HI WALLY!
KENT STATE
LET ME HELP YOU THERE!
MY, MY... WHAT HAVE WE HERE?
WELL I'LL BE-- VERONICA MILLER!*
BOY, I'LL ALWAYS BE SORRY WE DIDN'T HAVE SEX...
KENT STATE
LORD KNOWS, I GAVE YOU ENOUGH CHANCES!
I PROMISE THIS TIME I WON'T GET ON MY BIKE AND RIDE HOME LIKE A SCARED LITTLE RABBIT!
YOU'RE ON!
HELLO DEAR.
KENT

* See page 27

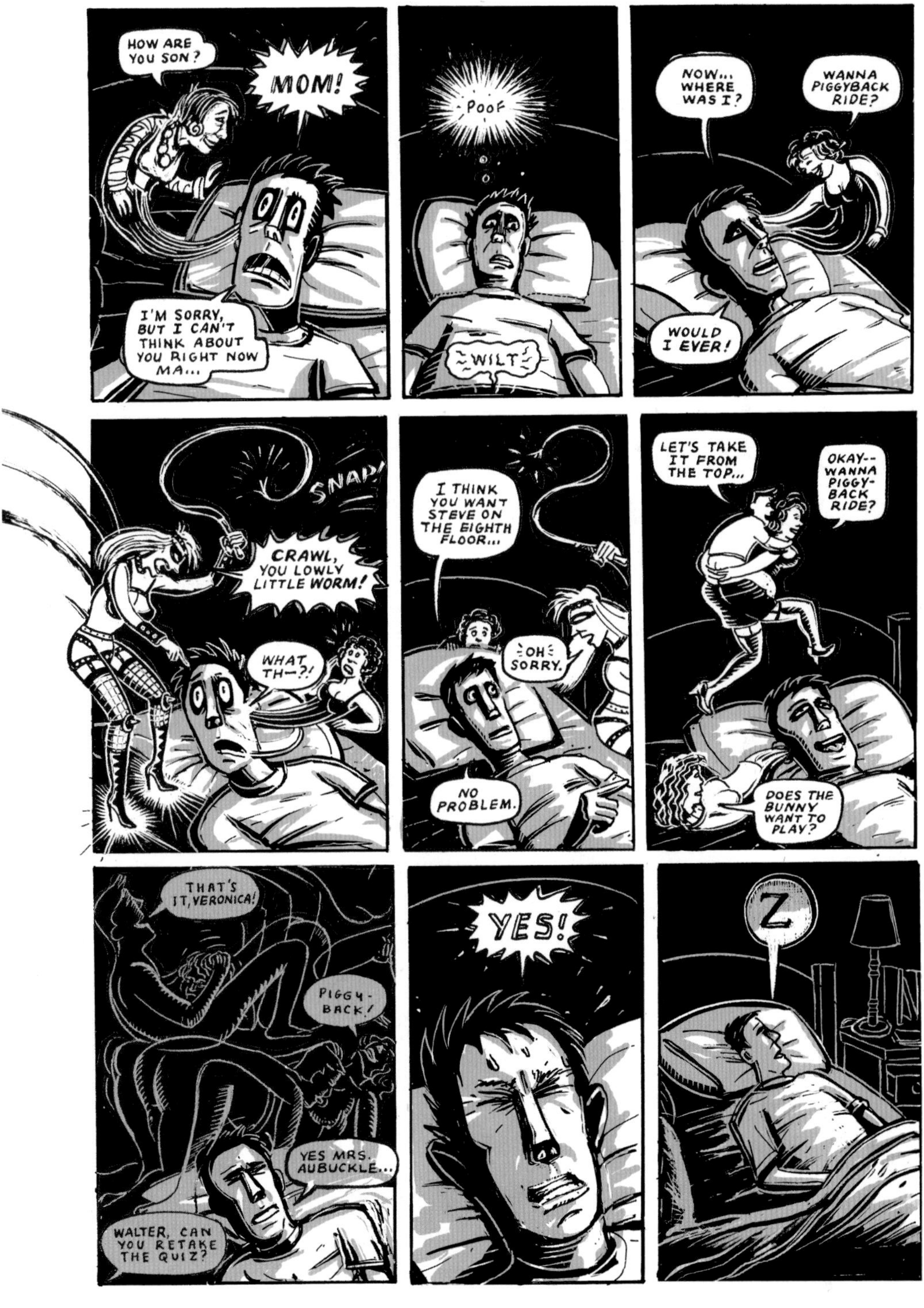
HOW ARE YOU SON?
MOM!
I'M SORRY, BUT I CAN'T THINK ABOUT YOU RIGHT NOW MA...
POOF
WILT
NOW... WHERE WAS I?
WANNA PIGGYBACK RIDE?
WOULD I EVER!
SNAP!
CRAWL, YOU LOWLY LITTLE WORM!
WHAT TH-?!
I THINK YOU WANT STEVE ON THE EIGHTH FLOOR...
OH SORRY.
NO PROBLEM.
LET'S TAKE IT FROM THE TOP...
OKAY-- WANNA PIGGY-BACK RIDE?
DOES THE BUNNY WANT TO PLAY?
THAT'S IT, VERONICA!
PIGGY-BACK!
YES MRS. AUBUCKLE...
WALTER, CAN YOU RETAKE THE QUIZ?
YES!
Z

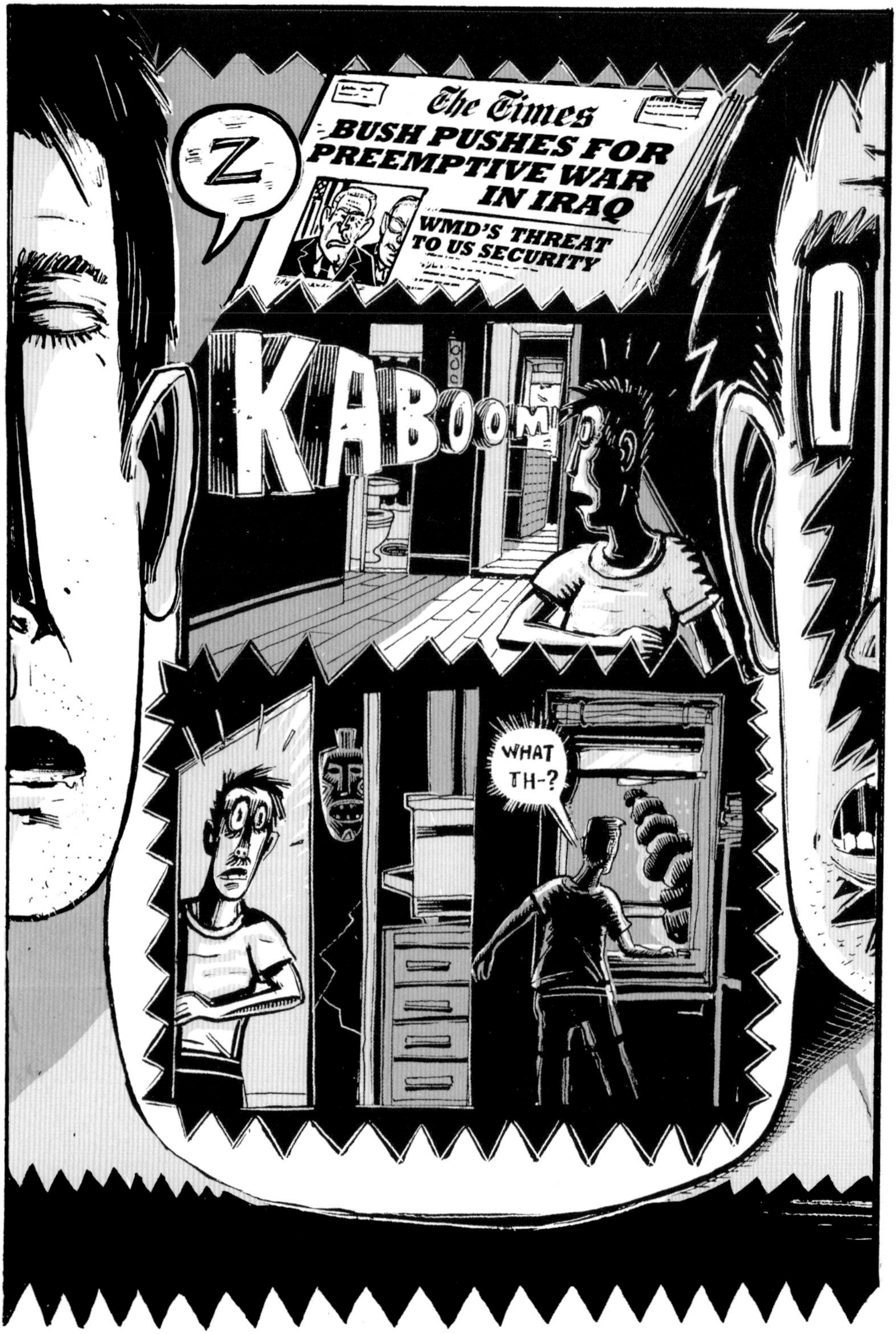
Z
The Times
BUSH PUSHES FOR PREEMPTIVE WAR IN IRAQ
WMD'S THREAT TO US SECURITY
KABOOM
WHAT TH-?

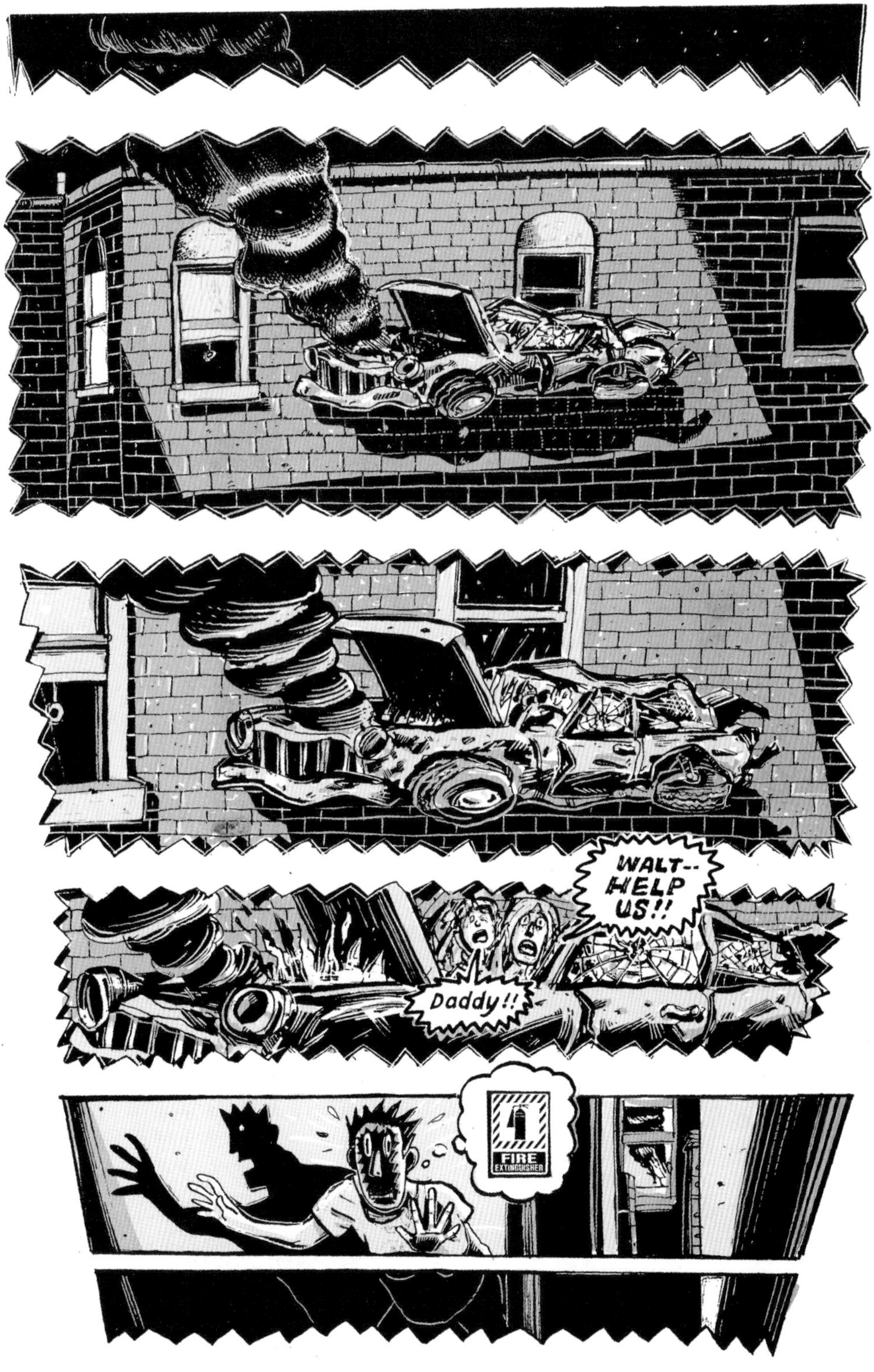
WALT-- HELP US!!
Daddy!!
FIRE EXTINGUISHER

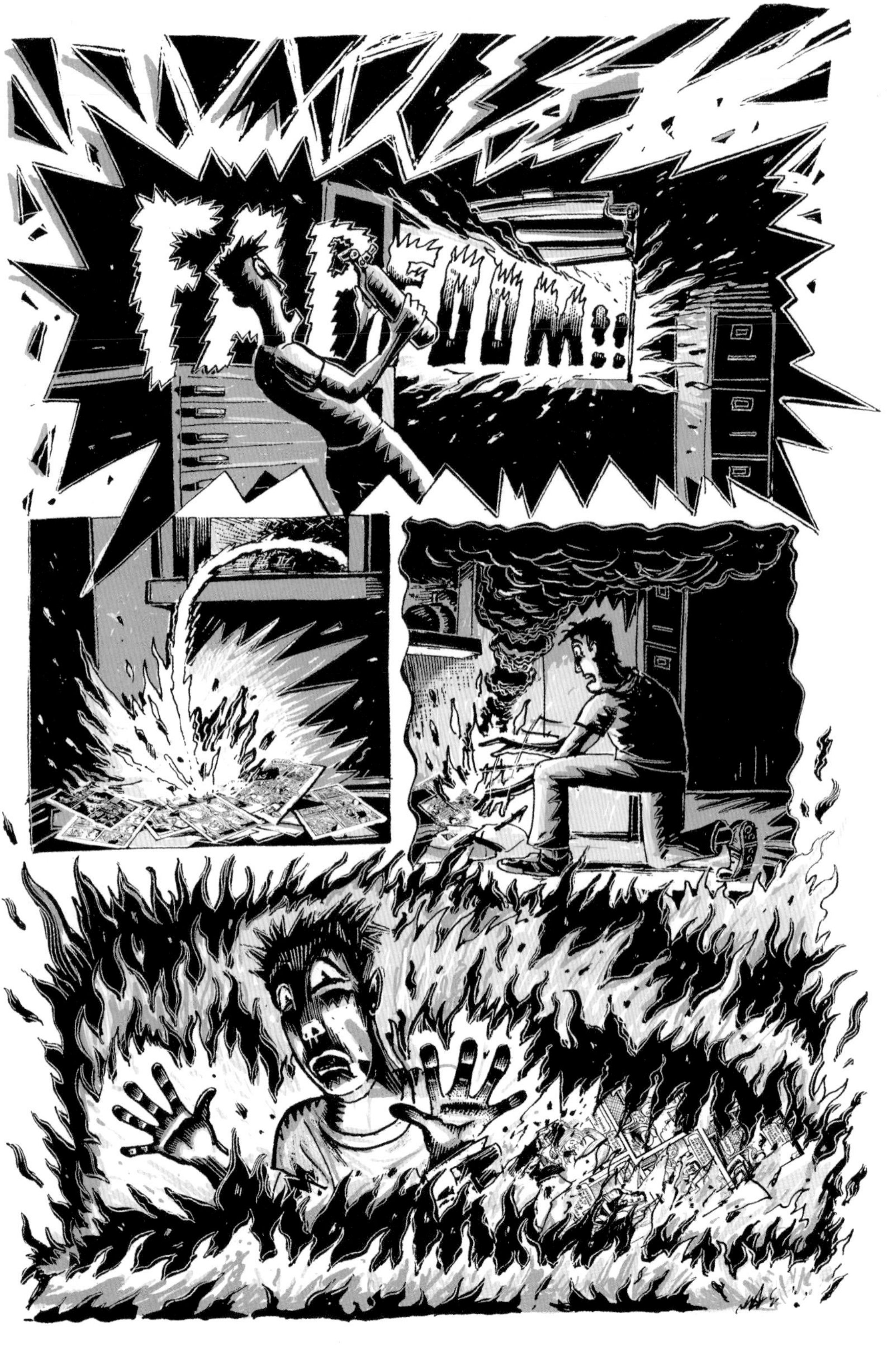
KA-DOOM!!

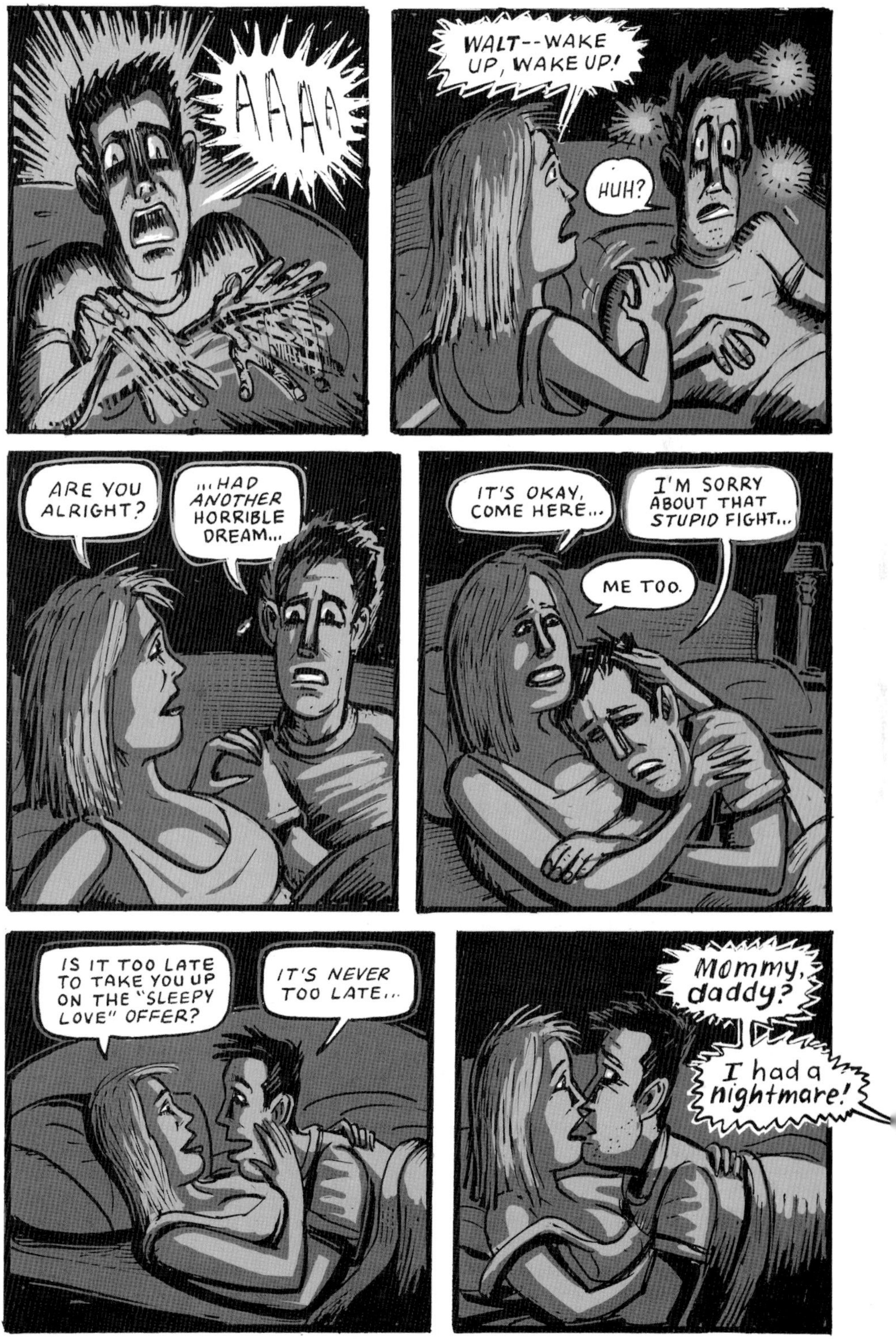
AAAA
WALT--WAKE UP, WAKE UP!
HUH?
ARE YOU ALRIGHT?
...HAD ANOTHER HORRIBLE DREAM...
IT'S OKAY, COME HERE...
I'M SORRY ABOUT THAT STUPID FIGHT...
ME TOO.
IS IT TOO LATE TO TAKE YOU UP ON THE "SLEEPY LOVE" OFFER?
IT'S NEVER TOO LATE...
Mommy, daddy?
I had a nightmare!

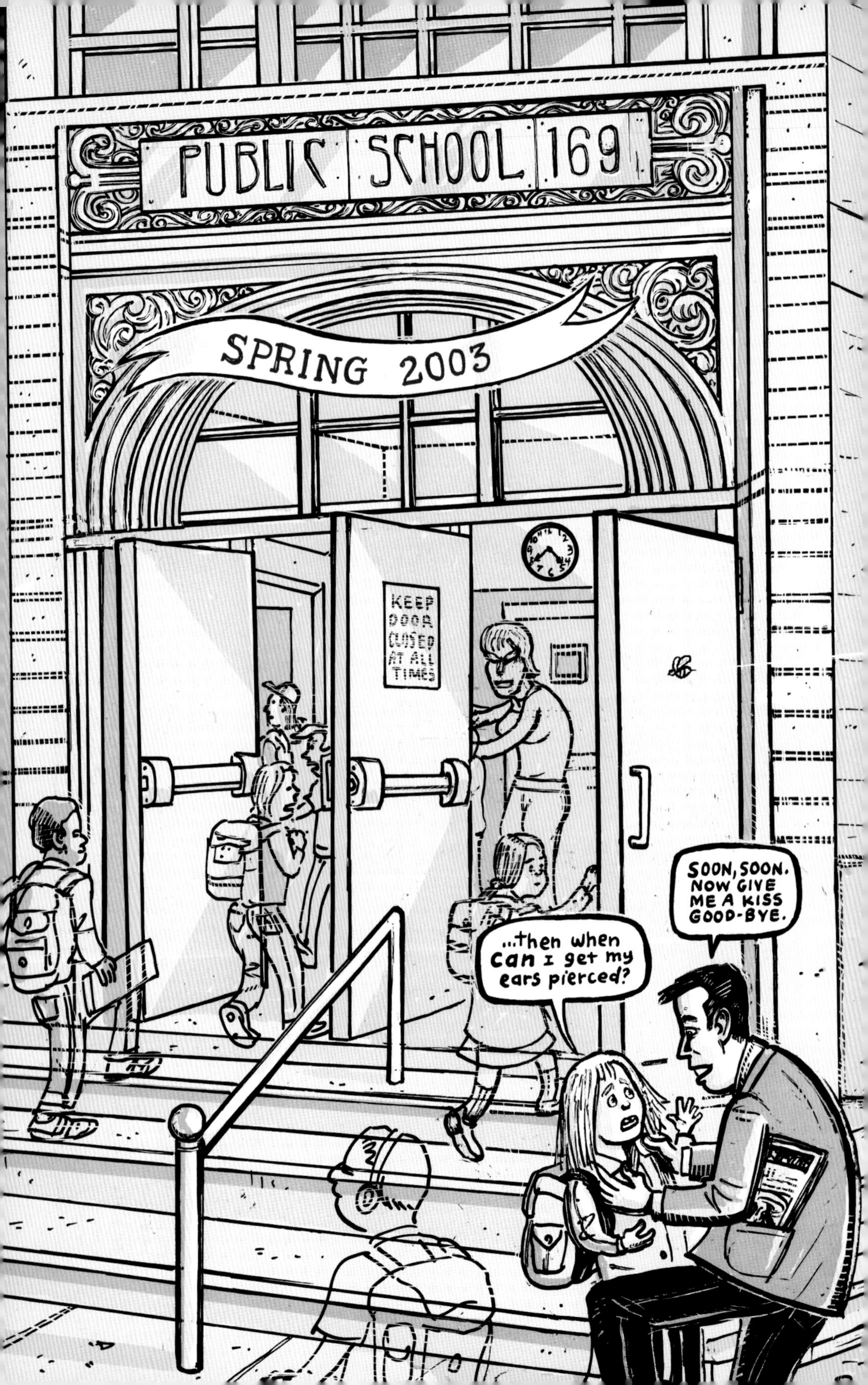
PUBLIC SCHOOL 169
SPRING 2003
KEEP DOOR CLOSED AT ALL TIMES
...then when can I get my ears pierced?
SOON, SOON. NOW GIVE ME A KISS GOOD-BYE.

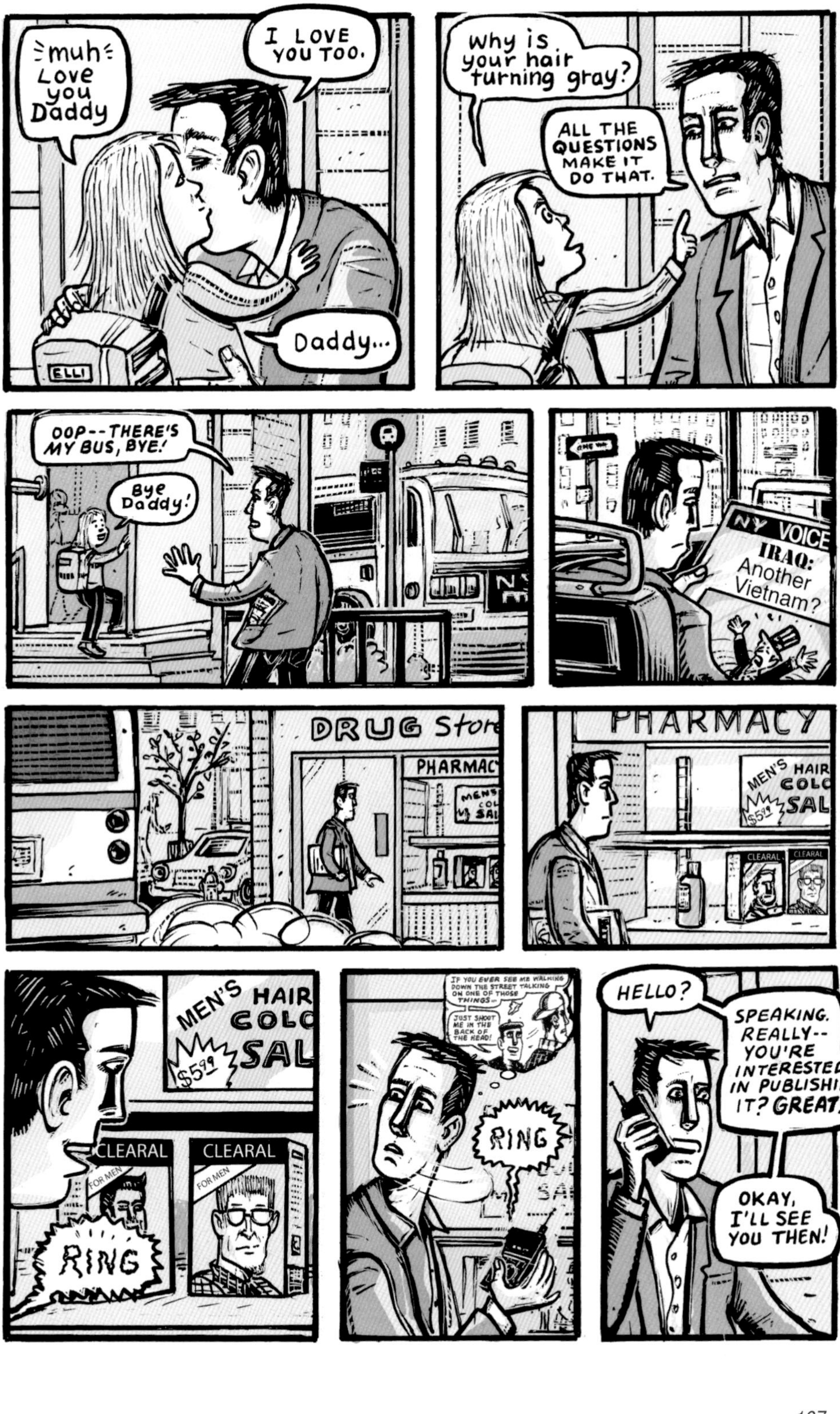
muh Love you Daddy
I LOVE YOU TOO.
Daddy...
ELLI
Why is your hair turning gray?
ALL THE QUESTIONS MAKE IT DO THAT.
OOP--THERE'S MY BUS, BYE!
Bye Daddy!
ONE WAY
NY VOICE
IRAQ: Another Vietnam?
DRUG Store
PHARMACY
PHARMACY
MEN'S HAIR COLO SAL
$5.99
CLEARAL
CLEARAL
MEN'S HAIR COLO SAL
$5.99
CLEARAL
FOR MEN
CLEARAL
FOR MEN
RING
IF YOU EVER SEE ME WALKING DOWN THE STREET TALKING ON ONE OF THOSE THINGS...
JUST SHOOT ME IN THE BACK OF THE HEAD!
RING
HELLO?
SPEAKING. REALLY--YOU'RE INTERESTED IN PUBLISHING IT? GREAT!
OKAY, I'LL SEE YOU THEN!

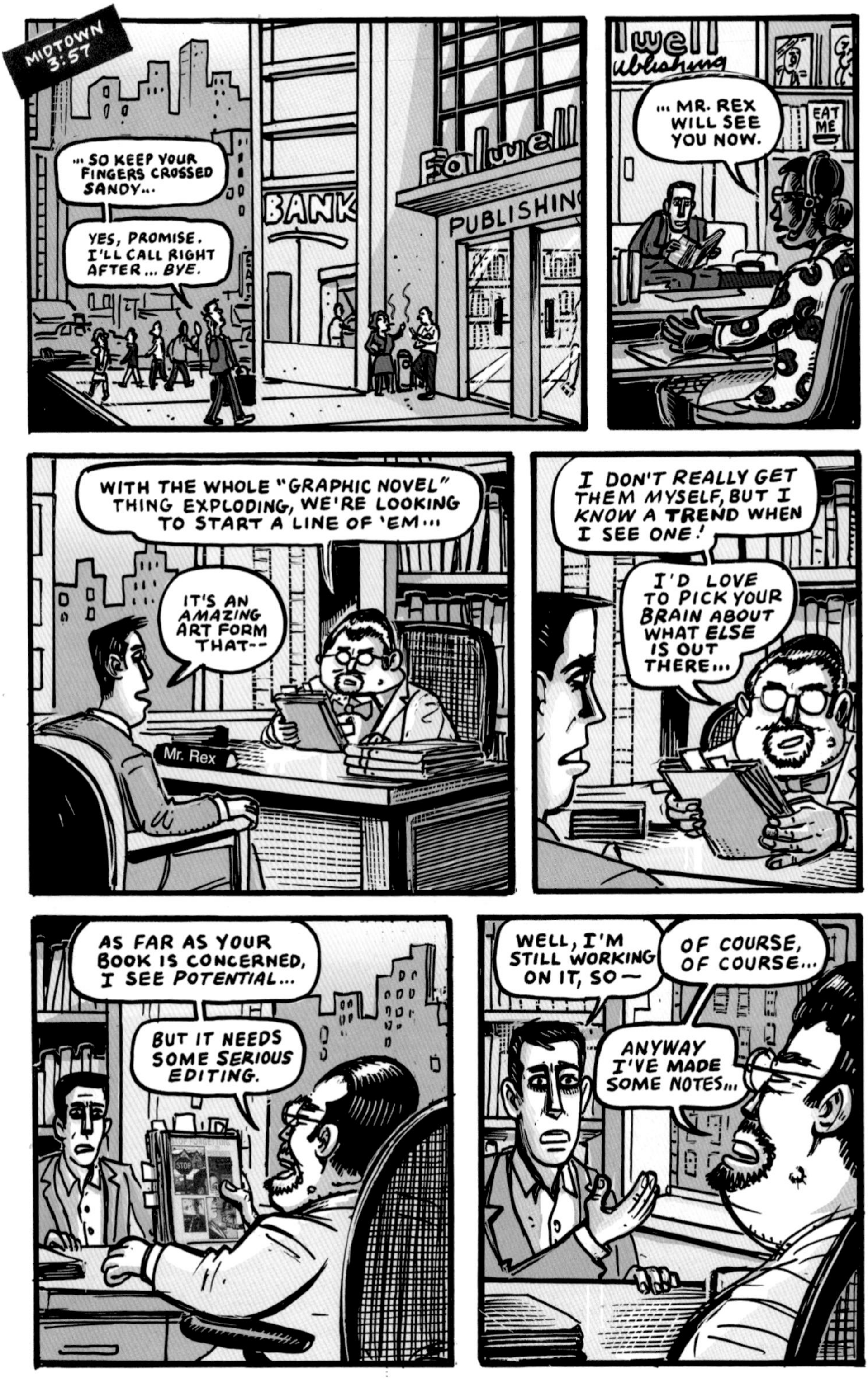
MIDTOWN 3:57
...SO KEEP YOUR FINGERS CROSSED SANDY...
YES, PROMISE. I'LL CALL RIGHT AFTER... BYE.
BANK
Falwell
PUBLISHING
...MR. REX WILL SEE YOU NOW.
EAT ME
WITH THE WHOLE "GRAPHIC NOVEL" THING EXPLODING, WE'RE LOOKING TO START A LINE OF 'EM...
IT'S AN AMAZING ART FORM THAT--
Mr. Rex
I DON'T REALLY GET THEM MYSELF, BUT I KNOW A TREND WHEN I SEE ONE!
I'D LOVE TO PICK YOUR BRAIN ABOUT WHAT ELSE IS OUT THERE...
AS FAR AS YOUR BOOK IS CONCERNED, I SEE POTENTIAL...
BUT IT NEEDS SOME SERIOUS EDITING.
WELL, I'M STILL WORKING ON IT, SO—
OF COURSE, OF COURSE...
ANYWAY I'VE MADE SOME NOTES...

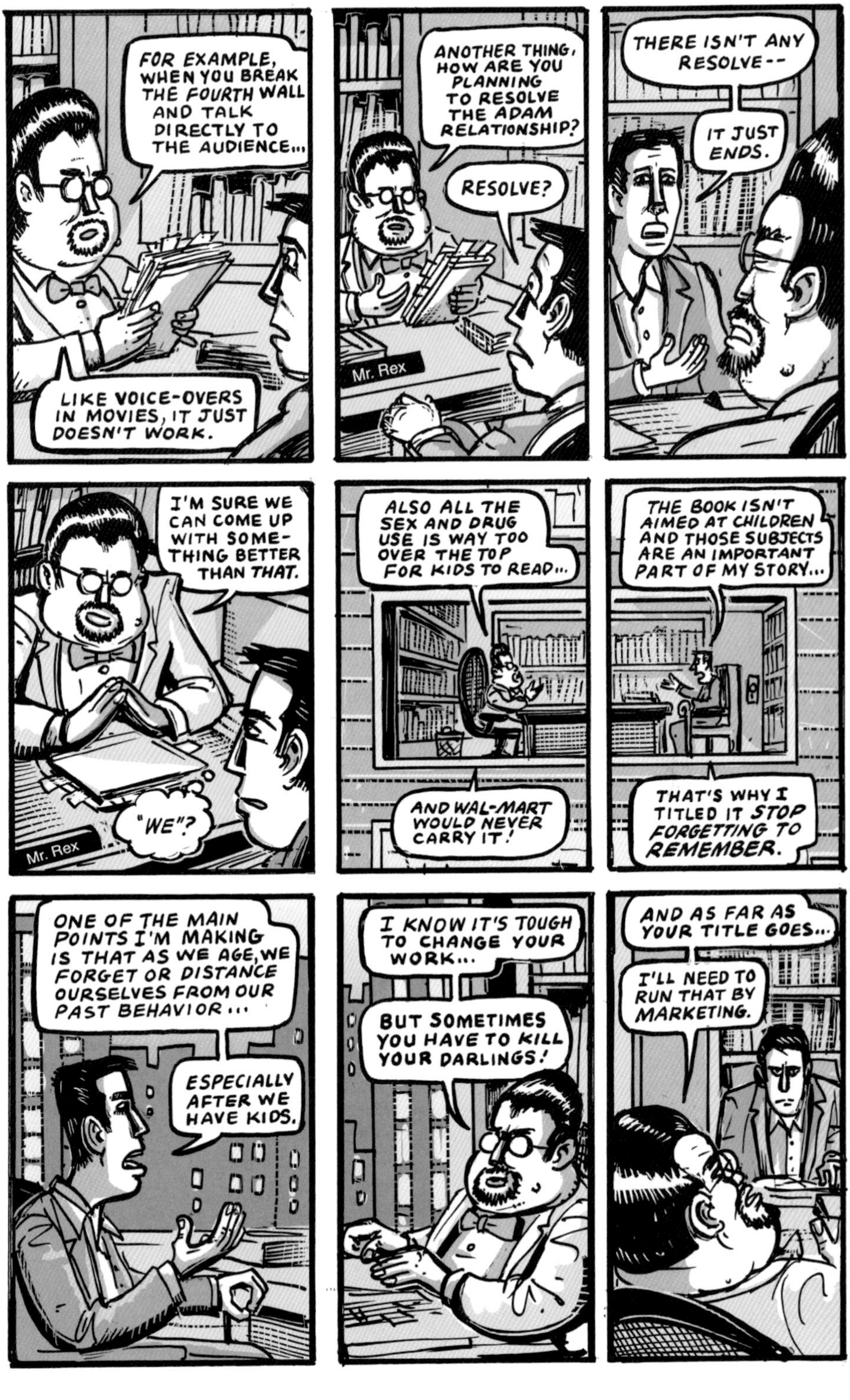
FOR EXAMPLE, WHEN YOU BREAK THE FOURTH WALL AND TALK DIRECTLY TO THE AUDIENCE...
LIKE VOICE-OVERS IN MOVIES, IT JUST DOESN'T WORK.
ANOTHER THING, HOW ARE YOU PLANNING TO RESOLVE THE ADAM RELATIONSHIP?
RESOLVE?
Mr. Rex
THERE ISN'T ANY RESOLVE--
IT JUST ENDS.
I'M SURE WE CAN COME UP WITH SOMETHING BETTER THAN THAT.
"WE"?
Mr. Rex
ALSO ALL THE SEX AND DRUG USE IS WAY TOO OVER THE TOP FOR KIDS TO READ...
AND WAL-MART WOULD NEVER CARRY IT!
THE BOOK ISN'T AIMED AT CHILDREN AND THOSE SUBJECTS ARE AN IMPORTANT PART OF MY STORY...
THAT'S WHY I TITLED IT STOP FORGETTING TO REMEMBER.
ONE OF THE MAIN POINTS I'M MAKING IS THAT AS WE AGE, WE FORGET OR DISTANCE OURSELVES FROM OUR PAST BEHAVIOR...
ESPECIALLY AFTER WE HAVE KIDS.
I KNOW IT'S TOUGH TO CHANGE YOUR WORK...
BUT SOMETIMES YOU HAVE TO KILL YOUR DARLINGS!
AND AS FAR AS YOUR TITLE GOES...
I'LL NEED TO RUN THAT BY MARKETING.

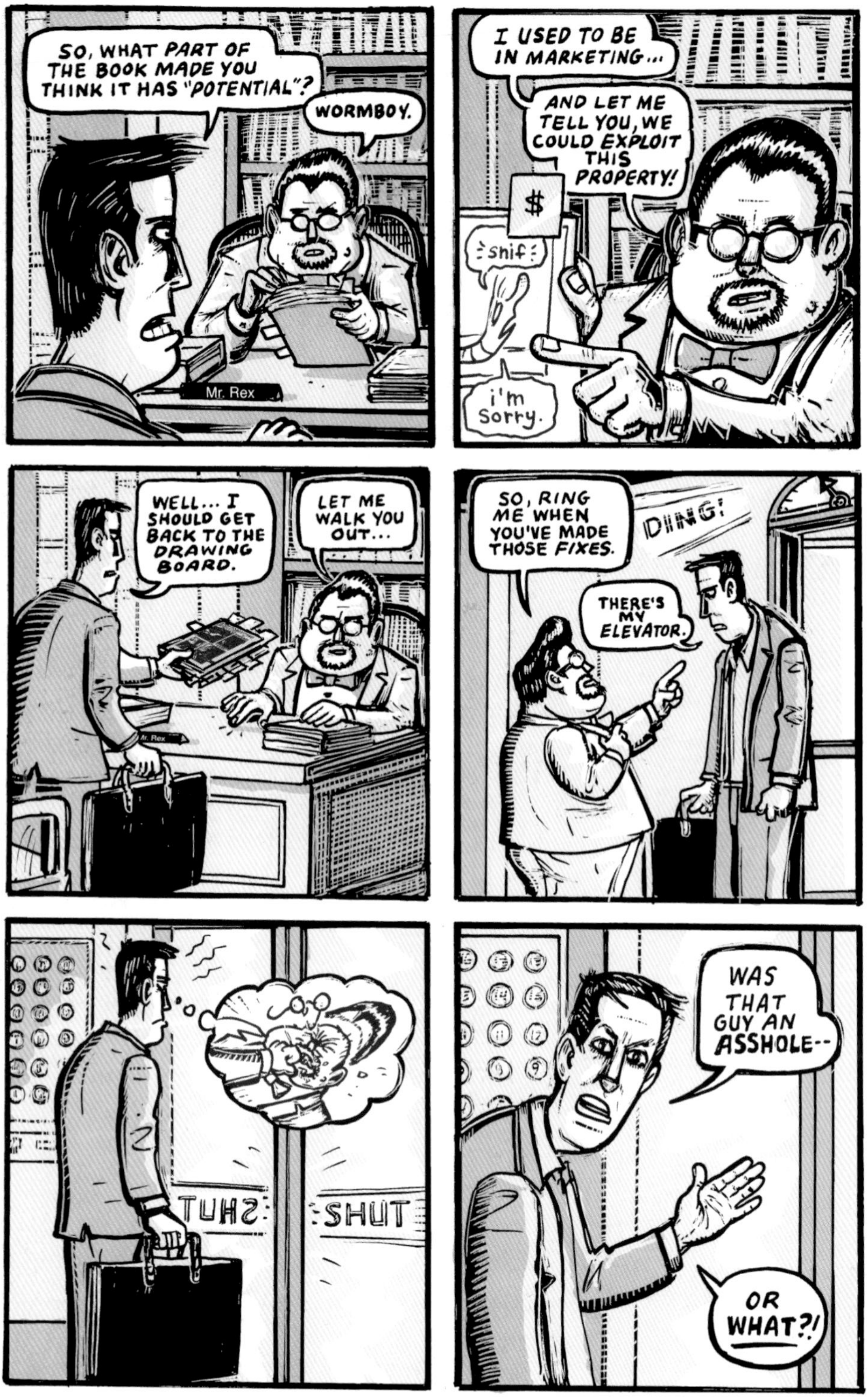
SO, WHAT PART OF THE BOOK MADE YOU THINK IT HAS "POTENTIAL"?
WORMBOY.
Mr. Rex
I USED TO BE IN MARKETING...
AND LET ME TELL YOU, WE COULD EXPLOIT THIS PROPERTY!
$
snif
i'm sorry.
WELL... I SHOULD GET BACK TO THE DRAWING BOARD.
LET ME WALK YOU OUT...
Mr. Rex
SO, RING ME WHEN YOU'VE MADE THOSE FIXES.
DING!
THERE'S MY ELEVATOR.
SHUT
SHUT
WAS THAT GUY AN ASSHOLE--
OR WHAT?!

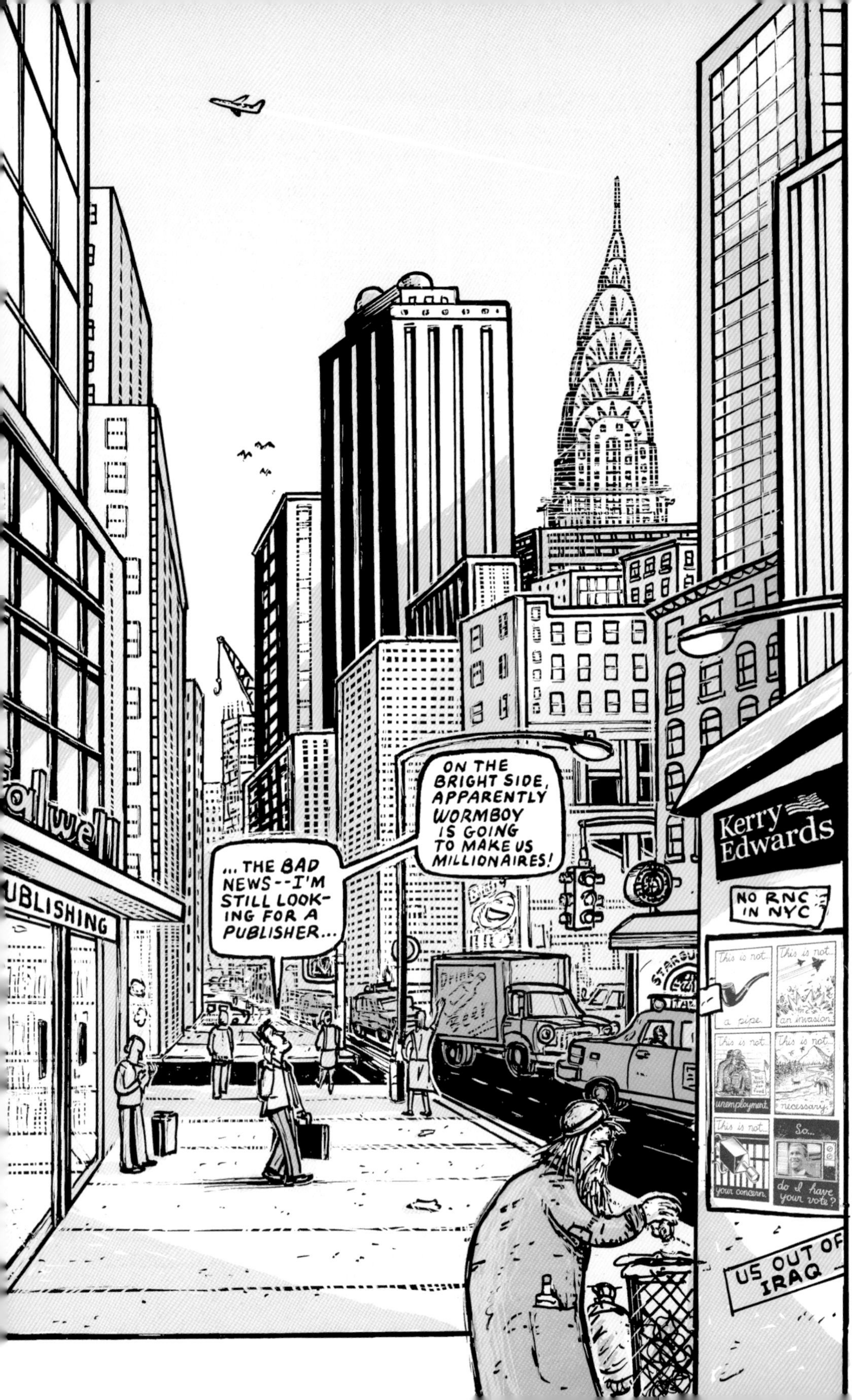
... THE BAD NEWS--I'M STILL LOOKING FOR A PUBLISHER...
ON THE BRIGHT SIDE, APPARENTLY WORMBOY IS GOING TO MAKE US MILLIONAIRES!
Kerry Edwards
NO RNC IN NYC
This is not... a pipe.
This is not... an invasion.
This is not... unemployment.
This is not... necessary.
This is not... your concern.
So... do I have your vote?
US OUT OF IRAQ

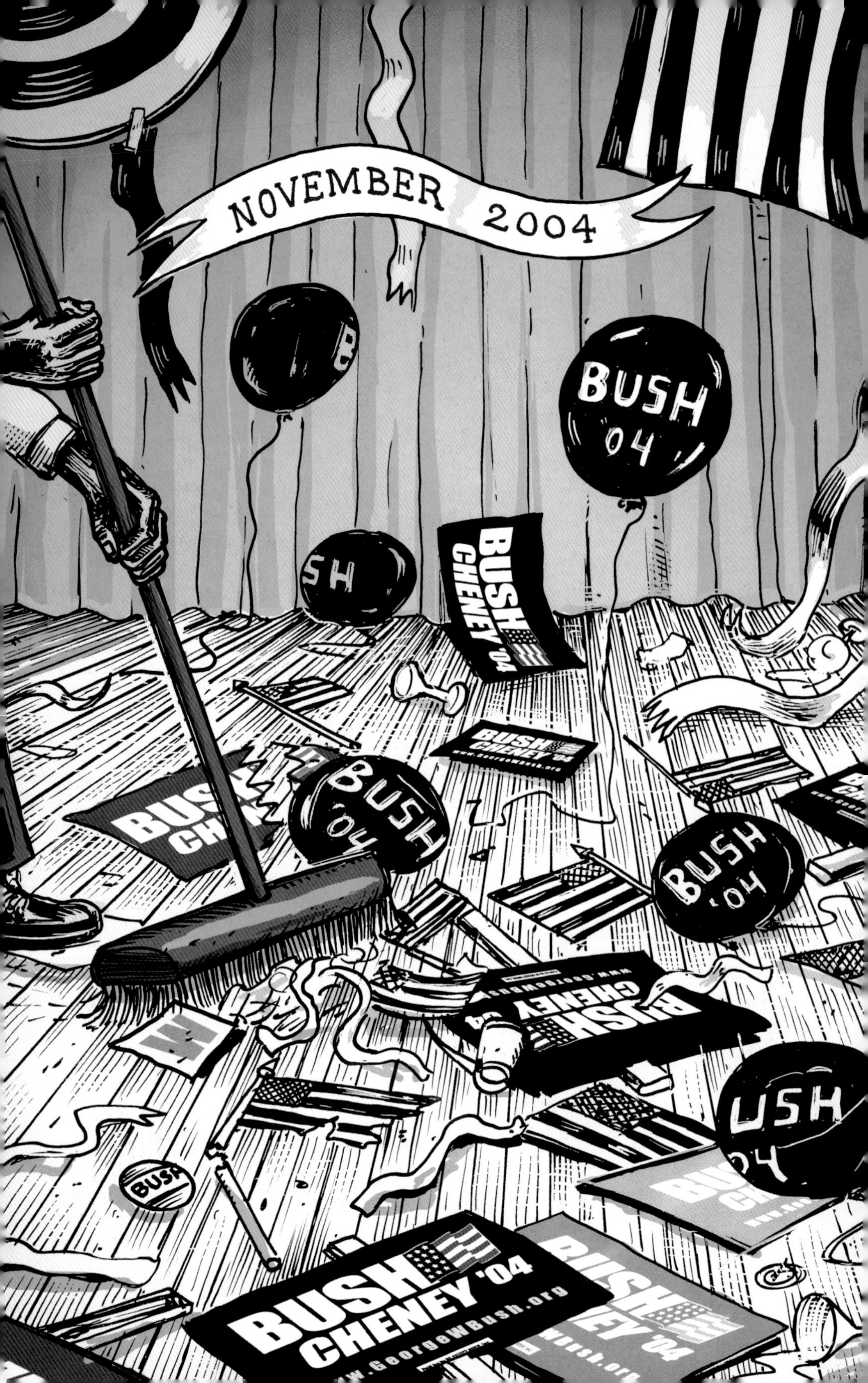

NOVEMBER 2004
BUSH '04
BUSH CHENEY '04
BUSH '04
BUSH '04
BUSH CHENEY '04
www.GeorgeWBush.org

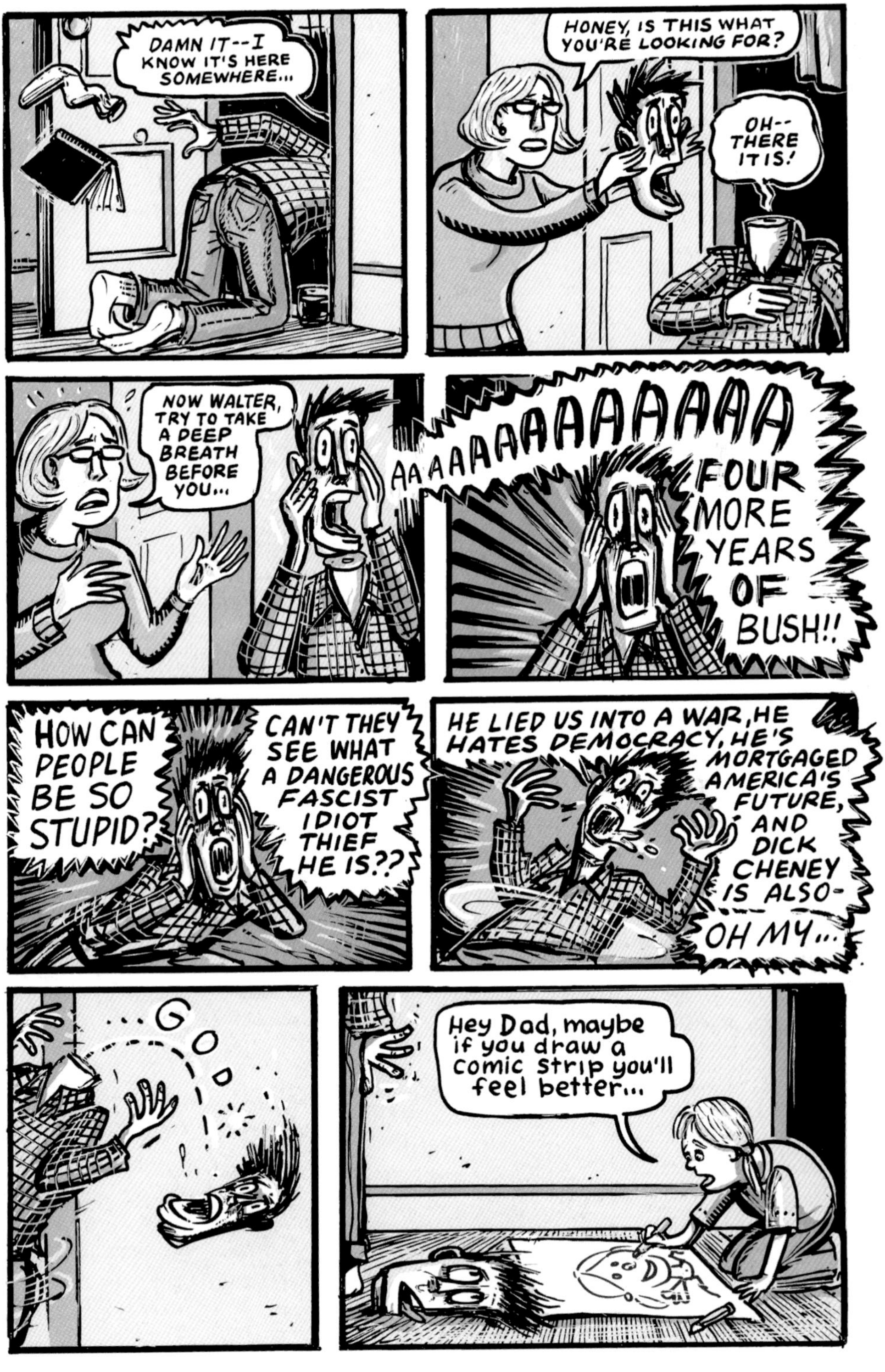
DAMN IT--I KNOW IT'S HERE SOMEWHERE...
HONEY, IS THIS WHAT YOU'RE LOOKING FOR?
OH--THERE IT IS!
NOW WALTER, TRY TO TAKE A DEEP BREATH BEFORE YOU...
AAAAAAAAAAAAA
FOUR MORE YEARS OF BUSH!!
HOW CAN PEOPLE BE SO STUPID?
CAN'T THEY SEE WHAT A DANGEROUS FASCIST IDIOT THIEF HE IS??
HE LIED US INTO A WAR, HE HATES DEMOCRACY, HE'S MORTGAGED AMERICA'S FUTURE, AND DICK CHENEY IS ALSO-
OH MY...
...GOD
Hey Dad, maybe if you draw a comic strip you'll feel better...

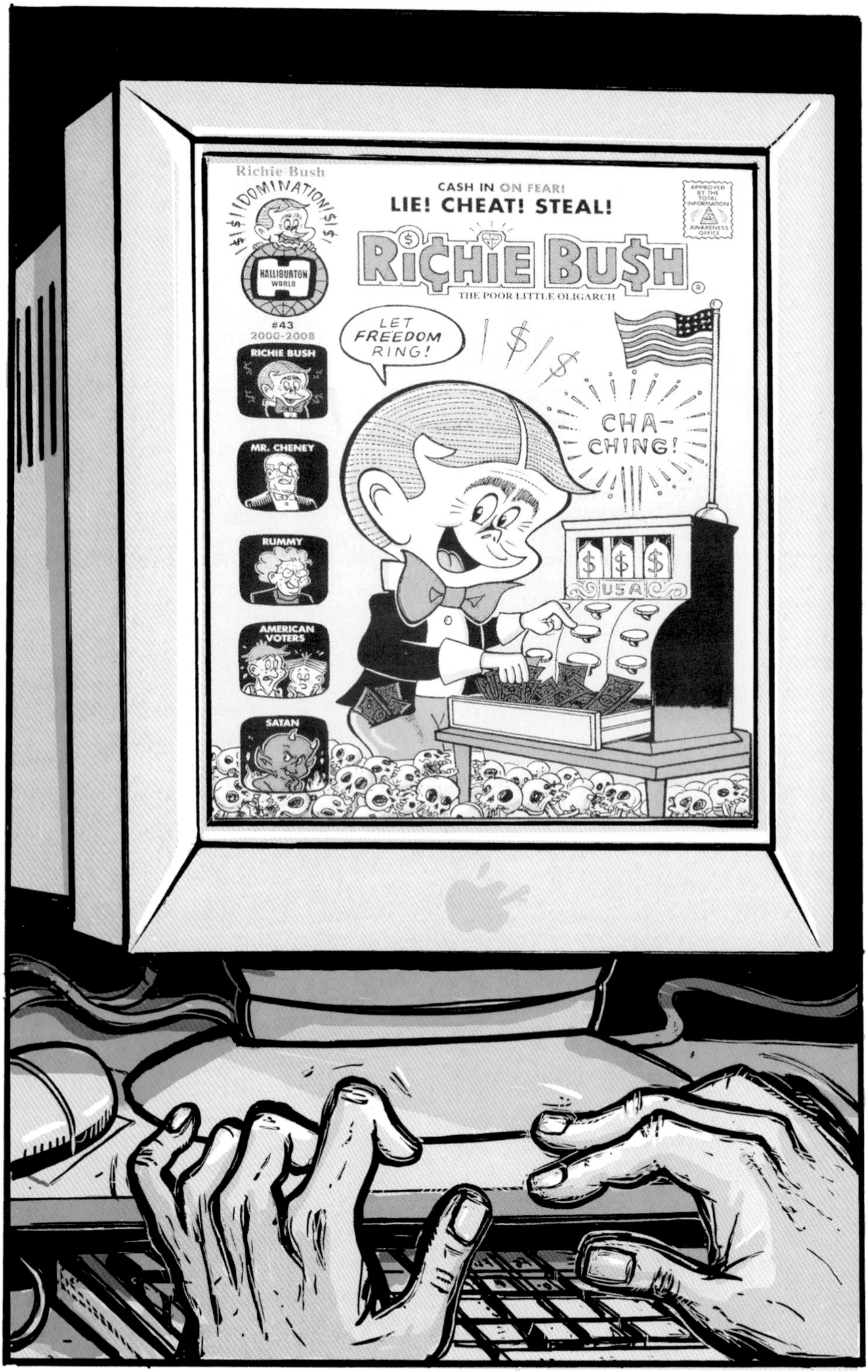

Richie Bush
$!$!DOMINATION!$!$
HALLIBURTON WORLD
#43
2000-2008
RICHIE BUSH
MR. CHENEY
RUMMY
AMERICAN VOTERS
SATAN
CASH IN ON FEAR!
LIE! CHEAT! STEAL!
APPROVED BY THE TOTAL INFORMATION AWARENESS OFFICE
RICHIE BU$H
THE POOR LITTLE OLIGARCH
LET FREEDOM RING!
$ $
CHA-CHING!
USA

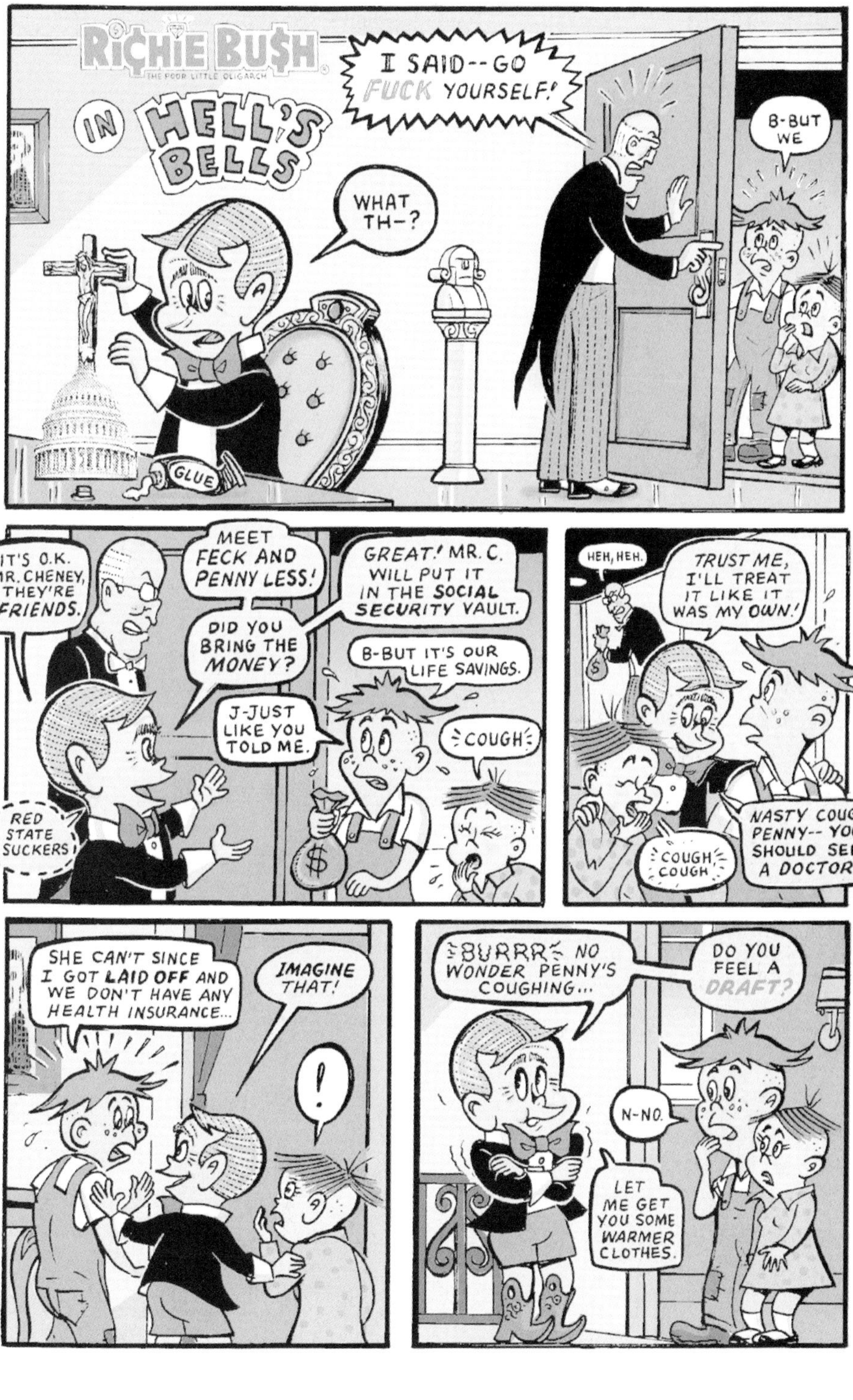
RICHIE BU$H
THE POOR LITTLE OLIGARCH
IN HELL'S BELLS
I SAID--GO FUCK YOURSELF!
WHAT TH-?
B-BUT WE
GLUE
IT'S O.K. MR. CHENEY, THEY'RE FRIENDS.
MEET FECK AND PENNY LESS!
DID YOU BRING THE MONEY?
GREAT! MR. C. WILL PUT IT IN THE SOCIAL SECURITY VAULT.
B-BUT IT'S OUR LIFE SAVINGS.
J-JUST LIKE YOU TOLD ME.
COUGH
RED STATE SUCKERS
HEH, HEH.
TRUST ME, I'LL TREAT IT LIKE IT WAS MY OWN!
COUGH COUGH
NASTY COUGH PENNY-- YOU SHOULD SEE A DOCTOR.
SHE CAN'T SINCE I GOT LAID OFF AND WE DON'T HAVE ANY HEALTH INSURANCE...
IMAGINE THAT!
!
BURRR NO WONDER PENNY'S COUGHING...
DO YOU FEEL A DRAFT?
N-NO.
LET ME GET YOU SOME WARMER CLOTHES.

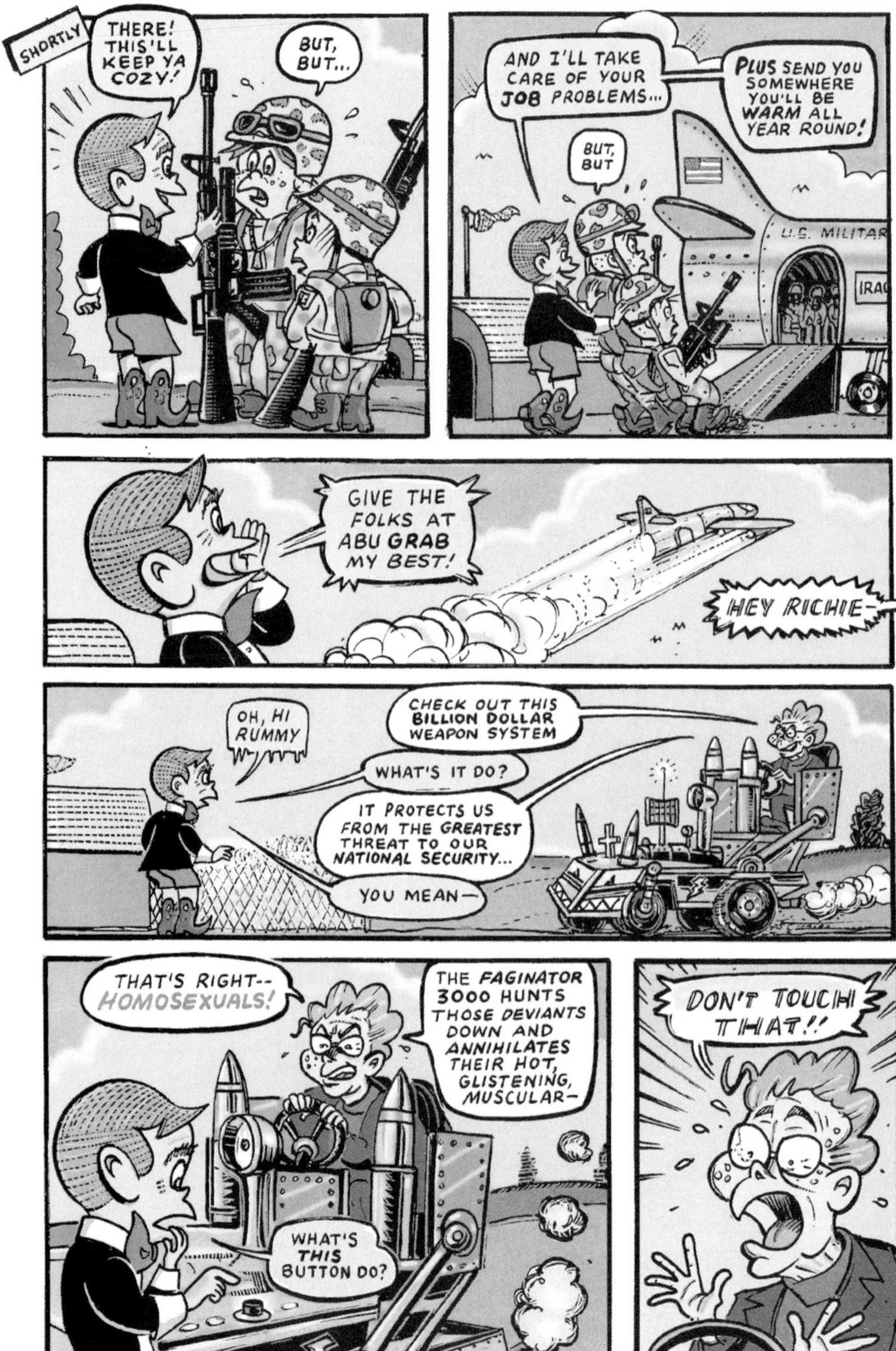
SHORTLY
THERE! THIS'LL KEEP YA COZY!
BUT, BUT...
AND I'LL TAKE CARE OF YOUR JOB PROBLEMS...
PLUS SEND YOU SOMEWHERE YOU'LL BE WARM ALL YEAR ROUND!
BUT, BUT
U.S. MILITAR
IRAQ
GIVE THE FOLKS AT ABU GRAB MY BEST!
HEY RICHIE
OH, HI RUMMY
CHECK OUT THIS BILLION DOLLAR WEAPON SYSTEM
WHAT'S IT DO?
IT PROTECTS US FROM THE GREATEST THREAT TO OUR NATIONAL SECURITY...
YOU MEAN—
THAT'S RIGHT-- HOMOSEXUALS!
THE FAGINATOR 3000 HUNTS THOSE DEVIANTS DOWN AND ANNIHILATES THEIR HOT, GLISTENING, MUSCULAR—
WHAT'S THIS BUTTON DO?
DON'T TOUCH THAT!!

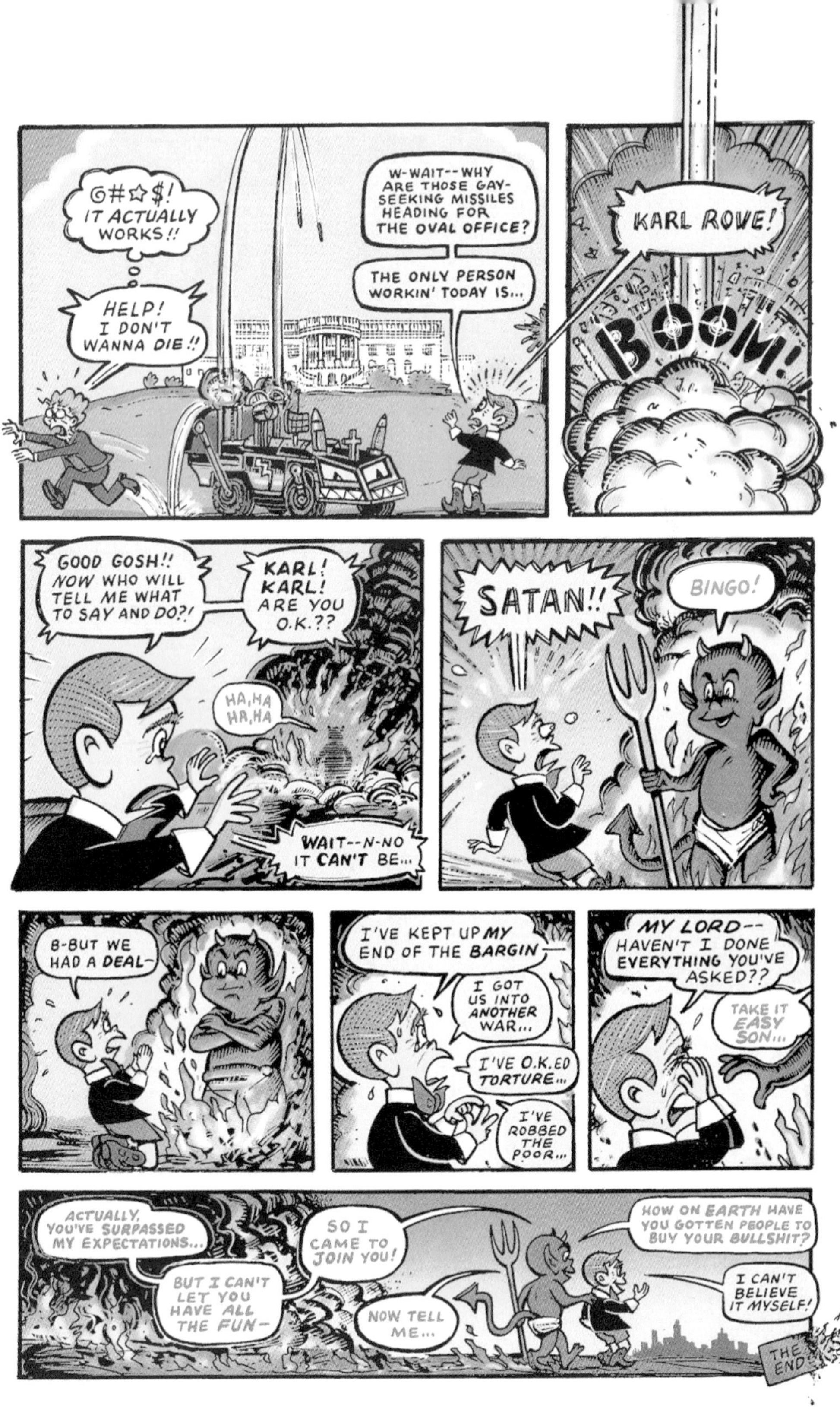
@#☆$! IT ACTUALLY WORKS!!
HELP! I DON'T WANNA DIE!!
W-WAIT--WHY ARE THOSE GAY-SEEKING MISSILES HEADING FOR THE OVAL OFFICE?
THE ONLY PERSON WORKIN' TODAY IS...
KARL ROVE!
BOOM!
GOOD GOSH!! NOW WHO WILL TELL ME WHAT TO SAY AND DO?!
KARL! KARL! ARE YOU O.K.??
HA,HA HA,HA
WAIT--N-NO IT CAN'T BE...
SATAN!!
BINGO!
B-BUT WE HAD A DEAL—
I'VE KEPT UP MY END OF THE BARGIN—
I GOT US INTO ANOTHER WAR...
I'VE O.K.ED TORTURE...
I'VE ROBBED THE POOR...
MY LORD-- HAVEN'T I DONE EVERYTHING YOU'VE ASKED??
TAKE IT EASY SON...
ACTUALLY, YOU'VE SURPASSED MY EXPECTATIONS...
BUT I CAN'T LET YOU HAVE ALL THE FUN—
SO I CAME TO JOIN YOU!
NOW TELL ME...
HOW ON EARTH HAVE YOU GOTTEN PEOPLE TO BUY YOUR BULLSHIT?
I CAN'T BELIEVE IT MYSELF!
THE END

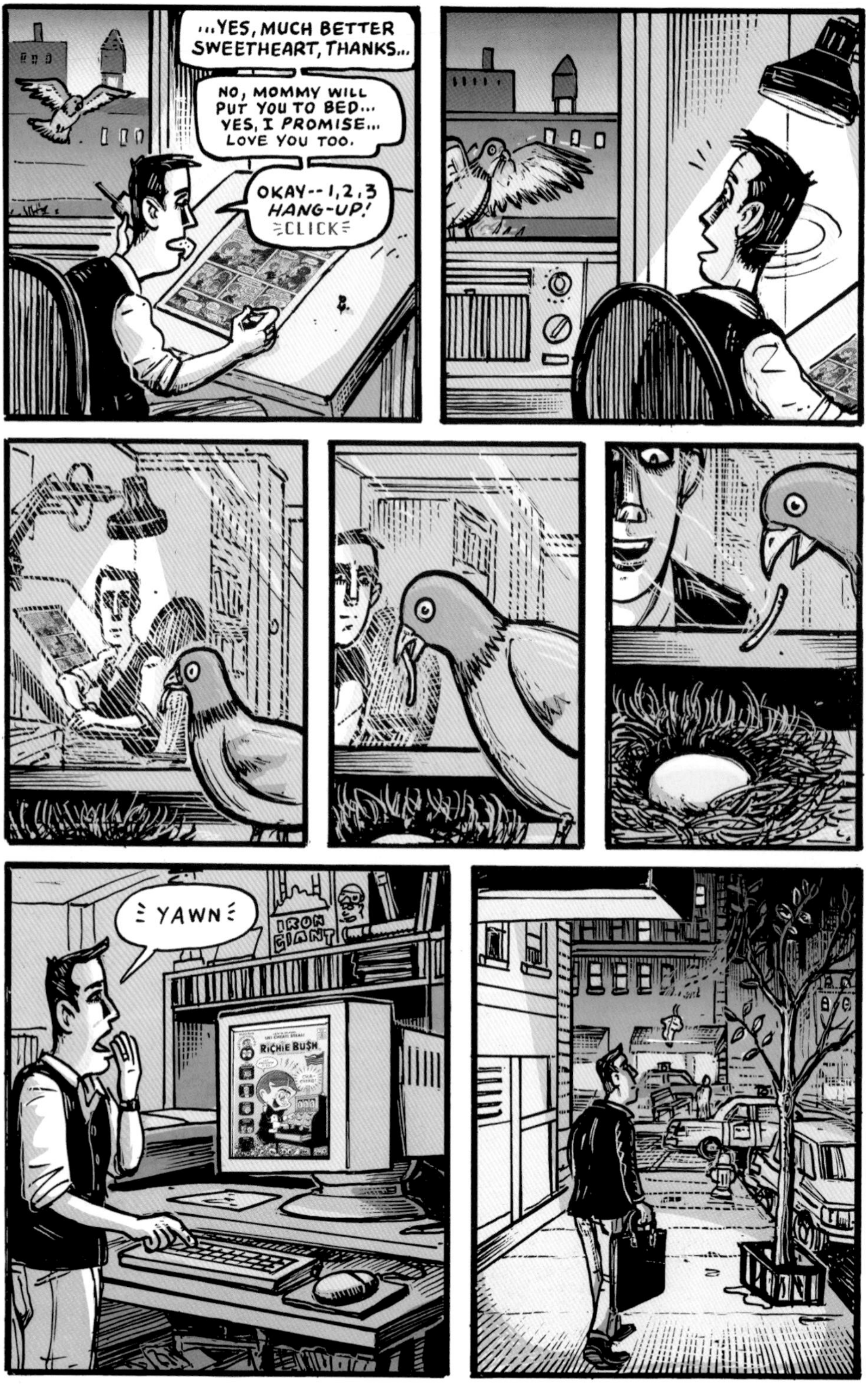
...YES, MUCH BETTER SWEETHEART, THANKS...
NO, MOMMY WILL PUT YOU TO BED... YES, I PROMISE... LOVE YOU TOO.
OKAY--1,2,3 HANG-UP!
CLICK
YAWN
IRON GIANT
RICHIE BU$H

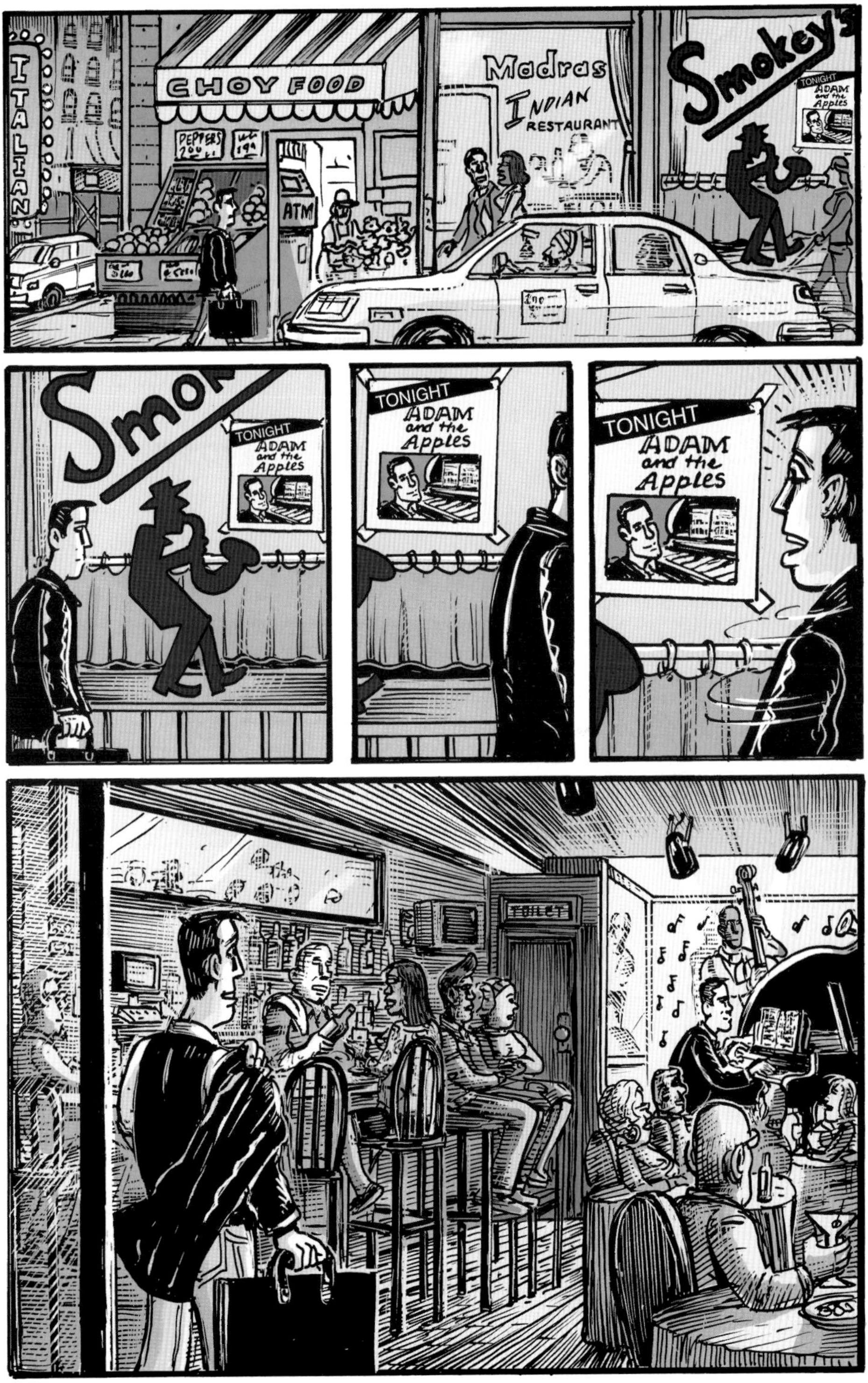
ITALIAN
CHOY FOOD
PEPPERS
ATM
Madras
INDIAN
RESTAURANT
Smokey's
TONIGHT
ADAM and the Apples
Smok
TONIGHT
ADAM and the Apples
TONIGHT
ADAM and the Apples
TONIGHT
ADAM and the Apples
TOILET

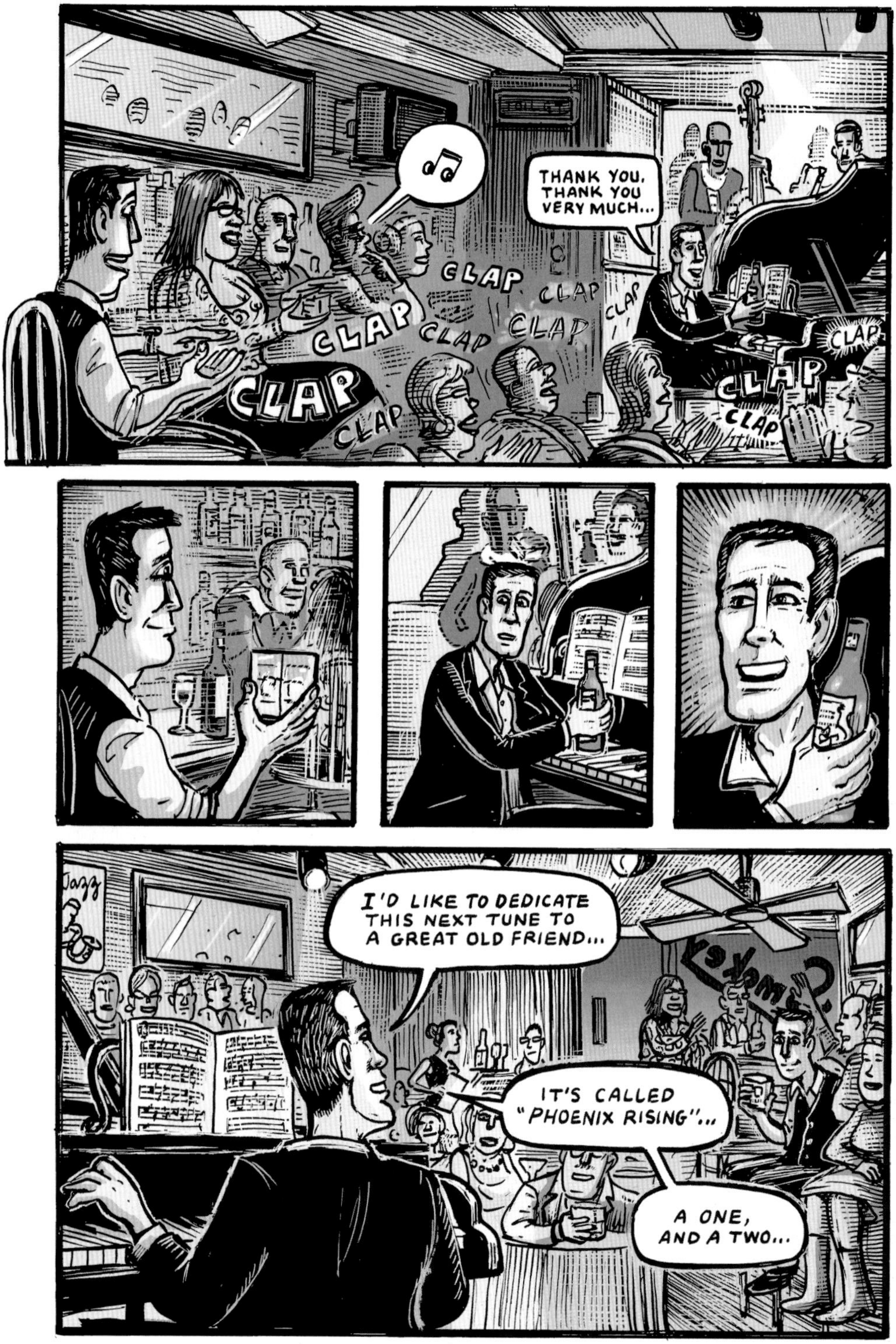
THANK YOU, THANK YOU VERY MUCH...
CLAP
CLAP
CLAP
CLAP
CLAP
CLAP
CLAP
CLAP
CLAP
CLAP
CLAP
Jazz
I'D LIKE TO DEDICATE THIS NEXT TUNE TO A GREAT OLD FRIEND...
IT'S CALLED "PHOENIX RISING"...
A ONE, AND A TWO...

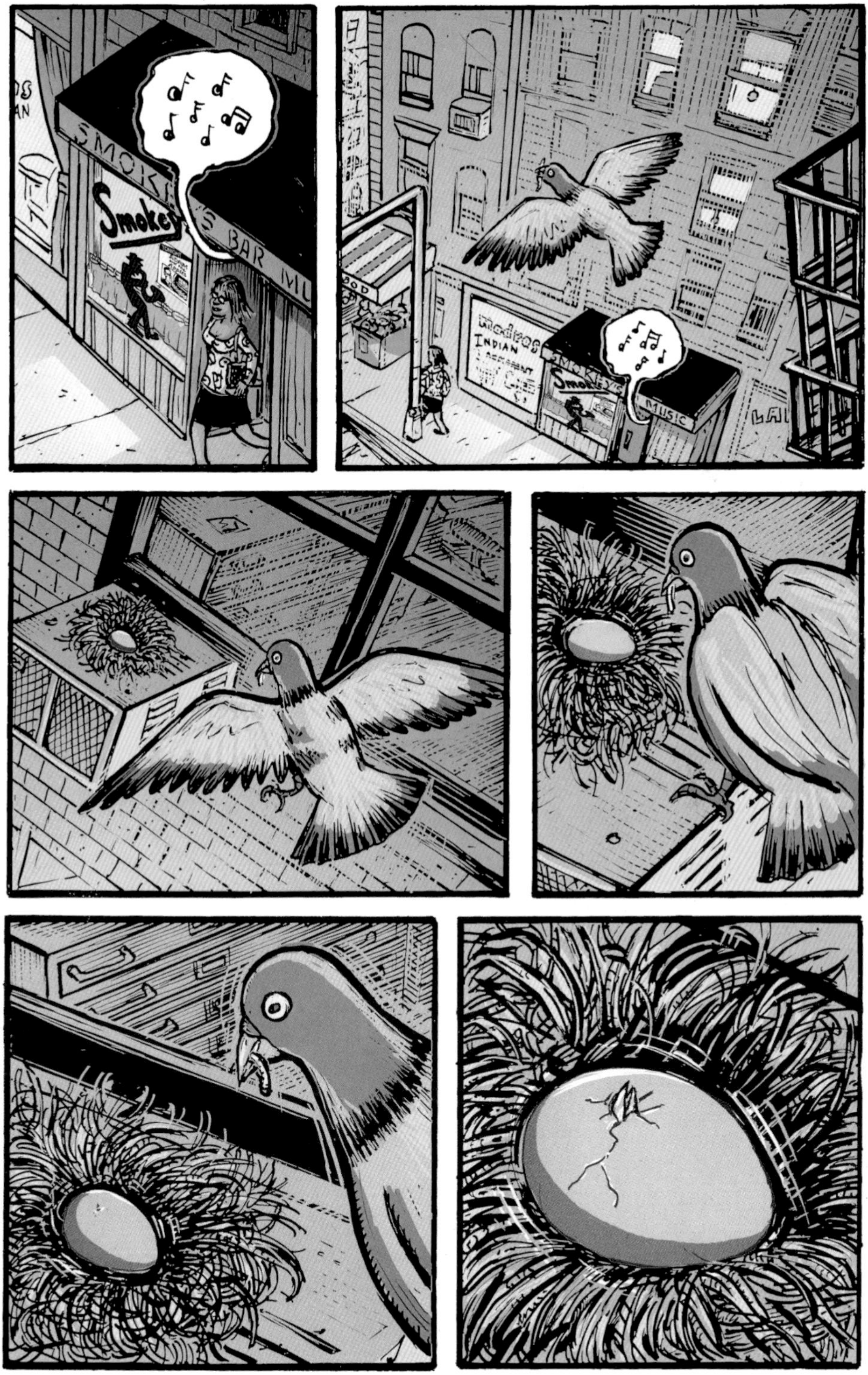
INDIAN
MUSIC

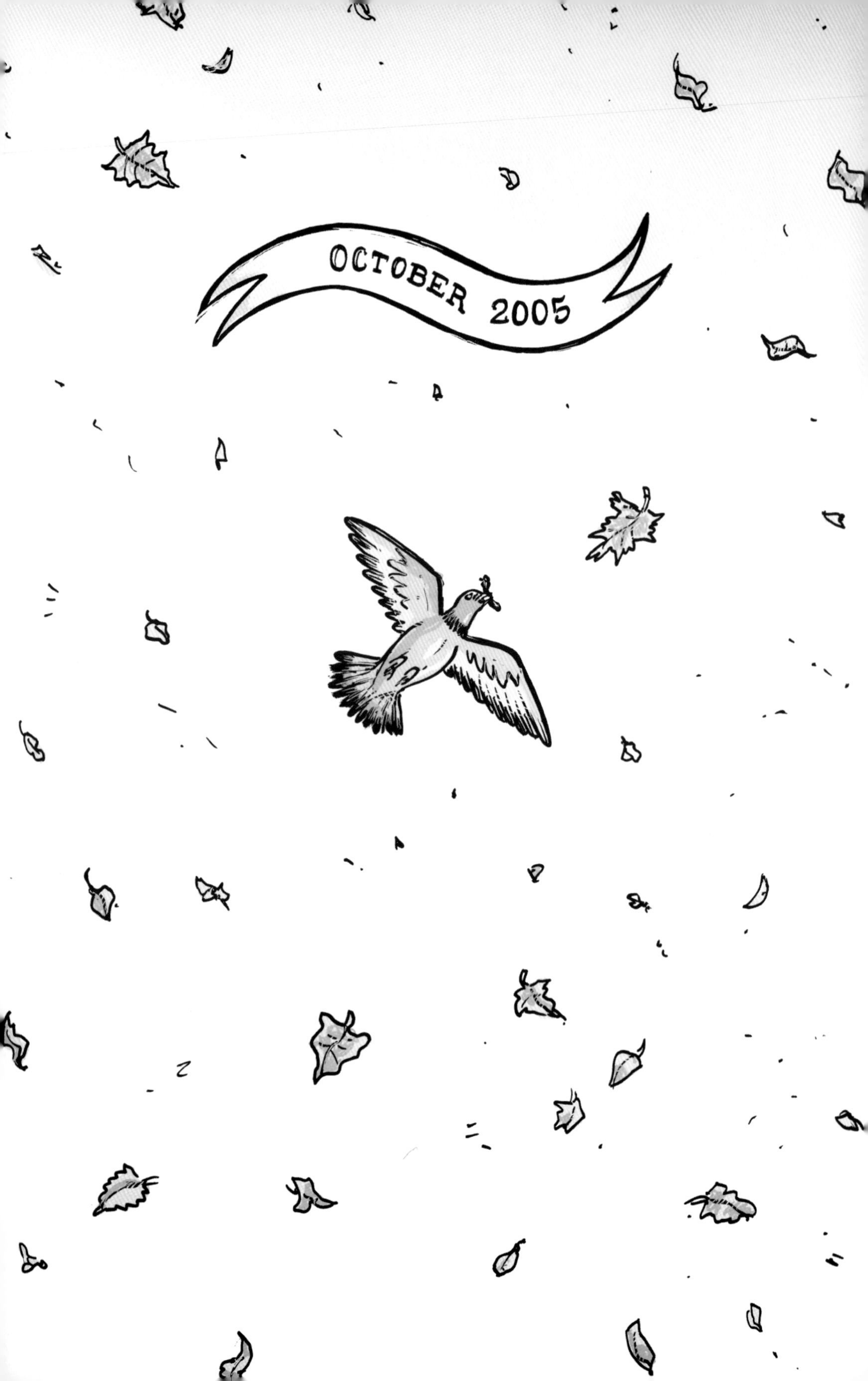
OCTOBER 2005

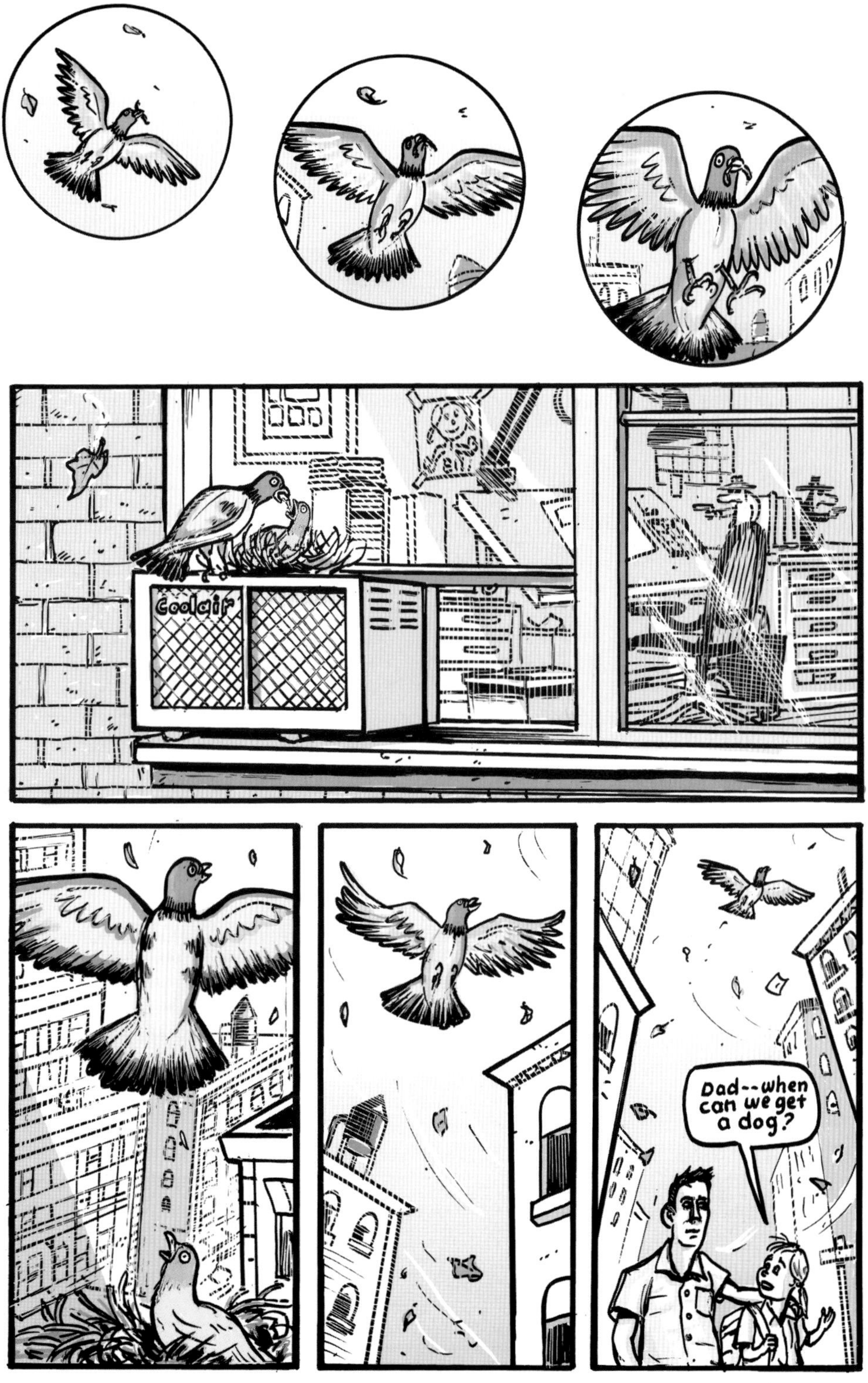
Coolair
Dad--when can we get a dog?

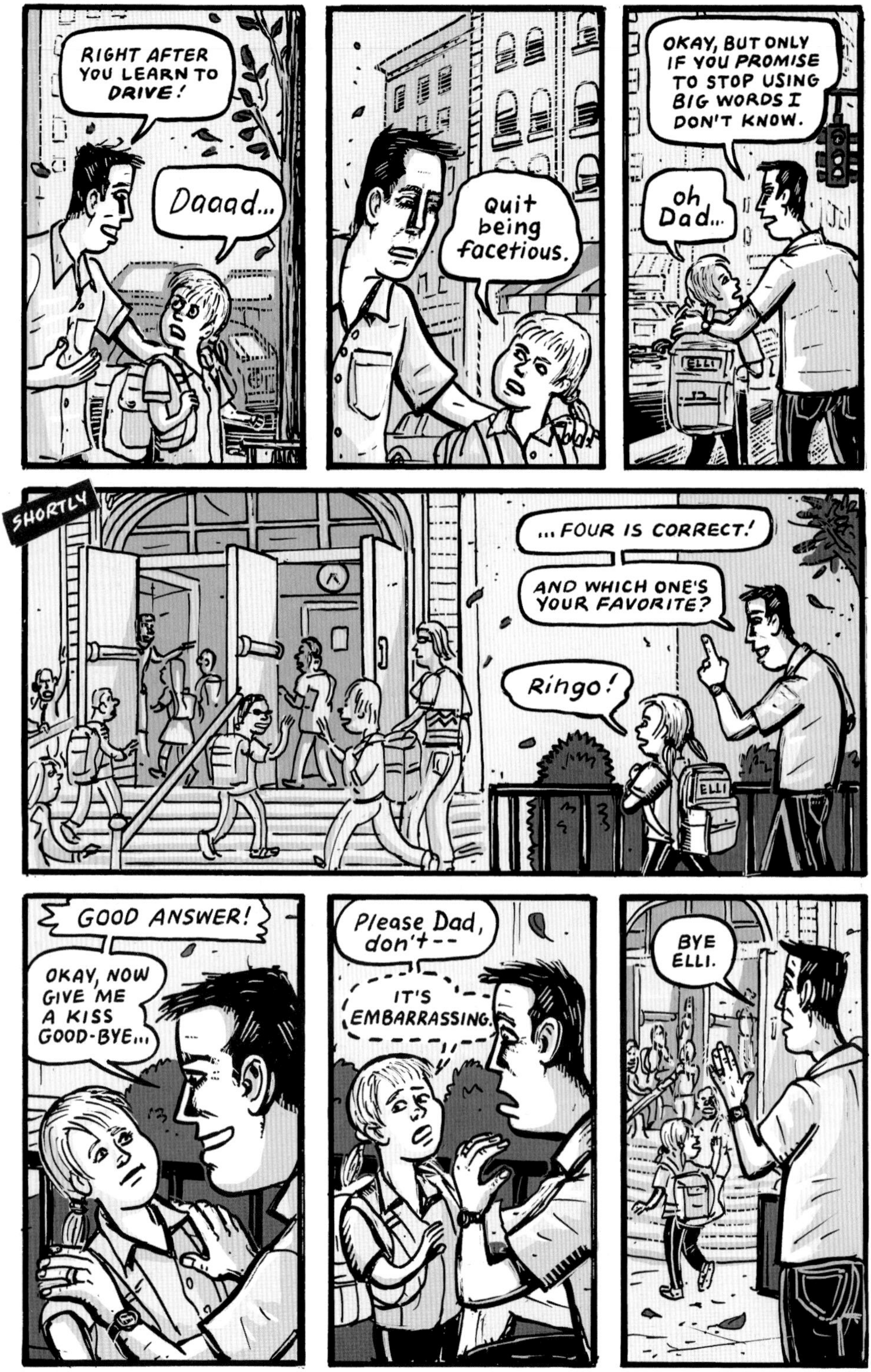
RIGHT AFTER YOU LEARN TO DRIVE!
Daaad...
Quit being facetious.
OKAY, BUT ONLY IF YOU PROMISE TO STOP USING BIG WORDS I DON'T KNOW.
oh Dad...
SHORTLY
...FOUR IS CORRECT!
AND WHICH ONE'S YOUR FAVORITE?
Ringo!
ELLI
GOOD ANSWER!
OKAY, NOW GIVE ME A KISS GOOD-BYE...
Please Dad, don't--
IT'S EMBARRASSING.
BYE ELLI.

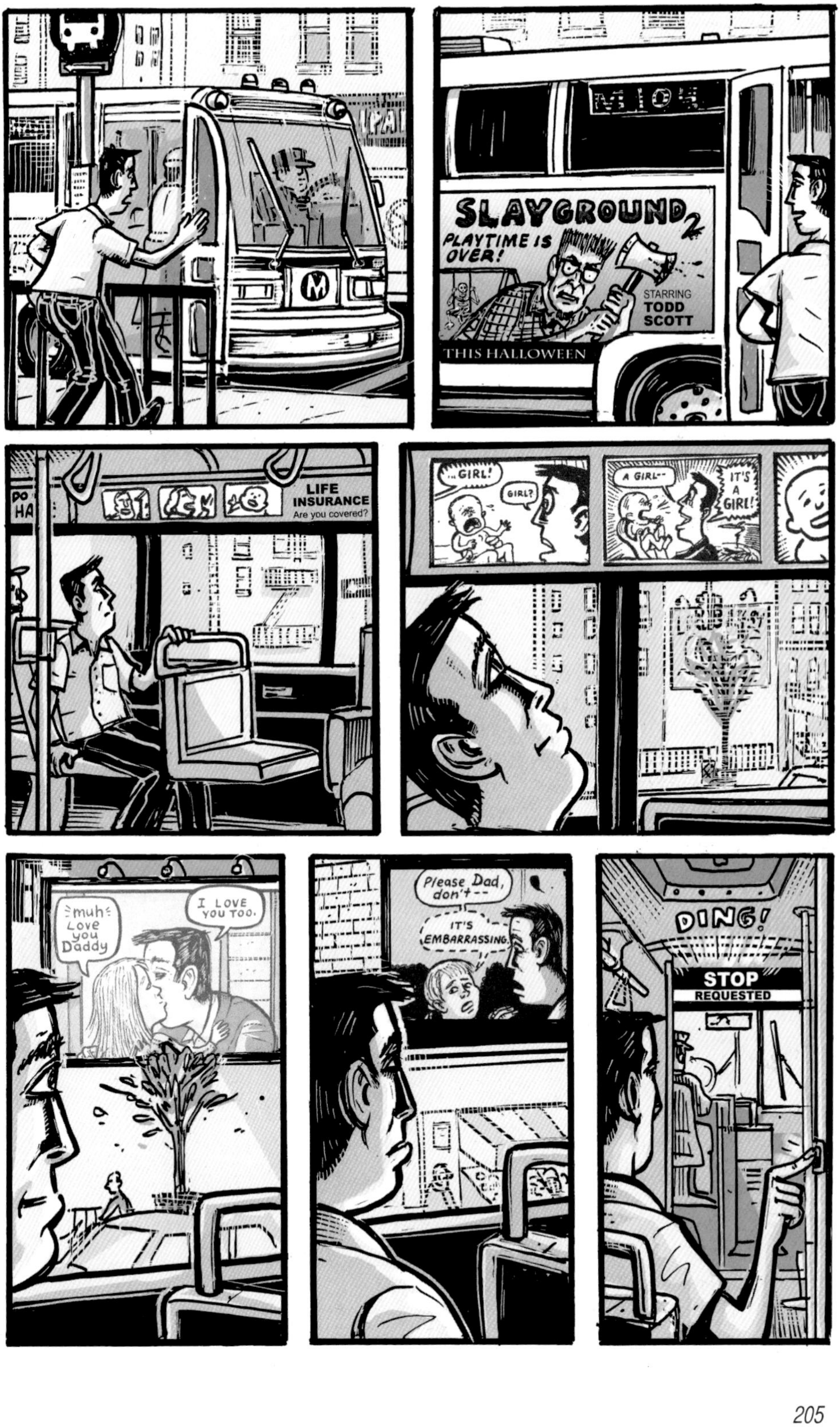
M104
SLAYGROUND 2
PLAYTIME IS OVER!
STARRING TODD SCOTT
THIS HALLOWEEN
LIFE INSURANCE
Are you covered?
...GIRL!
GIRL?
A GIRL--
IT'S A GIRL!
muh Love you Daddy
I LOVE YOU TOO.
Please Dad, don't--
IT'S EMBARRASSING.
DING!
STOP
REQUESTED

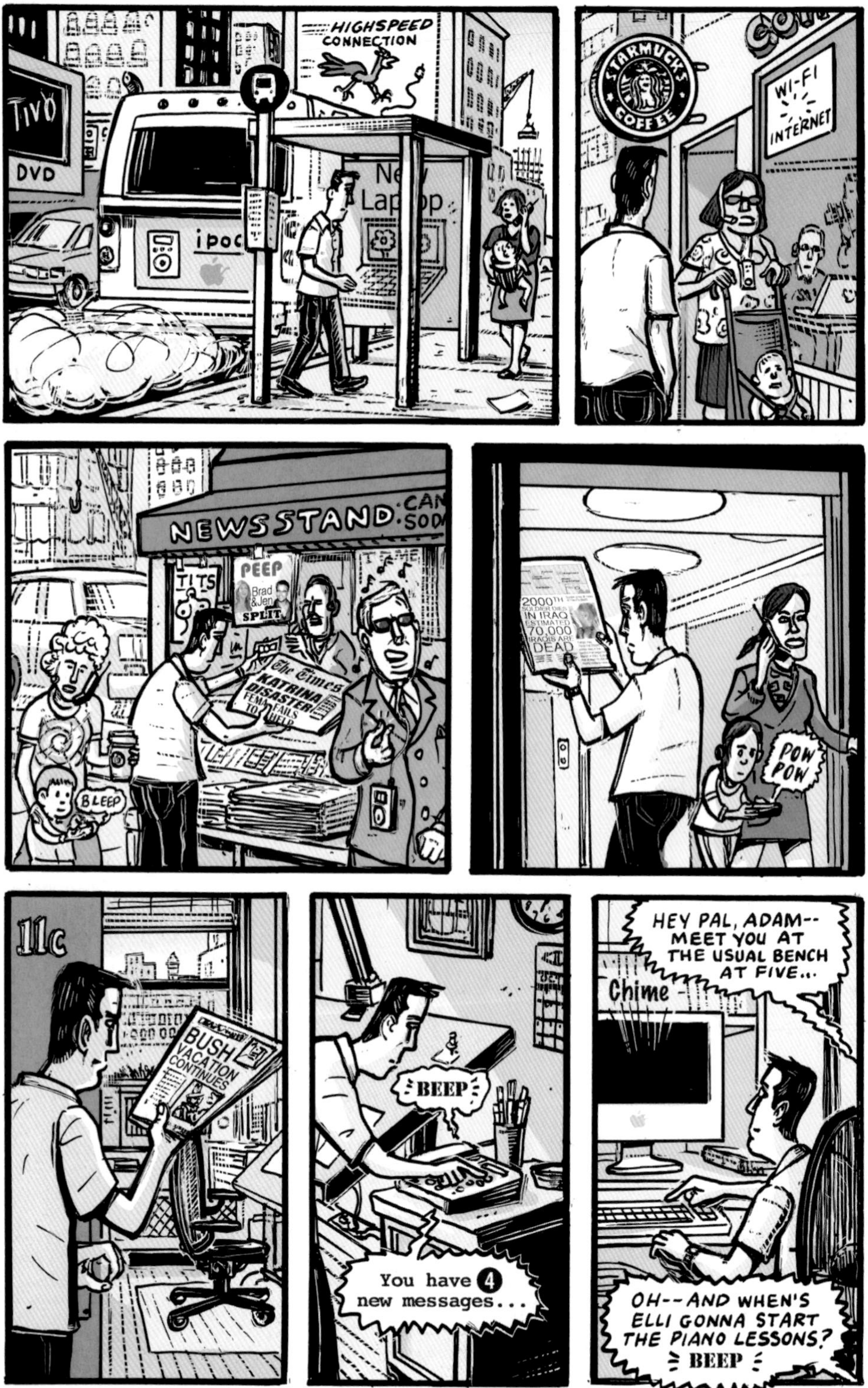

TiVo
DVD
HIGHSPEED CONNECTION
STARMUCKS COFFEE
WI-FI INTERNET
NEWSSTAND
PEEP
Brad &Jen SPLIT
TITS
The Times
KATRINA DISASTER
FEMA FAILS TO HELP
BLEEP
2000TH SOLDIER DIES IN IRAQ
ESTIMATED 70,000 IRAQIS ARE DEAD
POW POW
11c
BUSH VACATION CONTINUES
BEEP
You have 4 new messages...
Chime
HEY PAL, ADAM-- MEET YOU AT THE USUAL BENCH AT FIVE...
OH--AND WHEN'S ELLI GONNA START THE PIANO LESSONS?
BEEP

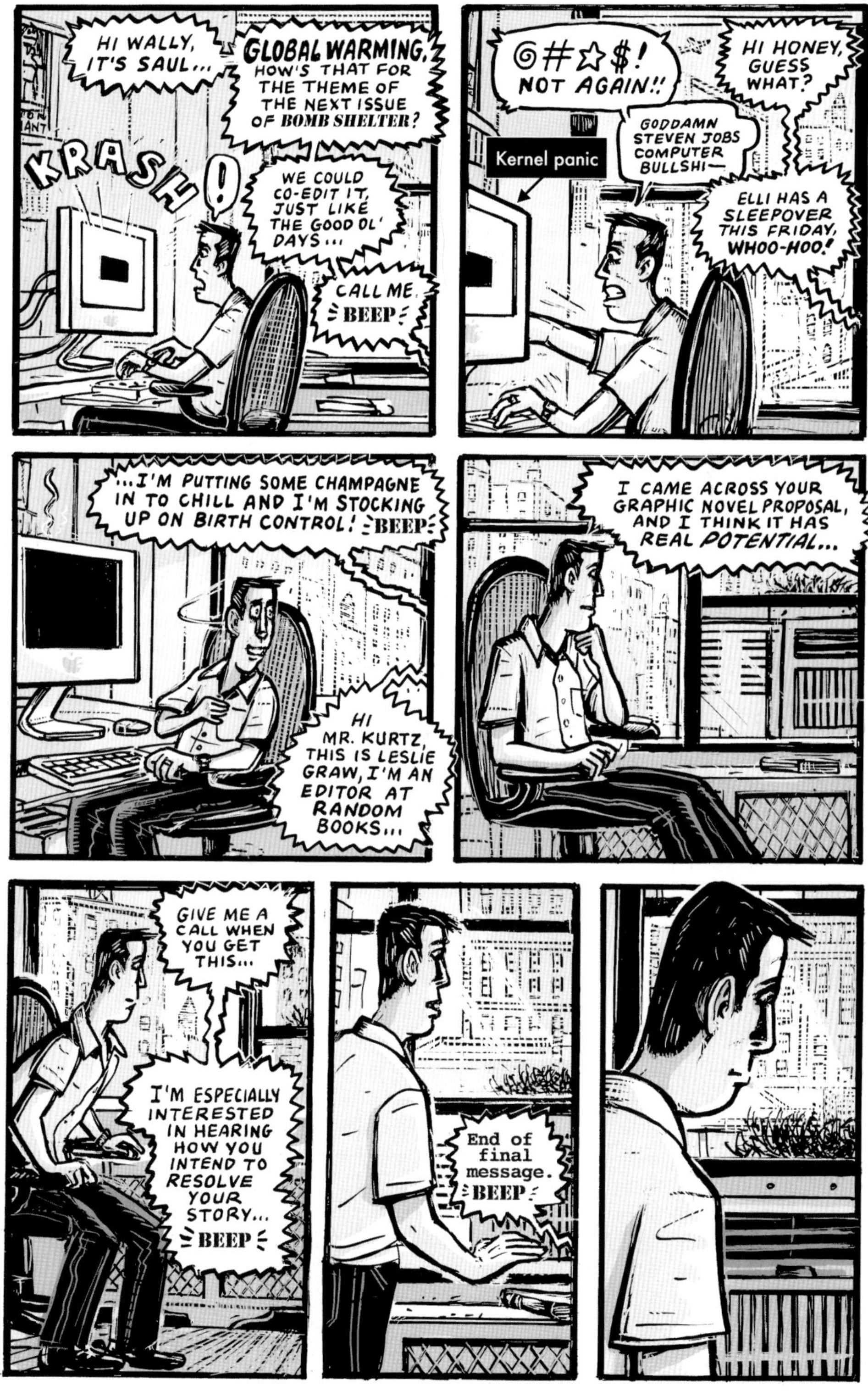
HI WALLY, IT'S SAUL...
GLOBAL WARMING, HOW'S THAT FOR THE THEME OF THE NEXT ISSUE OF BOMB SHELTER?
KRASH!
WE COULD CO-EDIT IT, JUST LIKE THE GOOD OL' DAYS...
CALL ME BEEP
@#☆$! NOT AGAIN!!
Kernel panic
GODDAMN STEVEN JOBS COMPUTER BULLSHI—
HI HONEY, GUESS WHAT?
ELLI HAS A SLEEPOVER THIS FRIDAY, WHOO-HOO!
...I'M PUTTING SOME CHAMPAGNE IN TO CHILL AND I'M STOCKING UP ON BIRTH CONTROL! BEEP
HI MR. KURTZ, THIS IS LESLIE GRAW, I'M AN EDITOR AT RANDOM BOOKS...
I CAME ACROSS YOUR GRAPHIC NOVEL PROPOSAL, AND I THINK IT HAS REAL POTENTIAL...
GIVE ME A CALL WHEN YOU GET THIS...
I'M ESPECIALLY INTERESTED IN HEARING HOW YOU INTEND TO RESOLVE YOUR STORY... BEEP
End of final message. BEEP

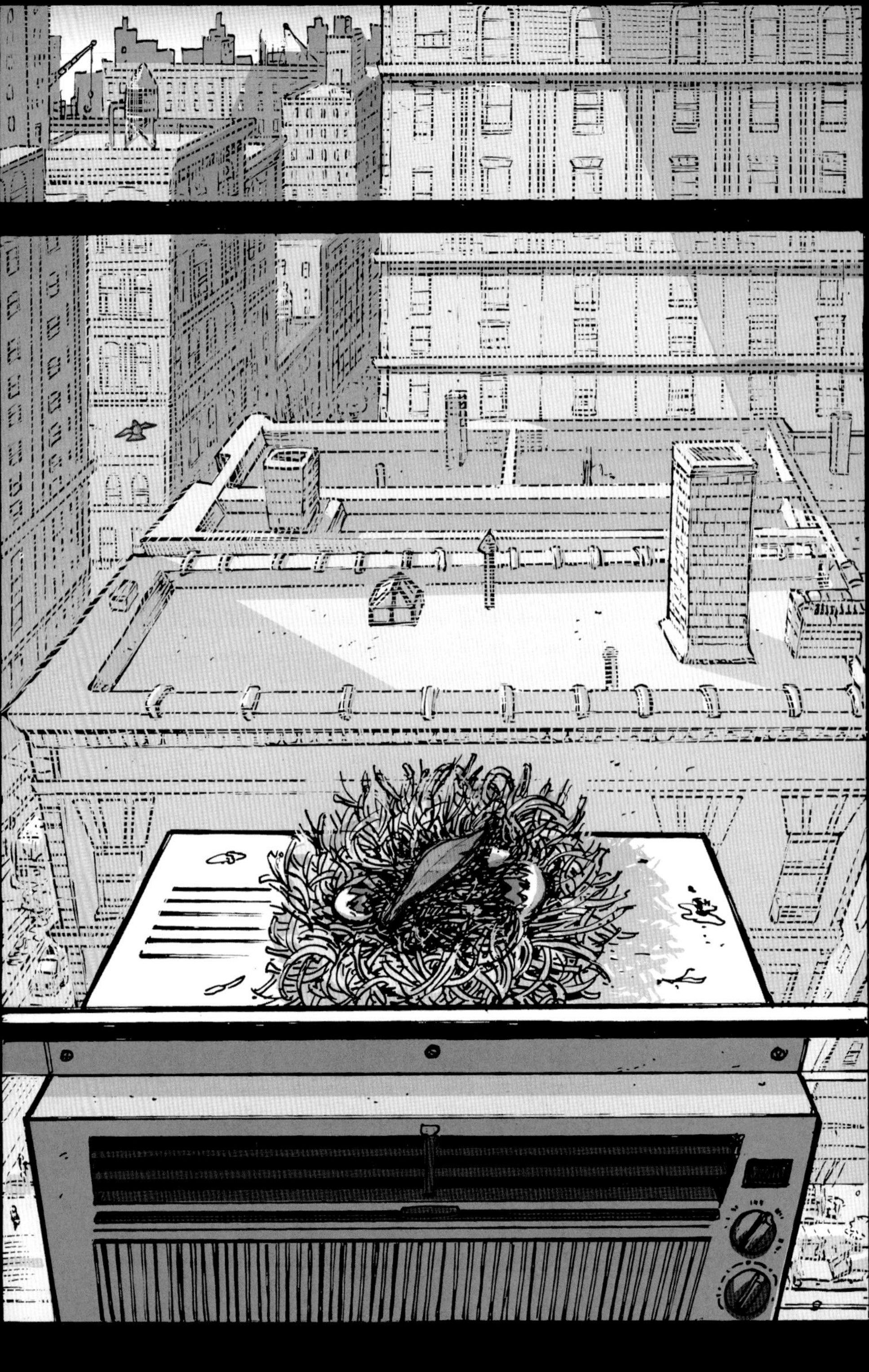

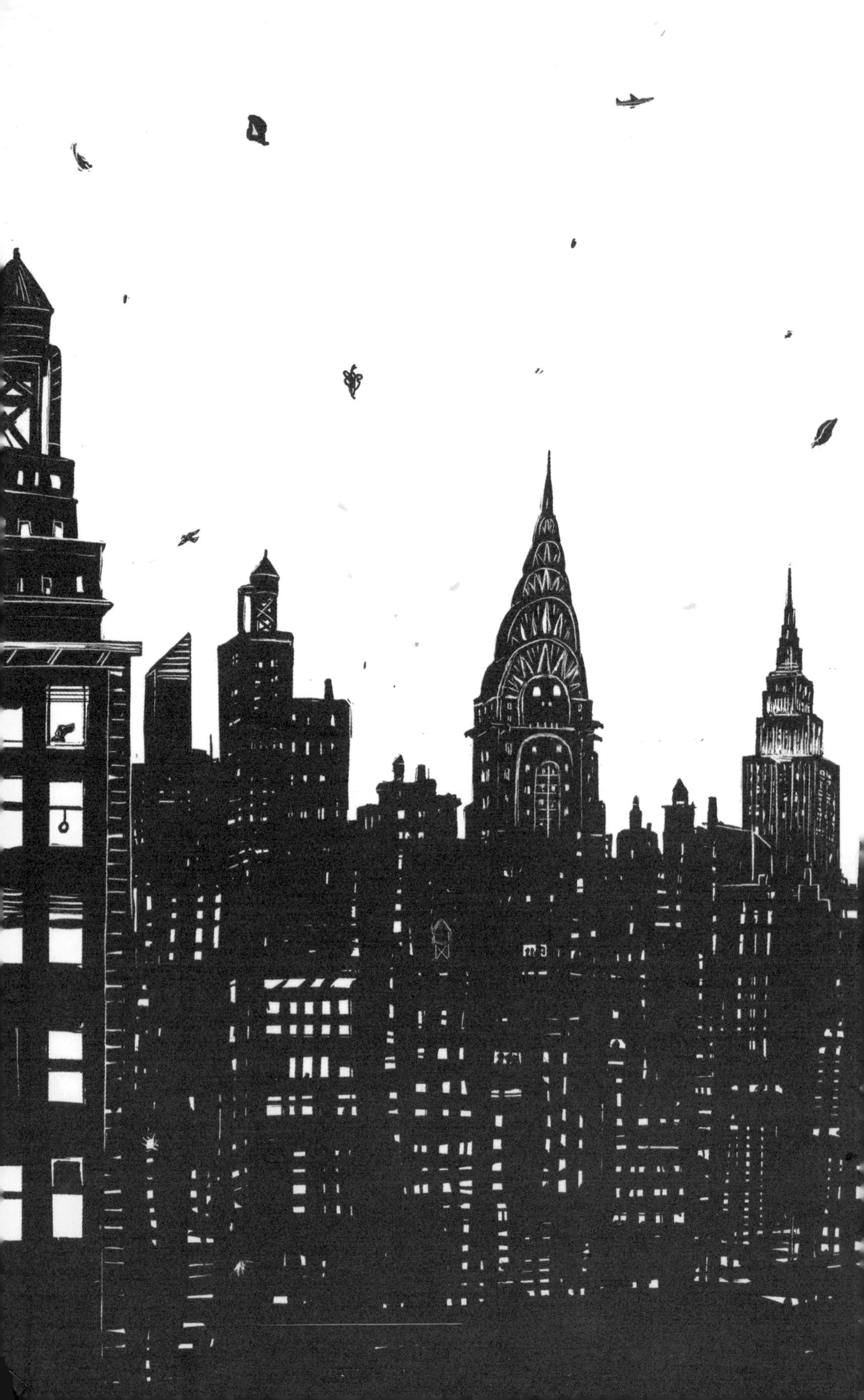